Boy-Wives and Female Husbands

Boy-Wives and Female Husbands

STUDIES IN AFRICAN HOMOSEXUALITIES

Edited by

Stephen O. Murray and Will Roscoe

With a New Foreword by

Marc Epprecht

Cover image: *The Shaman*, photographed by Yannis Davy Guibinga.
© Yannis Davy Guibinga. Subject: Toshiro Kam. Styling: Tinashe Musara.
Makeup: Jess Cohen.

The publisher gratefully acknowledges the generous support of the Murray Hong
Family Trust.

Published by State University of New York Press, Albany

© 1998 Stephen O. Murray, Will Roscoe

Originally published in 1998 by Palgrave Macmillan. Rights reverted to Authors in 2020.

Printed in the United States of America

For information, contact State University of New York Press, Albany, NY
www.sunypress.edu

Library of Congress Cataloging-in-Publication Data

Names: Murray, Stephen O., editor. | Roscoe, Will, editor.
Title: Boy-wives and female husbands : studies in African homosexualities /
    [edited by] Stephen O. Murray, Will Roscoe.
Description: Albany : State University of New York Press, [2021] | Includes
    bibliographical references and index.
Identifiers: LCCN 2020034064 | ISBN 9781438484099 (hardcover : alk. paper) |
    ISBN 9781438484105 (pbk. : alk. paper) | ISBN 9781438484112 (ebook)
Subjects: LCSH: Homosexuality—Africa—History. | Homosexuality—Africa—Public
    opinion. | Gay men—Africa—Identity. | Lesbians—Africa—Identity. |
    Homosexuality in literature. | Homophobia in literature. | Homophobia in
    anthropology. | Public opinion—Africa.
Classification: LCC HQ76.3.A6 B69 2021 | DDC 306.76/6096—dc23
LC record available at https://lccn.loc.gov/2020034064

10 9 8 7 6 5 4 3 2 1

For GALZ and African people everywhere
whose lives and struggles are testimony to the
vital presence of same-sex love on the African continent.

Contents

Part II. West Africa

Part III. Central Africa

Part IV. Southern Africa

Part V. Conclusions

Figures and Tables

Figures

Tables

New Foreword

MARC EPPRECHT

Steve Murray first approached me in early 1996 to invite me to participate in the second-ever panel devoted to queer topics at the African Studies Association (Amory 1997, 2017 provide succinct accounts of those early days of organizing). I was a junior lecturer at the University of Zimbabwe at the time, just embarking on this line of research. San Francisco, California, where the panel was being held, seemed like an awfully long way to go, but Steve convinced me. It proved to be a worthwhile investment, to say the least, to establish connections with people at the very beginning of what was to become a vibrant and critically important field of study. It was there that Steve mooted his idea to me for a book that spoke directly to my intentions in the paper I presented—that is, to provide a base of empirical evidence that confounded the emerging political homophobia in Zimbabwe and, subsequently, more widely on the continent; to balance the prevailing dominance of South Africa with material from other regions of Africa; and to challenge the silences and rhetorical claims about female-female sexuality. My eventual chapter in that book *Boy-Wives and Female Husbands* (*BWFH*) was my first substantive publication on the topic and helped set me on a most rewarding career path.

Steve and I had several small and enjoyable collaborations over the years that followed. I greatly admired his boldness and was thankful that I was never at the receiving end of his critical gaze. In 2017, when I heard that his health was failing, I contacted colleagues and friends to organize

xiv   Foreword to the Second Edition

some reflection on Steve's and his co-editor Will Roscoe's contributions to the development of sexuality studies in Africa. This became a lively roundtable discussion at the Canadian Association of African Studies annual conference held at Queen's University, Kingston, in May 2018, coinciding with the 20th anniversary of *BWFH*'s publication. This, in turn, became a forum in the *Canadian Journal of African Studies* (*CJAS*), which brought Steve together with two of the other original contributors to the book and several young African and Africanist scholars (Epprecht et al. 2018).

Authors to the forum acknowledged weaknesses (more on this below), but they generally saw the book as having had a powerful kick-start effect on research into same-sex sexuality and gender diversity in Africa. Among other outcomes, it led in an almost direct line through Deborah Amory to the creation of the International Resources Network (IRN)–Africa based at the Center for Lesbian and Gay Studies at City University of New York. IRN-Africa was an attempt to bridge the gaps between conventional academic research and activist or journalistic advocacy. Two further conferences aiming to mentor a new generation of African scholar-activists followed in Saly, Senegal (2005; the first time the topic was broached in a conference setting outside of South Africa) and Syracuse, New York (2009). Although IRN-Africa proved not to be sustainable, authors from those conferences went on to be published in Marc Epprecht (2004, 2008), Rudolf Gaudio (2009), Sylvia Tamale (2011), S. N. Nyeck and Epprecht (2013), Sokari Ekine and Hakima Abbas (2013), Zethu Matebeni (2014), Melissa Hackman (2018), and elsewhere. Most of the contributors to the *Global Encyclopedia of Lesbian, Gay, Bisexual, Transgender, and Queer (LGBTQ) History* (Chiang 2019; discussed below) acknowledge their indebtedness to *BWFH* either directly or through reference to these "spin-offs."

Will, whose work on Native North American sexual and gender diversity is well known (see Roscoe 1991, 1998), also contributed to the forum by alerting me to another spin-off from the book in the form of a powerful short play by award-winning British playwright Caryl Churchill. *Pigs and Dogs* was performed in 2016 to considerable acclaim at London's Royal Court Theatre (see Chapman 2016, Gardner 2016, Trueman 2016, for examples). It is surely rare that academic texts get interpreted for popular culture, although the spirit may be permeating a new generation of film and literature from Africa that explores the themes that Steve and Will intuited two decades ago (Coly 2019, Mathuray 2019, Osinubi 2019, Tcheuyap 2019, as entry points into that work).

Steve lived to see the *CJAS* forum published and was particularly moved by the expressions of appreciation if not epiphany by the new generation of scholars. Sadly, he died soon after. I was honored when Will reached out to me seeking help to fulfill one of Steve's enduring desires—to publish a second edition of the book and make it freely available online through an open licensing agreement. That this is now happening is a tribute to Will, Steve's partner, and executor Keelung Hong, Tim Stookesberry, and the team at SUNY Press, as well as another dear colleague from the early days (and yet another contributor to the original edition) Deb Amory.

Much water has passed under the bridge since those early days, which includes some dispiriting setbacks and tragic losses in the struggle for sexual and gender rights on the continent. But there have also been many achievements to celebrate. There are now activist organizations in virtually every country on the continent, with vibrant transnational networks, and a track record of success in overturning discriminatory laws (Botswana, at the time of writing, is the latest such success [Viljoen 2019]). The scholarship has also flourished across a diverse range of disciplines. Some of this new research identifies itself within the umbrella of "African queer theory" and makes a compelling critique of the coloniality of knowledge production, including in *BWFH*. Some of it, by contrast, is unabashedly empiricist. In the absence of good data and the presence of HIV and other sexually transmitted infections, empirical evidence is definitely not to be sniffed at.

My point here is simply to say that responding to such a diversity of new studies and theorization is not possible in this particular project. We, the editors, therefore decided to keep revisions to the bare minimum, otherwise sticking with the original. The book was never published in Africa, nor was it easily available, but it strikes me that there has been a significant trickle down of the book's main claims: that same-sex sexual relations and gender nonconformity historically existed in Africa in many forms; that contemporary articulations of homophobia in Africa bear the heavy stamp of Christian and colonialist ideologies; that research about these issues was feasible using a wide range of methods and sources; and that researchers need to challenge some of the claims and assumptions about sexuality and gender that are embedded in a Western theoretical framework.

Let me point to Aminata Mbaye's concluding assessment in the *CJAS* forum in that regard: "Reading Murray and Roscoe's book still seems essential for young researchers working on these themes, as it urges us to move beyond a Western view of homoeroticism" (2019: 358). We hope that the original still has that power to inspire.

That noted, we have made two small additions to this second edition: Steve's own account of the genesis of the book from his May 29, 2018, *Tangents Online* blog post as well as this foreword. I will use the remainder of the latter to acknowledge the limitations of the book as well as stress its importance as a historical document. We were aware of those limitations at the time of the first edition. But, with the imperative of getting out a forceful challenge to the homophobic rhetoric then coming out of Zimbabwe, we may not have taken due caution in some respects. Cautions, as well as unforeseen nuances and new evidence, are abundantly and insightfully articulated in much of the scholarship referenced above as well as the scores of entries on Africa in the *Global Encyclopedia of Lesbian, Gay, Bisexual, Transgender, and Queer (LGBTQ) History* (Chiang 2019) and in the annotated bibliography "Sexualities in Africa" (Epprecht 2020), among others. Let me limit myself to three simple observations drawing from that body of work.

First, the pool of African academic talent available for contributions to *BWFH* was negligible at that time. The sole black African scholar engaging the issues, to my knowledge, was Zackie Achmat (1993), and he was then leaving the academic field for activism in the fight against HIV. The editors of *BWFH*, and almost all of its original scholarly contributors, were white North Americans. My panel at the San Francisco conference was actually called "White Boys Do Southern Africa." The predominance of contributors to the book was male, and the disproportionate focus was on men.

Who can blame African scholars and particularly female scholars for not picking up the academic cudgels against political homophobia at that time? In my case, the homophobe-in-chief and president of Zimbabwe was also chancellor of the university. Research that promoted awareness of same-sex sexuality was a form of career suicide for Zimbabwean nationals. This is not to justify the obvious geographic and cultural gaps (nothing from the two largest countries in Africa south of the Sahara, nor the Horn of Africa, notably; nothing from Lusophone sources like the courts of the Portuguese Inquisition, etc.). But it does partially explain it.

Similarly, the use of the present tense when referring to historical situations could easily be interpreted as implying that we regarded African cultures as static. This is emphatically not the case but rather simply reflects conformity to a stylistic convention at the time that has since been largely, and appropriately, abandoned. Readers will note how change over time in relation to culture and political economy is a compelling theme in all of the original chapters of this book.

Many of the main obstacles to research on same-sex issues in Africa remain (Msibi 2014), but people's willingness to tackle them has dramatically changed over the past two decades. Over that period, and particularly as associate editor for Africa south of the Sahara in the above-mentioned encyclopedia project, I have gotten to know of an ever-widening circle of active researchers in Africa, or Africans based in the West, who are expanding the field of knowledge in very exciting ways. This includes developing more sophisticated language and theoretical/conceptual tools needed to capture nuances in the ways that sexualities have been constructed and contested over time.

Thus, my second observation follows: *BWFH* needs to read as a historic document in conjunction with the new scholarship, which it self-consciously hoped to kick-start. For example, one of the ways research has developed is somewhat to blur the line across the Sahara Desert that is so commonly drawn to package the region in a convenient analytic unit, on this topic as with most others. Steve had this in mind himself for a second edition. Rather than attempt to address that intention now by tacking North Africa onto this project, I would simply refer readers to the outstanding works of, for example, Jarrod Hayes (2000), Joseph Massad (2007), Sherry Gadelrab (2016), Rudolf Gaudio (2014), and Mehammad Mack (2019). Similarly, much of the new scholarship problematizes the translations and provenance of many of our key sources. Unravelling these issues in the ethnography that we drew on in *BWFH* is a whole other book. Again, rather than redo that task here, let me direct readers to the work of Evan Mwangi (2017), Xavier Livermon (2019), and Sureshi Jayawardene (2019), as well as my own attempt to follow the trail of silences and euphemisms back to their intellectual origins (Epprecht 2008). Undoubtedly, there are many other paths to the fuller understanding of the complexity of African sexualities, but these are themselves more richly understood when the pioneering works like *BWFH* are included.

Finally, it has always been a worry for me that academic research tends to circulate within a very narrow audience and that there remains a strong, if unintended, colonial-ish relationship between the West and Africa in knowledge production about Africa. We (academic researchers in the West and Africa alike) often make it easy for policy makers in Africa to ignore us. It is noteworthy, for example, that Uganda's Scientific Statement on Homosexuality in 2014 (Uganda 2014)—an important first by an African government to commission research on the topic so as to inform the polit-ical process—did not acknowledge *BWFH* or virtually any other academic research on the topic from Africa or by Africans. It is indeed humbling to spend decades of one's professional life creating work that seemingly makes no impact where it matters, although, admittedly, the government of Uganda may have purposefully looked the other way in this case for its own political reasons (Rodriguez 2018, Paszat forthcoming).

Getting the research into venues and a language that is heard and effective in moving nonacademic audience remains a core challenge (see Amory 2019 on "artivism"). Given the *Global Encyclopedia*'s cost, for example, it is unlikely that even its electronic version will get much consumption on African campuses. And yet, where it was once obscured by cultural silences and moralistic stereotypes and euphemisms, same-sex sexualities in Africa have now unquestionably entered the mainstream of knowledge production. Multilateral institutions like the World Bank and United Nations (Beyrer 2011, O'Malley et al. 2018, for example), undergraduate textbooks (Schraeder 2020), and many broad-based civil society organizations now actively engage with the struggle to advance sexual rights and sexual health for all. I am deeply grateful to Steve and Will, and to all the wonderful colleagues along the way, for facilitating my own participation in that project. May this new edition extend the conversation to the places it still most needs to be heard.

The Genesis of
Boy-Wives and Female Husbands

STEPHEN O. MURRAY

How two academic exiles (the euphemism is "independent scholars") who grew up in a homogeneous, all-but-monolingual Anglo-American society with no experience of Africa came to write a book about African homosexualities, *Boy-Wives and Female Husbands* (1998), I can explicate if not explain.[1]

I was a gay liberationist who read most anything I could find about homosexualities here, there, and everywhere. In 1974, in Montréal, I was one of the founders of the Sociologist Gay Caucus.[2] I was the one not doing research on homosexuality. I wanted to promote rather than do it, to read rather than write it.

As a graduate student at the University of Arizona, I had learned that research about homosexual men was seen as illegitimate advocacy. My first seminar paper bore the teacher's remark that "no one is interested in your lifestyle." This and some subtler pressure was supposed to turn my attention to other research topics, and neither my MA nor my PhD research focused on homosexualities. Nonetheless, I was perplexed that this pseudoradical sociology professor knew what my "lifestyle" was.

I can honestly say that I had no idea that I had a lifestyle. If asked in a more neutral way what my lifestyle was, I would have said, "That of a sociology graduate student restive at being turned into a certain—survey research—product." I was not then even aware that much of what we did was "secondary analysis," though the analysis was of US social materials.

Once relocated from Arizona to Toronto, I found at least tolerance of "gay topics" from my elders rather than automatic rejection and published my first "gay studies" as a graduate student in 1979 (based on data from Toronto).

As editor of the *Sociologists' Gay Caucus Newsletter* (*SGC*) in 1979—having been chosen as someone with no particular theoretical (or political) ax to grind—I persuaded Barry Adam, who though born a year after me was de facto my older brother within the University of Toronto sociology department as well as being a cofounder of *SGC*, to write about the emergence of modern homosexuality. I was impressed by the typology of kinds of homosexuality organized by differences in age, or differences in gender, or not organized by status differences that he produced in a reply to my comment. As I looked at the available material from world ethnography, I thought that it fit his typology. I eventually decided that his fourth type, "profession-defined," was not distinct from the age or gender stratifications of roles. (Others have suggested "class" and other categories.)

Crucial to my undertaking was encouragement of comparative thinking about homosexualities from Wayne Dynes, who so far as I could tell was the scholarship committee of the New York Gay Academic Union. He/they published my first critique of conceptions of (North American male) homosexualities *Social Theories, Homosexual Realities* in 1984 (there is a plural noun there, though not "homosexualities"), followed in 1987 by a book that was a model of the mix of analyses from me and some writings by others as *Male Homosexuality in Central and South America* (without the pluralization, alas).

Wayne edited the series in which the 1992 *Oceanic Homosexualities* appeared, as well as the *Encyclopedia of Homosexuality*, and *Gay Books Bulletin*, welcoming entries and reviews from me. Moreover, he published a two-page bibliography on homosexuality in Africa that aimed me toward many sources in the eventual elaboration of his two pages into *Boy-Wives*.

I considered myself a "Latin Americanist" and had done some "research" on Latin American male homosexualities, added some by others to the expansion that became 1995 *Latin American Male Homosexualities*. (It established the plurality of the phenomenon being studied once and forever more in my writings.)

I also had accumulated folders of material on Dar al-Islam and sub-Saharan Africa. Expecting myself to be dead before the millennium was, I was concerned that I would not be able to turn these into companion volumes (I skipped over Europe, which I thought better covered, especially by rising channels of historians' work, and persuaded the University of Chicago Press to publish *American Gay* [1996], which proceeded partly historically, but more topically.) At some point, I persuaded Will Roscoe to ensure that the Muslim and the sub-Saharan collections were brought through to publication. He did much to enhance readability and to spell out inferential steps that I tended not to explicate.

We worked on both books at the same time, though the publication order became Islamic then African entirely by the amount of time it took referees, editors, and publishers to bring out the books.

Will did not press, but he planted the notion in both me and the African text that role stratifications by age and gender were kinds of status, reinforcing the difference between each and what we called "egalitarian roles." The last has been interpreted as suggesting status equals across the boards, whereas what was definitional for us was the absence of a role hierarchy. What was popularly called "versatility in bed" or just the possibility of role-switching was sufficient for our analytical purposes. (The possibility of sexual relationships not being peripheral to self- and/or social identity was already central to Barry Adam's distinction of a "modern gay"/egalitarian type. There was never any belief that the "versatile" took the bottom role half the time, the top the other half—and some underestimation of intimacies not involving genitals, though I think the history of discourse has downplayed sex to talk about the less frightening (to social respectability) phenomena of "gender," so I have no regrets about my earlier goal of analyzing sex/sexualities.)

Along the way, Will's partner Bradley Rose translated some material published in German before WWII (though mostly after Germany's colonies were reapportioned after its defeat in WWI). (Then and more recently, I tried to figure out who Kurt Falk, who published two articles on same-sex sexual relations in 1925, was.)[3]

I remember that Will and I went to Stanford to hear a presentation by then graduate-student Rudi Gaudio on some of his research in Hausaland, which was of interest both as a Muslim and as a south-of-Saharan African setting.

I'm not sure how we met his Stanford graduate-student colleague Deb Amory, whose work was also interesting to us, not least in challenging the incoherent analyses of the same fieldwork by Gill Shepherd. I was puzzled by the different inferences Judith Gay drew about her material on Lesotho "mummies and babies" and that the difference in age was generally a few years rather than a generation. This fit with what we found elsewhere about homosexualities organized by age differences.

I can't ever remember being unaware that in one place (say Toronto), there might be a dominant discourse, but the other types also occurred (Barry Adam suggested as "minor traditions," though in this realm, the "great traditions" were not written ones, as in Robert Redfield's original contrast).

While we were delving in historical and ethnological records, some African despots, most prominently Robert Mugabe, were proclaiming that homosexuality (focusing on gender-defined relationships with denunciations focused on age) was "un-African" and was unprecedented recent seduction/corruption by jaded white devils. I don't know that anyone spoke quite so bluntly as that, but what we knew of early records, when there are very few white predators corrupting innocent black bodies, was that there were relationships between Africans who were like their same-sex sexual partners, including youngsters attracted to fellow youngsters.

We felt that we could make a contribution that was not just to scholarship but also to embattled practitioners of "un-African" perversion—and I think we did—with material from a range of places and times. The most persuasive and historically analyzed was what Marc Epprecht had started to do in the Rhodesian records, and I remember pleading with him to publish some of what he was finding in our book. He did so, and the historical material was supplemented by new material from the research of Amory and Gaudio after I heard a presentation at an American Africanist meeting in San Francisco.

∿

A book leaves the hands of it authors and is read and used by others, especially those with lived experiences of what had been noted by hostile or by sympathetic outsiders (ethnographers from the global North).

Only two chapters of the book were told from the perspective of Africans with intimate familiarity with living same-sex desires in Africa: Nii Ajen's casual survey of expatriates and my own interview of the young Kikuyu who chose the pseudonym of Kamau. In that the Kikuyu was one of the societies for which the most extreme claims of "never among us" had been made, it gave me particular pleasure. I wished that I had met a Yoruba who could belie the claims made about the Yoruba, but even though the African Africanist Niyi Akinnaso to whom I was closest was Yoruba, he was unable to connect me.

The publisher of the book wanted a stand-alone title that did not highlight it as being a part of a series, especially a later part, so "African Homosexualities" was retitled *Boy-Wives and Female Husbands*—a catchier title, I guess, though she also burdened us with a hardcover that infuriated me by making any same-sex connections invisible to any but a few Africanists familiar with textiles. I was mollified by the paperback cover (with wooden figures rather than opaque textiles). I was bemused that the African book received less attention than the preceding Islamic ones; I thought the interest in Africans loving other Africans of the same sex was larger, constituting more of a potential market. If I was right, that market was untapped and the book not well marketed (while 9/11 increased interest in *Islamic Homosexualities* [1997], though that book has even less of then-current patterns than *BWFH*).

The geographical breadth has been noted (sometimes with cavils about getting "native terms" rendered right, a criticism to which I would reply that we covered many here—and many more in *Islamic Homosexualities*—and are not area specialists). (What were the area specialists doing? Not writing a better, more comprehensive book, though one was supposedly being organized at the time of the American Africanist meeting that included some other good historical research in addition to Marc Epprecht's *Hungochani* [2004].) No one yet has refined the attempt to relate organizations of homosexuality with social structures, though I am well aware of the difficulty of statistical analyses in which an instance (that is, a society) might evidence all three values of the dependent value. That types A, B, and C coexist in society F is a problem for statistical analysis, but it remains a stubborn reality ("social fact").

Beyond that, there remains much to document about communities varying in the extent of being silenced/suppressed (and their post-1997 histories), and I find there to be too little on which to model either a singular or a plural African homosexuality. Deciding what is useful and supplanting what is not are tasks of researchers who are now active.

I can say that I'm still more interested in reading than writing about these historical and cultural complexities! I wish there was by now a larger historical and ethnographic literature on sub-Saharan African homosexualities to be analyzed, and I may have missed significant work, but I still find the bases for generalization and comparison there as elsewhere inadequate.

To close, if there is a single moral of the story, it may be that kicking back at the claim, "there's no there there," and looking for it sometimes is rewarded by evidence that the "there" has been ignored and invisibilized but evidence nonetheless can be found. Certainly, the claim that "homosexuality is un-African" was and is not useful, and I'd go so far as to claim that it has been refuted by our book and the material it drew on.

© May 2018, Stephen O. Murray

Notes

1. The Genesis of *Boy-Wives Female Husbands* was first published and copyrighted by Stephen O. Murray as a May 29, 2018, "*Tangents Online* exclusive."

2. SGC, later SLGC et al.

3 According to the Namibian historian Dag Henrichsen (Basler Afrika Bibliographien/University of Basel), who has recently launched a biographical project on Falk (b. 1892), Falk hailed from western Prussia in Germany (now modern Poland) and, being trained in colonial agriculture, emigrated to German Southwest-Africa (modern Namibia) in 1912. From there he re-emigrated to Angola in 1922 where he committed suicide in 1924. Apart from the two essays on homosexualities published in this book, he also wrote about reptiles in these two colonies (personal communication to M. Epprecht on August 7, 2020).

References

Epprecht, Marc. 2004. *Hungochani: The history of a dissident sexuality in southern Africa*. Montréal: McGill-Queen's University Press.

Murray, Stephen O. 1979a. "Institutional elaboration of a quasi-ethnic community." *International Review of Modern Sociology* 9: 165–177.

———. 1979b. "The art of gay insulting." *Anthropological Linguistics* 21: 211–223.

———. 1984. *Social theory, homosexual realities*. Gai Saber Monograph 3. New York: Gay Academic Union.

———. 1987. *Male homosexuality in central and south America*. Gai Saber Monograph 5. New York: Gay Academic Union and San Francisco: El Instituto Obregón.

———. 1992. *Oceanic homosexualities*. Garland Reference Library of Social Science 686. New York: Garland.

———. 1995. *Latin American male homosexualities*. Albuquerque: University of New Mexico Press.

———. 1996. *American gay*. Chicago, IL: University of Chicago Press.

———. 2000. *Homosexualities*. Chicago, IL: University of Chicago Press.

———. 2009. "Southern African homosexualities and denials." *Canadian Journal of African Studies* 43: 168–78.

Murray, Stephen O., and Will Roscoe. 1997. *Islamic homosexualities*. New York: New York University Press.

———. 1998. *Boy-wives and female husbands: Studies in African homosexualities*. New York: St. Martin's Press.

Roscoe, Will. 1988. *Living the spirit: A gay American Indian anthology*. New York: St. Martin's Press.

———. 1998. *Changing ones: Third and fourth genders in native North America*. New York: Palgrave Macmillan.

Preface

"All Very Confusing"

Among the many myths Europeans have created about Africa, the myth that homosexuality is absent or incidental in African societies is one of the oldest and most enduring. For Europeans, black Africans—of all the native peoples of the world—most epitomized "primitive man." Since primitive man was supposed to be close to nature, ruled by instinct, and culturally unsophisticated, he had to be heterosexual, his sexual energies and outlets devoted exclusively to their "natural" purpose: biological reproduction. If black Africans were the most primitive people in all humanity—if they were, indeed, human, which some debated—then they had to be the most heterosexual.[1]

The figures of "natural" and "primitive man" have proven indispensable to Western projects of self-definition since the Greeks imagined non-Greeks as darker, hairier, cruder, and more profligate than themselves—as *barbaros*. The valuation of the primitive can and has varied. The sylvan "wild man" of medieval folk belief was a monster and widely feared. The noble savage of Rousseau and others was idealized—"natural" man was healthier, better adjusted, the bearer of wisdom. But in all cases, the primitive serves the same function: to highlight that which distinguishes Western cultures by describing that which is not Western. Savagery proves indispensable to civilization, as does primitivism to progress, childhood to adulthood, deviancy to normalcy. Ultimately, every social difference that subdivides Western societies—ethnic, racial, national, and not the least sexual—has been mapped on to the ambidextrous figure of primitive man.

The sexualization of "primitive" Africans can be traced to Edward Gibbon's comments in the 94th chapter of his *History of the Decline and Fall of the Roman Empire*. When it was published in 1781, hardly any

Europeans had traveled more than a few miles into the African interior. Still, Gibbon wrote, "I believe, and hope, that the negroes, in their own country, were exempt from this moral pestilence [i.e., homosexual 'vice']" ([1781] 1925: 506). Belief and hope have been confounded in reports of African homosexuality ever since. A century later, Sir Richard Burton, who had observed homosexual practices firsthand in the Near East and South Asia, gave Gibbon's wishful speculation credence, reporting that "the negro race is mostly untainted by sodomy and tribadism" ([1903–04?]: 246). The boundaries of his so-called sotadic zone, that region where homosexuality was presumably indigenous, did not extend south of the Sahara in Africa.[2]

Yet, others acknowledged that "sodomy" occurred in Africa but claimed that it was introduced by non-Africans—Arab slave traders (Kagwa [1918] 1934: 98) or Europeans—or by another African group.[3] Eastern Bantu speakers claimed that pederasty was imported by the Nubians (Schneider 1885: 295–96); the Sudanese blamed Turkish marauders (Weine 1848: 120). Although such beliefs (which have counterparts throughout the world) may tell us something about perceived ethnic boundaries, they cannot be relied on as evidence for the actual origins or transmission of cultural traits, especially those that are stigmatized.

Unfortunately, rather than dispel the myth of African sexual exceptionalism, anthropologists have often reinforced it by not seriously investigating same-sex patterns, failing to report what they do observe, and discounting what they report.[4] Edward Evans-Pritchard, one of the most widely respected authorities on indigenous African cultures, said nothing about male homosexuality in his classic 1937 study *Witchcraft, Oracles, and Magic among the Zande*. Nor did he mention homosexual relations among the Nuer of southern Sudan in his equally influential monograph on that people.[5] Decades passed from the time of his fieldwork until he finally reported what he had learned about male homosexuality among the once-fierce Azande of the northern Congo.[6] In 1957, in a relatively obscure journal, and then in more accessible venues in 1970 and 1971, he related how Azande warriors routinely married boys who functioned as temporary wives. The practice was institutionalized to the extent that the warriors paid "bride-price" to the parents of the boys. This instance of age-stratified homosexuality, comparable in elaboration to the same-sex practices of ancient Crete or Sparta, had already lapsed by the time of Evans-Pritchard's fieldwork in the 1930s, although it was still remembered. The scope of these practices might be entirely unknown today had Evans-Pritchard not decided to finally write about them shortly before his death.

Other anthropologists, in Africa as elsewhere, have denied (or dismissed) the presence of homosexuality even when they observed it. Alan Merriam, for example, in one sentence stated that homosexual behavior was absent among Bala men and in the next reported native claims that the *kitesha*, a gender-defined social role, "is a homosexual" (1971: 93–94). When homosexuality is acknowledged, its meaning and cultural significance are discounted and minimized. By claiming that homosexual relations are solely due to a lack of women, for example, or are part of a short-lived adolescent phase, the possibility of homoerotic desire—that an individual may actually want and find pleasure in another of the same sex—is effectively denied. In the 1930s, Melville Herskovits asserted that homosexuality among Dahomey youths was merely situational and opportunistic: "[When] the games between boys and girls are stopped, the boys no longer have the opportunity for companionship with the girls, and the sex drive finds satisfaction in close friendship between boys in the same group. . . . A boy may take the other 'as a woman' this being called *gaglgo*, homosexuality." Yet, in the sentence immediately following, he reported, "Sometimes an affair of this sort persists during the entire life of the pair" (1938: 289).

Ethnocentric attitudes are often all too evident. In the 1930s, Geoffrey Gorer complained that among Dahomean royalty, "Sexual perversion and neurotic curiosity were developed to an almost European extent" ([1935] 1962: 141). Four decades later, Michael Gelfand employed the same judgments to claim the opposite for Zimbabwe: "The traditional Shona," he rhapsodized, "have none of the problems associated with homosexuality [so] obviously they must have a valuable method of bringing up children, especially with regards to normal sex relations, thus avoiding this anomaly so frequent in Western society" (1979: 201).

In fairness, the task of anthropologists, even the most conscientious, is daunting. Their research has always depended on the approval and material support of political authorities—originally those of the colonial powers, today those of both Western and African states. Indeed, as Sally Moore has pointed out, contemporary anthropologists are no less wary of offending the black governments under whose shadow they labor than earlier generations were of white colonial regimes (1994: 6). Given the overtly homophobic attitudes and policies of some African governments (see the discussion of events in Zimbabwe in part IV), it is not surprising that few anthropologists have made African sexuality, let alone homosexuality, a focus of their research.

The close identification of anthropologists with political authorities also means that ethnographer-informant relations are often fraught with tension.

xxviii   Preface

In this context, inquiries about sexuality typically result in a cat-and-mouse game, as Kurt Falk discovered in the 1920s:

> To begin with, it is difficult to judge the truth of stories and answers to questions. Secondly, those questioned, under the suggestion of the asker, often guess and readily answer not only the questions in the desired way, but exaggerates further, hoping to make the researcher happy. And then as the questions mostly touch on the subject of sex, they are very reticent and tend more than otherwise to disavowals and denials. It is easier to learn about the subject by questioning a knowledgeable member of a foreign tribe that has lived among them. Here also, however, caution is suggested and control is always to be exercised. (1923: 42)

Consequently, native denials of homosexuality should be regarded skeptically, as Brian MacDermot learned while conducting field research among the Ethiopian Nuer in the 1960s. MacDermot's informants told him in no uncertain terms that sex between men simply did not occur in their society, and he believed them. Then, one day, he noticed "a crazy old man . . . accepted by everyone in the village . . . [who] either tended the cattle or at other times helped the women harvesting corn or carrying burdens" (1972: 99). As the old man treaded off to join the women in their work, Doereding, MacDermot's primary informant, began to tell a story "which completely contradicted all I [MacDermot] had thought and learnt so far about Nuer homosexual relations":

> It had always been stressed by the tribesmen that homosexuality between men was impossible, for if discovered amongst them it could be punishable by death. Doereding now told me about a crazy man he had once known who lived near Nasir in the Sudan and who frequently dressed as a woman. This was different, Doereding explained, because "the man had actually become a woman"; the prophet of Deng had been consulted and had agreed to his change of status. The prophet had decided to call on the spirits and after consultation had declared that indeed the man was a woman. Therefore, he could dress in women's clothes and behave as a woman. From that time onward it was agreed that "he" should be called "she," and "she" was allowed to marry a husband. (99)

"All very confusing," MacDermont concluded with a note of exasperation, "and so totally against what the Nuer had been telling me, that I questioned Doereding carefully, but he failed to produce further explanation" (1972: 119).

For individuals from a society in which homosexuality is defined as a unitary, predominantly sexual phenomenon with fixed internal psychological motivations—and who have judged that phenomenon so harshly that even its leading social engineers and intellectuals are afraid to study or discuss the subject—the diversity of African homosexualities is, indeed, "all very confusing." But as this book shows, African homosexuality is neither random nor incidental—it is a consistent and logical feature of African societies and belief systems.

Today, especially where Western influences (notably Christianity and Marxism) have been strong, the belief that homosexuality is a decadent, bourgeois, Western import has become common. In the late 1970s, when the mother of South African Simon Nkoli discovered that he was gay, she said, "I knew I should not have sent you to that white school" (Bull 1990: 45).[7] Sensitized by missionaries and Western education, defensive in the face of stereotypes of black hypersexuality, and resentful of sexual exploitation in colonial institutions, the first generation of postcolonial Africans was extremely reluctant to discuss the subject of homosexuality.[8] For most, the negotiation of African identity remained tied to European standards of morality. In seeking to replace a "genuinely perverse" with a "genuinely normal" Other, they drew on the same rhetoric employed in colonial discourse on native sexuality (Bleys 1995: 4–9; see also Dunton 1989). As the medical model of homosexuality was being abandoned in the West, it was widely adopted in the developing world.

In the African diaspora, as well, the subject of homosexuality has evoked denials and just-so stories attributing it to alien sources. In the United States, where Afrocentrism—the movement among Americans of African descent to construct and embrace African history, customs, and values—has become influential; questions of what "tradition" does and does not include are highly politicized. In 1990, a member of the rap group Public Enemy asserted, "There's not a word in any African language which describes homosexual. If you want to take me up on that, then you find me, in the original languages of Africa, a word for homosexual, lesbian, or prostitute. There are no such words. They didn't exist."[9] In a similar vein, the Nigerian-English sociologist Ifi Amadiume denied the presence of lesbianism in what are otherwise described as marriages between women and decried Western black lesbians using "prejudiced interpretations of African situations to justify their choices of sexual alternatives" (1987: 7).

What began with denial has ended in a near taboo on the subject of African homosexualities—a taboo nonetheless based on European, not African, morality. The colonialists did not introduce homosexuality to Africa but rather intolerance of it—and systems of surveillance and regulation for suppressing it.[10] As the chapter by Marc Epprecht shows, however, these systems were not successful as long as the reaction of the colonized was simply to hide or deny such practices. Only when native people began to forget that same-sex patterns were ever a part of their culture did homosexuality become truly stigmatized.

Popular images of Africa—as the "dark" continent, the "cradle" of humanity, where distinctions between human and animal, civilized and savage, are tentative and easily reversed—continue to cloud Western views of the continent and its people (see Mudimbe 1988, 1994). The anthropological literature also offers changing and varied constructions of Africa. In the early 20th century, in response to the Victorian rhetoric of savagery and primitivism, anthropologists embraced functionalism and emphasized the integration, morality, and coherence of African societies—thereby redeeming them from an image of anarchy for their Western readers. In the postcolonial period, "change" has replaced "custom" in anthropological writings, and images of stable, traditional, and conservative African societies have given way to depictions of social "breakdown" in the face of urbanization and modernization. Africans are portrayed as emerging from stable social systems into a state of cultural disruption no longer "African" or fully European (Moore 1994: 57). Some anthropologists have suggested that the collapse of the tribal order is resulting in a new immorality (see, for example, the chapter by Günther Tessman). Many nonanthropologists have taken the next step in such a line of argument by naming homosexuality as one of the "immoralities" to be blamed on the effects of colonialism. Today, Western rhetoric about "African sexuality," with its myths of super-virile men and lascivious women, has found new life in accounts of AIDS in Africa and seems to underlie research agendas (see Chirimuuta and Chirimuuta 1987; Schoepf 1995).

Understanding African homosexualities requires not only abandoning these myths but also suspending certain deeply held Western beliefs and values concerning sexuality, love, and personal relationships. Although the ideals of voluntary marriage based on mutual choice, sexual attraction, and monogamy are now almost universally embraced in Western societies (and in a growing number of other countries), it has only been in the past century and a half that a majority of individuals could hope to attain them. A major impetus for egalitarian relationships has come from feminism, both during its first wave, in the 19th century, and its more radical second wave, beginning in the 1960s. For a growing number of Western women, the key to voluntary and mutual relationships with men has become the attainment of economic and legal independence from them. As these ideals have been more widely adopted, attempts to police the borders between voluntary and involuntary sexuality have become increasingly fine-tuned. Relationships between individuals of unequal status (between a powerful man and a woman employee, for example, or an older man and teenaged boy) have become increasingly suspect.

But in non-Western (and in earlier Western) societies in which arranged marriages prevail and strict rules limit and predetermine marriage partners, very different expectations exist regarding love, sex, and free will. In their personal relationships, not only women and girls but also boys and men lack choices that are taken for granted in contemporary Western societies. Love (intimacy, companionship, care), while welcomed in a primary relationship, is not necessary or always expected. We should not be shocked, therefore, that in some African societies, adolescent boys entered arranged relationships with older men without being asked if they were willing or what their sexual preference was (a concept that did not exist, in any case)— any more than the even more common practice of arranged marriages for adolescent girls with older men shocks us. We should also be prepared to find, as Epprecht shows, that such relationships had a range of meanings for their members—for some, being a boy-wife was almost a kind of slavery, for others a deep bond of love. Finally, it is important to remember that where there is power, there is resistance. Lila Abdul-Lughod, for example, has shown how women subjected to rules of seclusion in highly patriarchal cultures (desert Bedouins) find ways to resist and undermine the power of men (1986). We cannot assume that African boys any more than girls and women were passive victims of social forces. Indeed, some young people of both sexes actively seek relations with older adults. The black South African activist Zackie Achmat entitled his 1995 memoir "My Childhood as an Adult Molester."

Instead of attempting to forge yet another mythical African unity—a single, consistent homosexuality across a culturally homogeneous continent— this book offers multiple Africas and diverse patterns of same-sex sexuality. While we do attempt to make generalizations about patterns in appendix 2, the contributors to this book focus on specific groups and places, offering, if not always "thick" descriptions in the sense of Clifford Geertz, at least detailed and specific case studies, and they separate the description of practices and beliefs from generalizations about them. Indeed, if nothing else, the diverse backgrounds of the contributors ensure that no unified image of Africa emerges. They include anthropologists, sociologists, historians, linguists, and journalists. Several have had extensive firsthand experience in Africa (or are African themselves), and an oral history provides a detailed account of one contemporary African's same-sex life. These recent studies are supplemented with earlier ethnographies, which are reprinted here because of their value as primary sources and their inaccessibility. The authors of these reports include missionaries, colonial doctors, and anthropologists.

This book is organized geographically according to four broad regions of sub-Saharan Africa (see figure P.1): part I covers the Horn of Africa, the Sudan, and East Africa; part II, West Africa (including coastal West Africa and the interior Sudanic region); part III, Central Africa (from the tropical rain forests of the equatorial region to the Congo basin and east to present-day Tanzania); and part IV, southern Africa (from Mozambique and Zambia to South Africa and Namibia).[11] Each of the four regional sections begins with a survey by the editors of historical and anthropological reports. The book concludes with a review of the literature on woman-woman marriages, a general conclusion, and an appendix in which correlations between same-sex patterns and other features of African societies are analyzed.

Although this collection offers a wealth of evidence and insightful analyses of African homosexualities, the study of this subject has only been seriously undertaken in the past decade and a half. This book therefore necessarily reflects the unevenness of the research to date. Some of the regions considered are better represented than others (for example, West Africa compared to Central Africa), and certain traditions are examined in some detail by more than one contributor (for example, the gender-defined homosexual roles of coastal East Africa), whereas others are barely covered (such as the mixed- and cross-gendered healers and spirit mediums among Bantu-speaking groups in Angola and Namibia).

In every region, female same-sex patterns are poorly documented and often misunderstood. Infrequently revealed to men, especially outsiders, female-female sexuality has rarely been described by anthropologists working in the African countryside and almost never mentioned by observers of postindependence African cities. Still, Audre Lorde was surely right when she argued that sexual contact "has existed for ages in most of the female

Figure P.1. Key groups and places discussed.

compounds across the African continent" (1984: 50). With so many African men working away from their homes, it would be unusual for African women not to turn to each other, as indeed they do in the southern African homelands. Unfortunately, no one has seriously looked for parallels to South African woman-woman relations elsewhere in the continent, and very little has been published on female homosexuality in the labor reserves of Central Africa. Only in recent years has a body of retrospective accounts by lesbians in South Africa begun to appear, which describes their experience of growing up invisible to themselves (but not always to others).[12] Some work has been done in documenting marriages between African women (see the final section of this book). While this practice has been reported

for several African societies, it is poorly understood and the question of
sexuality within these relationships hotly debated.

Balance in presentation and discussion of male and female patterns
would be desirable, but no degree of commitment to that goal can produce
evidence that doesn't exist. At the same time, the reports on woman-woman
relationships in southern Africa by Kendall and others suggest that a rich
field for research does exist. It is our hope that the disappointment of various
readers in the subjects not covered (or not covered well) in this collection
will inspire the commitment on the part of researchers and institutions to
undertake the work needed to correct its shortcomings.

Despite these limitations, the studies included here make an important
contribution to anthropology, history, gender studies, and theories of sexuality (including the contentious field of "queer theory"). Taking their lead
from sociologists and historians, and inspired by feminist critiques of sex
roles and power, researchers have been asking provocative and productive
questions about how sexuality, that seemingly most private of all human
experience, is socially constructed. We are only beginning to ask the same
questions about other cultures. Recent works by Gil Herdt on homosexuality
in Melanesian initiations, Will Roscoe on the North American berdache,
Stephen Murray and Annick Prienr on Mesoamerica, Kira Hall and Serena
Nanda on the *hijras* of India, and Alison Murray and Saskia Wieringa on
Indonesia reveal how productive the social constructionist paradigm is when
applied to the analysis of non-Western homosexuality. At the same time,
these studies have raised some important challenges to certain assumptions
often made by social constructionist theorists. Although the homosexual
patterns of Western and non-Western societies are distinct, this diversity
is not infinite. It has become apparent that certain patterns tend to recur
across cultures and historical periods. Anthropological research on homosexuality raises the question, exactly *what* social and historical factors explain
both the occurrence of different same-sex patterns *and* the regularity within
these patterns?

Consideration of evidence on African homosexualities can help offset
the ethnocentrism of much recent research in sexuality and gender. Theorists
like Michel Foucault, Jeffrey Weeks, and Michael Warner, for example, consider only Western societies and, mainly, only the recent past of their own
countries. Occasionally, contemporary sexual identities are contrasted to those
of "tribal" societies—usually those of native North America, whose berdache
or alternative gender role has been well documented (see Roscoe 1998). A
more fruitful comparison, however, would be between Euro-American sexual

identities and same-sex patterns found in non-Western urbanized, agrarian societies, of which Africa provides several examples. Such comparisons could be critical in substantiating or refuting claims about the uniqueness of modern homosexual identity, and we hope the evidence herein will be so used. As Gaudio argues in his chapter, "Gender theory, and the ultimate goal of widening the scope of human beings' options for self-expression and survival, thus stands to benefit from the consideration of practices that do not derive from the same political or philosophical framework as the theories themselves."

In a 1987 article surveying evidence on African sexuality, Daniel Hrdy reiterated Gibbon's assertions when he categorically stated that "homosexuality is not part of traditional societies in Africa" (1987: 1113). Such claims are not merely a matter of scholarly interpretation. They have genuine social consequences because they stigmatize those who engage in homosexual behavior and those who are grappling with gay identities. Their implications are particularly ominous when it comes to preventing HIV transmission, which remains an ongoing concern for nations throughout the continent. With the publication of this book, we hope such claims will be finally acknowledged for what they are—wishful, unfounded prejudices.

Notes to the Preface

1. Rudi Bleys, Wayne Dynes, Marc Epprecht, and David Greenberg each suggested a number of sources. We are also indebted to the encouragement of and discussions with Nii Ajen, F. Niyi Akinnaso, Deborah Amory, Rudolf Gaudio, John McCall, J. Lorand Matory, and "Kamau." Thanks are also due to Chet Credier for identifying language names, the late Bradley Rose for unlocking Karsch-Haack's unreliable but fascinating 1911 survey of contact literature and missionary accounts, Everard C. Longland for patiently going over some other German materials, and Rico Buttermilch for assistance in completing translations.

2. Burton did acknowledge Dos Santos' report of cross-dressed *chibadi* in the Congo ([1903–04?]: 246–47).

3. Non-Indo-European and non-Semitic terms for homosexual roles reported early in the history of European contact make it unlikely that homosexual behavior was unknown before either Arab or European contact.

4. See Murray 1997a on anthropologists' determination to ignore ubiquitous evidence of homosexuality.

5. He consigned mention of the subject instead to a less important book (Evans-Pritchard 1951: 108–9).

6. Except insofar as Evans-Pritchard told his teacher about boy-wives in military camps (in Seligman and Seligman 1932: 506–7). He did mention relations between Zande women (1937: 56).

7. Elsewhere Nkoli (1995: 250–52) describes how his mother took him to a series of *sangomas* (native healers) to probe the origin and curability of his homosexuality. A more recent and especially vivid example of invoking white corruption of black innocence was the defense in Winnie Mandela's trial (see Holmes 1995).

8. Dagara spokesman Malidoma Somé (1994), who was molested by a priest in a French Catholic boarding school, noted that both before and after independence, "older students looked at young newcomers as girls and possible sexual partners. Their friendliness was stimulated by an attraction that could not find real girls to satisfy itself. So it settled on a substitute" (108) and that "others schooled privately as the protégés of white missionaries, arrived there still longing for their white fathers" (100).

9. Quoted in Conner (1993: 37). For responses to such claims, see Nero (1991), Simmons (1991), and Smith (1991)—none of whom were particularly well informed about the literature discussed here.

10. As they did in the Americas (see Roscoe 1991, 1998).

11. Africa north of the Sahara is generally treated as part of a distinct circum-Mediterranean culture area (see Murray and Roscoe 1997).

12. See Chan Sam (1993, 1995), Mamaki (1993), Radcliffe (1993), and Vimbela (1995).

Africa and African Homosexualities

An Introduction

"Just Because They Like Them"

In leading the exploration and colonization of Africa, the Portuguese became the first Europeans to realize that African sexuality and gender diverged in surprising and, to them, shocking ways from their own. In the early 17th century, their efforts to conquer the Ndongo kingdom of the Mbundu (Umbundu) were stymied by the inspired leadership of a warrior woman named Nzinga (ca. 1581–1663). Nzinga had become *ngola*, or king, by succeeding her brother, which was not unusual in a matrilineal society like the Mbundu. Less typical was the fact that she had ordered her nephew's death to prevent him from claiming his father's title. Nzinga proceeded to organize a guerilla army and personally led her warriors into battle. She successfully outmaneuvered the Portuguese for nearly four decades (Sweetman 1971, 1984: 39–47).

In the late 1640s, a Dutch military attaché observed firsthand what must have struck him as the strange organization of her court. As *ngola*, Nzinga was not "queen" but "king" of her people. She ruled dressed as a man, surrounded by a harem of young men who dressed as women and were her "wives." Wherever she appeared, her subjects fell to their knees and kissed the ground (Dapper 1670: 238). Nzinga managed to preserve Ndongo independence for a generation—indeed, it was not until the early 20th century that the Portuguese finally broke Mbundu resistance.

Other early reports from Angola, discussed in part III, make it clear that Nzinga's behavior was not some personal idiosyncrasy but was based on beliefs that recognized gender as situational and symbolic as much as a personal, innate characteristic of the individual. A result of these beliefs

1

was the presence of an alternative gender role among groups in the Kongo and Ndonga kingdoms. According to Andrew Battel, an English prisoner of the Portuguese in the 1580s, natives of the Dombe area were "beastly in their living, for they have men in women's apparel, whom they keep among their wives" (Purchas 1625, vol. 2, bk. VII, chap. 3, sec. 2, p. 973).

The reports from Angola set the tone for what followed. When natives like Evans-Pritchard's Zande informants told Europeans that men had sex with boys "just because they like them," Europeans were shocked, incredulous, and confused. They recorded but did not understand sexual and gender practices that epitomized for them how black Africans were different from (and inferior to) them. Although such reporting leaves much to be desired by way of objectivity and detail, European accounts nonetheless document widespread same-sex patterns and roles throughout the continent. In the introductions to each regional section that follows, this literature will be reviewed for the evidence it offers on same-sex practices and social roles. The remainder of this chapter provides an overview of African cultures and history and introduces key terms and concepts used in this book.

The African Continent

When the Portuguese made their first landfalls along the coasts of Africa, the continent was the home of racially and culturally diverse societies with ancient roots. In West Africa, the Songhay empire, centered in Mali; the Mossi and Ashanti (Asante) states to the south; the Hausa city-states to the west; and a series of kingdoms along the Sudanic belt south of the Sahara were flourishing, as were the kingdom of Kongo near the southwest coast and a string of Bantu-speaking states in the interior. In southeastern Africa, the great stone city of Zimbabwe was the capital of a trading empire with connections reaching to China. These black African states were typically ruled by divine kings and had complex political and legal systems. In other cases, large numbers of people were organized into societies without state institutions, on the basis of kinship groupings (the Tiv of Nigeria and the Nuer of Sudan, for example). At the same time, small bands, such as the !Xun (!Kung or "Bushmen") and Mbuti ("Pygmies"), pursued lifestyles similar to those of the earliest human occupants of the continent—which is to say the earliest humans, since the species is believed to have evolved in eastern Africa some three million years ago.

The distribution and types of societies in Africa reflect a combination of ecological and historical factors. The continent, more than three times the size of the United States, is transected by a series of distinct climatic zones that mirror each other as one proceeds north and south from the equator. The central equatorial region, from coastal West Africa to the Congo basin, is an area of high rainfall and tropical forests suitable for the cultivation of root crops, such as yams and manioc. Surrounding this area to the north, east, and south is a crescent of grasslands and woodlands known as the Sudanic zone, where cultivation of grain crops and herding are typical. North and south of this are deserts—the Sahara and the Kalahari. Finally, narrow zones of Mediterranean climate prevail along the northern and southern coasts.

Languages are also distributed in bands across the continent (see figure I.1). Arabic (and other Afro-Asiatic) languages are spoken along the coasts of the northern continent and in the Sahara, with large islands of Nilo-Saharan languages in the center of this area and along the Niger River. Below the Sudanic belt, a broad swath of Niger-Congo languages, including numerous

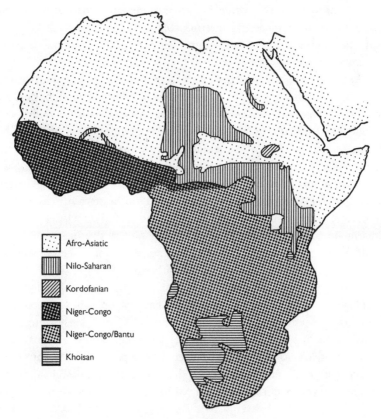

Afro-Asiatic

Nilo-Saharan

Kordofanian

Niger-Congo

Niger-Congo/Bantu

Khoisan

Figure I.1. Distribution of African languages ca. 1900.

Bantu ones, extends from western Africa, across the Congo basin, to the East African coast. Finally, Khoisan languages are spoken by the hunter-gatherers in the southwest and by a few other isolated groups. The distribution of Bantu is believed to reflect prehistoric migrations beginning as long as 3,000 years ago, when Bantu-speakers from the lower Niger River began to carry the technologies of digging-stick horticulture and, later, iron working south to the Congo basin and east to the Interlake region of Kenya and Tanzania, where cattle herding developed. Bantu-speakers continued to migrate southward down the east coast to the continent's southern tip. In all these areas, they are believed to have supplanted (or absorbed) older populations of hunter-gatherers.

By 1000 CE, the transition to sedentary, digging-stick horticulture was complete in sub-Saharan Africa. The majority of African societies were engaged in the production of plant and/or animal food, and the surpluses produced by these economies supported the emergence of powerful states, beginning with the Mande-speaking Ghana empire in Mali, from the 8th to 11th centuries. Indeed, while western Europe languished in the Middle Ages, devastated by plagues and interminable dynastic wars, black kingdoms based on a combination of agriculture, herding, iron working, and slavery were emerging throughout Africa.

Although African societies share economic, linguistic, and historic continuities, significant cultural diversity—and conflicts between both related and unrelated groups—exists as well. Most African societies traditionally depended on horticulture (that is, hoe-based agriculture) for most of their subsistence. The herding of cattle and other domesticated animals was also widespread in areas outside of the equatorial region and the Congo basin, where disease spread by the tsetse fly made it impractical. Many societies in the southern Sudanic belt, Interlake region, and southeastern Africa combined horticulture and husbandry, while Saharan and Sudanic societies depended primarily on pastoralism. A few groups in coastal and riverine environments depended on fishing, and in isolated areas, mostly in the deserts of southern Africa, groups engaged in hunting and gathering.

Throughout Africa, unilineal descent groups or clans—groupings of individuals who recognize kinship on the basis of presumed descent from an originary ancestor (or totem)—are common. Often, descent groups are the basic units of political systems for very large populations. Approximately 31 percent of "traditional" African societies have patrilineal descent groups; 20 percent have matrilineal groups; and 43 percent have descent groups in both lines. (Five percent are bilateral, without descent groups in either line

[Aberle 1961: 665].) Most patrilineal societies are also patrilocal and polygynous. The differences between societies in which descent is traced through the father, which are typically patrilocal and polygynous as well, and those who trace descent through the mother are significant. Women tend to be much less restricted in the latter, sexually or otherwise. Matriliny is most common in horticulture societies, where women do agricultural labor, and in savannah environments; patrilineal groups dominate in the tropical forests. A few matrilineal societies in Africa are based on mixed stock raising and agriculture, but as David Aberle commented, "The cow is the enemy of matriliny, and the friend of patriliny" (1961: 680).

Other differences among African societies reflect their various histories of contact and cultural exchange with non-Africans. By the second millennium, trade and migration from Southeast Asia by way of Madagascar resulted in the introduction of bananas, taro, and yams, which subsequently became staple crops throughout equatorial Africa. Arab contact along the east coast began in the ninth century. In the century that followed, it spread southward along the Nile and from port cities on the Atlantic coast of Africa westward to the Sudanic states. In these areas today, Islamic belief and practices and pre-Islamic African religions often coexist and are sometimes syncretized. Ethiopia, on the other hand, is the home of Coptic Christians.

European contact was inaugurated by the Portuguese, who established a foothold in Angola and the lower Congo basin in the early 16th century. The Portuguese, followed by other European powers, began to trade with African kings for human slaves. Between 1450 and 1870, more than 10 million Africans were transported to the Americas. Initially taken from western Africa, the trade eventually spread to east Africa and Madagascar. As late as 1879, however, most of sub-Saharan Africa—with the exception of southern Africa, where first Dutch (after 1652) then British colonists (after 1795) made significant inroads into the interior—remained unknown to Europeans, and few areas were under direct European control. All that changed with remarkable rapidity. Within two decades, the entire continent was claimed, fought over, annexed, and partitioned. Colonial rule did not end until around 1960 for Belgian, British, and French colonies and not until the 1970s for Portuguese.

The newly independent African nations inherited a wide range of European cultural and social institutions, ranging from language to legal systems, forms of government, military organizations, and educational systems. The legacy of British and French presence in Africa is particularly strong.

Same-Sex Patterns

Given the vastness of the continent and the diversity of its cultures and social forms, it comes as no surprise that same-sex patterns are diverse as well. Nonetheless, this diversity is not unlimited. In the past two decades, anthropologists and sociologists have shown that while homosexual behavior is probably universal, homosexual relationships, roles, and identities typically fall into three basic patterns, all of which are represented in Africa.[1]

The kind of identity and sexuality embraced by contemporary lesbian/gay Europeans and North Americans, in which both partners are members of the same social gender and differences of class, race, and age are *not* the formal basis for organizing the relationship (although such differences may exist), seems to be the most historically recent and least widespread pattern. Much older than the "gay" or "egalitarian" pattern of homosexuality are status-differentiated relations based on differences in either age or gender status. In age-based patterns, one partner is older (although the difference is usually not generational and, indeed, is often nominal). Typically, the older partner takes the inserting role in sex, and the younger partner is penetrated, anally or orally. In some societies, the younger partner is also expected to be less masculine or even overtly feminine, but this is not always the case. Although examples of institutionalized age-defined homosexuality include the *erastes-eromenos* relations of classical Greece, the relations between samurai and pages in medieval Japan, and those between age classes in New Guinea initiation rites, the social meaning and attitudes toward such practices vary considerably.

Unlike age-stratified relations in which both partners are regarded as still belonging to the same (male) gender (and, in some cases, such as in Melanesia, the younger partner is regarded as being masculinized by ingesting semen), in gender-defined patterns, sexually receptive males are categorized differently from other males. They are typically described as behaving, appearing, and working like women—or like stereotypes of women (which can have little to do with how women actually behave). The relative importance of sexuality, dress, and occupation in native definitions of these statuses varies. Outside observers—whether missionaries, anthropologists, travelers, or even natives other than those enacting these roles—rarely observe actual sexual behavior, whereas they are especially likely to notice a male dressing differently from other men or one who does what is regarded as "women's work."

Gender-based homosexuality is a widespread feature of Mediterranean and Latin American cultures. In this pattern, the "active" male in intercourse is not marked or regarded (especially not by himself) as "homosexual," whereas the penetrated male acquires a distinct identity, such as *ricchione* (southern Italy), *pasivo* (Spanish-speaking societies), or *bicha* (Brazil). In such patriarchal cultural contexts, individuals who are sexually penetrated (male or female), whether they enjoy penetration or are merely performing a sexual duty, are expected to conform to the behavior and social roles of women. Males identified as *pasivos* or *bichas*, however, are best thought of as "womanlike" rather than as "socially women." Their behavior is often an exaggeration of that of women, and they fulfill some but not all the social roles of women (for example, women's productive work but not their reproductive roles). Members of their communities are usually aware of their actual biological sex, and the medical and cosmetic technologies necessary for actual sex change are unavailable. Their social status is in some ways lower than that of most women (and akin to that of prostitutes), while they still retain some male prerogatives (such as freedom of movement).

As the marker of an inferior, not-man status, sexual receptivity is a pleasure that men in patriarchal cultures must forbear. Nonetheless, John Winkler has argued that classical Greeks were aware of such pleasure (1990: 67ff), and Gary Leupp has shown that the pleasures of anal receptivity were celebrated in Tokugawa, Japan (1995: 179–82). Precisely the fear of enjoying penetration is cited by Muslim men as a reason for not trying it (Murray 1995a: 5; 1997c: 17–18). Indeed, members of Mediterranean and Mediterranean-influenced societies take for granted (that is, consider "natural") the fact that some males won't attain masculinity and, therefore, will be sexually receptive. Although families may accept that a male member does not marry and produce children, they often make major efforts to discourage public gender nonconformity on his part, efforts that often succeed, because unmarried children live in their natal homes indefinitely.

In less patriarchal cultures, roles and identities for nonmasculine males who do not marry women and produce children are sometimes well-accepted and even honored. In native North America, for example, alternative gender roles for both males and females have been widely documented. Known as berdaches in the anthropological literature (and, more recently, as two spirits), the sexual and gender difference of these individuals was often sanctioned by religious beliefs. Indeed, male berdaches in some tribes fulfilled distinct religious roles and/or were believed to have special supernatural powers. Throughout North America, male berdaches specialized in certain work normally done by women (especially crafts) and were often said to do this work better than women (see W. Roscoe 1991, 1998). Comparable roles have been documented in Latin America, Oceania, Siberia, and Southeast and South Asia (see Murray 1992a, 1995a, 1999; Murray and Roscoe 1997), and as this book will show, parts of Africa. In some cases, the labeling and conceptualization of these roles constitute them as third and even fourth genders.[2]

Numerous reports also indicate that in the highly sex-segregated societies of Africa, homosexual behavior and relationships were not uncommon among peers, both male and female, especially in the years before heterosexual marriage (which, for men, was often delayed long beyond puberty). These kinds of relations were identified with specific terms and, to varying degrees, were institutionalized. Although the terminology of *active/receptive*, *older/younger*, and *male/female* was often used by those involved in such relationships and by others, in reality, sexual roles within same-sex peer relationships were often quite flexible and their adoption arbitrary.

In the chapters that follow, examples of all three patterns—age, gender, and egalitarian same-sex relations—are documented for both males and females. Although there are significantly fewer reports on woman-woman patterns, some detailed evidence is presented for societies in Sudan, Mombasa, and South Africa, and a chapter reviewing the literature on woman-woman marriages is included in part V.

Reading Colonial Texts on African Sexualities

Most of what is known of "traditional" African cultures was written by individuals who were part of a colonial system that disrupted those cultures (see Wolf 1982; J. Burton 1988). Given the absence of native writing systems before the late 19th century, there are few sources of evidence regarding African societies and cultures before European contact.[3] Because the overviews to each part of this book draw extensively from these accounts, some comments concerning their history and limitations are in order.

Father Antonio Cavazzi's reaction to the Ganga-Ya-Chibana, the presiding priest of the Giagues (Imbangala), a group in the Congo region, typifies the European response to African sexual diversity. In his 1687 *Istorica descrizione de' tre' regni Congo, Matamba, et Angola . . .* , Cavazzi described the Ganga-Ya-Chibanda as "a bare-faced, insolent, obscene, extremely villanous, disreputable scoundrel," who "committed the foulest crimes" with impunity. The funeral rites held for him were so indecent "that the paper dirtied with its description would blush." According to Cavazzi, the Ganga-Ya-Chibanda routinely cross-dressed and was addressed as "grandmother." The element *chibanda* in his title is certainly related to other terms used by Bantu-speakers in the region for nonmasculine males who are often shamans and have sex with other men (for example, *chibadi, chibado, jimbandaa, kibamba,* and *quimbanda*; see part III). In Cavazzi's account, however, the sexuality of the Ganga-Ya-Chibanda is ambiguous. Because he freely entered the precincts of secluded women, Cavazzi assumed that he indulged his "brutal passions" with them. But in most cases, where males in alternative gender roles have been observed associating with women, the situation is the opposite of what Cavazzi assumed: they enjoyed such access precisely because they lacked (or were assumed to lack) heterosexual desire (for example, the Omani *khanith,* the *mashoga* of Mombasa, and the Ila *mwaami* described in this book).[4]

In any case, Cavazzi's denunciation did not hinge on the sexual object choice of the Ganga-Ya-Chibanda. Phrases like "foulest crimes" were part of what Guy Poirier has termed a Western "rhetoric of abomination" directed not at particular forms of sexuality but at sexuality in general (1993: 223). Before the 18th century, European writings on sexuality were nearly always part of a moral discourse in which sexual identities, roles, and acts were represented in the terms of a Judeo-Christian code. In this code, all forms of extramarital sexuality and certain forms of marital sexuality were to one degree or another sinful and defiling, and everyone was believed to be at risk for the temptation and lust that led to such acts. The code was uninterested in why some sinners lusted for the same sex and others for the opposite—both were "foulest crimes." Indeed, the very nature of lust was believed to cause a breakdown of moral consciousness and the ability to discriminate between proper and improper sexual objects. Hence, homosexuality, incest, bestiality, and other sexual acts were all viewed as transgressions that occurred when individuals no longer recognized distinctions of gender, kinship, age, race, and species—an "undifferentiated" state of consciousness that Europeans also attributed to people they considered "primitive."

Only in the 18th and 19th centuries did interest develop in explaining same-sex desire as a special case. Even so, the influence of moral discourse remained—and remains—strong. Indeed, nearly all the texts that we might use to document and understand African same-sex patterns employ moral rhetoric—from late 16th-century Portuguese reports of "unnatural damnation" in Angola (Purchas 1625: 1558) to John Burckhardt's 1882 report of "detestable vices" in Nubia (364), an 1893 report of *copulation contre nature* in French Senegal (X 1893: 155–56), and the 1906 report of a German missionary who observed Herrero men forsaking the "natural use of women" (Irle 1906: 58–59). When one reads the more recent statements of Winnie Madikizela-Mandela in which she describes same-sex relations as "utter filth" and "alien to our culture" and an alleged homosexual as having "a very serious psychological problem," it becomes painfully apparent that discourse on African homosexualities has changed little since the time of Father Cavazzi—even though Africans now produce it.[5] The tropes of normal and abnormal, healthy and unhealthy, self and other (although the "other" is now reversed: a debauched West) reiterate a master trope of moral and immoral. European writings on African homosexualities have been eerily consistent over time and across nationality.

Accounts of North American sexual and gender diversity also employed moral rhetoric; however, these reached Europe much sooner and were often more detailed than those from Africa. They were repeatedly cited in European texts and eventually became part of discourses not limited to moral concerns. Will Roscoe has shown how such accounts became part of 16th- and 17th-century debates on the historical origins of the American natives, 18th-century debates on the occurrence of prodigies in nature, and 19th-century discourses of medicine and psychiatry. The medicalization of homosexuality in particular multiplied terms. Up to that time, most European words for homosexuality were derived from mythical originators and precedents—*sodomy* from Sodom, *catamite* from Ganymede, *lesbian* from Lesbos. The new taxonomy—*urning, homosexual, transvestite*—labeled people in terms of intrinsic psychic and physical traits they were believed to possess, which categorically distinguished them from others. Of course, natural scientists since the 18th century had been labeling plant and animal species on the basis of similar assumptions. In the 19th century, this taxonomic approach was applied to human racial groups as well. In *Geography of Perversion*, historian Rudi Bleys has persuasively argued that the construction of new sexual categories in the 19th century was closely linked to the construction of essentialized categories of race and gender, which occurred in the same period.

These developments are also evident in writings on African homosexualities. The earliest accounts, like that of Father Cavazzi, linked same-sex patterns to a general definition of African "otherness," which contrasted European restraint to African lasciviousness. In this regard, as Bleys points out, "Africanist discourse hardly diverged from constructions of American and Asian identity, as it equally turned indigenous sexuality into a metaphor of cultural difference" (1995: 35).

However, the overall body of references to African same-sex patterns is much smaller. Bleys speculates that the demand for black slave labor fostered a discourse on black masculinity that excluded evidence of nonmasculinity and homosexuality or made such behaviors less visible to Europeans. In addition, many reporters arrived in Africa already influenced by the statements of Gibbon and others that Africa lacked same-sex patterns. Consequently, no sustained discussion of African same-sex patterns was published until the early 20th century, and few reports ventured explanations for African same-sex patterns. Occasionally, one encounters a pseudohistorical etiology, for example, that same-sex relations were imported by Arabs or adopted due to their influence.[6] Ulterior motives for such assertions are usually obvious, however, whether it is Christian Europeans blaming homosexuality on Muslims, French blaming it on Italians, or the member of one African society blaming it on another.

Because of the paucity of reports from Africa and their predominantly moralistic tone, the appearance of medical-psychiatric terminology is striking. Phrases like "morbid eroticism" in A. Corre's 1894 report on homosexuality in French Senegal and Guinea (59), and "contrary sex occurrences" in Michael Haberlandt's 1899 article on Zanzibar are borrowed directly from the medical-psychiatric terminology of Karl Ulrichs, Richard von Krafft-Ebing, Albert Moll, Magnus Hirschfeld, and other German authorities, beginning in the 1860s.[7] By the end of the century, familiarity with this terminology was widespread among German and French writers. It is evident in texts by Lasnet (1899), Haberlandt (1899), Kandt (1905: 150), Roux (1905), Hammer (1909), Bieber (1909), Falk (1923, 1925–26), and Tessman (1921). English writers, in contrast, were slower to adopt the new terminology. Through the 1920s, texts in English (including those of anthropologists) continued to describe African same-sex patterns in terms of "pederasty" (Smith and Dale 1920), "unnatural rites" (Talbot 1926), and "pederastical practices" (Butt-Thompson 1929). In his contribution to this book, however, Epprecht reports testimony in Zimbabwe courts in the 1920s that indicates that English colonial authorities were beginning to employ psychiatric language—and that natives were refuting it. Epprecht quotes one native as saying, in reference to his cross-dressing son, "I have never thought him mentally affected." Once Anglo-American anthropologists adopted sexological terminology, they were slow to abandon it. When Evans-Pritchard finally published his observations of Azande homosexuality in 1970, he did so under the rubric of *sexual inversion*—a term from pre-Freudian sexology.

Medical-psychiatric theories treated male homosexuality as an innate condition—one in which nonmasculinity was linked to same-sex desire. This determined that a central focus of the discourse on homosexuality would be arbitrating the discrepancies between the ideal type and specific instances, whose relations to the ideal were not always clear. Egalitarian and age-defined patterns involving noneffeminate men, for example, did not fit into the third-sex paradigm dominant in medical discourse until the 1920s. Still, other concerns arose from disagreements as to whether homosexuality was inborn or acquired, genuine or situational, natural or unnatural, pathological or normal. Earlier ethnographic literature was cited in all these discussions, while new reports came increasingly to be framed in terms of these debates (see W. Roscoe 1995).

Haberlandt's 1899 article on Zanzibar, for example, is concerned with distinguishing inborn (*angeborne*) "contrariness" (a psychological condition rather than an act, like sodomy) from that which is "acquired" (*erworbene*). One of the preoccupations of medical-psychiatric discourse at this time was reconciling an older theory of homosexuality as acquired (through degeneracy, which was conceived simultaneously as a failure of morality and physiology, a favored 19th-century explanation for both group and individual behavior) and the newer theory of homosexuality as an inborn orientation. There is no evidence, however, that these distinctions were used by the natives of Zanzibar—Haberlandt does not quote natives on the subject, nor does he provide case histories that might elucidate how and why individuals came to be engaged in the behaviors he reports. Indeed, from the perspectives of the discourse Haberlandt relies on, contrariness is an essential psychic condition that can occur in any human population and is the same phenomenon in each case. Native understandings can only be misunderstandings in relation to the facts of Western scientific discourse.

Consequently, Haberlandt's statement that "the adolescent slaves that are selected [for use as 'catamites'] are kept away from any work, well pampered, and systematically effeminized" reflects his reliance on the tropes of degeneracy theory, which require him to assume that effeminacy and homosexual desire *followed* social selection (1899: 668). He does not consider the possibility that such traits *preceded* selection and were the basis for it—a conclusion that can just as easily be supported by his data. The need to account for noncommercial homosexuality by individuals who are not slaves and therefore not "selected" for such relations, but willingly pursue them, requires Haberlandt's second theory—that of congenital homosexuality. Congenital "contraries," Haberlandt reports, are individuals who from youth have "no desire for women and only find pleasure in female occupations." He then makes a curious statement: "In outward appearance, inborn contrary men are not distinguishable from male prostitutes, but the natives make a sharp distinction between them: the professional catamites are despised, while the behavior of the inborn-contrary is tolerated as *amri ya muungu* (the will of God)" (669). Here, Haberlandt admits that his theoretical distinctions between inborn and acquired cannot be verified empirically, but then he claims that the native view agrees with his. What is apparent on close reading is that the distinction he attributes to the natives has nothing to do with beliefs about inborn or acquired homosexuality but rather with the difference between consciously chosen immoral behavior (prostitution) and that which is God's will. This is quite a different idea from that of congenitalism, and it implies a different moral outlook as well. In the West, it has been rarely claimed (until recently by lesbian and gay Christians) that God wills the existence of homosexuals.

German discussions of same-sex relations in Africa written in the 1910s and 1920s reflect the influence of a discourse paralleling that of the medical authorities, which sought to construct a nonstigmatized identity for homosexuals. In fact, the medical-psychiatric construction of homosexuality as an essential, inborn disposition was first fostered by homosexuals, such as Ulrichs. Among other things, it allowed them to argue that, being inborn, homosexuality should not be subject to legal and moral persecution. However, when the medical and psychiatric establishment adopted the congenital model, it insisted that such a condition was a disease. Thus, a debate over the status of congenital homosexuality developed—whether it was pathological or normal, diseased or natural, changeable or inherent.

Echoes of this debate are evident in Kurt Falk's articles about homosexuality in Angola and Southwest Africa, included herein. In a variation of Haberlandt's distinction between congenital and acquired homosexuality, Falk tries to distinguish "true" from "pseudo" (or "situational") homosexuality. While he acknowledged widespread homosexual behavior on the part of *Bisexuellen* and *Pseudohomosexuellen*, he considers this incidental to that of "true," congenital homosexuals, who, following the Ulrich-Hirschfeld model, represent an intermediate or third sex and were therefore nonmasculine.

This distinction between "true" and "pseudo" homosexuality had become important in debates over the German law banning homosexuality, in paragraph 175. The reformers who sought to repeal this law felt compelled to argue that not all homosexuality needed to be allowed. The behavior of those who engaged in homosexuality only because they lacked heterosexual outlets, or to obtain money, or out of libertinism, or to debauch minors should be punished. But allowance had to be made for "true" homosexuals, whose desires were inborn and who therefore could not help themselves. To attempt to legislate against a congenital condition was pointless, and to deny such individuals the opportunity of sexual release and emotional relationships was not only cruel but also psychologically and physically harmful. Falk's conclusions clearly reflect his involvement in this discourse: "Anyone who refutes inborn homosexuality should take a look at native people and he will soon change his mind" (1925–26: 214).

Günther Tessman, himself a repressed homosexual (Klockmann 1985), argues similarly in his 1921 article (translated in part III): The existence of widespread homosexual relationships among the Bafia of Cameroon, he suggests, supports the conclusion that "homosexual desires are firmly established in human nature" (Tessman 1921). Both Falk and Tessman drew on a well-established counter-discourse with roots in the Enlightenment that sought to criticize Western civilization by reversing the usual values attributed to "nature" and "civilization." What was "natural" and "primitive," rather than being inferior to the civilized, was portrayed as superior—simpler, healthier, and more democratic in comparison to civilization, which was artificial, stultified, and static. The "noble savage" was an implicit critique of the ruling nobility of Europe.

With this, discourse on homosexuality comes full circle—from the citation of African homosexualities in debates on the moral, cultural, and racial inferiority of Africans, to its citation in texts constructing homosexuality as an essential (albeit pathological) condition, and finally, its appearance in discourses constructing a nonpathological homosexual identity in terms of the sexual politics of Western societies in the 20th century.

Given the history of Western discourse on sexuality, using colonial and anthropological reports requires a strategy of double reading—first, to identify the tropes of the discourse in which the ethnographic data are represented and, second, to identify the ethnographic data. Of course, some might consider the project of disentangling "data" from the tropes of ethnographic writing impossible. Discourse, they might argue, constructs its data; there are no transcendental signifieds, let alone "hard facts," whose meaning will be transparent to all readers, regardless of the language used to describe them. What we are suggesting, however, is a more modest goal—that of seeking to *control* the effects of Western discursive regimes on what observers of African sexualities write.

Accomplishing this double reading requires familiarity with the history of European texts on sexuality, including their terminology, rhetoric, and the internal contradictions that generate (and constrain) their debates. This makes it possible to identify and control for discursive effects in the reporting of observations. Thus, if a writer states that "unnatural crimes are unknown" for a given group, we know that the terminology *unnatural crimes* is part of Judeo-Christian discourse. This alone, of course, does not warrant claiming that same-sex relations are present despite the writer's report, but it does require us to ask various questions about the original statement. If, for example, an observer uses a phrase like "unnatural crimes" in questioning natives about their practices, and if the social group to which those individuals belong does not view same-sex relations as "unnatural crimes," then it is quite possible that they will respond, "No, we don't do that," when in fact homosexual patterns do occur.

Statements purporting to report native attitudes toward homosexuality must also be analyzed in this way. Same-sex behavior and relationships may indeed by disapproved of in some groups, but too often, Western reporters fail to determine the basis (or extent) of the disapproval and assume that it is derived from the same moral precepts that underlie Western disapproval (for example, that such behavior is a sin, a crime, or a sickness).

Having separated what can be attributed to discursive imperatives from what *might* be attributable to something actually seen or heard in Africa, it is then necessary to "test" the "data," to the extent possible. New fieldwork and reports from Africans themselves are, of course, highly desirable and can help verify and contextualize earlier reports. Contemporary reports, however, cannot always verify past practices and beliefs about them—and postcolonial writers, European and African, have been no less constrained by regimes of moral discourse than earlier writers. In any case, contemporary reports, if available, should be combined with a thorough review of all available literature on a given social group. The greater the familiarity of a reader with a culture, the better she or he is able to evaluate any given statement about it. A writer, for example, might state that "the X people believe that male homosexuality causes a disease." The reader, well-grounded in the history and culture of that group, will know whether or not such a statement is plausible; whether it is consistent with beliefs about the body and sexuality, health, disease, and so forth; and what the group's attitude toward this belief is—its moral, social, and religious implications. Such a reader will know not to assume that any given African group's belief about disease and sex parallels the Western medical model of homosexuality as a disease or that the association of same-sex practices with a disease necessarily implies a moral judgment.

In addition to ethnographic literature, a variety of primary source materials can also be used to reconstruct historical roles and practices. Epprecht's chapter is an excellent example of how even such seemingly biased records as those of colonial courts can be used to recover something of the practices and voices of native Africans who engaged in same-sex relations.

These are the procedures we have applied in reviewing the ethnographic literature in the introductions for each region. Explanatory schemes and rhetoric shape what is reportable, but careful reading often can extract valid data even from biased reporting. When we do relate the various theories and etiologies offered in the texts of the colonial era, it is not to lend them credence but merely to remind readers of the historical and discursive context from which the data are drawn.

Notes to the Introduction

1. For additional background on the development of this typology, see Murray 1995a: 1–16; 1999.

2. The priests of the Greco-Roman gods Cybele and Attis, the *galli*, were termed a *medium genus*, while classical Sanskrit texts refer to "eunuchs" and "impotent" males as a *trhytiya prakrhyti* (third kind) (see Roscoe 1996).

3. Arabic sources have yet to be scrutinized for what was found in the way of sexual practices as Islamic traders descended the coasts of Africa beginning as early as the ninth century.

4. Missionaries in California also assumed that native males who cross-dressed did so to gain access to women for sexual purposes—until they discovered a male berdache having sex with a man (Palou [1787] 1913: 215).

5. These statements are quoted in "Submission by the National Coalition for Gay and Lesbian Equality on Homophobia in the Conduct and Defence of Winnie Madikizela-Mandela," Truth and Reconciliation Commission, Johannesburg, November 24–December 4, 1997.

6. See, for example, J. Roscoe (1907), Junod ([1912] 1927), Corre (1894: 80 n. 1), Schneider (1885: 295–96), Haberlandt (1899), and Messing (1957: 551).

7. On the emergence of the medical model of homosexuality, see A. Davidson (1990) and Chauncey (1982).

Part I

Horn of Africa, Sudan, and East Africa

Overview

Societies throughout the Horn of Africa and the Sudanic belt combine agriculture and pastoralism. In Ethiopia and Eritrea, long-standing contact with the Near East accounts for the early presence of metallurgy and weaving, an extensive market system, and Christian and Islamic religions. Islamic influence is strong among the Bantu-speaking populations of coastal East Africa, especially in port cities, such as Mombasa and Zanzibar. Patrilineal Bantu-speakers also occupy the highland savannas of Kenya, where agriculture is the dominant subsistence pattern, and the grasslands of the great lakes region, where pastoralism and agriculture are combined. Amid these Bantu-speaking groups is a wedge of Nilotic pastoralists, speaking eastern Sudanic languages, that extends from north of Lake Victoria in Uganda south through western Kenya and northern Tanzania. Several kingdoms flourished in this region.

Horn of Africa

The Italian Paolo Ambrogetti, at the beginning of the 20th century, reported age-based homosexual relations between Eritrean men and what he called *diavoletti* (little devils) (1900: 16). Regarded as being no more than a mild fault, these relationships were pursued quite openly and tolerated by the boys' fathers since it was a source of income. After puberty, the boys generally began to have relations with females, but *diavoletti* especially attached to their patrons might continue their relations with them until they were 20 years old. An unusual case was a 25-year-old married chief who continued to have receptive intercourse with men *senza lucro* (not for payment). Ambrogetti also reported that many apparently effeminate Eritreans were not "sexual inverts" (16), echoing other writers of this period who argued that same-sex behavior among "nature peoples" was situational and that few, if any, were "real" or "constitutional" homosexuals (see Bleys 1995: 185–92).

A few years later, Friedrich Bieber described what he termed "Uranism" among the Islamic Harari, Semitic-speaking agriculturalists near the Ethiopian city of Harar (Harer). According to Bieber, "Sodomy is not foreign to the Harari" (1909: 404). Such relations appear not to have been organized in terms of age or gender status, however—"Uranism" occurred as often between adult men as between men and youths. He also reported similar practices among the Cushitic-speaking Galla, pastoralists in southern Ethiopia, and their neighbors, the Somali, "albeit not as commonly" (405). In addition, both sexes and all ages in all three groups (Harari, Galla, Somal) practiced mutual masturbation. More recently, Frederick Gamst reported homosexual relations among shepherd boys of the Cushitic-speaking Qemant (Kemant) of central Ethiopia (1969: 106).

In the 1950s, Simon Messing encountered males with alternative gender identities among the nearby Coptic Amhara peasants. Viewed as "god's mistakes," they were generally well accepted. Such *wändarwäräd* (literally, "male-female"), as they were termed, were believed to be physically defective (1957: 550). They "live as individuals, not forming a society of their own, for they are tolerated. Only their kinfolk are ashamed of them, so they go to live in another province. Women tolerate a transvestite 'like a brother'; men are not jealous of him even when he spends all his time with the womenfolk. Often the transvestite is an unusually sensitive person, quick to anger, but intense in his personal likings, sensitive to cultural diffusions from the outside world, especially those carried by Arab traders; and Muslim Arab traders are often the only male contacts he tolerates" (551). He also found "mannish women" (*wändawände*) suspected of attempting to abrogate male privileges (550), although he did not inquire into their sexual conduct.

Christopher Hallpike conducted fieldwork in the mid-1960s among the Cushitic-speaking Konso, agriculturalists living in walled cities on the southern edge of Ethiopia. He found a complex of beliefs concerning the danger to men of contact with women. Konso men believe that "women have an emotionally as well as physically deleterious influence on men," and one told Hallpike, "Some girls' vaginas are so strong that they can snap off a man's penis" (1972: 153, 152). These beliefs are reflected in restrictions on when and how often marital intercourse could occur that are as severe as those of the Melanesian societies that have served in anthropological literature as the prototypes of sexually antagonistic cultures (see Herdt 1984).

The Konso have "two words each for penis, vagina, and sexual intercourse, but no less than four for 'effeminate man'" (Hallpike 1972: 150).
One of these categories, *sagoda*, includes men who never marry, weak men,
and men who wear skirts.

> Men who actually wear skirts are very few, and those who do
> are clearly incapable of acting as men. I knew one in Gaho,
> who earned his living curing skins, a female occupation. He was
> very effeminate in voice and manner. . . . I was told that *sagoda*
> liked to play the passive role in sodomy, and the description I
> was given of the manner in which a *sagoda* would induce a man
> to perform this upon him in the night was so detailed that it
> could not have been invented. The question is whether normal
> men only practice sodomy with *sagoda* or among themselves.
> I am strongly inclined to think it is not confined to relations
> with *sagoda*. (151)

Although Konso men "were generally very reluctant to talk about sexual
matters," Hallpike heard "coarse remarks on occasion" that included jokes
about taking a man reputed to be a *sagoda* into the fields and raping him.
Hallpike concluded, "This sort of occasion, the conduct of transvestites,
and the sexual strains put on men by society, lead one to suppose that
they seek relief among themselves on occasion. But this is not to say it is
approved of" (1972: 151).

Among the Maale of southern Ethiopia, Donald Donham observed that
"a small minority [of men] crossed over to feminine roles. Called *ashtime*,
these (biological) males dressed like women, performed female tasks, cared
for their own houses, and apparently had sexual relations with men" (1990:
92). Donham interviewed an *ashtime*, who described his status in terms of
a distinct gender conception: "The Divinity created me *wobo*, crooked. If I
had been a man, I could have taken a wife and begotten children. If I had
been a woman, I could have married and borne children. But I am *wobo*;
I can do neither." Although this individual was the only *ashtime* Donham
knew, Maale men told him that more had existed in the 19th century:
"Indeed, part of the Maale kin's traditional installation had consisted of a
ritual ordination of an *ashtime*." By 1975, however, the Maale considered
ashtime "abnormal" (92).

Donham suggested that rather than discrete gender categories, the
Maale recognize a continuous gradation of maleness from the ritual kings

to subchiefs on down (1990: 112). The ritual king "was the male principle incarnate." Consequently, no woman of childbearing age could enter the king's compound. Domestic labor generally done by women was performed instead by *ashtime*, who in traditional times were gathered and protected by the kings. On nights before royal rituals, when the king was prohibited from having sexual relations with women, "lying with an *ashtime* was not interdicted." Thus, Donham concluded, *ashtime* constituted "part of the generativity of maleness in Maale" (113).

Sudan

In his study of non-Islamic Nuban groups in Sudan who traditionally combined agriculture and cattle herding, Siegfried Nadel contrasted the sexuality of the Heiban and the Otoro. Among the former, he found "no expected corollary of homosexual acts" (that is, no role or social identity based on homosexuality), but among the latter, a recognized role for males who dressed and lived as women was noted (1955: 677). In an earlier report, Nadel also mentioned gender-differentiated homosexuality among the related Moro and Tira, as well as the Nubian Nyima to the north (1947: 242).[1] Nonmasculine males were called *londo* by Nuban Krongo (Korongo) and *tubele* by the Mesakin, and they could marry men (285).[2] Such marriages required a "bride-price" of one goat, and the generally young husband might also have female wives: " 'Wife' and 'husband' lie together and keep a common household. The 'marriages' rarely last long: the 'husband' is as a rule a young man who will outgrow his homosexual learnings, or who had been induced to play this part by the promise of an easy life. He would soon tire of the unnatural life and abandon his male 'wife.' The fact that he had lived in this homosexual union does not disqualify him for marriage in the eyes of the women. In fact, I heard of two Mesakin men who had each for a time lived with two 'wives,' one male and one female" (285).

Although Nadel did not specify whether *londo* and *tubele* were older than their husbands, his use of "young" suggests they were. According to Nadel, in these societies with "widespread homosexuality and transvesticism," men feared heterosexual intercourse as sapping virility. Consequently, they were often reluctant to abandon the pleasures of all-male camp life for the fetters of permanent residence: "I have even met men of forty and fifty who spent most of their nights with the young folk in the cattle camps instead of at home in the village" (1947: 300).[3]

Brian MacDermot's 1972 report of denials of homosexuality by the pastoralist Nuer of Sudan—despite the presence of a gender-defined role for males that could include marriage to men—was cited in the Preface. Although he found Nuer statements confusing, there was no contradiction from their point of view. The old man who did women's work had changed his gender, as far as they were concerned. Thus, intercourse with him was not viewed as an encounter between two men.

In Khartoum, Carolyn Fluehr-Lobban observed premarital peer homosexuality during fieldwork from 1970 to 1972. "If a man dares to gain some sexual experience before marriage," she noted, "he must do it in the prostitutes' quarter or through temporary homosexual liaisons that are tolerated before marriage" (1977: 134). She did not indicate whether involvement in homosexual activity is temporary for both partners or what they do sexually.

Anthropologists also have documented gender-defined roles for males in contemporary Sudanese possession cults.[4] In the 1970s, among the Muslim riverine peoples of northern Sudan, Pamela Constantinides witnessed male participation in a healing cult called *zaar*, which is otherwise the domain of women: "Some men are regular participants at cult rituals, and a few become cult group leaders. Of this male minority, some are overt homosexuals, while others may initially have symptoms, such as bleeding from the anus or penis, which tend symbolically to classify them with women" (1977: 63).[5] According to Constantinides, while "men who attend zaar rituals regularly are suspected by both men and women of being homosexual," there is also suspicion that some men may "dishonourably [be] gaining access to women by feigning illness"(63). (Similar accusations are made regarding *'yan daudu* in the *bori* cult of the Hausa; see part II.)

Zande

The (A)Zande are an Islamic-influenced forest people occupying a region where tsetse flies preclude stock raising—in southwestern Sudan, the Central African Republic, and the northeastern Congo. Although they resemble other forest-clearing peoples in the importance of their secret associations, they are distinguished by having created a monarchical state (actually a loose confederation of chiefdoms) supported by a nobility. Zande society as a whole recognized patrilineal descent, although ruling families gave preference to the maternal line (Maquet 1972: 173–74).

References to Zande homosexuality were already published at the time
Edward Evans-Pritchard undertook his fieldwork. In the 1920s, P. M. Larken
had referred to the practice of chiefs having sex with youths because they were
presumably free of diseases (1926–27: 24), while Jan Czekanowski rejected
the claims of European residents that pederasty was an Arabic introduction
and not an indigenous practice (1924: 56). Evans-Pritchard's data, although
late in reaching publication, are more detailed. Describing traditional Zande
culture as remembered by his informants, he wrote:

> Homosexuality is indigenous. Zande do not regard it as at all
> improper, indeed as very sensible for a man to sleep with boys
> when women are not available or are taboo. . . . In the past
> this was a regular practice at court. Some princes may even have
> preferred boys to women, when both were available. This is not
> a question I can enter into further here beyond saying I was told
> that some princes sleep with boys before consulting poison oracles,
> women being then taboo, and also that they sometimes do so
> on other occasions, just because they like them." (1971: 183)

Evans-Pritchard's informant Kuagbiaru stated: "Men used to have sexual
relations with boys as they did with wives. A man paid compensation to
another if he had relations with his boy. People asked for the hand of a boy
with a spear, just as they asked for the hand of a maiden of her parents.
All those young warriors who were at court, all had boys" (1970: 1430).

Kuagbiaru also told Evans-Pritchard that when a "boy"—that is, any
male between the ages of 12 and 20—appealed to a prince, the prince would
summon the boy as a page. Later, the prince "provided bridewealth for his
pages when they grew up," although "when a prince dies they do not let
his pages escape; they kill them after the prince is dead, for they have eaten
the prince's oil. People call them 'the prince's old barkcloth,' for, because he
used to summon them all the time, they are like his old barkcloth" (1971:
185). Institutionalized relationships with youths were not limited to princes
and their pages, however:

> Many of the young warriors married boys, and a commander
> might have more than one boy-wife. When a warrior married a
> boy he paid spears [bride-price], though only a few, to the boy's
> parents, as he would have done had he married their daughter.
> The warrior in other ways acted towards the parents as though

he had married their daughter. . . . He addressed the parents as
gbiore and *negbiore*, "my father-in-law" and "my mother-in-law."
He gave the boy himself pretty ornaments; and he and the boy
addressed one another as *badiare*, "my love" and "my lover."[6]
The boy fetched water for his husband, collected firewood
and kindled his fire, bore his shield when traveling. . . .[7] The
two slept together at nights, the husband satisfying his desires
between the boy's thighs. When the boy grew up he joined the
company and took a boy-wife in his turn. It was the duty of
the husband to give his boy-wife a spear and a shield when he
became a warrior. He then took a new boy-wife. Thus, Kuagbiaru,
a member and later a commander of one of Prince Gangura's
companies, married three boys in succession. (1971: 199–200)

Another commander, Ganga, told Evans-Pritchard that "there were
some men who although they had female wives, still married boys. When
a war broke out, they took their boys with them, although they were left
in camp, as befitted their wifely status, not their future status as fellow
warriors" (1970: 1431). The warrior paid bridewealth (five or more spears)
to the parents of the boy and performed services for them as he would have
done had he married their daughter. If another man had relations with the
boy, the husband could sue the interloper for adultery (1429).

Evans-Pritchard maintained that "it was on account of the difficulties
of getting satisfaction in heterosexual relationships that boy marriage was
recognized." As evidence he pointed to the fact that, as marriage between men
and women became easier and earlier, "boy-marriage has in post-European
times entirely disappeared," but so had the military companies and the
royal court, which were its context. Despite these changes, Evans-Pritchard
reported, "I have never heard anyone speak of sleeping with a boy with
distaste" (1970: 1429).

Evans-Pritchard's account of Zande age-stratified homosexuality shows
such relationships to be the product of both individual motivations (sexual
and other) and a complex set of social expectations and practices. Earlier
authors less credibly attributed it solely to situational factors, discounting
the involvement (or possibility) of homosexual desire or preference. R.
P. Graere, for example, blamed Zande homosexuality on the monopoly
of women by rich and powerful men (1929: 362). Similarly, the French
colonial administrator Adolphe Cureau attributed the origins of pederasty
among the Sandeh (that is, Zande) to the Turks and the continuation of

the practice to the monopolization of women in the vast harems (*bodimoh*) of Sandeh royalty. Vassals, soldiers, and servants had to make do with what the rulers left. Consequently, Cureau argued, boy *nsanga* (*servants d'armes*) took the place of women. Wearing their hair artfully parted, with arms and necks loaded with decorations, a woolen skirt around the hips, and their bodies oiled and glistening, the boys were at the disposal of soldiers. Called *ndongo-techi-la*, they followed their husbands on their marches, carrying their rifles and provisions. In the camps, they cooked and managed household finances (1904: 644–45).

Zande Woman-Woman Relations

Among the Zande, the Seligmans reported that sisters who married brothers "have a reputation for lesbian practices" (1932: 515). According to Evans-Pritchard:

> All Azande I have known well enough to discuss this matter have asserted that female homosexuality was practiced in polygamous homes in the past and still [ca. 1930] is sometimes. . . . One of the many wives of a prince or of an important commoner in the past might not have shared her husband's bed for a month or two, whereas some of the dozens, even hundreds, of wives of a king must have been almost totally deprived of the sex life normal in smaller homes. Adulterous intercourse was very difficult for a wife in such large polygamous families, for the wives were kept in seclusion and carefully watched. . . . Wives would cut a sweet potato or manioc root in the shape of the male organ, or use a banana for the purpose. Two of them would shut themselves in a hut and one would lie on the bed and play the female role while the other, with the artificial organ tied around her stomach, played the male role. They then reversed roles. (1970: 1429, 1431–32)

In the same article, Evans-Pritchard reproduced texts from two male informants about special friendships between women that mimicked male blood brotherhood relations. Two women would break a cob of blood-red corn (*kaima*) and utter a spell over it: "After this they should not call each other by their proper names, but they call each other *bagburu*. The one who is the wife cooks porridge and a fowl and brings them to the one who is the husband. They do this between them many times. They have sexual intercourse between them with sweet potatoes carved in the shape of a circumcised penis, with carved manioc also, and also with bananas" (1970: 1432). This relationship was not approved by Zande men. Evans-Pritchard asserted that "it is a further indication of male dominance that what was encouraged among males was condemned among females. Zande men, princes especially, have a horror of lesbianism, and they regard it as highly dangerous" (1432).

Closer to the time of his fieldwork, Evans-Pritchard reported the Azande belief that women had sex with *adandara*, a species of wild cat considered female and unlucky: "Both are female actions which may cause the death of any man who witnesses them" (1937: 56). Without offering much insight into how the women involved understood the practices, he noted:

> Zande women, especially in the homesteads of princes, indulge in homosexual relations by means of a phallus fashioned from roots. It is said that in the past a prince did not hesitate to execute a wife whose homosexual activities were discovered, and even today I have known a prince to expel wives form his household for the same reason. Among lesser folk, if a man discovers that his wife has Lesbian relations with other women he flogs her and there is a scandal. The husband's anger is due to his fear of the unlucky consequences that may ensue from such practices. Azande therefore speak of them as evil in the same way as they speak of witchcraft and cats as evil, and they say, moreover, that homosexual women are the sort who may well give birth to cats and be witches also. In giving birth to cats and in Lesbianism the evil is associated with the sexual functions of women, and it is to be noted that any unusual action of the female genitalia is considered unlucky. (56)[8]

Coastal East Africa

The Swahili-speakers on the Kenyan coast provide an instance where reports of same-sex patterns are not only detailed but also have some historical depth. A vigorous debate has developed over the exact interpretation of this evidence, which appears to document gender-defined roles as well as age-differentiated and even egalitarian homosexuality. These reports come primarily from the port cities and surrounding regions of Zanzibar and

Mombasa. The indigenous population of these areas speak Bantu languages, but as Muslim domination of Indian Ocean trade—and cultural and political influence—increased after 1000, they became Muslim city-states with close ties to Arabia, especially the sultanate of Oman. The integration of African and Islamic culture in these cities is extensive, as evidenced by the large number of Arabic words in Swahili, a Bantu language that was long used for African-Arabic trade.

European reports of homosexuality in Mombasa and Zanzibar date to the 19th century. The first Swahili-English dictionary, published in 1882, included the term *mumémke* (*mume*, "man"; *mke*, "woman") along with *hánithi*, defined as "catamite," which is clearly related to *khanith*, the term for an alternative gender status in Oman (Krapf 1882: 891).[9] The latter also has been transcribed as *hanisi* and defined as "effeminate" (Madan 1902: 92).[10] At the beginning of the 20th century, Michael Haberlandt reported that on Zanzibar "homosexuals of both sexes are designated in the Swahili language as *mke-si-mume* ('woman, not man'). However, the expressions *mzebe* and the Arabian-derived *hanisi*, which actually mean an impotent person, also apply" (1899: 670). (See the translation of Haberlandt's report that follows.) According to Haberlandt, such males were prominent in Ngambo, especially at dances, although their dress and deportment was variable—some cross-dressing, some distinguishing themselves by headdress alone, yet others dressing as men. They derived their income from prostitution.

A half century later, Godfrey Wilson described an occasion in Lamu, a Swahili town north of Mombasa, when boys dressed as women performed a striptease and then paired off with older men from the audience (1957: 1; cited by Shepherd 1987: 269, n. 9).

Based on observations during her 1970s field research in the Comorian community (individuals from or descended from the Comoros Islands), Gill Shepherd published two reports on Mombasan same-sex patterns—and sparked a lively debate over their interpretation. In her first report, she described male homosexuality as largely a matter of prostitution: "Mombasa's *mashoga* [sing. *shoga*] are passive male homosexuals offering their persons for money. They advertise themselves in bright tight *male* attire in public places, usually, but may, when mingling with women at weddings, don women's *leso* cloths, make-up and jasmine posies. *Mashoga* have all the liberties of men and are also welcome in many contexts otherwise exclusive to women" (1978a: 133). She concluded that although "there are long-lasting relationships between homosexuals in Mombasa, most homosexual acts are fleeting, paid for in cash" (1978b: 644).

In a subsequent report, Shepherd modified this description somewhat:

The Swahili [word] for a male homosexual is *shoga*, a word also used between women to mean "friend." Homosexual relations in Mombasa are almost without exception between a younger, poorer partner and an older, richer one, whether their connection is for a brief act of prostitution or a more lengthy relationship. In the former case, there are fixed rates of payment, and in the latter, presents and perhaps full financial support for a while. But financial considerations are always involved and it is generally only the person who is paid who is called *shoga*. The older partner may have been a *shoga* himself in his youth, but is very likely to be successfully married to a woman as well as maintaining an interest in boys. Only if he is not married and has an apparently exclusive interest in homosexual contacts will he perhaps still be referred to as a *shoga*. The paid partner usually takes the passive role during intercourse, but I think it is true to say that his inferiority derives from the fact that he is paid to provide what is asked for, rather than for the [specific sexual] role he adopts. . . . The paying partner is usually known as the *basha* [pl. *mabasha*]—the Pasha, the local term for the king in packs of playing cards. (1987: 250)[11]

According to Shepherd, "both male and female homo-sexuality is relatively common among Muslims, involving perhaps one in twenty-five adults" (1978a: 133). Without explanation, she subsequently raised the estimate to 1 in 10 (1987: 240).

Shepherd's consistent thesis is that rank is more important than gender in the Mombasan construction of homosexuality. Indeed, she has argued that trading sexual compliance (that is, being penetrated) for money or aid is simply a case of "patron-client relations given a sexual dimension" (1987: 255). The emphasis on wealth is apparent in the passage just quoted. However, it is immediately followed by a description of the Mombasan belief that some boys become homosexual because they are nonmasculine (that is, "pretty"): "People say that they can predict who will be a homosexual, even with boys as young as 5 or 6 years old at times. They seem to base their prediction upon prettiness and family circumstances; boys reared in all-female households by a divorced mother and several sisters are likely to become homosexuals, they say, and the prediction is self-fulfilling since these are the boys whom men are certain to approach. 'If he's not a homosexual yet, he will be,' say women of teenage boys from such households" (250–51). Shepherd may be correct that economic status is the primary means of differentiating *basha* from *shoga*, but clearly more than economics is involved.

Although Shepherd (1978a,b) strenuously objected to Unni Wikan's (1977) suggestion that *mashoga* represent a transsexual or third-gender conception, she acknowledged some gender variance in their dress, if not as part of an attempt to pass as women.[12] Rather, *shoga* "tend to employ the gait and voice which are the international signals of homosexuality" (Shepherd 1987: 259–60). (Exactly what these signals are she does not say.) Her point is that "these seem to be imitated from other homosexuals, not from women, and the modest and quietness of ideal Swahili womanhood are quite absent in homosexual behaviour."[13] Consequently, *shoga* are not classified as women. They do not do women's tasks, "but are rather used as junior male kin are" (253). In fact, their participation with women in weddings is not typical of everyday interaction (1978b: 664). On most occasions, "when the mood is less playful—at a prayer-time, for instance, or at a funeral—the *shoga* must attend with men or not attend at all." Shepherd concludes, "It would be quite wrong to suggest that homosexuals ought always to be in the company of women in situations where there is formal segregation" (1987: 253).

Mary Porter conducted research in Mombasa in the late 1980s. Like Shepherd, her primary research focus was not on *mashoga*; however, she did work in the Swahili community. Porter is admirably clear that what she has described are "discourses on homosexuality," not the self-understandings of Kenyans involved in same-sex sexual relations. According to Porter, in addition to *(ma)shoga* and *hanithi*, both of which have Arabic roots, and *(ma)basha*, which is derived from Persian, two other terms are used: *msagaliwa*, which has a Bantu root and "refers literally to men who grind *liwa*, an aromatic wood," to produce a cosmetic paste, and *rambuza*, a seemingly Bantu-based word for effeminate males (1995: 142). She saw *mashoga* in women's dances at wedding celebrations, playing *pembe* (a female musical instrument) and doing *chagkacha*, a "woman's dance form that entails hip rotation in an exclusively female way" (141). They sat with women at funerals and took flamboyant parts, sometimes wigged and dressed in women's clothes, in religious celebrations. They were "said to engage in women's domestic tasks such as cooking and sewing" (141). And contrary to the ready acceptance Shepherd presented, Porter observed that at least by the late 1980s, *mashoga* were targets of verbal and physical violence and that some people's animus for them was so great that they would not attend weddings at which they performed (142).

Deborah Amory's chapter, based on actual research and interviews with *mashoga*, is a significant contribution to this debate. As she shows, the role of *shoga* serves to mark the boundaries of conventional behavior for men and women. At the same time, individuals who assume *shoga* identity express a variety of traits, behaviors, and interpretations of the role.

Having absorbed Arabic and Muslim influence in the past, coastal East Africa is now responding to influences from the West, including the influence of Western gay sexual patterns. Amory found that the English terms *gay*, *boyfriend*, and *girlfriend* are frequently employed by coastal East Africans today.[14]

"Grinders"

In arguing against a third-sex or -gender conception in Oman or Mombasa, Shepherd noted that "lesbians [in Mombasa] are known as *wasaga* (grinders). . . . The dominant partner . . . is not seen as a man" (1978a: 133). However, she reported that "there is almost always a dominant and subordinate economic relationship between them" (134). She later revised her transcription: "The word in Swahili glossed as 'lesbian' is *msagaji* (plural *wasagaji*)—'a grinder.'[15] The verb *kusaga* (to grind) is commonly used for the grinding of grain between two millstones . . . The upper and lower millstones are known as *mwana* and *mama* respectively: child and mother" (1987: 254). In this relationship, one woman is typically older and wealthier than the other. Shepherd did not indicate, however, whether these distinctions affect sexual behavior inside the relationship.

According to her later account, "Lesbians dress entirely as women. Their wealth enables them to dress in a rich and feminine way, and though dominant lesbians are more assertive in manner and conversation than most other women, they make no attempt to look like men. When they go out they wear the veil (*buibui*) like all other coastal women. . . . Dependent lesbian women are expected to behave like ordinary women. Dominant lesbian women display energetic personalities very similar to those of active, intelligent non-lesbian women" (1987: 259–60). However, Shepherd also claimed, "Women who are dominant lesbians do not obey strict seclusion rules. As household heads they welcome male visitors to the house and sit with them in the reception room, and they frequently go out of the house" (260). In short, her analyses of homosexuality among women, as among men, are contradicted by the behavior she reports.[16] *Msagaji* seem to be bidding for some male privilege beyond that of having sex with submissive women. That is, they do not entirely conform to Mombasa conceptions of how women should look and act.

As in the case of *mashoga*, gender variance is more salient than sexual behavior for labeling women *misago/wasagaji*. According to Porter, women who resist marriage and are interested in education and careers are labeled "*misago* regardless of the erotic preferences of the women. They are being condemned for behaving in ways that are inconsistent with being a woman and for challenging the gender/status system" (1995: 144).[17] She also heard the derogatory term *lezzies* used, which she interpreted as a diffusion of the Western view of close female-female relations as pathological and evidence of continuing colonial consciousness among Kenyans (144). More systematic data is needed to settle the question of whether gender or sexuality is primary in Swahili conceptions of lesbianism—especially among any self-identified *misago*.

The Interlake Region

Nilotes (Eastern Sudanic Languages)

According to Jean Buxton, the Mandari (Mondari, Mundar), an Islamic society of southern Sudan, connected witchcraft and homosexuality: "Homosexuality is viewed as a ludicrous and non-productive act. Thus while all perverts are not necessarily thought witches, since the latter know the aberrant or harmful nature of those habits, they exploit them designedly, in accordance with their wish to obstruct normal development" (1963: 103; also see 1973: 209). Although folks' fear of witches is widespread in Islamic cultures, this particular association has not been reported elsewhere.

In what was regarded in early 20th-century English social anthropology as an exemplary ethnography, Jack Driberg uncritically passed on the folk explanation of the Nilotic Lango, agriculturalists north of Lake Kwania in Uganda, that impotence is the basis for assuming the alternative gender status of *mudoko dako*.[18] Such males were treated as women and could marry men. Although Driberg thought that they were rare (estimating 50 out of 17,000 people), his Lango informants told him that their behavior was very common among groups to the east—specifically the pastoralist Iteso (Teso) and the Karamojan (Karamojong) of northwestern Kenya and Uganda (1923: 210).

(Similarly, in southwestern Uganda, Nkole informants told Musa Mushanga that the Bahima [but not themselves] practiced homosexuality [1973: 181].)

In fact, in the 1950s, Jeremy Laurance asserted that among the Iteso, "people of hermaphroditic instincts are very numerous. . . . The men are impotent and have the instincts of women and become women to all intents and purposes; their voices are feminine and their manner of walking and of speech is feminine. They shave their heads like a woman and wear women's ornaments and clothing. They do women's work and take women's names" (1957: 107). He wrote, "I myself know of no cases in which they live with men as a 'wife'" but added that in Serere prison, one was kept with the women because "the male prisoners would assault him were he imprisoned in the men's cell." He also published a song with the title, "The Fellow Who Pinches a Hermaphrodite Is a Fool" (160–61). Group masturbation by young Iteso males also has been reported but with no information on its frequency (Karp and Karp 1973: 392).

Cross-dressing is not always part of an ongoing social identity. In the mountains of western Kenya, Alfred Hollis observed circumcision festivals among the agriculturalist Nandi in which boys wore women's clothes for about eight weeks (1909: 52–56). He also published Massai texts that describe initiates, called Sipolio, who "like to appear as women and wear the *surutya* earrings and garments reaching to the ground. They also paint their faces with chalk. When they have all recovered they are shaved again and . . . discard the long garments and wear warrior's skins and ornaments" (1905: 298). However, homosexual relations in this region were not limited to those between normatively masculine and nonmasculine males. Felix Bryk referred to "homoerotic bachelors" among the Nandi and nearby Bantu-speaking Maragoli, and he described the case of a Nandi boy whose affair with a white farmer continued even after the boy married, so that he "shared his bed between wife and master" ([1928] 1939: 151). He also reported that some adult Nandi women "satisfied each other alternately" using wooden dildoes ([1928] 1939: 149).

Bantu Groups

Evidence exists of both gender-defined and peer homosexuality among Bantu groups of the Interlake region, most of whom combined agriculture and pastoralism (or were agriculturalists in symbiotic relationships with Nilotic pastoralists). Rodney Needham noted a religious leadership role among the agriculturalist Meru of the Kenyan highlands called *mugawe*. *Mugawe* wore women's clothes and hairstyles and sometimes married men (1973a: 116). Among the related Kikuyu, men who took the active role in sex with other men were called *onek*. (See the oral history of Kamau that follows.)

In the late 19th century, Haberlandt reported a nonmasculine member of the Wganda (Waganda, Ganda, Baganda) in southern Uganda who was "totally given to passive pederasty" (1899: 668). Bryk wrote that "in Uganda I saw two boys, a Mgisho and a Baganda, lying in bed together, whereupon another boy sneered at them with the words, 'They love each other like husband and wife.' When one of the embarrassed boys objected, the boys deriding them answered quite rightly, 'A man does not sleep with another boy in broad daylight'" ([1928] 1939: 151).[19] More recently, Martin Southwold noted that Baganda acknowledged homosexuality but attributed its introduction to Arabs and tended "to regard it primarily as foolish: why fool around with a man when women are freely available?" (1973: 170).

In western Kenya and Tanzania, Bryk claimed that among the Bagishu (Bagish or Gisu), so-called hermaphrodites "are quite numerous and are called *inzili* [pl.]; among the Maragoli [Margole] *kiziri*. A seventeen year old boy told me, without being at all embarrassed, that he had such a *mzili* in the posterior. The passive fellow called him and gave him ten shillings for this. While he was with him, the pederast had his flabby penis tied to his stomach" ([1928] 1939: 151). The boy claimed to have received (and rejected) many such offers from other *inzili*.

Two decades later, Jean La Fontaine found that the Gisu "scorned but did not regard with revulsion transvestite *buyazi*." However, "it is said that today transvestism is associated with homosexuality, whereas formerly it was not." La Fontaine observed three men and one women who cross-dressed and reported that they were "not mentally disordered" nor were they believed to have special magical powers (1959: 60–61).

In contrast, Needham suggested that in the culture of the Nyoro, a Bantu group led by divine kings east of Lake Albert, a relationship exists between "sexual reversal (by homosexuality, feminine accoutrements, putative child-bearing, or by other less dramatic means)" and the power of diviners (*embandwa*; the root *nda* being a term for "womb") (1973b: 316). According to Needham, "at the ceremony of initiation into the Cwezi cult the novice is given to believe that he must demonstrate his genuine possession by the spirits by becoming a woman." (Although Brian Taylor [1962] did not mention homosexuality in his sketchy account of Bantu cults in the Interlake region, the resemblances of the Toro *mbandwa*, Tkiga *mandwa*, and Haya *Baharambwa* ceremonies to the Hausa *bori* cult—and all these, in turn, to Afro-Caribbean possession cults—are noteworthy [see Fry in Murray 1995a: 193–220].)

In a chapter based on the observation of a Ugandan prison, Ralph Tanner wrote that the "majority could understand but not tolerate homosexuality in others, and they constantly referred to the practice in admonitory terms" (within earshot of colonialists) (1969: 301). "A few made quasi-normal adjustments by adopting homosexual practices while in prison in order to get material advantages. A few entered the prison with homosexual traits already in existence and provided service for the previous group; they were mainly Arabs or Somali. They were not usually identifiable by ways of dressing or mannerisms. The majority of all fights were over what prisoners call their 'wives' " (302).

Age-structured and gender-based homosexuality also existed in various royal courts. According to John Faupel, the Ugandan king Mwanga's persecution of Christian pages in 1886 was largely motivated by their rejection of his sexual advances (1962: 9–10, 68, 82–83). He found it increasingly difficult to staff his harem of pages and supposedly was especially enraged when Mwafu, his favorite, refused to submit to anal penetration any longer.[20] In the early 1960s, male homosexuality was described as common among Hutu (Bantu agriculturalists) and Tutsi (Nilotic pastoralists) in the kingdom of Rwanda, especially among young Tutsi being trained at court, who were sexually available to court guests (Maquet 1961: 77–78). More recently, Cary Johnson reported a conversation with a young Tutsi: "Mutabaruka, a 19-year-old college student told me that, traditionally, in his tribe there was an extended period during which boys lived apart from the rest of the village while they are training to be warriors, during which very emotional, and often sexual, relationships were struck up. . . . 'Sometimes these relationships lasted beyond adolescence into adulthood,' he told me. Watusi still have a reputation for bisexuality in the cities of East Africa" (1986: 29).

An early 20th-century dictionary includes the Rundi terms *umuswezi* and *umukonotsi*, translated as "sodomite," and at least five Rundi words for male-male sexuality (*kuswerana nk'imbwa, kunonoka, kwitomba, kuranana inyuma, ku'nyo*). The dictionary also appears to document gender-mixing priests among the Mirundi (Hutu and Tutsi), called *ikihindu* and *ikimaze* (translated as "hermaphrodite," a very imprecise label at that time) (Burgt 1904: 20, 107).

One of the few reports of woman-woman relations in this region comes from Thomas Beidelman, whose male informants among the Bantu-speaking Kaguru of central Tanzania told him that "some Kaguru women practise lesbian activities during female initiation, women taking both the roles of men and of women in demonstrating sexual congress to initiates. Women were unwilling to discuss this in detail with me, but conceded that women did demonstrate with one another how to have proper sexual congress" (1973: 266). Rudlp Geigy and Georg Höltker (1951) also mentioned sexual education in the three-year-long seclusion of young women following menarche in the Ulanga district.

Lesbianism in a Kenyan Novel

An African novel in which female-female passion is represented, albeit very negatively, is Rebeka Njau's *Ripples in the Pool*, originally published in 1975. Set in postindependence Kenya, the novel has two urban villains: a corrupt member of parliament and an educated woman, Selina, who follows her earnest husband Gikere back to his natal village, where she is not accepted by his mother (who holds title to the land). After Gikere beats her, Selina wants to have no further dealings with him and focuses her passions on a young sister-in-law Gaciru, who keeps house for her. Njau represents Selina's passion for her young sister-in-law as deeply pathological. Proper women produce children. A woman who turns away from her husband (even if she keeps her affection inside his family) is a menace to herself and others in Njau's representation, and the passionate relationship between females is "shameful to talk about" (1975: 64).[21] What Gikere sees of the relationship between his wife and his younger sister disgusts him, though he does not know how to stop their relationship: "Whenever Gaciru appeared, Selina would run towards her, embrace her tightly, and kiss her all over the face, her heart beating wildly. It was a nightmare for Gikere to watch her. He could not understand that kind of passion. It worried him to see a young girl drawn into an emotional kind of love that was strange for human beings" (64).

Selina, who had had extensive heterosexual experience in the city, tries to argue, "It's not a crime to love her [Gaciru]. She gives me joy. Peace." She also claims that the demons in her are afraid of Gaciru (1975: 65). Njau does not buy such an argument, stressing innocent youth in contrast to corrupt homoeroticism and serving up some stereotypical homosexual fretting over aging by having Selina fear that Gaciru is growing tired of her (103). Selina warns Gaciru not to marry: "Men are beasts. All they want is to ruin you, especially if they discover you have a brain" (111), but Njau seems to side with patriarchy, to have little sympathy for Selina's pains (psychological or physical), and none for what she characterizes as "Selina's mad grip" on Gaciru, from which Gaciru finds it difficult to disentangle herself (118).

Karuga, Selina's closest relative, who has come to help Gikere build a clinic, falls in love with Gaciru. Gikere tells Karuga that Selina has ruined Gaciru—"How can a girl like that go on living with a mad woman and remain normal?"—and warns Karuga that Selina "is a jealous woman. She wants to keep her [Gaciru] only to herself. Her passion is sickening. It is not the normal type of love" (1975: 118).

When she recognizes that Gaciru and Karuga love each other, Selina (in a frenzy, not in cold, calculation) strangles Gaciru and, after retreating to the bush, eventually kills Karuga as well. Both of the young lovers are victims of "abnormal love" lashing out at "normal love," destroying a beloved in preference to losing her (even to a kinsman—whom she does not set out to slay but does when he hunts her down). The view from Njau's novel is that female-female passion is possible; however, it is not only wrong but also very dangerous.

Notes

1. S. R. Steinmetz had already reported it among the Kadis of the Nioro (1903: 111).

2. The terms for male homosexual in these two languages also mean "coward" and "weakling."

3. Apparently, even male wives were excluded from the all-male camps.

4. According to Ioan Lewis (1973: 434), Somalis make a categorical distinction between two kinds of men: *waranleh* (warriors) and *waddado* (men of God). The latter have a kind of imperfectly realized manhood in Somali eyes. They are ideally, if not often so in reality, "weak" (*masakiin*) in physical and martial strength and correspondingly endowed with mystical power. Consequently, Somalis suspect the masculinity of orthodox (Sufi) religious virtuosi, not just men involved in possession cults.

5. See also Messing's discussion of the preponderance of women in the *zar* or *zaar* cult (1959: 327). Enrico Cerulli contended that the cult is a marginalized residue of the ancient Cushitic religion, which was displaced by Christianity and Islam (with their patriarchal leaders) (1923: 2). I. Lewis (1966), in contrast, sees an elective affinity between patriarchal Islam and preponderantly female possession religions. Janice Boddy notes that in Khartoum and Omdurmum, where deities are female, men who are possessed by them cross-dress, whereas in the Hofriyat area of northern Sudan, where deities are male, they do not (1989: 210, n. 4).

6. Elsewhere, without explanation, Evans-Pritchard reported that the boy addressed his husband as *kumbami* (my husband) and was called in turn *diare* (my wife) (1970: 1430).

7. They did not cook porridge for their husbands; rather, they fetched it from their natal household (Evans-Pritchard 1970: 1430). Generally, the boys were with their husbands only at night.

8. It is not clear from this whether Evans-Pritchard was arguing that the sexual behavior was not problematic or whether he was rationalizing male fear of women. C. R. Lagae did not elaborate on the cosmology of the recurrent sexual relations between wives (1923: 24).

9. See Wikan 1977. Krapf's dictionary also includes the phrase *asiewesa ku kuéa mke*, laconically translated as "catamite" (1882: 266).

10. Charles Sacleux reported *kaumu luťi* for "sodomite" in Swahili ([1891] 1949: 95). The usual etymology for *luti* in Arabic is "Lot's people" (see Murray 1995b: 624; 1997c). Arthur Madan added *watu wa Sodom* (men of Sodom) (1902: 376).

11. Mary Porter (personal communication to S. O. Murray, November 11, 1996) rejects the idea that Mombasans view those who are sexually penetrated as inferior to those who do the penetrating, stating, "The only top and bottom would be the social hierarchies, which are much more subtle and graded than simple top and bottom." At the same time, she also attests (in comments reported by Amory 1996) the Mombasan belief that *mabasha*, as suggested by the Arabic/Persian-derived label for them, were originally colonialists "exploiting an indigenous class of innocent Africans," who were called by the Bantu-derived term, *shoga*.

12. In describing the *khanith* role in Sohar, Oman, Wikan vacillated between calling it an "intermediate" gender and a "third sex" (1977). The controversy following Wikan's article is discussed by Stephen Murray (1997b). Shepherd (1978b) closed by defining the *shoga* (and, by ready extrapolation, the Omani *khanith*) as an instance of age- rather than gender-defined homosexuality. As Wikan justly noted, this departure from an original emphasis on poverty is "startling" (1978b: 669). Nor does Shepherd's statement that "many passive homosexuals, far from viewing their activity as joyless, are brought to orgasm by it" (1978b: 664) fit with her scenario of dire economic necessity. It also reduces "sexual pleasure" to ejaculation (see Carrier 1980).

13. Will Roscoe (1988: 28) has cautioned against a widespread failure in writing about what Frederick Whitam and Robin Mathy (1986) call "transvestitic homosexuals" to distinguish female behavior from the stereotyping and exaggerations of flamboyant male performances of "femininity."

14. Moreover, Khalid Duran has reported that "the picturesque township of Malindi [off the Kenyan coast] has been turned into a German sex colony frequented by single men and homosexuals," many of whom seek liaisons with local blacks (1993: 186). According to Duran, an Islamicist backlash has developed against what is viewed as foreigners corrupting young males (see also Porter 1995: 148–50).

15. Porter renders the singular as *msago*, the plural as *misago* (1995: 141; *wa-* pluralization is not correct for the nonhuman noun class discussed in Porter 1995:152 n. 12). It derives from *kusaga* (grind), the same Bantu verb root as for *msagaliwa*, but "refers to the sexual activities of women, as 'grinders,' rather than to grinding wood for facial products" (145). In kindly supplying the following description of top and bottom in Mombasa millstones, Porter stressed that social hierarchies are much more subtle and graded than simple top and bottom: "They consist of two dinner plate (or larger) sized discs about an inch thick. Dried corn 'niblets' are scattered on the bottom one, the second one laid on top. The top stone has a hole in it at one side. A stick is inserted into it and is used to rotate the top stone above the stationary bottom stone" (personal communication to S. O. Murray, November 11, 1996).

16. Margaret Strobel (1979: 166) was not clear about sexual aspects of the Mombasa Muslim women's dance, *lelemama*, which she discussed. See the translation of Haberlandt (1899) in this book on women using dildoes with other women in Zanzibar.

17. Murray has argued that in Thailand, as in Latin America, effeminate male homosexuals are "taken for granted and no threat to the social order or even to authoritarian military castes. Indeed, in their widely-recognized womanly inferiority, they visibly reinforce gender stratification" (1992b: 393–94). In contrast to "craven," "fallen" men who take women's socially devalued roles and are seen as reinforcing the link between gender and status, "uppity" women aspiring to male privileges are seen as threats to the sexual order. It seems that men can lose male privilege, but women cannot legitimately gain it even if they dress and behave like men (and/ or take women as sexual partners). In the Swahili hierarchy, *msago* ranks above *mabasha*, according to Porter, who suggests that "unnatural," "un-African" sexuality will be used to inhibit female friendships (1995: 142, 151).

18. Cf. Melville Herskovits 1937a (117). This is reminiscent of the frequent confusion about the biological basis of the berdache role in native North America (see W. Roscoe 1998). See also the controversy about the "impotency" of *hijra* in India (Murray 1999; Nanda 1990; W. Roscoe 1996).

19. Bryk attested the Arabic term *hanisi*, used for Nandi, Badama, and/or Baganda men "whose penises had died" (1934: 150).

20. Also see J. A. Rowse (1964) and Ronald Hyam (1990: 186–89). The Gandan kingdom was founded in the early 16th century by Luo herder-warriors. It grew and prospered in subsequent centuries (see Maquet 1972: 152).

21. By dedicating a novel that is about the catastrophic consequences of resisting domination by a husband to her own husband and children, the author ensures that readers know she is not like Selina.

"A Feeling within Me"

Kamau, a 25-Year-Old Kikuyu

STEPHEN O. MURRAY

What follows is the sexual life history of one young man from a people about whom particularly absolute claims concerning the lack of homosexuality have been made. Born in rural Kenya, Kamau was raised and educated there until the age of 23, when he left to reside in London. The interviews occurred in December 1994 in San Francisco, California. I have done nothing to edit out the fuzziness, particularly about his use of the term *gay*. I think Kamau's oscillation between using and denying the term provides insight into homosexuality without any gay world or self-identification in contemporary Africa. My questions are italicized. In addition to the notes, bracketed passages are my own, although Kamau vetted the text.—S. O. Murray

When I was about 11 I started watching men. When I went to the toilet with a brother or somebody, I'd be interested in, look at, check out their groins. Then, when I grew up, when I was 14, I went to a [government, secular] boarding school. The first year nothing happened. The second year we would share beds with friends—not in a gay manner but to keep warm in the cold nights of the rainy season. The dormitory was too open for you to feel warm. We only had a small blanket, so would share a bed with friends. That's when I started actively being gay or something like that—interested in men.

I was a school prefect, and each prefect had his own corner in the dormitory. The first time it happened to me, I was sleeping. This boy,

41

Momaui, the *kamini*, the school head-boy slept in a decker-bed above mine. He was in fourth year, when I was in second year. He would come down to me so we could keep warm, holding each other to warm up. Then we would leave each other and sleep. But once we would leave each other, he would stretch his hand down. Since I was a light sleeper, I would wake up. I wouldn't wake up startled, but I was interested, curious, so it must have been in me already, just being brought out. So, he stretched his hand and started trying to discover areas within me that could excite him. Once, I felt him leaning behind me with a hard-on. I didn't know what to do, so I pretended still to be sleeping, so I could know what it was all about. He stretched his hand until he cupped my person and then he started playing with me—slowly by slowly, because he doesn't want to wake me up, but he wants to excite me, slowly by slowly. At the same time, he's playing with himself. He was a big man, and I was only small, but he was very, very interested in making sure that I would release. Momaui was a sweet father!

That went on for some time. I kept pretending to be asleep. One time I was sleeping in the top bed up—his bed. He removed everything. He uncovered me slowly and started giving me a blow job. It felt very exciting. I was still pretending to sleep. The lights were off, and it was quite dark. I didn't realize when he came and sat on me. I was still thinking that he's still playing with his mouth, he's still using his mouth, while I was still pretending to be asleep. I opened my eyes slowly. When I noticed what he was doing, I decided to become active, and I held him. I had seen movies and pictures, but I had never kissed a man or a woman. (You don't have to go to school to learn these things!) So I held his hand while he was sitting on me and pulled his head down to me, and we started kissing. I told him "I know! I've known all along." I told him that "I'm sorry, but I didn't want to make you feel like a fool, but I didn't know what to do. I've always been interested to know. I enjoy it. It's quite good," because I did enjoy it. So from then, then we started becoming very actively like partners. Sometimes we'd say to someone we were interested in, "You go and sleep with Kamau in the cubicle. Go and sleep with Momaui, the school captain, in the cubicle." Then we would see what would happen. If he was not interested, then nothing would happen: he'd push your hand away, you know? We were trying to know things, venture into more things in school. That is how I started.

You tried everyone in the school?

No, not everyone; I tried some that I was interested in. There were at least three of them who did that. When we were having showers, I would admire bodies. I would look at their naked bodies and I would be interested in their private parts and bodies: everything. And I thought, "I'm becoming—Oh, my God, something is wrong here. I'm becoming more attracted to men than to women," even though I had a girlfriend and was seeing her and doing things together, having sex. I wouldn't mention anything about my interest in men. I wouldn't discuss anything about men with her. That would look crazy or stupid or something like that. It was quite interesting. School was quite an experience.

When I came out, I didn't know what to do, because I thought school was playing about. Always to me it ended up being like playing about in school—not serious.[1] I'm not actively gay, because there is no issue like "gay."

Did you know that gay people existed?

No. I didn't know that there were gay people. The whole thing about gayness came to me when I went to London. I stayed in Kenya and went to college and then worked for three years in Nairobi before going to London to continue my studies. In college nothing ever happened. I would go and play with myself at home. No one looked like that to me in college. I still didn't think anything about gayness, but I would see men in cottages [public restrooms]. I was more interested in going to cottages so I could see men, and I could do the same thing that I used to do when I was 11: check on them and things like that. I had quite many experiences going to pick someone in a cottage. Then, we would go to a hotel, because no one has somewhere to go to. Most of the ones I went with were married men. They considered me a young bird, a young person, and they want to take the opportunity, because they have been there on the scene for some time. I couldn't even tell you what they called the gay scene, because they never mentioned it. We would go to the cottage and look at each other in the cottage. We would leave the cottage after eyeing each other, moving your head to say, "Can we meet outside or something?" No touching [in the cottage], no nothing. There were many, many other straight people in the cottage. Though, who knows, even the straight ones—you couldn't tell whether they were interested or not. I mean, why are they using cottages? Why would a straight person go and use what looked like a gay cottage? I could tell by their behavior or the way they would eye me, looking and wanting, like they are hungry. Even if you're looking away, you can feel it if someone behind you is eyeing you terribly.

So, I had a couple of experiences. My first experience of going with a man from a cottage in the city, he didn't have a place to go to. We didn't go to his car. We went to the toilet of one of the two big hotels, 680, I think. In the toilet, we went inside the loo, and he closed the door behind, and he started sucking me. (I didn't know it was called a "blow job" until I went to England.) And I did the same thing. I was curious, but it felt horrible! It felt so disgusting! I hated it and swore that I would never do it again, but I was interested in doing it and trying it again and again. I came, and he played with himself and he came, and I didn't see him after that. He just left and I was there hating myself, brushing my teeth like all eternity, because I thought that I had done the most horrible thing. And there was no one to speak to. There was no gay community. There was nowhere I could go for advice to try to find myself. I couldn't go and tell a G.P. about it, 'cause he'd think I'm crazy—at least to my young mind I thought he'd think I was crazy, so I kept away.

I went back to the cottage. It wasn't enough! Even though I'm brushing my teeth for all eternity because I felt like I'd done something horrible, very dirty, I kept going to the cottage. People meet in Nairobi at the cottages. They don't meet in any other place. They won't cruise somebody when he is passing by in a car, no—it's either you go to a cottage, or you stand outside a cottage eyeing someone leaving the toilet who's got the looks. You can tell someone like that! It's not at any exploited level like it is in the European or Western style whereby you can obviously tell that someone is really gay, so you have to be careful, because someone might come to you and slap you and do something horrible to you. It never happened to me, but people said that it happened. I never saw it myself.

Most of the people I looked at coming from the cottage or going into the cottage or passing around the cottage, just pretending, I could tell. They're just there standing, looking around, I guess you'd call it cruising.

My neighbor happened to be like that. We were very good friends. He was much older than me: I was 19 and he was 36. I didn't know why he was so much interested in me. He was attracted to me, though I didn't know about it until I went to one of the cottages and I met him there. Funny enough, he wasn't doing anything that would kick me a lot and let me know that really he's like that. What my neighbor did, immediately after leaving the cottage, he stood somewhere by a hotel and waited until I left the toilet. We said hello to each other in the loo. "Hello, how are you? Are you still at work?" It was lunchtime, so I thought, maybe he's on his lunch break and was stopping at the loo before going to the restaurant or something. I was always curious about why people would go to the cottages instead of going to the loo at work and then go somewhere else.

He went and waited for me outside the restaurant, but I didn't know that he was waiting for me. It was still in the young time, when I'm not very into it yet. All this is happening in the first year that I was in the city, because I was brought up in the countryside, and I did all my studies in the countryside. I came to the city to do my college work. I did not use those cottages for two years, until I finished my college and went to work. Then, on my lunch break, I would go to the cottages.

So, when I found him, I just said hello, but from then I knew that he was like that. Something just told me: the eyes he gave me, the looks he gave me, like a hungry hyena. He wants to know a bit more. What happened is that he offered to give me a lift home that night. He had never given me a lift before. He left early, and I left late. This time he said he would wait in his office and give me a lift, so I passed by his office so I could come by there in the evening. It was very close.

So, I went back to work, finished working, went back, and got my lift home in the evening. During that time, he did not hide anything. I think he decided, "What the heck: whatever happens, I don't care." He stretched his hand and put it on my lap. He continued stretching it until he touched me, and I was interested as well. I was saying to myself, "Oh, gosh, how convenient! He's just my neighbor. When his wife is away we can be doing funny things, and when my sister (who I live with) is away, we can be doing funny things as well."

So he got home. During the time in the car we did so many things. I played around with him. He was driving, getting excited. We had to use a sort of rug to cover him and dim the lights so that people on busses couldn't see anything inside the car and nobody passing can see and wonder, "What are those two doing?" It's not acceptable: it's happening though it's a norm in the community to pretend that it doesn't happen, that it doesn't exist, there's no man-to-man thing, and you have to hide, not go out from under the cover.

He played around with me, and I played with him. He came. I didn't. I was too nervous, because it was my first time in the car. He, obviously, had done it so many times. He enjoyed it terribly.

I thought are most men like this? They're all hiding behind marriages, most of the ones I met, 75 percent at least were married. They all had a wife and one or two children.

The next day he wasn't working, because it was Saturday. My sister was away, and her children were upstairs playing, and his wife had gone to the countryside to get the children who were on holiday. He called me and I went to his house. He sent the house-help to shops far away to buy something, so that she would be gone a long time. His whole idea was getting me into his wife's bed. It was strange to me, but I was curious, so I went to his bedroom. He removed his clothes, and he had a beautiful body. He excited me almost immediately. He wanted to fuck me, and I said "I can't"—because I'd never done it. I'd never taken it. I'd always given it. So I refused completely and he sat on me—and I was like smiling and decided: "Let me enjoy this. This is now out of school, it's not a playing thing, like we used to play in school, this is really happening out in the world now, and it's like going to get a girl and get her into bed and we'd enjoy sex and now it's happening to me with men, as well," because I was going with girls as well. He came and he came and he came. He came like forever: he was really enjoying it, and I asked him, I felt free to ask him because he was very open and he made me feel relaxed, the way he talked to me, he made me relaxed then. It was my first time in a house where you can enjoy it without worrying about anything. The shops that he sent the girl to were very far away so that I knew it would be at least an hour or an hour and a half before she comes back. He asked me so many things, and I told him so many things. He told me that he enjoyed it very much. He told me that sometimes when he's sleeping with his wife, he doesn't get hard, because he really enjoys taking it, yeah? He's got a wife and three children, but when he's doing it with his wife, he feels like she's enjoying it too much and she doesn't deserve it, you know? Something like that, because the way he was enjoying it and the way that he saw that I was enjoying it, because he was watching to see if I enjoyed it. He said, "That's the way my wife acts. I could even be worse than her, even more enjoying it than I've seen her enjoy it." Because there is no foreplay in our community when someone is sleeping with a woman, but with men there is a little foreplay. When you're sleeping with a woman, you just get her into bed. There's no kissing. There's no playing with anything. You just sort of get her clothes off immediately and you're lying on her and start sticking it in. There's nothing! I never even knew that a woman comes. I didn't know, because I didn't do any foreplay. I never heard a woman screaming and saying they're coming, though I now know that it happens.[2]

So, we played there in the room together. The girl didn't find us. We were lucky. As the time got closer and closer to when I thought she'd get back, I was getting worried. I went back to my sister's flat, had a quick shower. I felt clean from the shower and so happy within me. I was so, so happy. That's when I first started seeing Martin. Don't forget, I never saw my school captain again. We exchanged addresses, but since it was school play for me, I threw them all away. I don't need them. I didn't keep any of the addresses of the boys from school.

My neighbor, we kept seeing each other, even 'til now. He still lives there today, he's still a neighbor. He's a very nice person. He's the first person I felt really liking in the manly, the gay lifestyle, the way you'd say "I love—I like the man." He was much older than me. If I went to Kenya today, I would still see him. I wouldn't cross off anything, because I enjoyed it with him and we had too much fun together.

After he spoke to me about how he enjoyed taking, being on the receiving end as we call it in England, I became more curious how it's like, how it feels like.

What would you call it in Kenya?

I don't know; you see we never talk about it. I don't know—it's just when a man takes a woman's position, but there's this feeling of dirt, that it's going to be dirty and all that. When I did it in school, it was sometimes messy. With two of the boys, it wasn't messy, and with this one, he wasn't messy as well, and that's when I enjoyed it, really. Everything is clean and fine. He was a nice person.

He started taking me to many places, to many cottages. Cottages in Kenya have numbers, so he would say, like, "Today I'm going to take you to number five and you can see what happens around there." In the evening after work, he would go and park his car and we would go together. He wouldn't play with himself in the toilet. I would have known if he was playing with himself. He would just go in there and eye someone he likes. He was much more experienced. He'd been in this city 15 years, so he was much-experienced. He would eye the person and use his hand to wave, "Let's meet outside." Then we went to the cottage. He was going to show me how they do it. He was the first person I could go to for counseling to be explained to about all these things. He was the first person to explain to me about everything that happens in the gay community in Kenya—which to me never existed: there was no gay community in Kenya, there were no gay people in Kenya for me, but yes, they were there, it was all happening. So he showed me a couple of toilets to go to. The very first one we went to, we went in, we saw someone we liked, he saw someone he liked, I saw one I liked, and we all went back to the car. We went to a very dark place, drove out into a dark part of the city. There are no cars driving by, like in a park with many trees. They are in the front of his car, and me and my friend, the one who I had just cruised are in the back of the car. We are playing about, and he is young like me, and it felt good to be with some person of the same age, playing around together. That time we exchanged numbers. He gave me his home number, but he said I have to be extremely careful, because if anybody knows about it, he would never forgive me, so I never called him. I got my friend to call him for me.

My neighbor told me how I should be careful with all these people, like if it got back to my family, it would be very wrong and that he wouldn't like anyone to know about what he does, that it would affect his marriage and like that and that I should be more cautious with anyone that I would meet that I should not give my phone number—which I had not done anyway because I was scared to death of my sister finding out anything like this. We were very close, but for her to know that I was like that I thought would be prejudicious to everything we ever shared together, that it would slow everything down. So what I did when he explained that I should not give my number out was, I decided I wouldn't give my number out. He was just giving me fatherly advice, because he was much older than me. What he was doing himself contradicted what he told me. What he was doing with *me* wasn't contradicting, but I would see him doing it with other people, but it didn't bother me, because I was like someone he was taking care of, and I felt nice to be fathered that way. I was looking more on him for advice, and I would say that even if he's doing it, he's smart and he's got his children. Maybe he decided he can mess about because he's already got his children, and he doesn't want any more because he's got so many, and sex with his wife has become hopeless for him. He was a frustrated man to me because he can't do it with his wife totally, and he feels that he's locked up, tied up in a marriage he doesn't want because he's more interested in men than women. He was really gay, not bisexual. He had stopped having children with his wife. He told me that he did not expect any more children. His last child was about six years old, and it was about four years since they had enjoyed sex together properly. I never got a chance to ask him about his sex life or when did he first experience it and such things. I should have asked him what was in his mind when he was fucking his wife: what was he thinking, since he was not sexually attracted to a woman any more—he was now very, very much gay—how does he do it with her? Now, I would be able to ask him so many things that I would like to know which I never did ask him then. He and his wife were very close. Leaving his wife was out of the question. It's just that he felt tied in this marriage because he still has to act straight. He was a born-again

Christian. The funny thing about these gay people in Africa is they are all so religious. He was a born-again Christian and he was the choirmaster in his church, and that is considered to be very, very important in Kenya: if you're a choirmaster, then you're a respectable person in the community. So, me doing these things with him and seeing what he's doing is really giving me a different view of life in the city, and I felt that everybody in the city, that most of the men in the city are promiscuous, and they are all hiding; they're in these big jobs and beautiful lands and different respects of life—most of them are hiding behind marriages. It's a pity. Some friends have told me how they've been with men who are big directors and have to act very, very straight because they are married, most of them are married. Once they get married and have one or two children, they decide to slow down in getting children and in doing anything with their wives, and they start acting more with men and looking about and really chasing each other in big hotels. It happens a lot, yeah.

Back at the back of the car, we played with each other. I sucked him: I was curious because he was my agemate and I gave him a blow job and he gave me one and we both came, but there was no fucking or anything. My neighbor was in front getting screwed by this guy he'd only just met, and they weren't using anything: they didn't have any condom or anything. It wasn't safe. Safety needed to be there because the AIDS thing was still about, yeah? And it had already been advertised in Kenya to try and be careful.

After he came, the one I was with left the car, and I told my friend that I'm going to a hotel, which is around the corner, to have a cup of tea and to meet me there when he's finished getting fucked. We went to a cheap corner restaurant for French fries and enjoyed having French fries and tea. I was just going to have tea, but I ended up having something to eat so I can completely get this thing out of my mouth, you know? These experiences are like really weird to me, but I was getting very much into it. From there, I went to one of the cottages on my own, without him, and that's when I met my Londoner [a Ugandan who lives in London] in a toilet.

What did you think about your neighbor getting fucked by other people?

It didn't affect me. It didn't in the love sense—I wasn't jealous. Not at all. But I was concerned about safety. When I did it with him, we would use something, but when he did it with others, he didn't bother. So I felt like he was taking care of me, so I was fine, so why should I be jealous of his being screwed by someone else? Because when he was with me, he's using safety precautions.

When you lived in Nairobi, how often would you go out cottaging?

About twice a week. I would when I think I was safe, that no one would see it.

Alone or with your neighbor?

Eighty percent of the time on my own.

OK, I'd met the first Londoner [sigh]. That's when I fell in love with a man for the first time. I've always wanted to go to London. I've not been to London at the time. I've not even flown anywhere.

I met him in cottage number eight in Nairobi. I'll never forget, because he was the most beautiful thing that ever happened to me. I'll tell you what happened. I walk into this toilet, this cottage. He was there having a wee, but, naturally, I don't think he was really having any wee: he knew what he was doing! I walked through, he saw my face, and we exchanged looks, yeah? He cruised me, and I decided why not? I didn't know that he was a Londoner, then, because he was a black Ugandan. He's lived in England about 20 years. He was about 34, and I was about 21. So what we did is that he showed me to go out, like "Let's get out of here." We went out. He gave me his number. He asked me to call him in the afternoon, so I called him and we arranged to meet the next day outside Wimpy, a big, big restaurant in Nairobi. And we had a beautiful meal. I felt, "Hmm, this is a different way to look at things, the whole idea of being gay," because no one had ever taken me out for a treat and no one had brought home to me the idea of having sex in a passionate way whereby the two of you agreed before on what you're going to do before you even go into the hut or wherever you're going to do it. We went to his friend's home—he was staying with a friend in Nairobi who is in England and has a home in Kenya. We went to his friend's home, and there it happened. So after that, we met often in the evening, and he told me that he was a father, that he was training to be a priest in England. I was going through a crisis with my faith, because I'm a strong Christian. I was going through a crisis, and I asked him what he thinks about it, being a Catholic priest, what he would tell me to make me feel at ease with whatever I was doing. And he explained to me that it's only natural, because, it's not anything that I chose to do, I'm not doing it for money, I wasn't doing it for anything else, I was doing it for pleasure, and it's a feeling within me, it's not a feeling without, it's a feeling within me that makes me lust for men and not to lust for anything else, and I couldn't control that, it was a power beyond my control. So, he gave me a nice lecture, and I thought it was quite advisable. And I asked him about what London is like, and he told me that in London, the gay people live like in their own sort of world—there's a community of gay people whereby they all live in themselves, and they have their rights, and are accepted by people—straight people—which has never happened in Kenya, so I thought, "Hmm, that's strange!"

So, did he consider himself gay?

Yes, he considered himself very gay. [Inaudible]

Anyway, I went to him and met him, and he was the first person to show me around. And the best thing about him was that he never penetrated me. Never, because I had never done it, and he thought that he wouldn't violate that right, because he had a bit more knowledge coming from the West that it's not nice to violate someone, so he didn't.

So, who did?

Who did? Someone in London—that's a completely different area. In London, yeah. [Laughs.] Anything else you want to ask?

What is the reason your family thinks you're not married?

I'm only 25. I'm too young to marry. According to my father's advice, according to the Kikuyu tradition, a man shouldn't get married before the age of 30. That's very, very traditional. And I love my dad so much and my mom that whatever advice they give me I take.

Even though your younger brother is married?

Even though my younger brother is married, I'm still too young. It happens that many men get married early. All of my brothers have gotten married before the age my dad recommends, but my big sister kept her word to get married at the age of 25, which is what my dad thinks, according to the Kikuyu tradition, is the age for women to marry. A man is given a bit more time. You know men! They are always up and about looking for girls and playing about, so they're given enough time to mess about, so that when they get married, they are ready to settle down and take more responsibility as a man of the house. Girls mature quicker than men and can settle down. And so my sister got married at 25, and I thought I could look upon her as an example. She listened to my dad. We're eight children in the family and she's the firstborn, and she waited until she was 25 to get married and set a good example. My dad preferred that the girls get married at 25 and the boys at thirty. I said, "I'll get married when I want to get married. If I want to get married at 21, I don't care, I will! I don't think you should interfere with that"—that's what I told him, because if I fall in love, I can't stop myself from getting involved, so that's why I say that in Kenya maybe by now I'd have gotten married, but, when I'm coming to think about it, I got closer and closer to my dad. When I was in school, when I grew up, I got closer and closer to him and to my mom, so I felt that I wouldn't do anything to upset them, so I held back and said I'll get married around 30. Today, if I got a girl in the family way, I would get married, but I'm not ready yet. I don't feel that I'm ready yet. I feel that maybe I could be ready by 30, like he said. Yeah, I feel that I could be ready by then, but you never know. I might get married before then. That would be like hiding my complete other life, once I get married. To me it would be like I'm hiding behind everything. To the Western friends that I have, it would seem like I'm hiding something, but truly I would be getting married because I wanted to. To my family, it would be like a blessing, because they're happy that I'm married and that I'm settling down. They don't realize that I'm the most confused person, because I have two double lives that I'm trying to lead. I love being with men and I love girls. This girl that I've been with the last seven years, she's very close to me. I've told her I'm not in a hurry to get married, so if she loves me so much, she can wait until I'm ready.

Does she know that there are also men in your life?

No. She doesn't know about it, because she lives in Kenya. She comes to London and visits me, and I've been to Kenya every year since I came to London, but I've never asked people any questions about gay life and I've never got involved. I always keep away in Kenya, because I don't want anything. I feel like I could be active in Kenya and bring out what I've learned in the West about this whole thing and sort of my independence on the issue and show it off there. I could have let it loose, but I thought, "No. If I do, it might go the other way around and people would start saying, 'Oh, see he went to London and this is what he's bringing to us,'" you know? So I keep it all; it doesn't have to happen, anyway.

This time, I want to speak to my neighbor and know more, because he's older than me. I want him to explain to me about whatever happened because it must have been more difficult, because now, according to him, there are more people than when he was there, when he was younger, when he was my age. Now there are more people. When he was my age, they used to go with white people. They wouldn't go with a black person, but with white people, tourists visiting. So I would like to know more about that, because I never asked him. I'd like to know much more.

So your relations with men in Kenya was in school, in cottages, and with your neighbor. No sort of organized gay life?

No, there's no organized gay life. I'm sure it's still the same. But on the coast, on the Kenyan coast, Mombasa, because we've got all these American and British tourists coming in and all the ships docking on the coast, there are so many of these things happening, where you see boys—I've never been to the coast in a similar situation, but I'm told that the boys come wrapped up with laces. I saw this once when I went to the coast to visit my brother who lives there. I saw it once but I didn't take it in mind, it was never in my mind. So, boys with laces: they have a big flowered sheet tied around and they have nothing under, but they have a T-shirt on top and that thing underneath. They go to the hotels where the tourists are and that's how they excite, how they get men doing very, very weird things. There are places on the coast where these things are really alive, it's happening, the gay life is very active and is more accepted by the Arab community. There's a very big Arabic community in that area, the coast. But once you leave the coast province, it's not the same when you come to the inland. It's a completely different story.

Are there transvestites?

On the coast, yes.

I mean inland.

In Nairobi, I'm sure they are there, because I was interested in trying women's clothes when I was growing up, when I was going home on school holidays and all that, I would be so interested. I would see my sister's new dress, and when they were not in, I would go and try it on and have a look in the mirror. All those quite interesting things.

What age?

When I was in boarding school, up to the age of 14, 15, 16. I even tried squeezing my feet into their shoes and all that. Today, I wouldn't be comfortable in it, but at the time when I was changing, when I was really getting involved in this type of feeling, when my feelings were really coming out, at that time I really was interested in trying them on. When I'd hear someone coming, I'd close the door and get them off and say, "My, you have a very nice dress here" and things like that, but panicking that maybe they saw me. I was scared.

If they'd seen something, would they say something or would they pretend not to have seen?

I think they would have pretended not to have seen it, because there is nothing I would say, because I'm too young at the time, and it's just a matter of messing about, yeah.

Did your father or anyone ever warn you about sex with men?

No. He would never have thought of it. We don't expect it to happen in our community, the Kenyan community, or my Kikuyu community if

I would put it more precisely. It's not expected to happen, so he would not talk about it.

There weren't transvestites in rural Kenya?

No, no cross-dressing. I never saw any cross-dressing. Maybe at the coast, yes. Up in the cities, I don't think so. In Nairobi, I would see men, men who are hairdressers—not barbers. Hairdressers are thought to be gay, but they don't put it as *gay*, they put it as they sleep around with men. They are all considered to be men who sleep with men for money. But that's not the truth, because they don't sleep with men for money. They sleep with men because they like it, but other people think that they sleep with men for money. It seems like one is a prostitute if a man does a hairdressing job. They do women's hair. No men go into hairdressing salons in Kenya. I would like to go to a salon in Kenya and sit down and listen to what they talk about—these men who do hair, because I've never listened to it, but I know they're there. One of my sisters is a hairdresser, and where she works, there was a boy who was like that. But I never thought of it like that and my sister never mentioned it, because he was a nice person. I don't know anything else about it, because I wasn't interested. I wouldn't want to be anywhere my family is. I don't want to know anything more. I just keep out, and it doesn't even affect me. Even though you want to, it dies off. It dies a natural death quickly. The feeling is completely gone. I'm not interested, that's it.

In Kenya, they are thought to be, they really are—because in Kenya anyone who does anything that is feminine is really like that, is thought to be a male prostitute who goes with men for money.

In the Kenyan view, why would a man want to pay a hairdresser, why would anyone pay money to go with . . . ?

Not the Kenyan men. The tourists are the ones who go with these hairdressers to the big hotels. They believe these are male prostitutes for foreign tourists, because they always hang around in the big hotels. No Kikuyu, no traditional man, no native (would you say it that way?) would be interested. They *believe* that no native Kenyan would be interested, but it happens. I'm sure that a lot of it happens, and they just hide behind their marriages and their big jobs and all that.

Do some of the rich ministers keep boys on the side?

I think that's what happens.

But it's impossible for men to live together as lovers?

Yes, it's impossible for men to live together as lovers. But, you see, a man sleeping with another man in our community? There's nothing wrong with that. No one would think anything. Often there's only one bed available, and it's a single bed and things are happening, but nobody knows. Even in the city. I had a very good friend in college, and he decided that when he leaves college, we're going to leave our parents' home and get a flat together and become roommates. If we are like that, then no one will ever know, no one will ever know that we are sharing. Never! But it would still be happening and nobody would know. So a man sharing a room, sharing a bed, with another man is not seen as taboo. I could hold your hand or hug you in the street. There's no problem with holding your hand and not releasing it if you're a man. If it's a lady, she should release my hand quickly, and it's a taboo for a man to kiss a woman. It's such an issue in the streets: it's terrible. Even today, I would be very surprised if I saw a man kissing a woman in the street in Kenya. I'd think, "I don't believe it. This is wonderful." I'd be excited by it.

What about if you hold hands with a white man?

No, I'd be seen like I'm going with you for money. Even walking in the street with a white man in Kenya, I never did, In Nairobi I was afraid I might be seen by an uncle or cousin or somebody and go and say, "Oh, I saw Kamau with this white guy. How come he's got a white friend?" Because most of the white men who have boys as their friends are believed to be having them as their rent boys.

But now? Now that you've lived in England, aren't you supposed to know white people?

Yes. Now if we were in Kenya and walking in the street, I could hold your hand. People will still think that I am a rent boy, but my family wouldn't have anything because they know I've already been here. Anyone who knows me wouldn't worry about it but other people would, but I don't care because I know you and my family knows that I know you because I've been living in the West. But before then, it would have been an issue. I would have been called home by my mom and my dad, and they would sit there and ask me questions: "Who is this man? And what are you doing with him? Is there anything we haven't given you that you'd like us to give you, because we don't want you to do . . . ," you know what I mean?

Why do you think you're interested in men?

It's already in me, I was born with it. It's not that I got to a time whereby I became seriously confused and ended up with men rather than being with women. It's from when I was born. It must always have been in me. When I was small, I wanted to stay more with girls, watch every single thing they are doing. I was interested in watching my sisters knitting, cooking. My dad would stop the boys from going to the kitchen, because he'd say it's women's work, cooking. They have all these funny beliefs in Africa, like it's women's work to cook, and man's place is not in the kitchen, a woman's place is in the kitchen. So, I would always go there and he'd come and tell me. He even locked the kitchen sometimes so no man goes into the kitchen when there are no girls in the house, he would lock it. Not with the way that you would say he is being mean or something like that, he would just naturally do it. Even today I wouldn't think there was anything wrong with it, if he came and locked the kitchen, I wouldn't find anything wrong with it, because it's a very traditional thing to do to keep men away from the kitchen completely. Always, if you wanted porridge, someone does it for you, brings it to the sitting room because you're a man. Food is always done, clothes—you never wash them. Ladies do it, so it's like a little heaven on earth for men in Africa, yeah.

So your father wasn't concerned with your masculinity in particular, just the general pattern?

Yeah.

He didn't think there was anything suspicious or funny about you as a child?

No. I was just a butch little thing toddling about, messing about, although I was more interested in being with ladies a lot. I would watch my mom cook and, even if dad didn't want us to do it, men, when there was no lady around, I'd say, "Dad, that man is busy and I'll do it. Why are you making her do all the cooking and all that?" you know? Because we used to get on very well, so it was very easy for me to tell him anything I wanted. I'd tell him, "Dad, I'm going to cook, and you're not stopping me. Today I'm cooking for everybody. If nobody wants to eat it, you can all go and throw that food away, but I'm going to cook for everyone, yeah? It's going to be a man's food today, so watch it." So I would go into the kitchen and do the whole cooking. Today, I'm not a very good cook, but then, ages 14, 15, 16, 17, 18, I was a very good cook. I don't know, I sort of drifted away from it—naturally—drifted completely from being interested in the kitchen, in cooking. Even today, as I am, I know men more, and I know that men who like other men are regarded as feminine, it's looked at as a feminine thing, it's not looked at as masculine.

You mean in Kenya? In England?

I think everywhere, because you find gay men calling each other "she" [like] "Oh, look at her!," you know? It's more on the feminine—I don't know how you'd put it.

Do you think it's true?

I don't know. I don't know what is right and wrong now with all these gay community. I don't know.

So in Kenya, I would cook, and dad enjoyed the food and mom and everybody. There you are: I did it. So when I grow up and I live in my own place, I can cook by myself. I don't want anybody watching me.

Would you consider moving back to Kenya?

Yeah. I plan to move back. I would like to live in Canada, but I'm content with what I have. I'm working in England, steady, and I'll be going back to Kenya next year. I'm happy for now. When I decide what I want to do—I haven't decided. For now I want to get enough money to do my degree, even though I intend to buy a flat in London so I can always have a flat in London. That's my dream—whether I settle in Canada or Kenya—I always want to have a flat in London.

And I'd love to travel. I want to see how people live in all different communities. The funny thing, Steve, is that I'm not more interested in what's happening in the gay community in the cities of the world, just visiting, interested in sightseeing, seeing how people live, not necessarily gay—gay is just part of it, but I don't just have to go and get another man. I'm just interested in seeing. It just attracts me, the scenery and the mountains. I'm more interested in such things than in anything else. Most gay men say they want to travel because they want to see all these men in all these countries. Some of them do that; most that I know do that!

You're not a sex tourist?

No. Since the whole AIDS thing came on, it scared me too much. In Africa, it's happening, and so many people have caught the illness, and it's believed to be a heterosexual community, so it has to be a heterosexual AIDS. I would never associate the whole thing that men hide behind their marriages as the reason, no. No, I don't know what I would say. I don't know.

Was there any discussion in Kenya media about AIDS and homosexuality?

No. I've never seen it or heard about. I'd like to, but I haven't seen or heard about it. I haven't seen it in newspapers, no. There was a lot of publicity in the middle-[19]80s and even today but only for the heterosexuals—you and your wife and you've got to protect your family if you're a man, because they believe that a man will go out with another girl and do everything and bring it to the wife, or the wife would go around and get this thing and bring it to the man, I know that, but it's not man-to-man, no, apart from the rent-boys who are getting it from the white folks who are visiting or something like that.

Has there been any attempt to crack down on them?

Maybe there will be, but I haven't heard it. When the AIDS came out, they wanted to find who has it and incarcerate them, put them all away, but they didn't do it.

Were you initiated? Did you go through irua?

Yes, I was circumcised at the age of 14. Kikuyu boys usually get circumcised at the age of 15 or 16. In the old Kikuyu community, people used to get circumcised at the age of 25: boys were considered to be grown-up men. They would take a look at life from a different angle, like adults. [Inaudible] now can be married.

Besides circumcision, what else happened in your initiation? Were you isolated and taught anything?

That used to happen before the British colonized the country. That used to happen a lot, to keep you away from everybody else, but it didn't happen in our time because we are sort of like a new generation. Ours was the hospital one. What my dad went through was the traditional one, where you have to go through a traditional circumcising. Where first you're incarcerated away from everybody for about a week, then you're all taken into a river very early in the morning and the river is really cold. You're dipped into the river so you're genitals can get like anesthetized, then you'd come back, and they would perform the circumcision. But I had it in the hospital.

Was there any other part of initiation for you?

Lots of advice from my parents and from my brothers that now I'm going to be a man. Yes, it happened in the hospital, and before that I had about a week's training whereby they observe you and your behavior and how you approach adults and how you give them the respect they deserve, how you treat the younger ones, how you give them the attention they want. You have to be looked at in all angles: your mom, your dad, your brothers are all checking on you to see your behavior and who your friends are and all that—to check on you, on what you're doing.

And if they didn't like what they saw, they would have waited another year?

They would have waited another one year, yes.

Kenyatta[3] and Leakey[4] wrote about ngweko between unmarried men and women . . .

[It's pronounced] Ngweke. Oh yeah, when a woman sleeps with a man before marriage—a man sleeping with a woman before marriage is called *ngwecke*, I think. I can't remember very well, but if a woman sleeps with a man before marriage, we call that *gicikio* [K's spelling—it sounded like *ishokio*]. They would keep you away from the tradition once you do that. Traditionally, they wouldn't marry you off if you do that.

According to Kenyatta, in ngweko, *the naked man would lie with his penis tucked between his legs and rub his breast against the woman, and her genitals would be covered.*[5]

In their days, not in our days. That's long, long gone.

There is no kissing, there's nothing to do with kissing between man and woman up to today, apart from the educated ones. It wouldn't happen. If I go to the countryside and I find someone in the countryside, I wouldn't expect them to be kissing in public, or even in bed. They wouldn't do it.

How about sex with uncircumcised women?

Sex with uncircumcised women is OK now, but before it wasn't.[6] A woman had to be circumcised at the age of 20, I think, and a man at age 25, before they married. and your dad would choose for you your wife to be; you wouldn't choose it for yourself.

But you've chosen your own?

Yes, because I believe that if I'm going to live with a woman who I've got to get married to, it's got to be somebody I love. I'm making a commitment here to live with a woman for the rest of my life, so I don't expect anyone else to choose for me what they think is good taste for me.[7] If my parents think someone is great, then they can keep her, I don't want her. That's true.

Do they approve of your choosing?

They don't mind that now in our community. My dad doesn't have to choose my wife—although at least he has to accept her into the family. If he doesn't accept her, then I'll have to think twice before I take her about, because they still believe in giving the parents the respect they deserve, for they're older and more experienced.

Do your parents know your fiancée?

Oh yeah, they know my girlfriend for the last seven years.

Everyone is just waiting for you to turn thirty?

I'm going to wait until the right time, until I'm ready. If she gets married before, in the next five years, too bad—[laughs] for the man to be! She knows that. If she can't wait, if she gets married before I get to her, then she wasn't meant to be my wife. If she was meant to be my wife, she would wait for me, until I think I'm ready for it. It's a bit mean on my side, but if she wants children from me, she can get them and I'll take care of them—I don't mind—but I won't say we're married. She'll be taking a chance—until I think I've reached the right age to get married.

She wants children by you now?

She wants children—anytime, but I postpone it. I don't want a lot of children, not yet.

Has she been circumcised?
No.
Will she be circumcised?
No.
You want her to have pleasure when you have sex?
Yes. We both enjoy it, the sex.
So, there are no gay bars in Nairobi?
No.
Or bars where men go to find other men interested in sex?

Not that I know of, but when I go back, I'll check for you. If there's any, I'll fax you from my cousin's office. [As far as I know, he has not been back since these interviews.]

Notes

1. In an earlier generation, competitive masturbation was "given up after the initiation ceremony," according to Jomo Kenyatta, who maintained that "the practice of homosexuality is unknown [and 'unnecessary'] among the Gikuyu" (1938: 155–56).

2. "It is considered taboo even to have sexual intercourse with a woman in any position except the regular one, face to face" (Kenyatta 1938: 155).

3. Kenyatta 1938: 149–54.

4. Leakey 1977: 2:584–85.

5. "The chief concern in this relationship [*ngweko*] is the enjoyment of the warmth of the breast, *orugare wa nyondo*, and not the full experience of sexual intercourse," according to Kenyatta (who, like Kamau, stressed that Kenyans do not kiss) (1938). Also see Gretha Kershaw (1973: 49).

6. "No proper Gikuyu would dream of marrying a girl who has not been circumcised and vice versa," Kenyatta wrote in his defense of clitoridectomies as the sine qua non of the whole teaching of tribal law, religion, and morality (1938: 127). "It is taboo for a Gikuyu man or woman to have sexual relations with someone who has not undergone this operation." Kershaw noted a steady decline in girls undergoing the operation (1973: 50).

7. According to Kenyatta, even in his day, marriage was "a free choice of one another by the boy and girl" (1938: 156, 302).

Occurrences of Contrary-Sex among the Negro Population of Zanzibar (1899)

M. HABERLANDT

Translated by Bradley Rose

M. Haberlandt sent the following letter to his deceased friend Dr. Oskar Baumann.[1]

> Occurrences of contrary-sex [*conträre sexual-erscheinungen*] among the Negro population of Zanzibar, inborn as well as acquired contrariness, probably exists only in rare instances.[2] The rather high frequency in Zanzibar is doubtless attributable to the influence of Arabs, who together with Comorosans, and the prosperous Swahili mixed-breeds, account for the main contingent of acquired contraries. Typically engaging in sex at an early age, oversaturation soon occurs among these people, and they seek stimulation through contrary acts, in addition to normal acts. Later they lose desire for the female sex and become active pederasts. With the occurrence of impotence, they then cross over to passive pederasty. Their [love] objects belong almost exclusively to the black slave population; only rarely do the poor freeman, Arabs, "Belutschen" and others submit to it out of greed. The adolescent slaves that are selected are kept away from any work, well pampered, and systematically effeminized (*ku/*

ainishwa). In the beginning they take pleasure in normal sex acts, as well, and remain normal if they aren't used for too long as catamites [*Lust-Knaben*]. If this happens however, then the scrotum gradually shrinks, the member loses the capacity for erection, and the individual finds pleasure only in passive pederasty. In parallel to this custom the Negroes of Zanzibar also come to engage in contrary acts. Since slaves are often not available to them for this purpose, male prostitution has developed, which replenishes itself partly from the former catamites of the Arabs, and partly from other Negroes. The aforementioned mainly live in Ngambo and ply their trade very openly. Many among them wear female clothing; at almost every dance in Ngambo one can see them among the women. Others go about in male clothing, but wrap a cloth around their heads in place of the cap. Many otherwise reject that distinctive sign.

Most of them get rectal problems, which they seek to hide in the beginning through kerchief pluggings and applications of perfume. —All, active as well as passive pederasts, are considered sturdy drunkards to such an extent that the Swahili designation *Walevi* (drunk) in many cases can be used for "pederast."

Inborn contraries of the male as well as the female sex exist. From youth on, the former show no desire for women and only find pleasure in female occupations, such as cooking, mat-weaving, etc. As soon as this is noticed by their relatives, they reconcile themselves without further ado to this peculiarity. The person concerned puts on female clothes, wears the hair braided in female fashion, and behaves completely as a woman. He associates mainly with women and male prostitutes. He seeks sexual satisfaction mainly through passive pederasty (*kufira*, "to pederast"; *kufirwa*, "to be pederasted") and in coital-like acts. In outward appearance, inborn contrary men are not distinguishable from male prostitutes, but the natives make a sharp distinction between them: the professional catamites are despised, while the behavior of the inborn-contrary is tolerated as *amri ya muungu* (the will of God).

Contrary-sex aligned women are likewise not rare. Eastern custom makes it impossible, of course, to wear men's

clothing, but they do it in the privacy of the home. They
spot other women by their masculine bearing and when
their female clothing "doesn't fit" (*hawapendezwi na nguo za
kike*). They show preference for masculine accomplishments.
They seek sexual satisfaction with other women, sometimes
contrarily disposed ones like themselves, sometimes normals
who give themselves over to it from coercion or greed. The
acts performed are: *kulambana*[3] (to lick one another); *kusagana*
(to rub the private parts up against each other); and *kujitia
mbo ya mpingo* (to furnish oneself with an ebony penis).
This last kind is remarkable because a special tool for it is
necessary. It is a stick of ebony in the shape of a male member
of considerable size, which is fashioned by black and Indian
craftsmen for this purpose and is sold secretly. Sometimes it is
also made from ivory. There exist two different forms. The first
has below the end a nick where a cord is fastened, which one
of the women ties around her middle in order to imitate the
male act with the other. The stick is pierced most of the way
and it then pours out warm water in imitation of ejaculation.
With the other form, the stick is sculpted with penis heads at
both ends so that it can be inserted by both women into their
vaginas, for which they assume a sitting position. This kind
of stick is also pierced. The sticks are greased for use. —In
addition to its use by contrary-sexes, this tool is employed in
the harems of the Arabs, where the women, because of strict
seclusion, find insufficient sexual pleasure. It is considered an
Arabic invention.

Homosexuals of both sexes are designated in the Swahili
language as *mke-si-mume* (woman, not man). However, the
expressions *mzebe* and the Arabian-derived *hanisi*, which
actually mean an impotent person, also apply. Arabic law is
somewhat "tolerant" in the persecution of male contraries,
although the Qur'an strenuously forbids pederasty. Female
contraries are punished, as are the craftsmen who supply
the ebony penis, which is consequently acquired only with
difficulty and at a considerable price.

Of other perversions, bestiality (with goats) occurs here
and there; on the other hand, masochism and sadism are
unknown; also I was never able to hear of an occurrence that
somehow could recall necrophilia.

Notes

1. Originally published as "Conträre Sexual-Erscheinungen bei der Neger-Bevölkerung Zanzibars," *Verhandlungen der Berliner Gesellschaft für Anthropoligie, Ethnologie und Urgeschichte,* ed. Rud. Virchow (Berlin: A. Scher & Co., 1899) (*Zeitschrift für Ethnologie* 31[6] [1899], 668–70). Oskar Baumann (1864–99) was an Austrian explorer of Africa.—B. Rose, Translator

2. Only two cases came to my attention of *effeminatio* and passive pederasty, of which one concerned a man from Unyamwezi and the other one from Uganda.

3. The verb *(ku-)lamba,* "to lick," might come from a Portuguese word that passed into the Swahili language.

Mashoga, Mabasha, and Magei

"Homosexuality" on the East African Coast

DEBORAH P. AMORY

This chapter is a preliminary report[1] on current research concerning cross-dressing, homosexual behaviors, and the emergence of contemporary "homosexual" identities on the East African coast.[2] The study focuses on the socially recognized (and stigmatized) category of *mashoga*, men who are reputed to be passive homosexuals,[3] who wear women's clothing or select articles of women's clothing at particular social and ritual events, men who in many ways appear to be the Swahili-speaking society's equivalent to Euro-American drag queens. The research was conducted in the summer of 1995 in East Africa, in a large coastal city that I will generically refer to as "Old Town." (I refrain from naming my research site or the people I talked to there out of concerns for everyone's safety.) These neighborhoods are found in the older cities along the Swahili-speaking coast, distinguished from the greater cosmopolitan area by their architecture (typically featuring stone houses) and longtime resident families.[4] Even though this report should be taken as provisional, pending further research, it represents the first attempt by any scholar to conduct ethnographic research concerning *shoga* identity in a coastal, Swahili-speaking society.

My aim was to explore how *mashoga* identity is currently understood in coastal society. Research questions included: What is the relationship between contemporary same-sex practices, gendered practices such as cross-dressing, and the historical, socially recognized category of "male transvestites" (referred to as *mashoga* in Mombasa, and sometimes *makhanith* or *mahanisi*)? How do *mashoga*[5] conceive of themselves and their place in the world, and what about *mabasha*, their "masculine" partners? Finally, two new questions emerged: How are contemporary communities of people who engage in same-sex relationships being constructed with reference to transnational popular culture, and how are new social identities being constructed today? For during the course of this research, I learned a new Swahili word, *magei*, referring to "gay" people, both male and female.

Below, I outline the wider context of my research and report my findings, reviewing the literature concerning cross-dressing and "homosexuality" on the East African coast. Based on interviews with informants, I describe the categories currently in use and comment on two of the life histories that I recorded. Rather than focus on sexual identities per se, I emphasize an understanding of gender as a complex set of social practices that includes but certainly is not limited to sexual behaviors. The complexity of gender as a process and a lived practice is betrayed by select, stable categories ("man," "woman," or even "third gender")[6] and by ideas of static sexual identities ("homosexual" and "heterosexual"). I join with other scholars of "homosexuality" in calling for an integrated analysis of gender and sexuality that locates these social practices within specific historical and cultural contexts (see Blackwood 1996; W. Roscoe 1994; Weston 1993). In Swahili-speaking societies, the emergence of *magei* indicates that important changes are taking place in local constructions of social identity.

The Swahili-Speaking Coast of East Africa

The Swahili-speaking coast ranges from southern Somalia to northern Mozambique, including offshore islands, and is characterized by a shared set of cultural practices that includes Swahili or Kiswahili being the first language, observance of Islam, and an economy centering on trade, agriculture, fishing, and tourism (Middleton 1992). Elite ideology has historically emphasized the importance of urban centers to cultural life on the coast and contacts over the sea toward Arabia. Notwithstanding colonial and elite ideologies that insist on the fundamentally Arab orientation of Swahili-speaking societies, the coast has been the meeting ground for diverse peoples for centuries, including various African groups from the hinterland and interior, Arabs and Asians involved in the Indian Ocean trade, Portuguese explorers and conquerors, and European colonizers. The coast is a "borderland" in Gloria

Anzaldúa's (1987) sense: a meeting point for peoples and cultures where identity becomes more than the sum of all the parts.

In these coastal towns, people identify themselves in a number of ways. Some call themselves "Arabs," thereby staking a claim to various important lineages, some of which can be traced back to an Arab forefather who arrived from the Hadhramaut or Oman. Today, these claims to Arab descent also invoke the wealth of the Gulf states. Others call themselves "Africans" or "Swahilis," typically reflecting a nationalist political awareness that predominates in Tanzania as opposed to Kenya. Identifiable Asian groups also exist, collectively referred to as "Wahindi" (the Hindi people), most of whom maintain a somewhat separate cultural and political identity from "Arab," "African," and "Swahili" groups. Local people also identify with a smaller collection of ethnic subgroups, often associated with a particular place: "Shirazi" refers to indigenous inhabitants of Zanzibar and Pema; "Bajuni" to the indigenous peoples of the Lamu archipelago; "Washihiri" for families whose lineage originated in Yemen; and so on (see Amory 1994).

This historical and cultural complexity is reflected in recent scholarship that highlights multiple ideologies and discourses at work on the coast. In terms of kinship and descent, Swahili society is a patrilineal one with preferred cousin marriage, although matrilateral kin retain important roles, and in some (typically rural) areas, descent may be reckoned cognatically (see, for example, Caplan 1982; Middleton 1992; Shepherd 1987: 246–49). Other social practices, such as traditional healing and spirit possession cults, coexist with Islam (Alpers 1984; Giles 1987). Strict male control over female kin is normative, and veiling and (modified) seclusion remain elite ideals, but women earn income through informal economic activity, own property, and therefore are able to exercise some independence from male kin (see Bujra 1975).

In this context, I would suggest, it is particularly important to attend to both dominant ideologies and subordinate ones. This is particularly true for the social construction of gender, as a number of scholars have suggested (Askew 1992a; Biersteker 1996; Caplan 1975, 1982; Porter 1992; Strobel 1975, 1976, 1979). In many ways, the elite ideology is a specifically male one: "The personal qualities and acts marking the most respectable and highest status person have been, by definition, more easily achieved by men than by women" (Porter 1995: 138). Indeed, the central notion of *heshima,* or respect, effectively works to maintain a highly stratified social system in which proper behavior and comportment are fundamentally gendered and serve as the key to social status. Within this world there exists the social institution of *mashoga*, male transvestites reputed to be "passive" homosexuals.

Research on homosexuality and cross-dressing constitutes one important method of examining the ways that borders historically have been crossed and confounded on the East African coast—geographic borders, gendered borders, social, and sexual borders. Mary Porter's (1995) insightful analysis of discourses on homosexuality in Kenya provides an important starting point: ethnographic research reveals the ways in which meanings are produced in particular places and points in time and precisely how *shoga* identity serves as a gendered arena of sometimes violent struggles over power.

"Transvestites" and "Homosexuals" in Swahili Society

There is frequent mention of male transvestites, sometimes described as passive homosexuals, in the historical and ethnographic literatures on the Swahili coast, along with references to "sodomites," the occasional "pecadillo," and "transsexuals." Clearly, the terminology is confusing and all too often reflects the observers' preconceptions. It is also important to note that these references typically occur in footnotes or asides, literally at the margins of the ethnographic literature. For the sake of clarity, I divide these references into three categories: (1) rituals of inversion, (2) male performers who cross-dress, and (3) *mashoga*. Interestingly, this typology hints at increasing shades of implication in homosexual behavior.

Rituals of Inversion

A variety of rituals occur on the coast that constitute rituals of inversion marked by male cross-dressing. Peter Lienhardt, for example, notes a high incidence of cross-dressing in spirit possession dances (1968: 39). The New Year's festival of Mwaka Oga is another event at which cross-dressing typically occurs, although these celebrations are now only observed in a few locales. In 1988, I attended the Mwaka Oga festival in the southern town of Makunduchi on Zanzibar. This annual event constitutes a sort of harvest festival and New Year's party that emphasizes ridding the town of unhealthy tensions that have built up over the year. A central part of the festivities included men and women, and men dressed as women, chasing one another around with sugar cane sticks, beating one another. The celebrations that I saw involved huge crowds of people, numbering in the thousands, who watched and cheered (and ran out of the way at times) as the battle raged. There were too many men dressed in women's clothing to suggest that they were all *mashoga*. Rather, this event seems to mark the centrality of gender to social organization and social hierarchies, as the crossing of gendered boundaries becomes an important part of challenging, expressing, and reinventing the social order.

Transvestite Performers

James de Vere Allen notes that the *mbenda* dance is performed by men in women's dress and so may be the "preserve of transsexuals" (1981: 243). John Middleton (1992) refers to "transvestite musicians" as ritually power-ful and socially ambiguous people. Specifically, there is a certain category of male performers and musicians who are employed to sing and play at the otherwise sex-segregated women's part of wedding celebrations. Some of these men are referred to as *mashoga*, and this is one way in which the *mashoga* role is a profession-defined one, although also explicitly marked by gender.[7] Porter notes that *mashoga* are identifiable because they are the only male performers who play the *pembe*, a woman's instrument, and participate in women's dances (1995: 140–41). Indeed, only these type of non-kin (biological) "men" can cross the gendered line of sexual segregation into women's space on a regular basis.

Another place where cross-dressing regularly occurs is in the plays performed by local culture groups during Islamic holidays, such as the Idd al Haj (see Amory 1994). At these performances, a crowd of women and children are entertained by half-hour morality plays that focus on the themes of spirit possession and adultery (both men's and women's infidelity). Cross-dressing men play prominent roles in these plays that are seen as part of a low-class, "African," or indigenous tradition, as opposed to high Arab culture. Again, while some of the men who perform in these plays may be *mashoga*, some are not; they simply play the part of a man dressed in wom-en's clothing. While I was researching these performances, I repeatedly asked friends why these men were wearing dresses. The reply was always the same and always entirely obvious to everyone but me: "Because they want to."

"Male Homosexuals"

Finally, there are occasional references to "male homosexuals" in Swahili societies. A report by an American consular officer in Zanzibar in 1860, after the installation of Sultan Bargash, noted that "numbers of sodomites have come from Muscat, and these degraded wretches openly walk about dressed in female attire, with veils on their faces" (Russell 1970: 342, quoted in Murray 1997b: 253, n. 9). This report mirrors both a scholarly emphasis on homosexuality in Islamic societies and local reports that homosexual behaviors are the result of Arab influences (see also Porter 1995: 148).[8] More recently, Kelly Askew observes that "male homosexuals" perform the female ritual of *kutoa mapasho*, "to give tips," that is, walking forward from the audience to present money to singers during *taarab* concerts (musical performances, identified with Arab culture) to convey messages to other members of the audience (1992a: 15). Askew describes this practice as a form of "hidden gossiping" otherwise only associated with women (1992b: 10, n. 6).

Both Gill Shepherd and Porter have written about "homosexuality" on the coast. Shepherd (1987) emphasizes the importance of rank in Mombasan society, downplaying the significant gendered implications of men who dress in women's clothing, perform women's work, and have sex with other men, sometimes in exchange for money. Rather than considering *mashoga* to be members of a third-gender category, she characterizes *mashoga* as essentially rational economic men (and local "lesbians" as rational economic women) in pursuit of higher social status. This is an inaccurate representation of *mashoga* identity and, as Porter (1995) argues, misses the possibility that discourses on "homosexuality" constitute an important site where struggles over power are explicitly gendered.

In a persuasive critique of Shepherd's article, Porter demonstrates how talk about "homosexuality" serves as an important "vehicle for expressing political conflicts" (1995: 145), mapping out two distinct discourses in Mombasa and within the nation-state of Kenya. Indeed, Porter transforms the greatest weakness of Shepherd's article into a strength by analyzing gossip about "homosexuality" as a specific form of discourse and not necessarily any kind of truthful representation. Porter argues that *shoga* identity is most highly stigmatized precisely because it represents visible evidence of violations against gender and status norms. She also identifies a second and, in some ways, competing discourse that marks the site of postcolonial political struggles, whereby "Swahili people have become a Muslim 'homosexual' Other in opposition to which non-coastal Christian Kenyans may construct an identity" (147).

Porter's analysis demonstrates how discourses about "homosexuality" become arenas for discursive and political struggles, and my research supports that view. I argue, following Porter, that *shoga* identity is fraught with discourses and dangers, precisely because it involves crossing gendered, sexual, and status boundaries. Moreover, ethnographic research provides the key to analyzing "homosexuality" cross-culturally in terms of desire as well as economic gain and in terms of local belief systems as well as Western cultural and professional—that is, anthropological—beliefs. Emotions and desire are certainly difficult to analyze cross-culturally, or even to understand; nonetheless, they are crucial components to the social construction of gender (see, for example, Abu-Lughod 1986) and, indeed, of sexuality.

The Omani Khanith (Xanith)

Also of relevance to a study of *shoga* identity is the work of Unni Wikan (1977, 1982; see also Murray 1997b), who has described and analyzed the Omani *khanith* tradition of male cross-dressing, prostitution, and "homosexuality."⁹ Wikan argues that the social institution of the *khanith* constitutes a "third gender," that is, an intermediate gender between "man" and "woman." She emphasizes both the punishments for boys who display gender transgressions at an early age and the eventual acceptance of that behavior as boys mature. Grounding her analysis in the Omani concept of personhood and proper behavior, Wikan argues that local conceptions of an individual's identity embrace a complex combination of traits, all of them considered to be "natural," with homosexual behavior as only one of many attributes, something to be accepted if not condoned. Thus, the *khanith* stands as a third-gender category precisely because people see the behavior as occurring naturally, within the rubric of Islamic cosmology.

Wikan's discussion of the Omani *khanith* is important because of long-standing ties between Oman and the East African coast. Oman has been a key player in coastal politics for several centuries, joining with local forces to oust the Portuguese from Mombasa by 1700. Subsequently, the sultan of Oman ruled over parts of the coast, and in 1840, the sultan moved his base from Muscat to Zanzibar. The sultanate continued on Zanzibar under British indirect rule, ending only with the revolution in 1964. Many people currently living on the East African coast have close ties to the Gulf states, as young men work in the oil industry and young women marry into wealthier families there. Particularly on Zanzibar, when the economic and political isolation of the island ended in the mid-1980s with the adoption of structural adjustment policies, increasing amounts of people and capital from Oman returned to Zanzibar. Finally, on Zanzibar in particular (and to a lesser extent in Mombasa), the term *khanith* or *hanisi*—a borrowing from

Arabic—is used alongside *shoga*. These historical ties are demonstrated by the 1860 report, noted above, of "sodomites" arriving from Muscat, wearing women's clothing and veils.

"Homosexuality," Gender, and Identity in Old Town

When someone asked me how long it took me to find "the gay bar" in Old Town, I replied 2 weeks—and 10 years. Actually, I hesitated for years before openly asking questions about *mashoga*, and I carefully avoided any appearance of knowing anything about homosexuality in East Africa or elsewhere for that matter. Finally, in 1995, I took the plunge. Along the way to Old Town, I picked up a "husband" in Nairobi, an American friend who doubled as both research assistant and convenient heterosexual cover.[10] After a few days in residence, we casually broached the topic with everyone—from old friends to recent acquaintances. The reply was always the same: "*Mashoga? Wasagaji?* (Lesbians?). Of course, everywhere." And as it turned out, these initial responses to our inquiries were quite accurate. I was often astounded by the openness and ease with which most people discussed these topics.

Lest I paint too rosy a picture, the same type of (official and unofficial) homophobic discourses that Porter describes (1995) were evident during my fieldwork in 1991–92, in Tanzania as well as Kenya. In 1995, when I openly asked questions about *mashoga* in Old Town, the people who voiced concern about my research were younger elites rapidly rising in social and economic status. They worried about possible government censure. Also, the one reputed *shoga* who refused to talk with me and who actively seemed to avoid me was also elite, and it was rumored that he had recently left a neighboring country in a hurry, presumably because he had been attacked, either personally or professionally, because of his homosexuality. I had also heard of stories of gay bashings.

But after a week or two at our research site, we had found a bar where *mashoga* congregated, and we soon learned to spot the same among unknown passersby. Initially, I approached two individuals identified (without discernable hostility) by others as *mashoga*, stated my research topic, and asked if they would be willing to talk with me. Both agreed to interviews, and it was primarily through these two individuals that we met a wider circle of people. I spent one of the most enjoyable months I have ever spent doing research, going out with my new friends, comparing notes on life in the

United States and Old Town, and trying to understand local constructions of gender and sexuality.

An identifiable community of individuals who engage in homosexual behavior and to a certain extent identify as "homosexuals" exists in Old Town. The individuals I interviewed acknowledged that they were *mashoga* but also referred to themselves (and their friends) as *magei*—that is, gay and lesbian—using the English word with the Swahili prefix *ma-* to indicate the plural. The social center of one particular network included two friends, a man and a woman, who worked together in a local business. (This business was owned by another divorced woman who also had a girlfriend.) The network included the respective boyfriend and girlfriend of the two close friends, a wealthy friend/roommate who was also identified as a *shoga*, and other pairs of boyfriends and girlfriends in town, as well as a few individuals identified as straight. They all congregated at the same local bar, at the same two tables every week, to listen to music, to socialize, and for some, to work. The bar was owned by a woman who was married to a man but was identified to me as a "lesbian."

Why was I first directed to the two perhaps best-known *mashoga* in town when I made my initial inquiries? Most important, both were "out" or "open" about their identity. The phrase in Swahili, *yuko wazi*, "(s)he is open/clear," stands in opposition to *anajificha*, "(s)he is hiding," referring to the individual's identity/sexual practices. These phrases seem to be similar to Anglo-American talk of being "out" versus being "in the closet." I was also directed to these two *mashoga* because they displayed a cluster of characteristics that quintessentially defines *shoga* identity. One, at least, was known to engage in homosexual behavior precisely because it was common knowledge that (s)he earned a living through sex work. The other individual was renowned as a local singer, and (s)he sometimes performed in women's clothing. Both, indeed, crossed gender boundaries in subtle as well as more obvious ways. As I came to understand more about *shoga* identity, I came to see gender as a complex rendition (see Weston 1996) of identity that involved and signified not only sexual practices but also dress, status, and division of labor.

Swahili Terms for "Male Homosexuals"

There are a number of different terms in use that constitute categories of identity relating to sexual practices. I was told, repeatedly, that differences within specific categories are the result of dialect rather than meaning. That is, informants explained to me that four different words could be used to refer to "passive" homosexual men: *(ma)shoga* (Kimvita, the Swahili dialect spoken in Mombasa); *(ma)khanith* or *(ma)hanisi* (Kiunguja, the Swahili dialect spoken on Zanzibar); and *m(i)senge* (Swahili, dialect unspecified from the Tanzanian mainland). I heard all of these terms used in conversations or in response to my research questions, referring to a man who is "entered" by his partner. In some ways, then, the definition of *shoga/khanith/msenge*[11] centered on that individual being a "passive" partner during anal intercourse.

As explained to me by informants, the active partner to the *shoga* is known as the *basha* (pl. *mabasha*) or *haji* (pl. *mahaji*). Again, these terms are identical in meaning; the *basha* is said to refer to the king in a pack of playing cards (Shepherd 1987: 250), and the term *haji* presumably refers to a powerful man, one who has made the pilgrimage to Mecca. The definitions provided by informants included, for *basha*, "mwanaume anamwingilia mwenzake," a man who enters his friend/partner, and for *haji*, "mwanaume rasmi, rijali," that is, a true man, a real man. Further, the two terms, *shoga* (or *khanith*) and *basha* (or *haji*) form a pair—"kuna shoga na basha wake," that is, there is the *shoga* and his *basha*. Because the *basha* is seen as a "real man," his identity remains unmarked unless he is paired with a *shoga*. For example, the *sumsumia* dance only involves *mashoga* and *mabasha* dancing together. This dance was performed by Washihiri sailors (from Yemen) upon their annual arrival at the Old Town port during the 1920s and 1930s (Laura Fair, personal communication). I was told that today these dances still occur but mostly for fun and only in private settings. *Mabasha* remain "invisible" unless seen with *mashoga*; as Porter puts it, "*Mabasha* are powerful, high ranking men, consistent with what a Swahili man is supposed to be: they spend their time with other men, they are sexually 'active,' and they are not significantly contravening their gender position" (1995: 145).

Shepherd (1987: 250–51) states that the term *shoga* refers to a younger, poorer man who takes the passive role in sex with an older, wealthier *basha*, typically for payment, and claims that "financial considerations are always involved and it is generally only the person who is paid who is called *shoga*" (250). Porter also reports differences in wealth, status, and age. I agree with Porter that these are accurate representations of talk about *mashoga* and *mabasha*, but in practice, the situation is far more complicated.

While some *mashoga* certainly are sex workers and are paid for being penetrated by older, wealthier men, *mashoga* are not *only* sex workers, and money or presents are not always involved in sexual encounters. Rather, definitions of *shoga* and *basha* identity rely on the "active" versus "passive" roles in sex that are specifically gendered in coastal society and that correlate with other gendered behaviors, such as dress or speech. The section that follows outlines four important ways in which *mashoga* are gendered beyond the realm of sex: naming practices, work, dress, and greetings.

Mashoga Identity: Practicing Gender

Names. Significantly, in the Swahili language, the gender of a person cannot be indicated grammatically through the use of a pronoun; all pronouns are gender neutral and instead indicate the noun class of the person or object being referred to. Thus, in discussions with informants and friends about *mashoga,* there was no way to tell if the person being referred to was considered a "he" or a "she."[12] Alternatively, it was noticeable that *mashoga* were often called by feminine names or chose alternative feminine nicknames. In many cases, the gender of a name is indicated by the presence or absence of the suffix *-a.* For example, an individual born as Seyyid (boy's name) would be referred to as Seyyida (girl's name). Others, who were performers, took stage names of famous women singers or movie stars (both Western and Hindi). Thus, while gender was not grammatically indicated, the feminine gender of an individual *shoga* could be indicated through the assignment or choice of nicknames or stage names.

Work. Most of the literature on coastal societies reports male transvestites and homosexuals working as musicians during women's events at weddings (Porter 1995: 140–41) and as sex workers (Shepherd 1987). These may be the two most visible forms of employment for *mashoga*: first, because they entail the crossing of specifically gendered lines, as in joining women's celebrations and, second, because sex work places sexuality (and gender) in the realm of public knowledge. Other *mashoga* that I encountered during my research worked in a variety of professions, most of which carried some gendered implications. Thus, some worked in beauty parlors performing such services as hair styling and skin and hair bleaching. (As in Western society, there is a distinction in East Africa between male barbers and female beauticians.) Another *shoga* who worked as a beautician was also renowned for their skill at decorating wedding stages, where the bride and groom would be displayed. Another was not employed at all but earned an income from house rentals. Another worked as a performer and also as a traditional healer, skills learned from a grandmother. (Both men and women served as healers

in Old Town.) Another relied on income from sex work at local bars to
survive. My point is simply that the *mashoga* I encountered in Old Town
came from a wide range of social and ethnic backgrounds and worked in
a wide range of occupations.

If social space helps construct gender, then the spaces that *mashoga*
occupy in Old Town mark their gender as being significantly different from
("real") men, more allied with women, but not exactly the same as women,
either. *Mashoga* did tend to spend more time working and socializing in
women's space and were able to cross the rather strict lines of sexual segregation in ways that ("real") men could not. Nonetheless, as Porter notes,
these crossings were not always uncontested; some women would refuse to
attend weddings where *mashoga* played prominent roles (Porter 1995: 142).
In many ways, it seemed to me that *mashoga*, along with their *mabasha* and
their *wasagaji* (lesbians) friends, created alternative spaces where men and
women met and mingled in ways unimaginable for "respectable" society.
These mixings and crossings occurred, for example, at the local bar or in
private homes where *magei* congregated to socialize. Dominant ideology, which
clearly demarcates social space in Swahili-speaking societies as women's versus
men's, becomes confounded by the practices of *mashoga* at work and play.

Dress. Hanging around with *mashoga* friends taught me that gender
as a practice is performed through ways of clothing and dress, not simply
in terms of the specific (women's versus men's) articles worn. This added
distinction may help clarify the debate between Shepherd and Wikan about
dress, and therefore gender, for the *shoga/khanith*. Shepherd states that
Mombasan *mashoga* wear "bright, tight male attire in public places" (for
the purposes of sex work) but also "may, when mingling with women at
weddings, don women's *leso* cloths, make-up and jasmine posies" (1978a:
133). Wikan notes the difference with Omani *khanith*, who "always wear
characteristic clothes intermediate in a number of features between male and
female" (1978a: 473), and that, in fact, the *khanith* is "not allowed to wear
the mask [a part of local veiling practices], or other female clothing" (1977:
307). For Wikan, intermediate clothing becomes evidence of an intermediate
gender, and for Shepherd, the lack of intermediate dress demonstrates the
lack of an alternative gender.

The *mashoga* whom I observed wore a variety of clothing, some of
it male and some of it female. Dress varied specifically according to the
occasion and ranged from full veiling (at a local bar, interestingly enough)
to shorts and T-shirt (the casual attire one *shoga* wore when welcoming
me to the house for an interview). Typically, I would say that *mashoga*

who were dressed for the evening (sometimes including sex work), or for visiting with friends, would choose a somewhat intermediate ensemble: a blouse (women's) and pants (men's) or slacks (women's), lots of gold jewelry (women's), and makeup (women's; kohl to highlight the eyes, for example). Footwear was also important; one *shoga* I noted on the street was dressed in expensive, gold, high-heeled, women's sandals, as part of a becoming slack and blouse outfit. In this sense, the *mashoga* I observed wore a combination of masculine and feminine clothing, some of it more traditional and some of it more modern, mixing and matching the pieces in ways that neither ("real") men nor women do.

More importantly, *mashoga* also wore their clothing, even if it was men's clothing, differently from other ("real") men. It took my trusted research assistant, an American man who on occasion wears the typical male Islamic gown or tunic, the *kanzu,* to point this out. Although this article of clothing is specifically (and only) worn by men—even if it resembles a house dress to American eyes—the wearing of the thing is explicitly gendered. So my assistant took his *kanzu* and demonstrated how a masculine man would walk around a mud puddle: one simply grabs the bottom edge of the *kanzu* skirt with both hands, hauls it up over the knees, and tromps through the mess. Alternatively, a *shoga* would delicately grasp the side of the *kanzu* skirt, draw its edge carefully away from the mess, and tiptoe around the edge. Another indication would be how one sits, even in a *kanzu;* knees spread apart and hand on the crotch, or legs crossed and knees together. When I did see a *shoga* in a *kanzu,* it was readily apparent that the practice of wearing the *kanzu* was radically different. A *shoga'*s sense of style in terms of how an article of clothing is worn underlines the fact that gender is a social practice, performed in a unique way by *mashoga.*

Finally, when I asked an informant if all *mashoga* wore women's clothing, (s)he said it depends; some wear women's clothing, some wear men's—*vile wanavyopenda tu* ("just the way they like it, that's all"). It seems an obvious point but one worth repeating: *mashoga* dress as they want, as they want to be seen, in ways that are intended to attract male sexual partners. The point is not to be a woman, or even to be like a woman, but to attract men, because "that's the way they like it." It is part of the pleasure of being a *shoga,* an important part of the construction of *shoga* identity, gender, and desire.

Greetings. Another important social context where behavior is explicitly gendered is the way in which individuals greet one another. On the East African coast, where great emphasis is placed on *heshima* (respect or modesty), greetings constitute an important social institution that allows for the demonstration and negotiation of everything from friendship to status and gender. Women greet one another in particular ways, men have their own greetings, and children are always expected to show the deference due adults in the way that they speak to and greet an elder. Men will oftentimes avoid touching unrelated women, acknowledging them instead with a nod or a verbal greeting. Women, and particularly female friends, perform a specific handshake: the right hand of each is extended, hands briefly clasp, and then one raises her own hand up to her lips for a quick kiss. This greeting demonstrates fondness and closeness between women (particularly younger ones). It may be a modified form of the child's greeting for an adult, where the child extends both hands, palms together and up to the adult, and then takes the adult's right hand and kisses it. Grown men do not greet others this way, and men and women would *never* demonstrate this degree of intimacy in public. Significantly, when I greeted one *shoga* friend, (s)he initiated the handshake appropriate among young female friends. This act signified and established a specific social relationship: that of intimate female equals.

Life histories. I also interviewed at length two *mashoga* about their life experiences. What struck me about both of their stories was that they immediately recounted incidents of gender crossing at an early age, whether it was playing with girls or being captivated by girls' clothing and chores. Both were severely reprimanded for this behavior by adult kin. Also, both informants talked about the experience of "being ruined" (*kuharibikwa*; the term typically describes a girl's loss of virginity before marriage, but in this case, it refers to anal penetration by an older male). In both accounts, the informants recounted this as a painful experience, emotionally and physically. One *shoga* described being repeatedly beaten as punishment for "being ruined"; (s)he sought refuge with a sympathetic grandmother, threatened suicide, and repeatedly ran away from home as the beatings (and, I think, the penetration) continued. (S)he eventually left home for good when (s)he finished school, at about the age of 12 years. In both of these cases, it seems that early crossings of gender boundaries, although (sometimes severely) punished, were permanently marked and eventually accepted through the experience of penetration by an older male, typically a school teacher, Islamic teacher, neighbor, or relative.

In reference to the experience of "being ruined," both informants also reported that after being penetrated by an older man, repeatedly, they "got used to it." They used the same phrase, *nimezoea*, "I became accustomed/

got used to it." In fact, I was struck by how many times this phrase was used; it led me to question whether I really understood the term, for it has (I think) slightly negative overtones. It seems to offer an important complement (from those penetrated early and often rather than from those avoiding being penetrated) to the Arab (indeed, circum-Mediterranean) view that the pleasures of being fucked are addictive and uncontrollable once awakened (Murray 1997c: 18–20). It was always specifically used in conjunction with the description of "being ruined." In this sense, because it is only women (technically) who can be "ruined," it may refer to simply "getting used to" being in a passive, feminine position with older, more powerful men.

Other people also talked about the cause of these individuals' homosexuality in similar terms, that is, it seemed a common assumption that the experience of "being ruined" had something to do with the *shoga*'s eventual assumption of *shoga* identity and practice of homosexual behavior. I would describe this as a common local discourse concerning the cause of an individual's "homosexuality" but also one that is fundamentally gendered, as noted above. These statements accord with Wikan's discussion of sexuality and gender identity in Oman in which she emphasizes that "it is the sexual *act*, not the sexual organs, which is fundamentally constitutive of gender" (1977: 309). Here, too, discourses on the cause of *shoga* "homosexuality" represent it as a specifically passive act, that is, being penetrated as a woman would be penetrated. The irony, of course, is that *mashoga* I talked to reported that the biggest, butchest man in town—a *"basha"*—would turn into a screaming bottom once safely behind bedroom walls. During an interview with one friend, we laughed about this fact for a long time. "Do it to me! Do it to ME!" squealed "the *shoga*," mimicking and mocking "the *basha*," and we laughed some more. Here, indeed, is where "sexuality" as well becomes a fundamentally performative practice: variations on the sex act that may not accord with dominant ideology demonstrate precisely how constructed that ideology is.

For *mashoga* and *mabasha* alike, there is far more to sexual identity than simply being the penetrator or the penetrated. Evidence of the many pleasures involved would include the elaborate rituals of preparing for an evening out: choosing a costume, applying makeup, selecting jewelry, and then starting over again after posing in the mirror. In Swahili societies, women's wedding celebrations include explicit discussions of how to provide sexual pleasure for a partner, and this knowledge is graphically demonstrated in various women's wedding dances. *Mashoga*, given their central role in women's wedding celebrations, have access to this information and participate actively in its elaboration. There is far more to sex and pleasure than meets the eye, particularly for the allegedly "passive" partner.

Finally, the general acceptance, by neighbors, family, and friends of *mashoga*, is explained in terms of a general (although sometimes begrudging) acceptance of an individual's basic "spirit" (*roho*) or "nature" (*umbo*).[13] Here, too, Wikan's description of Omani attitudes (1977: 311) seems similar to what I encountered in Old Town. That is, homosexuality was thought to spring from a basic nature that may be imperfect and indeed sinful but permanent and unassailable nonetheless. Interestingly, one *shoga* reported that other *mashoga* had not provided any advice or assistance as (s)he made his/her way in the world. No, (s)he said, (s)he hadn't been taught or mentored by other *mashoga*; instead, (s)he used the English term *natural* to describe the process whereby (s)he had assumed a *shoga* identity. I was struck by how this statement accorded with others' accounts that attributed a particular *shoga*'s identity to their basic "spirit" or "nature."

Again, I would argue, it is here that desire and pleasure enter the story, too, because sexual desire was seen to spring from this same innate, "natural" place. The irony, of course, is that dominant ideologies of "being ruined" fail to account for the full range of practices, let alone pleasures, that constitute *shoga* identity. As much as I learned about and saw the real dangers, the pain and anguish that was part of *shoga* identity, I also saw the familiar pleasures of how a small group of individuals bent the rules of society, laughing (and crying) as they went. These are all important elements to *mashoga* identity, as important, I would suggest, as any functionalist explanation centering on a theory of rational economic strategy (Shepherd 1978a, 1987).

Transnational Popular Culture and New Identities

I was also struck by the influences of American popular culture on local *mashoga*. When I asked one *shoga* if (s)he could have anything (s)he wanted, or be anyone (s)he dreamed of, what would it be, (s)he replied, without hesitation: "I would be Madonna" (the American singer). For this *shoga*, being Madonna meant being wildly successful, enjoying enormous commercial success and a glamorous lifestyle with throngs of devoted followers. This dream highlights the importance of a global popular culture and notions of beauty, glamor, and success framed by the international entertainment industry. It is a reflection of the ways in which the current world economic

system makes a commodity out of identity, and current information technologies extend the realms of cultural contacts across ever-wider frontiers
(see also Braiterman 1996).

The AIDS epidemic has played an important role in the internation-
alization of gay and lesbian liberation movements and seems to have had
some impact on local constructions of (and living of) *mashoga*/gay/lesbian
identity. Matthew Roberts (1995), for example, suggests that in several
developing countries, the establishment of AIDS organizations has served
as a catalyst for the broader growth of gay social movements. In Old Town,
two of the individuals in the circle of friends that I met had started doing
AIDS education among their circle of friends—both "straight" and "gay"
sex workers—and had recently been employed by the government to carry
out this work in local bars. Although AIDS research in Africa is adamantly
heterosexual, in this particular case, it was *magei* working in the sex industry
who initiated AIDS education in their community.

There was an obvious reason for this initiative. In Old Town, almost
everyone whom I met, and eventually visited in their homes, pulled out their
picture books as part of a friendly visit. These collections of photographs—a
few dating back perhaps 20 years, but most more recent—outline the important
social networks of any given individual. It was striking to me that only people
who identified as *gay*—at times using the English words, *gay* and *lesbian*, to
describe themselves and their acquaintances—showed me photo albums that
included pictures of people who had died of AIDS. Not all of the deceased
were "homosexual," but most had worked in the sex industry. I was struck by
how they openly identified these people as having died of AIDS. While many
governments, to be sure, are using the AIDS epidemic to label "homosexuality"
a "Western" disease and perversion, it was only *mashoga* in Old Town who
would openly discuss the deaths and their implications.

Indeed, it seems that Western discourses of gay liberation are in
the process of transforming the possibilities for *mashoga* identity. While
interviewing *mashoga*, I was much more likely to use the terms *shoga* or
basha than were my informants. I even thought that I saw an occasional
wince when I asked, "Is this person a *shoga*?" As noted earlier, some of my
informants used the term *magei* (pl. "gay") interchangeably and, I sensed,
with more pride than *mashoga* or *mabasha*. While this difference may have
been a function of the fact that they were speaking with an American, I
noticed, too, that when one informant in particular—who had also been
involved with AIDS education work—showed me a picture, (s)he stated
spontaneously and quite happily, "Huyu ni boyfriend yangu" (This is my

boyfriend). Porter rightly notes the derisory use of English terms (*lezzie*, for example) by others to refer to alleged "homosexuals" in Mombasa and that the use of a Western condemnatory discourse may be overshadowing local, "traditional" discourses (1995: 150). What I observed, however, indicates that a liberatory discourse is also emerging, complementing, and perhaps competing with other discourses on "homosexuality" that exist on the coast.

Conclusion

Mashoga identity, as a locus of cross-dressing and "homosexuality" on the East African coast, marks a struggle over gender that is also a struggle over power. Practices of gendering are strictly policed precisely because they can challenge dominant ideologies central to social structures of inequality. Through these practices, dominant ideologies of sexuality, status, and gender are contested, reified, and subverted all at once.[14] The evidence presented here demonstrates how individuals actively gender themselves and others as *mashoga*. Young boys are punished for displaying gender-inappropriate behavior, but if they survive to adulthood, they can assume the socially stigmatized but still-recognized identity of *mashoga*. Indeed, they may come to describe themselves as *magei*. *Mashoga* and *magei* are taking part in social practices that are always remaking the terms of gender within coastal society.

Notes

1. This article grows out of a paper originally delivered at Yale University in December 1995 at the Agrarian Studies Conference on Indian Ocean trade. I would like to thank Bruce McKim for encouraging me to present the original paper, Stephen O. Murray for encouraging me to revise it and for his helpful comments, "Arthur" for the insights that only a local expert can provide, and Jared Braiterman and William C. Bissell for comments. *Magei* was misspelled in the original article. The correct spelling is *"gei/magei"* (sing./plural) in Standard Swahili.

2. Quotation marks here are used to indicate some distance from historically specific Western constructions of "the homosexual." I argue that the categories of identity described here (*"mashoga," "mabasha," "magei"*) must be understood as historically and culturally specific constructions. Moreover, while sexual behavior is an important component of these identities, other important aspects include gender and economic roles.

3. "Passive," that is, in terms of being penetrated (and therefore, allegedly passive) during anal intercourse. This characterization should not be understood

too literally, as demonstrated below. See also Braiterman (1996), who argues that discourses on "the passive homosexual" are crucial to the construction of "active" masculinity for "real men."

4. For example, see Porter (1995: 136–37) for a vivid, contemporary description of Mombasa's Old Town.

5. Whereas *hanisi* (pl. *mahanisi*) or *hanith* (pl. *mahanith*) and *shoga* (pl. *mashoga*) are terms for the same phenomenon in two different dialects of Swahili (Kiunguja and Kimvita, respectively), I have chosen to use the term *(ma)shoga* throughout, largely because the extant literature refers only to *(ma)shoga*.

6. Gilbert Herdt (1994) provides an excellent review and range of arguments concerning the notion of a "third gender" in the cross-cultural study of "homosexuality." He not only provides a compelling argument for the utility of this concept for the purposes of critiquing dominant ideologies of sexual dimorphism but also acknowledges the dangers of this approach, as do several authors in the volume (see also Murray 1994).

7. On profession-based homosexualities, see Murray (1992a: 257–72).

8. The question of where cultural practices come from is an interesting one and too complicated to address here at any length. Clearly, there are important ties between the social institution of the *khanith* in Oman and the *shoga/hanisi* on the East African coast, as Stephen Murray originally suggested to me. Porter notes that homosexuality is said to be "unheard of" anywhere other than the Kenyan coast (1995: 147), although based on my own interviews with informants in Nairobi, it seems that homosexual behaviors are known to be practiced by members of various pastoralist groups such as the Massai and Samburu. Innovative sexual ideologies and practices were also clearly brought to the coast in the 19th century by members of enslaved groups, as evidenced by the role of *makungwi* (sexual instructor for girls) in Mombasa (Strobel 1975). While the social institution of the *shoga/hanith* may have its origins in Oman or the southern Arabian peninsula, I would also caution against too hastily dismissing other possible influences from or origins within the African continent.

9. Following Murray (1997b), I use the more standard romanization, *khanith*, in lieu of *xanith*, the spelling employed by Wikan (1977, 1982).

10. My experiences conducting research in Swahili-speaking societies over the past 10 years have convinced me never to conduct research alone again. Young, single Euro-American women traveling and working alone in Muslim societies are subject to forms of harassment and stigmatization that can severely limit research activities.

11. Porter lists two additional words used to "describe or refer to" a *shoga* that I am unfamiliar with: *rambuza* and *msagaliwa* (1995: 142). Similarly, I was told that *(ma)haboo* was another term used in Zanzibar, with the same meaning, although I never heard it used in conversation.

12. Wikan (1977: 309) reports that Omani *khanith* are referred to in the masculine grammatical gender in Arabic.

13. Thanks to William C. Bissell for his comments on semantic fields in reference to this point.

14. It seems important to note that only men can engage in this "play"; it's not funny when women do it. Accordingly, women tend to cross gender lines in more subtle ways (see Porter 1995).

Part II

West Africa

Overview

West Africa includes portions of both the Sudanic belt and the equatorial rain forest. In the Savannah areas, cattle herding is widespread, and grains and other foodstuffs are grown as well. Most of the societies based on herding are nomadic or migratory. Although many groups are Muslim, others, such as the Mossi and the Tallensi, have retained traditional religions, and some Islamic groups, such as the Hausa, have flourishing non-Islamic possession cults. Sudanic societies are typically patrilineal, ranging in scale from small, independent units to kingdoms and empires.

Coastal West Africa (the Guinea coast) has a similar climate, although rainfall is concentrated in the months from June to November, followed by a dry season. Societies in this area are primarily based on the production of root crops and, for a few, fishing. The region is characterized by a wide range of social and political forms. Patrilineal descent groups are common. Some societies, such as the Yoruba, the Dahomey, and the Asante, formed large political states (prior to European colonialization), whereas others, such as the Kru and the Igbo/Ibo, were organized on a smaller scale.

Sudanic West Africa

Relationships organized by both age and gender (even more so than those of the Zande) were observed in the Mossi (Moose) royal court—in what is now Burkina Faso—in the early 20th century. *Soronés*, or pages, were chosen from among the most beautiful boys aged 7 to 15 years old. They dressed as women and assumed other feminine attributes, including women's sexual role with the chiefs, especially on Fridays, when sexual intercourse with women was prohibited to them (Tauxier 1912: 569–70).[1] The *soronés* who proved their discretion were entrusted with state secrets. However, they had to undergo annual tests to determine that they had not been sexually intimate with women. After a boy reached maturity, the chief gave him a wife. The firstborn of such couples belonged to the chief. If a boy, he would follow his father in becoming a *soroné*; if a girl, she would be given in marriage by the chief (as her mother had).

Not far from the Mossi, between the lower Senegal and Niger rivers in contemporary Mali, are the Bambara millet farmers. A report from the 1890s refers to a pair of young Bambara archers who took turns with each other while they were enslaved and even after being freed (until they were able to share a wife of an absent fellow archer) (X [1893: 258] 1898 2:165–66).

Religious Vocations in West Africa

Malidoma Somé, a member of the agricultural Dagara of southern Burkina Faso, is among the few contemporary Africans to comment on the subject of homosexuality in traditional culture. Somé reports that many individuals who filled spiritual roles in his society are "gay," and he credits this to their capacity to mediate based on the ability to bridge gender roles:

> Gender has very little to do with anatomy. . . . The Earth is looked at, from my tribal perspective, as a very, very delicate machine or consciousness, with high vibrational points, which certain people must be guardians of in order for the tribe to keep its continuity with the gods and with the spirits that dwell there—spirits of this world and spirits of the other world. Any person who is this link between this world and the other world experiences a state of vibrational consciousness which is far higher, and far different, from the one that a normal person would experience. This is what make a gay person gay. This kind of function is not one that society votes for certain people to fulfill. It is one that people are said to decide on prior to being born. You decide that you will be a gatekeeper before you are born. And it is that decision that provides you with the equipment that you bring into this world. So when you arrive here, you begin to vibrate in a way that Elders can detect as meaning that you are connected with a gateway somewhere.[2] (1993: 7)

In Dagara belief, Somé explains, the survival of the cosmos depends on such gatekeepers: "Unless there is somebody who constantly monitors the mechanism that opens the door from this world to the Otherworld, what happens is that something can happen to one of the doors and it closes up. When all the doors are closed, this Earth runs out of its own orbit and the solar system collapses into itself. And because this system is linked to other systems, they too start to fall into a whirlpool" (1993: 8).

Somé's 1994 book *Of Water and the Spirit* relates some of his own experiences during (a belated) initiation. After years of study in the West (earning doctorates from the Sorbonne and from Brandeis), he returned to his village. He began to wonder about Dagara, "who feel the way that certain people feel in this culture that has led to them being referred to as 'gay.'" When he asked one of them, "who had taken me to the threshold of the Otherworld [as one of the elders supervising his initiation cohort], whether he feels sexual attraction towards another man, he jumped back and said, 'How do you know that?' He said, 'This is our business as gatekeepers'" (1993: 7).[3] As a result of such beliefs, Somé reports that "the gay person is very well integrated into the community" (8). (The particular gatekeeper he spoke to had a wife and children.)

Somé also reports that among the related Dogon of Mali, "a tribe that knows astrology like no other tribe that I have encountered, the great astrologers . . . are gay," and he argues that, with the exception of Christendom, "Everywhere else in the world gay people are a blessing" (1993: 8).[4]

Unfortunately, other reports of West African homosexuality come from much less sympathetic chroniclers, namely Christian Europeans. One early 20th-century observer, for example, described a ceremony performed by a secret society variously known as Obukele, Obukere, and Oweu among the Igbo/Ibo and Abuan peoples of Nigeria whenever the Niger and adjoining rivers were at their crest. It included "unnatural rites performed during the ceremonies and sympathetic magic practiced in order to secure fruitfulness for human being, animals and fishes" (Talbot 1926, 3:766). Yet another colonial-era author, in discussing phallic signs "in Oro, Egbo, Nimm, Katahwiriba, Orisha, and other societies" in Sierra Leone and West Africa, obliquely mentioned "pictures in some of the council houses of old pederastical practices" (Butt-Thompson 1929: 175).

Hausa

The once-fortified Muslim city-states of the Hausa represent the westernmost extension of Chadic-speakers, who reached their present location some

500 years ago (Newman 1995: 199). Although substantially converted to Islam by the 16th century, many Hausa today participate in a possession religion—the *bori* cult—that some believe to be a survival of pre-Islamic religion.[5] Gender-marked homosexual men are prominent in this cult, which is strikingly similar to possession cults in Brazil and the Caribbean founded by descendants of West Africans.

As in the Haitian voudou(n) cult, the Hausa speak of those who are possessed as being horses "ridden" by the spirit. Homosexual participants are called *'Yan Daudu* (son of Daudu). Fremont Besmer explains that Daudu is a praise name for any Galadima (i.e., a ranked title). It specifically refers to the *bori* spirit Dan Galadima (literally, son of Galadima; the Prince), who is said to be "a handsome young man, popular with women, a spendthrift, and a gambler" (Besmer 1983: 30, n. 4).

In fact, according to Besmer, *'yan daudu* are not actually possessed by Dan Galadima or any other spirits (1983: 18). Rather, their role is to make "luxury snacks"—such as fried chicken—which are sold at cult events (Pittin 1983: 297).[6] They also serve as intermediaries between female prostitutes and prospective clients.

Christin Pittin offers some additional observations of this role: "The economic enterprises of the *'yan daudu* are centered on three related activities: procuring, cooking, and prostitution. . . . Procuring, the mobilisation of women for illicit sexual purposes, clearly demands close ties between the procurer and the women. The *dan daudu* [sing.], in his combination of male and female roles, can and does mediate between men and women in this context" (1983: 296–97). In fact, living among women in the strangers' quarters of Hausa towns provides "a cover for men seeking homosexual services. The *dan daudu* and his sexual partners can carry out their assignations with greater discretion than would be possible if the *'yan daudu* lived together, or on their own outside the *gidan mata*" (297).

In patriarchal Hausa society, the *bori* cult provides a niche for various low-status persons. As Besmer notes, "Women provide the bulk of membership for the cult and are stereotyped as prostitutes," while "jurally-deprived categories of men, including both deviants (homosexuals) and despised or lowly-ranked categories (butchers, night-soil workers, poor farmers, and musicians) constitute the central group of possessed or participating males." In addition, the cult attracts "an element of psychologically disturbed individuals which cuts across social distinctions" (1983: 18–19; see also Hill 1967: 233; M. F. Smith 1954: 64).[7] Besmer explains the decision to join the *bori* cult in terms of labeling theory, as an instance of "secondary deviance":

One whose status identity is somewhat ambiguous, arising
from some personal characteristic . . . specific social condition,
or regularly recurring condition associated with the life cycle,
can seek either to have his social identity changed or his social
status regularized and defined through participation in bori rituals. Marked by "abnormality" and accepted as a candidate for
membership in the cult through an identification of iskoki as the
cause of the problem, a person's behavior becomes explainable,
and simultaneously earns a degree of acceptability, after the
completion of the bori initiation. Symbolic transformation from
a suffering outsider—outside both the society and the cult—to
one whose status includes the description, horse of the gods is
achieved. (1983: 122–23)

In other words, the *bori* cult provides its members with a social niche
and an alternative source of prestige. Even so, the cult remains marginal.
According to Besmer, "Status ambiguity is not completely eliminated through
involvement in the bori cult. While an initiated individual achieves a specific, formal status within the cult since possession is institutionalized, it is
not possible for him to escape the general social assessment of his behavior
as deviant" (1983: 21). Besmer did not determine, however, if members of
the cult accepted this devaluation. His account provides some indications
of "tertiary deviance," that is, rejection of stigma (18).

In the end, Besmer fails to explain how and why certain Hausa
come to define themselves or others as different, let alone as homosexual.
Research by Salisu Abdullahi in the early 1980s provides some insight into
this question. He interviewed 140 *'yan daudu* and reported that 56 percent
cited economic reasons to explain why they became a *'dan daudu*, whereas
22 percent cited the influence of friends and associates, and only 7 percent
attributed their role to "nature."[8]

These findings led Gerald Kleis and Abdullahi, researchers at Bayero
University in Kano, Nigeria, to conclude that economic rewards are "sufficient
to account for recruitment without assuming a personality predisposition"
to dress and behave like a woman (1983: 52). In their view, prostitutes
provide a "safety valve" in Hausa society, in which female seclusion has
been increasing since the 19th century. *'Yan daudu*, rather than being
prostitutes themselves (like the Omani *khanith*), function as procurers,
recruiting runaway women, "socializing them in the seductive arts" and then
"soliciting suitors, arranging contacts, extolling and advertising her charms,

and managing relations with the authorities." The intermediary role of *'yan daudu* is crucial, because female prostitutes live and work outside the walled city core. For these services, the *'dan daudu* is paid by both the prostitutes and his customers. According to Kleis and Abdullahi, these commissions constitute "the bulk of his daily income" (45).

Kleis and Abdullahi treat the *'dan daudu* as a wholly secular role, an economic niche for poor emigrants (not all of whom are Hausa) from the countryside, not as a refuge for males seeking sex with males.[9] Following a long line of anthropologists and others who discount the possibility of homosexual desire in the occurrence of homosexual acts (yet never raise the same question about heterosexual desire), Kleis and Abdullahi assert, "Many *'yan daudu* are assumed also to be homosexuals, although this does not seem to be the major feature of their social status, which hinges more on their self-identification as females" (1983: 44). For them, the nonmasculine behavior and dress of *'yan daudu* are products of purely practical considerations: "A male with masculine gender identity and pronounced heterosexual interests would be less suitable as a broker because he might well find it difficult to separate his personal and professional involvements with the prostitute and would risk becoming a rival of her customers" (46). (Apparently, it did not occur to them that a homosexual *'dan daudu* could also have conflicts, since he could be a rival for the female prostitutes' customers. They do not report who the sexual partners of *'yan daudu* are.)

Kelis and Abdullahi note that there is no Hausa or Omani role for women who live or act like men, and they stress that both the Hausa *'dan daudu* and the Omani *khanith* are conceived as a type of male. Indeed, "They occupy these positions precisely because they are anatomical males."[10] Further, like the *khanith*, *'yan daudu* "can temporarily, alternately, or permanently switch back and take up conventional male roles—a course definitely unavailable to anatomical females" (1983: 49).

In his chapter, Rudolf Gaudio reports on his research in the 1990s in the "gay male community" of the predominantly Hausa city of Kano. Although he follows Kleis and Abdullahi in de-emphasizing the connection between *'yan daudu* and possession cults, his view of the Hausa sexual landscape is more nuanced. In addition to the gender-defined role of nonmasculine *'yan daudu*, Gaudio describes *k'wazo*—older, well-to-do men, generally masculine in behavior—and their younger partners, called *baja*, who are generally sexually receptive (that is, penetrated) and receive presents as would female lovers. Although the labels for these roles are grammatically gendered, the actual behavior of individuals in such relationships is variable. Age, wealth, and temperament are not always neatly bundled. Indeed, Gaudio heard of nonmasculine males having sex with each other, which was considered to be a form of *kifi*, or "lesbianism" (1996b: 132). Even sex between two masculine males was viewed as *kifi*. As Gaudio notes, such labeling reveals the belief that valid sexual encounters involving "real" men normally entail a distinct power asymmetry. At the same time, while sex between *'yan daudu* is derided, sex between two masculine-identified men is not condemned. In other words, in Hausa terms, valid sex requires at least one masculine partner—but not necessarily a female or feminine partner.

Gaudio believes that there has been little if any non-African influence on Hausa same-sex patterns. In 1994, when a local Muslim newspaper characterized homosexual marriages as a Western practice alien to Hausa Muslim culture, Gaudio heard members of "Kano's gay male community" speak of "homosexuality and homosexual marriage as practices that are indigenous to Hausa Muslim culture [even] as they are marginal within it" (1996a abstract).

The Hausa men that Gaudio describes significantly differ from most contemporary North American and European gay men in that they do not see homosexuality as incompatible with or excluding heterosexuality, including marriage and parenthood. This observation is key for understanding African patterns of sexuality. The assumptions behind modern Western forms of voluntary or "choice" marriage, in which the partners freely choose each other based on personal desires and criteria, have led many to imagine that marriage everywhere "naturally" flows from heterosexual desire. But in societies in which marriage is required and viewed as a fundamental obligation of kinship and citizenship, whether or not the partners are attracted to each other—or to each other's sex in general—is irrelevant.

Arranged or mandatory marriage does not require heterosexual orientation or desire, and consequently, heterosexuality is not fetishized in traditional societies as "normal" or "natural" or even a necessary (or recognized) state of being. Traditional societies do not need "heterosexuality"—the idea, the word, the symbol, the ideology—to ensure the union of men and women and the production of new generations. Familial intervention and kinship obligations guarantee that marriage will happen. Consequently, such societies do not need to suppress homosexuality, as long as it does not threaten the directive to marry and reproduce (specifically, in patrilineal societies, sons). The freedom for men to pursue extramarital heterosexual or homosexual relations can be quite extensive, provided such affairs remain secondary and socially invisible. Homosexuality must never exclude heterosexuality (see, for example, Badruddin Khan on contemporary Pakistan [1997]).

As Gaudio found, Hausa "gay" men regard their homosexual desires as real and as intrinsic to their nature, but they also regard their reproductive obligations as real and, ultimately, more important than their homosexual affairs, which they considered merely *wasa* (play). Not surprisingly, Gaudio did not encounter any *'yan daudu* who expressed an interest in surgical sex reassignment. In Muslim belief, removing one's genitalia would not only make it impossible to fulfill the role of parent, it would be a kind of sacrilege to one's God-given body. In this regard, even the most effeminate *'dan daudu* is understood by all Hausas to be male.

Yoruba

In the early 1960s, a psychiatric team surveyed villagers around Abeokuta, Nigeria—the region of the Yoruba, non-Islamic Savannah agriculturalists who have long been intensely hostile to the Hausa—to identify symptoms thought by the Yoruba to indicate or constitute mental and emotional illness. "Homosexuality was not mentioned; and when we asked about it, we were told it was extremely rare, probably found only in changing parts of urban centers" (Leighton et al. 1963: 111). However, the failure of Yorubans to mention homosexuality when questioned about illness is not the firmest basis for drawing conclusions about its presence. Such responses could just as easily suggest that rural Yoruba did not consider homosexuality an "illness."[11]

As among many other African peoples, Yoruba spirit possession (*òrìsà gìgún*) is primarily associated with women. Most Sango priests are female and those who are not dressed in women's clothing, cosmetics, and jewelry and sport women's coiffures when they are going to be possessed (Matory 1994: 6–7, also see 183–215; H. Baumann 1955: 33–35; Matory 1986: 51).

The Yoruba verb for possession *gun* ("to mount") "often implies suddenness, violence, and utter loss of self-control. . . . Sango will 'mount' the initiand bride, an act whose sexual implications are clear. Not only do gods 'mount' priests, but male animals 'mount' females in the sex act. . . . It does not normally apply to human beings. Applied to human beings it suggests rape. Hence, its application suggests metaphorically the violence and absolute domination implicit in Sango's command" (Matory 1994: 175, 198, 270 n. 16). Initiates of both sexes are referred to as a "bride" (*iyawo*) of the god (179).

For the Yoruba—in marked contrast to their religious and political antagonists, the Hausa (and Yoruba emulators in the Bahian possession cults of Brazil and many other peoples)—the priests who are mounted by gods are not assumed to be mounted by men as well. Of the *elegun* Lorand Matory wrote, "They regularly have multiple wives and children, and no one seems to wonder if they engage in sex with other men" (1994: 208). Matory actually broached the subject of homosexuality with Yorubans—so that in this instance, lack of evidence cannot be blamed on lack of inquiry. In his research on Afro-Brazilian possession religion, Matory observed that

> there is an extensive public discourse suggesting that males who are possessed by spirits tend also to be the *type* of men (i.e., *bichas*) who habitually get penetrated sexually by other men. By contrast, my point about the Nigerian possession religions is that they and their [non-believing] neighbors present no *public discourse* suggesting this link. To me the absence of such a discourse does not by itself mean that no Sango priest is penetrated by other men. It just means that few people, if any at all, in this socio-cultural context recognize penetrated men as a type of social personality and that sexual penetration is not the aspect of the sacred marriage that Oyo-Yoruba royalists highlight in the construction of god-priest relations or, incredible as it may sound, husband-wife relations. . . . I do not mean to infer that these men never have sex with other men [although] I doubt that they do, based upon my limited but deliberate investigation of the possibility. (Personal communication to S. O. Murray, April 12, 1996)

In short, there does not appear to be a Yoruba role in which homosexuality is an expected feature.[12] It does appear, however, that Yorubas contrast their own sexuality (both Christian and "traditional") to the "corrupt" sexuality of the Islamic Hausa in the same way that highland Kenyan Kikuyu (who are mostly Christian) contrast their sexual mores to the perceived acceptance of gender-defined homosexuality in Islamicized coastal areas. These alleged differences have over time increasingly become a "marker" in ethnic-religious conflicts in colonial and postcolonial multi-ethnic states. However, while noting the contrast between the Hausa's ready acknowledgment of (and gossip about) the involvement of leading men in homosexuality and Yoruban denials of any corresponding practices, Gaudio "categorically reject[s] the idea that there is no homosexual self-identity in contemporary Yoruba communities":

I met at least two Yoruba self-identified "gay" men in Kano,
neither of whom had ever lived abroad, who told me about the
many other "gays" they knew in such cities as Ilorin, Ibadan,
and, of course, Lagos where there is a "Gentleman's Alliance"
with pan-Southern membership. My Kano Yoruba contacts told
me that GA members have private parties at each other's homes,
and that there is a division of Yoruba gay male social circles into
"kings" and "queens." . . . When I asked one of these Yoruba
"queens" whether there was any Yoruba equivalent to the Hausa
'yan daudu, he said that no, Yoruba queens had more "respect"
than the 'yan daudu, insofar as Yoruba queens keep their outrageous, feminine behaviors a secret from other people. (Personal
communication to S. O. Murray, March 13, 1997)[13]

Tade Akin Aina, a sociologist at the University of Lagos, has written
about male concubines and male prostitutes (many of whom double as
pimps for female prostitutes) in contemporary cities such as Lagos and
Kano. Patrons often "operate plural relationships with a retinue of young
men," who may use the resources they derive from their homosexual liaisons
to pursue heterosexual sex: "They are often identifiable as big spenders and
playboy socialites" (1991: 88). The male prostitutes that he interviewed in
Kano and Lagos

> still believe that there are magical and witchcraft effects associated
> with male homosexual intercourse. They also believe that if the
> dominant partner is a businessman, such associations confer spiri-
> tual benefits to his business. This, they state, affects the price they
> place on their services. Also it is felt that homosexuality conveys
> some unique advantages on its practitioners; for instance, they feel
> that homosexuals tend to be rich and successful men. . . . [They]
> feel that they are at risk of becoming impotent (the "eunuch
> effect") or permanently incapable of conventional heterosexual
> relations once any of their clients exploit the relationship for
> ritual or witchcraft purposes. . . . Among the Nigerian prostitutes
> spoken to, modern risks such as AIDS or sexually transmitted
> diseases did not carry weight as sources of fear. (88)

As Gaudio reports below, there are Hausa lesbians, some of whom
know of and use the terms for male homosexual roles, and Hausa gay men

claim that lesbians engage in the same types of relationships they do—that is, they exchange gifts and assume active/receptive sexual roles. In 1942, Siegfried Nadel made passing mention of Nupe lesbian behavior in Nigeria (152; see also 1954: 179).

Coastal West Africa

Eunuchs, Amazons, and a Sometimes Lifelong "Adolescent Phase" in Dahomey

Historical reports refer to same-sex patterns in the royal court of the Dahomey kingdom (in present-day Benin), which emerged in the 18th century. In the 1780s, Robert Norris saw castrated men during his journey through the region (1789: 422). A century later, Richard Burton reported that "it is difficult to obtain information in Dahome concerning eunuchs, who are special slaves of the king, and bear the dignified title of royal wives" ([1865] 1924: 123). About the same time, a privileged role for nonmasculine males was observed in the Dahomey court at Ouidah (Whydah) (Langle 1876: 243). Called *lagredis*, they were chosen from among the sons of the country's best families. In their youth, they were forced to drink potions that stifled their passions. Reportedly, they had unlimited powers, and their headman played an important part at court and in the king's council. Two *lagredi* accompanied any emissary of the king's, monitored his negotiations, and reported what they observed directly back to the king. All of this is reminiscent of the role of eunuchs in the courts of the Near East, and the practice may, indeed, have been adopted as a result of Islamic influence. Earlier observers, however, speculated that pederasty among the Dahomean royalty was inevitable given the king's monopolization of women (Bastian 1879, 305; Gorer [1935] 1962: 141).

Another unique feature of the Dahomean state system was the presence of military troops of women. In his account of his 1863–64 mission, R. Burton devoted a chapter to "the so-called Amazon" troops of King Gelele (1864, 2: 63–85). In Burton's view, "the origin of the somewhat exceptional organisation" of the women troops, which he estimated to number about 2,500, was "the masculine physique of the women, enabling them to compete with men in enduring toil, hardship and privations" (64). He also offered an historical explanation—the female troops were organized after the early 18th-century King Agaja depleted the ranks of male soldiers (65).

Alfred Ellis, noting that Dahomean women "endured all the toil and performed all the hard labour," elaborated on the historical evolution of the Amazon institution:

> The female corps, to use the common expression, the Amazons, was raised about the year 1729, when a body of women who had been armed and furnished with banners, merely as a stratagem to make the attacking forces appear larger, behaved with such unexpected gallantry as to lead to a permanent corps of women being embodied [by King Trudo]. Up to the reign of Gezo, who came to the stool in 1811, the Amazon force was composed chiefly of criminals, that is criminals in the Dahomi sense of the word. Wives detected in adultery, and termagants and scolds were drafted into its ranks; and the great majority of the women "given to the king" by the provincial chiefs, that is, sent to him as being worthy of death for misdemeanours or crimes, were, instead of being sacrificed at the Annual Custom, made women soldiers. Gezo, who largely made use of the Amazons to keep his own subjects in check and to promote military rivalry, increased and improved the force. He directed every head of a family to send his daughters to Agbomi for inspection; the most suitable were enlisted, and the corps thus placed on a new footing. This course was also followed by Gelele, his successor, who had every girl brought to him before marriage, and enrolled those who pleased him. ([1890] 1965: 183)

Burton reported nothing, and Ellis next to nothing, about the sexuality of these "Amazons." They were distinguished from the king's numerous wives, and "two-thirds are said to be maidens" (Burton 1864: 64, 68). In his "Terminal Essay" to his translation of the *Arabian Nights*, Burton wrote, "In the Empire of Dahomey I noted a corps of prostitutes kept for the use of the Amazon-soldieresses" ([1903–04?]: 247). In his 1864 account, he merely noted, "All the passions are sisters. I believe that bloodshed causes these women to remember, not to forget LOVE" (2:73).

Commander Frederick Forbes's journals of his 1849–50 missions to King Gezo of Dahomey (published in 1851) also failed to describe the sexual behavior of the "Amazons," but they are clearer than Burton about their masculine gender identification:

The amazons are not supposed to marry, and, by their own statement, they have changed their sex. "We are men," say they, "not women." All dress alike, diet alike, and male and female emulate each other: what the males do, the amazons will endeavour to surpass. They all take great care of their arms, polish the barrels, and, except when on duty, keep them in covers. There is no duty at the palace except when the king is in public, then a guard of amazons protects the royal person, and, on review, he is guarded by the males. . . . The amazons are in barracks within the palace enclosure, and under the care of eunuchs and the camboodee or treasurer. (1:123–24)[14]

Indeed, in a parade on July 13, 1850, Amazon troops sang about the effeminacy of the male soldiers they had defeated:

We marched against Attahpahms as against men,
We came and found them women.
What we catch in the bush we never divide. (2:108)

Some 2,400 Amazons joined the parade, pledging to conquer Abeahkeutah (a British ally in Sierra Leone) or to die trying. An Amazon chief then began a speech by referring to their gender transformation: "As the blacksmith takes an iron bar and by fire changes its fashion, so we have changed our nature. We are no longer women, we are men" (2:119).

In the 20th century, the Fon, the predominant people in Dahomey, were studied by the anthropologist Melville Herskovits. According to Herskovits, the Fon considered homosexuality an adolescent phase: "[When] the games between boys and girls are stopped, the boys no longer have the opportunity for companionship with the girls, and the sex drive finds satisfaction in close friendship between boys in the same group. . . . A boy may take the other 'as a woman' this being called *gaglgo*, homosexuality. Sometimes an affair of this sort persists during the entire life of the pair" (1938: 289). The last statement shows the insufficiency of either the native model or Herskovits' understanding of it. As the need to carefully conceal homosexual relationships that continue beyond adolescence demonstrates, the Fon model is prescriptive rather than descriptive.

Herskovits also reported that "homosexuality is found among women as well as men; by some it is claimed that it exists among women to a greater extent" (1938: 289). Male suspicion of what women are up to among themselves, on the one hand, and women's formation of emotionally intense relationships as shelters from men, on the other, are common patterns in West African cultures.

Togo, Ghana, Ivory Coast, Liberia

J. P. Froelich's mention of a separate (and longer) initiation rite, called *kpankpankwondi*, for Moba girls in northern Togo who refuse to marry the husbands selected for them is especially tantalizing (1949: 115–18). Among the Fanti of Ghana, James Christensen observed gender-mixing roles for both males and females, which were based on the belief that those with heavy souls, whatever their biological sex, will desire women, whereas those with light souls will desire men (1954: 92–93, 143). David Greenberg has related Evan Meyerowitz's (unconfirmed) report, based on her fieldwork in the Gold Coast (now Ghana), that "lesbian affairs were virtually universal among unmarried Akan women, sometimes continuing after marriage. Whenever possible, the women purchased extra-large beds to accommodate group sex sessions involving perhaps half-a-dozen women" (1988: 66).[15]

The Ashanti, another matrilineal Akan people who reside in present-day Ivory Coast, created a powerful state in the 18th century. According to a 19th-century report, they used male slaves as concubines, treating them like female lovers. Male concubines wore pearl necklaces with gold pendants. When their masters died, they were also killed (Hutchinson 1861: 129–30). Meyerowitz, who observed the Ashanti and other Akan peoples from the 1920s to the 1940s, recalled that "at that time men who dressed as women and engaged in homosexual relations with other men were not stigmatized, but accepted." She believed that there were good reasons for men to become women, since among the matrilineal Akan, the status of women was particularly high (a situation that she believes has changed due to missionary activity).[16]

More recently, Anyi informants in the Ivory Coast (Côte d'Ivoire), members of another Akan people, told Paul Parin that "in every village there are some men who, for neurotic reasons, do not have sexual relations with women. A number of them are known to practice occasional reciprocal masturbation with boys" (Parin et al. 1980: 204). Parin asserted that bisexuality was even more common among women, and he published a case study in which the approaches of a gift-giving sorcerer to another man are ambivalently recounted (289–95).

In the early 1970s, Italo Signorini described age-stratified homosexuality among the Nzema (Nzima), traditionally an agricultural and fishing people living near the mouth of the Tano River in Ghana. Nzema same-sex couples speak frankly about their attraction to the physical beauty, character, and oratorical skills of their partners. They "fall in love," contract relationships, and share beds. The husband pays bridewealth to the male wife's parents, as he would for a female bride, and celebrates with a wedding banquet. The same incest taboos that restrict availability of women apply, and divorce requirements for male couples are the same as for male-female ones. The male wives are younger than their husbands, but usually the difference is not generational—for example, a 30-year-old marrying a 20-year-old (Signorini 1971). Vinigi Grottanelli also has noted the role of age differences. *Agyale*, or "friendship marriages," were "usually between a man and a male teenager, more rarely between two women." In either case, "preliminaries similar to those of real marriage are performed, partners cohabit for short periods, exchange presents, and share the same bed or mat" (1988: 210). However, Italo Signorini reports that Nzema men acquired same-sex partners for "social, not sexual consumption" and that they persistently denied practicing "sodomy."[17]

Wilhelm Hammer noted that homosexual relations were not rare among Liberian Kru youths (1909: 198), whose domestic services to men of other tribes included being sodomized, according to Freidrich von Hellwald (1886, 4:591). In the 1930s, Wilfred Hambly noted that "homosexuality is reported" (without specifying by whom) in the Grand Porro in Liberia and Sierra Leone (1937: 500).

Gender-Defined Homosexuality in and around Senegal

In Senegal in the 1890s, A. Corre encountered black men with feminine dress and demeanor, who, he was told, made their living from prostitution; in Boké, Guinea, he saw a prince's dancer miming a sexually receptive role (1894: 80 n. 1). In the 1930s, Geoffrey Gorer reported that among the Wolof in Senegal, "Pathics are a common sight. They are called in Wolof men-women, *gor-digen,* and do their best to deserve the epithet by their mannerisms, their dress and their make-up; some even dress their hair like women. They do not suffer in any way socially, though the Mohammedans refuse them religious burial" ([1935] 1962: 36).

Twenty-five years later, Michael Crowder saw young males waiting to be picked up in the Place Prôtet, the main square in Dakar (since renamed

Place de l'Indépendence), and he reported that the Wolof word for homosexual was *Gor-Digen*. "The elders and faithful Muslims condemn men for this," he noted, "but it is typical of African tolerance that they are left very much alone by the rest of the people" (1959: 68). Another observer in the same period noted that homosexuality was rare in the countryside but well established in large towns (Gamble 1957: 80). In 1958, Michael Davidson observed a cross-dressing male prostitute in a Dakar bar who was well accepted (see "A 1958 Visit to a Dakar Boy Brothel").

In the early 1970s, a nonrandom survey of Sengalese found that 17.6 percent of the males and 44.4 percent of the females reported having homosexual experiences (Schenkel 1971: 343). The visibility of homosexuality in Dakar was also noted (379).

More recently, Gerben Potman and Huub Ruijgrok referred to "militant transvestites and other uninhibited types in bigger cities" in Senegal and Burkina Faso. They reported that "one of us took part in a ceremony where two male couples married in front of their friends. Each of the friends delivered a speech and rings were exchanged. The married couples, however, did not have the means to live together in the same house. Only a few rich urban men have the opportunity to live together" (1993: 169).[18] They also noted that there are men who "will never consider or identify themselves as homosexuals, even if they have sex with other men regularly" and others who "clearly prefer homosexual contacts" but "will never label themselves publicly as homosexual because of the consequences. They therefore hide both their identity and activities."[19] Within their relationships, "traditional male/female casting plays an important part. Partners characterize themselves as 'the man' or 'the woman'; this choice of social role is reflected also in sexual intercourse, with an active and a passive partner" (169).

In 1990, Neils Teunis observed similar role dichotomization in a Dakar bar. The men he met referred to themselves as *homosexuèles* in French and *gordjiguène* in Wolof (cf. *gor-digen*), which Teunis translates as "manwoman" (1996: 161). However, the term was applied to both sexual insertors (*yauss*) and insertees (*oubi*, literally "open"). According to one informant, "When two men have sex, the one who acts as inserter is the one who pays money or gives gifts to the other." Sometimes, however, one *oubi* may "play" sexually with another *oubi*—perhaps because *oubi* "were able to support themselves and were often wealthier . . . [and therefore] not economically dependent on the *yauss*" (161). Such "play" was distinguished from "sex" (that is, anal penetration), although Teunis did not learn how roles or sexual acts between *oubi* are negotiated.

Teunis claims that physical appearance is the sole basis for assigning a male to the role of *yauss* or *oubi*. His evidence for this is tenuous, however. He describes a big, strong *yauss*, whom he calls Babacar, who told him of "his desire for lightskinned (not white) men with big chests and huge muscles, like Rambo" (1996: 164). (Although Teunis assumed that Babacar desired such a man to take the insertive role in sex with him, he could just as easily have desired to be the penetrator.) Babacar's sexual partners were boys around the age of 17 who were not part of the bar subculture and who were paid by him to be sexually receptive. Thus, his visible gender and sexual behavior were consistent.

Teunis' other reason for concluding that role assignment by others is immediate and permanent is that he himself was typed as an *oubi* by the hustler/pimp who led him to the bar and by its denizens. (It would have been interesting if he had tested this judgment by claiming that he was a *yauss* or that he was a European gay man and therefore neither or both, which he could have done while still maintaining his chastity.) Given that some of Babacar's boys offered to be anally penetrated by him, he was apparently seen by some Senegalese insertees as a possible insertor (1996: 164).[20]

Notes

1. There is nothing in Louis Tauxier's report indicating sexual unavailability the rest of the week. He did stress that only the chiefs were forbidden women on Fridays.

2. Permission from Bert Hoff to quote passages from his interview (©1993) of Malidoma Somé is gratefully acknowledged.

3. Somé does not suggest that sexual relations with such gatekeepers conveyed spiritual benefits. He also describes the Dagara disinclination to ask questions as a means of attaining knowledge and the tendency to respond to questions with indirect answers: "Grandfather never tackled a question directly. He had the habit of introducing an answer by way of a whole bunch of stories that often placed the question being asked into a wider context. Your answer would arrive when you were least expecting it, nestled into the middle of a litany of fascinating narrations" (1994: 17, 29; see also 264, 287, for examples of anti-questioning).

4. Earlier, Calamé-Griaule (1986: 409) mentioned that some adolescent Dogon males engaged in homosexual relations, though these were socially condemned.

5. Joseph Greenberg (1941) echoed by Ioan Lewis ([1966: 324] 1986: 38). It is notable that Besmer writes about an urban cult, especially in light of mistaken claims that *voudou(n)* in the New World is confined to the countryside. Also see

Mary Smith (1954). According to I. Lewis ([1966: 317] 1986: 35), the *bori* cult has spread to Tunisia, Syria, Egypt, and even Mecca.

6. In other words, although doing women's work, they use more prestigious raw materials and/or serve more elite customers, which suggests that they retain some male status and distinguish their role from true gender crossing. Access to superior materials and customers may be the basis of the common claim (as among native North American groups) that men who do women's work do it better than women (although male observers are often willing to believe that anything men do, even men of dubious masculinity, will be better than what women do).

7. Rudolf Gaudio has cautioned against inferring theological or institutional approval of homosexuality from a concentration of gender- or sex-variant priests in cults any more than is the case with Roman Catholicism (personal communication to S. O. Murray, February 23, 1995)—although in Latin America (and probably in Mediterranean Europe as well) not particularly masculine boys and/or those not showing signs of being sexually interested in females traditionally have been channeled into the priesthood. Thus, there *is* a social view of the priesthood as a niche. Moreover, for many men in Latin cultures, the manhood of priests is suspect. Respect for them is frequently low; jokes about their "dresses" and lack of *cojones* (testicles properly bursting with semen) are commonplace.

8. Kleis and Abdullahi (1983: 53, n. 10), based on Abdullahi (1984: 71).

9. According to Moses Meyer, " '*Yan daudu* are not the same as homosexuals. There is a distinct homosexual identity in Nigeria that is different from the '*yan daudu*. They overlap socially because both communities practice same-sex sex" (personal communication to Harry Hay, 1993).

10. Kleis and Abdullahi add a functionalist explanation premised on the necessity for consistency in culture: "If they were fully recognized as social females, anatomy would be irrelevant, but the premise 'anatomy is destiny' is too critical to the maintenance of the social order to be so easily compromised" (1983: 49).

11. Eugene Patron (1995: 24) reported the establishment of a Metropolitan Community Church (MCC) in the Nigerian state of Imo in the late 1970s ("hiding nothing of MCC's mission to welcome all peoples—including homosexuals") and the subsequent founding of more than 20 MCC churches in Nigeria. Whether there are identified "homosexuals" for these Nigerian churches to accept is not clear.

12. In addition to Matory's patient explanation of what underlay "no one seems to wonder," the Yoruba linguistic anthropologist Niyi Akinnaso described growing up in Yorubaland not knowing that males could have sex with males and knowing of no indigenous homosexual roles (personal communications to S. O. Murray, 1990, 1992). Both mention rumored occurrences in cities, especially the capital.

13. In regard to claims made by some Edos that "there's no such thing as homosexuality or 'yan daudu in our place [in southern Nigeria, adjacent to Yorubaland] because such a man would by physically attacked," Gaudio wondered "how 'unimaginable' can a phenomenon be if people can vividly report or imagine the

cruel fate of men accused of such a thing?" (Personal communication to S. O. Murray, March 13, 1997).

14. Forbes (1851, 1:77–79; 2:59–60, 106–21, 123–24, 168, 226–27) describes parades of bellicose Amazon troops, the parallel ranks in male and female troops, and the competition for greater glory between them.

15. D. Greenberg adds that according to Meyerowitz, "There was no change of gender, that age differences were minimal and did not play a role in these interactions, nor did differences of status or rank. Nothing she [Meyerowitz] said indicated that she herself had participated in these group sex sessions, so I am assuming her remarks were based on what women told her about them" (personal communication to S. O. Murray, November 1, 1994).

16. Interview reported by D. Greenberg (1988: 87).

17. We have relied on the summary of Nzema male-male marriage in Robert Brain (1976: 62–64). He also reports on nonsexual friendships between males and females "to have the pleasure of their companionship." These friends become "like brother and sister" and may sleep together (53–54; quoting from Signorini 1971).

18. The authors are exceptionally vague about both the place and time of their observations.

19. These are social pressures, rather than fear of legal penalties: "We never met homosexuals who mentioned legal oppression as a constraint to their sexual life," and "despite clearly defined religious guidelines for human conduct, we seriously doubt whether religion has a great influence on the sexual lives of West Africans" (Potman and Ruijgrok 1993: 168).

20. Stephen Murray (1996b) has argued that intercultural sexual relations provide an uncertain basis for reaching conclusions about what "natives" generally do with each other. We are not criticizing Teunis for failing to take up invitations for either "sex" or "play" but for his failure to inquire about departures from the neat cultural scenario described by his informants. Reports of masculine customers eager to be penetrated by effeminate male prostitutes in North and South America cannot be extrapolated mechanically (see, for example, Braiterman 1992; Kulick 1998) but should prompt at least some curiosity about whether normative sexual role dichotomization by perceived gender presentation in Senegal is sufficient to predict actual sexual practices.

A 1958 Visit to a Dakar Boy Brothel

MICHAEL DAVIDSON

In 1949, Dakar was still the administrative capital not only of Senegal but also of a number of vast tribal territories [French West Africa], which today are sovereign nations.[1] The French still ruled, and Dakar was already the "gay" city of West Africa. When I returned nine years later, the French rulers had gone, and Dakar was gayer than ever. . . . For some reason, buried in history and ethnography, the Senegalese—the people who inhabit the vast plains on either side of the Senegal River, raising livestock and harvesting the easy-growing peanut—have a reputation in all those regions for homosexuality, and in Dakar, one can quickly see that they merit this reputation. . . .

The Dakar of 1958 was the Paris of Africa. . . . That one didn't have to be shy in Dakar, and even less furtive, if one was queer, became pretty plain to me almost my first evening there. . . . I'd been introduced to an official of some sort in one of the Ministries: a middle-aged Senegalese of great charm and culture—and himself a lover of boys. Would I care to see a very special side of Dakar night-life, off the regular beat of most foreign visitors to the city? And so, one night after dinner—it must have been toward 10 o'clock—we set off in his car for some outlying suburbs. We soon left the "modern" town beyond and drove through miles of dimly lighted districts of the *ville indigène*—long acres of "native quarters": low-walled cantonments containing, according to tribal customs, either thatched beehive huts or parallelograms of one-room dwellings built of sunbaked brick. Then we came into a world of *bidonvilles*—a twilit, dismal, shanty-town constructed of corrugated iron and empty oil drums and any sort of do-it-yourself material that the owner-builder could lay his hands on. From the endless rows of dark and unwelcoming hutments there came a low muttering of human life—the life of the crowded families that lived in them, and, here and there, the throbbing of some deep-voiced drum, beating for a wedding or other family festival. But there was nothing festive in the aspect of these sad districts: behind the general air of squalor and dejection, I got the impression of latent hostility and watchfulness: a notion that all these sullen shells, which were the scene of human love and passion and family devotion, were on the defensive, on the lookout, in a state of mental siege. That sort of peripheral slum always attracts police interference, to say nothing of those little government busybodies obsessed with things like rates and taxes. . . .

Somewhere near the core, it seemed, of this labyrinth of sad—and even a little sinister—dreariness, my friend stopped his car and said: "Here we are. There are a couple of places we can look at here. I think you'll see something to amuse you."

He parked the car and locked it, and I got out and stood in the sultry, near-tropical night and suddenly found that I was listening to the muffled rhythms of some kind of dance music. There were drums of course, there are always drums in Africa, and I love drums, but I also heard the nasal noise of something like a saxophone. . . . Full of misgivings, what with the rather weird surroundings, now almost pitch dark, and the saxophone, I followed my guide along a number of narrow and unlit alleyways, branching off abruptly at right angles one way or the other, till suddenly he stopped at a wooden door at the end of a blind alley—and now, all at once, I became aware of a large arc of illumination being thrown into the night from whatever might be beyond the door.

The door was opened. My friend talked to somebody or other—whether it was a club with an entrance fee I can't now remember—and then we were let in and walked across what was an open-air dance-floor of polished and hard-trodden earth, veneered and admirably dressed with cattle dung, and found a table handily adjacent to the door whence the drinks came and as far as possible from the saxophone. We sat down, ordered some beer, and looked around. Couples were dancing vaguely European dances—after all, Europeans had been dancing in Dakar, among their other European activities, for two or three hundred years; people were sitting in tables round the dance-floor in twos and threes—and a few in solitary expectance. The whole small circular arena was brightly lit. Our beer was brought. By now I was really looking around.

The place was full of adolescent Africans in drag.

In drag. I mean that most of them were indeed in girls' clothes: some in European, some wearing the elaborate headdress of the West African mode. It was in fact a drag party, and apart from ourselves and perhaps two or three African onlookers of adult age, nobody there, I judged, was more than 18 years old and most were around 15.

They danced together. They camped around like a pride of prima donnas. They came to our table and drank lots of beer with us, simpering, blinking their white-powdered eyelids, widening their great carmined lips. . . . They have pleasant manners, these transvestite Senegalese boys. They were friendly and undemanding and bubbling with jokes of a tartish kind. They seemed, on the surface, to be as cheerful as boys of that age ought to be. But one couldn't, through all that paint and camp hilarity, see beneath the surface—

We went to a couple of such places, and about midnight drove back to Dakar through the same dark, sinister, shanty-towns. I went home with what's called a nasty taste in my mouth—not, of course, from any moral biliousness, but because temperamentally I dislike a display of effeminacy in boys and am repelled by an extreme exhibition of it. . . .

The most interesting lesson of the evening was that these boy-brothels, for that's what they were (I forgot to ask whether accommodations could be got on the premises) hadn't been set up for a special branch of the tourist trade. Their remote and dingy situation alone was evidence of that. They were the spontaneous acknowledgment of a native demand, an African taste. For some reason, which I don't pretend to know, homosexuality, including the love of adolescent boys, seems to be immeasurably more widely and more conventionally inveterate among the Senegalese than among any other African people that I have knowledge of.

Note

1. © 1970 and 1988 by the estate of Michael Davidson; excerpted with the estate's permission from the 1988 corrected edition of *Some Boys* (London: Gay Men's Press), 167–68. A degree of American punctuation has been imposed. In the chapter that this excerpt is drawn from, Davidson speculates at length about differences in the visibility of male-male sexual relations in Timbuctoo and Dakar.

Male Lesbians and
Other Queer Notions in Hausa

RUDOLF P. GAUDIO

As a student of Hausa, the most widely spoken language in West Africa, and a graduate student researcher in northern Nigeria in the late 1980s and early 1990s, my initial encounters with Hausa Muslim culture—those mediated by teachers and texts in the United States and those I had in the field—were dominated by stark, foreboding images of veiled women, conservative imams, and a rigid segregation of the sexes in daily life. Hausaland was not a place in which I expected to encounter gay people, much less a community even remotely resembling the gay communities I am affiliated with in the West. Not long after I began my doctoral fieldwork, however, I became aware of a considerable degree of ambiguity and contradiction in Hausa Muslim discourses about gender and sexuality, and I was especially surprised to find out that Hausa society has a reputation in Nigeria for homosexual activity. Many southern Nigerians, for example, who scoff at the suggestion that there might be men or women in their region who engage in homosexual behavior,[1] claim it's only "those Muslims" up north (as well as decadent Westerners and Arabs) who do that sort of thing. For their part, Hausa people are less inclined to deny the existence of homosexuality in their society than they are to gossip about it, usually in disparaging terms. Living in Kano, the largest city in Hausaland, I heard rumors about the homosexual proclivities of prominent local men, read sensationalistic newspaper stories about homosexual scandals in boarding schools, and heard reports of police raids on bars and nightclubs frequented by homosexuals.

Yet, I knew of no acknowledged homosexual individuals, communities, or institutions. I had, however, seen tantalizing references in the ethnographic and sociological literature on Hausa society to 'yan daudu, a term that was usually translated as "homosexuals" or "transvestites."[2]

In the earliest stages of my research, when all I knew about 'yan daudu was what other people had written or said about them, it was hopeful intuition that made me think that I, as a gay man, might be able to become involved in their largely hidden social world in a way that I suspected previous academics and my (presumably) heterosexual Nigerian acquaintances had not. I was intrigued, therefore, the first few times that I saw 'yan daudu dancing and sashaying at nightclubs and outdoor festivities, chattering and laughing in grand, seductive ways, and I could not help but compare these images to my recollections of gay life at home. Although subsequent events forced me to reconsider—but not to reject outright—the naïve idea that 'yan daudu were men with whom I could communicate on the basis of a shared sexuality, my interactions with them introduced me to a thriving social world of Hausa men who acknowledged and acted on their sexual attraction to other men. In Hausa communities throughout Nigeria, the elaborate social-occupational network of 'yan daudu, who self-identify as men who act "like women" (kamar mata), constitutes a matrix for what can arguably be called a homosexual community in Hausa society, though this differs in important ways from gay communities in the West. One apparent similarity, however, is that, as drag queens and "fairies" did for straight-acting gays in mid-20th-century New York (see Chauncey 1994), 'yan daudu's visibility and social proximity to female karuwai (courtesans, prostitutes) attract otherwise unidentifiable "men who seek men" (maza masu neman maza) and permit them to meet and socialize without blowing their cover.

These two groups, that is, "feminine-" "and "masculine"-identified men who have sex with men, comprise what I construe as a gay Hausa subculture. This chapter focuses on one of the key cultural practices that characterize this subculture, namely, the terms and labels that 'yan daudu and their masculine associates use to characterize their male-male sexual relationships.[3] Drawing on my own ethnographically informed understanding of the meanings of these terms and the ways they are used in everyday conversations, I consider the extent to which these men's sexual and linguistic practices can be said to constitute a challenge to dominant cultural discourses about gender and sexuality. My analysis of this sexual lexicon—some elements of which derive from heterosexual Hausa discourses, while others are unique to the gay Hausa subculture—reveals a dialectical pattern of adherence to and subversion of Hausa Muslim cultural norms, which makes it difficult to judge particular forms or practices definitively as subversive, resistant, or conformist. To make this discussion understandable to an English-speaking North American audience, my analysis points to apparent convergences and divergences between the discourses of gay speakers of Hausa and those of American English. Without claiming a definitive perspective on gay Hausa culture, I pay critical attention to the claims various academics have made regarding homosexuality and transgenderism in Hausaland and describe how the cultural practices of gay and "womanlike" Hausa men are more diverse and more complicated than scholars have acknowledged.

Despite the lack of significant communicative contacts between Hausa and North American gay communities, certain similarities in the discourses of both groups are sufficient to justify my use here of "gay" and related terms to refer to Hausa men who have sex with men. If "gay" is seen to refer only to the overt, politicized gay communities that have emerged in the West in the past 100 years, it surely does not apply to the Hausa men I met in Nigeria, most of whom have little if any knowledge of Western gay life. If, however, "gay" is understood to refer to men who are conscious of themselves as men who have sex with men and who consider themselves to be socially (if not temperamentally) distinct from men who do not have this kind of sex, then these Hausa men are undoubtedly "gay," and it is in this sense that I use it. This is not to say that Hausa gay men understand their sexuality as do North American gay men.[4] For example, Hausa people generally refer to homosexuality as an act rather than a psychological drive or predisposition, and homosexual men are more often described as men who *do* homosexuality than as men who *want* other men sexually. The most common in-group term for men who have sex with men is *masu harka*, "those who do the business," often abbreviated to *masu yi*, "those who do [it]."[5] Moreover, homosexuality is not seen to be incompatible with heterosexuality, marriage, or parenthood, which constitute strong normative values in Hausa Muslim society. At some point in their lives, most of the men I am calling "gay"—including those who identify as "womanlike"—marry women and have children, even as they maintain their more covert identity as men who have sex with men.

I have chosen not to use the term *bisexual* to refer to married gay Hausa men because I understand bisexuality to refer to an individual's acknowledged capacity to be sexually attracted to both women and men and to the assertion of one's prerogative to act on such attraction; this implies a degree of choice regarding sexual matters that is not recognized in Hausa society. Specifically, most Hausa people do not see marriage as a choice but rather as a moral and social obligation. My own refusal to marry based on my lack of sexual desire for women typically did not follow the cultural logic of my gay Hausa acquaintances, who did not see a necessary connection between marriage and heterosexual desire. Common usage of both the mainstream and in-group Hausa terms referring to male homosexuality (see note 5) usually presumes that gay men have sex with women at least to father children and not necessarily for sexual pleasure. Although many men do acknowledge enjoying sex with both women and men, these men do not constitute a distinct subgrouping in gay Hausa communities, since men who do not desire women sexually are unlikely to admit this except to their closest friends.[6] "Bisexuality" can thus be seen as normative for all Hausa men who have sex with men, whether or not they actually desire or enjoy sex with women.

Though virtually all Hausa people are aware of the presence of 'yan daudu in cities, towns, and villages throughout Hausaland, few students of Hausa society have addressed the subject, and fewer still have offered more than popular stereotypes regarding 'yan daudu's sexuality. Various scholars allude briefly to 'yan daudu's presence as "homosexuals," "pimps," or "transvestites" in the contexts of female prostitution (karuwanci) and spirit-possession (bori), but they present little ethnographic evidence to explain their use of these terms (for example, Besmer 1983: 18; Mary Smith [1954] 1981: 63; Pittin 1983: 296–98; Yusuf 1974: 209). Only Gerald Kleis and Salisu Abdullahi, drawing on Abdullahi's original field research, make 'yan daudu the central focus of their discussion, yet they too skirt around the issue of sexuality (Kleis and Abdullahi 1983, based on Abdullahi 1984). Abdullahi notes that the English terms commonly used to describe 'yan daudu—"homosexual," "transvestite," "pimp"—have connotations that do not apply in the Hausa context, but neither he nor any other scholar details just how these terms do and do not pertain to 'yan daudu (1984: 32).

The short shrift given to 'yan daudu's homosexuality owes a great deal to Hausa and Western scholars' discomfort in addressing the issue, but it also reflects the fact that although 'yan daudu do commonly (though discreetly) engage in sexual relations with other men, the practice of daudu is culturally understood in terms of gender rather than sexuality.[7] Through their everyday use of stereotypically feminine speech and gestures and their performance of women's work, such as cooking and selling food, 'yan daudu present themselves as "womanlike" without sacrificing an essentially male sex identity. Because they usually do not adopt women's clothing or hairstyles and are most frequently addressed as men by others, they are not, properly speaking, "transvestites." Most 'yan daudu earn money by cooking and selling food and/or through their association with karuwai.[8] At nightclubs and celebrations where traditional-style Hausa music is played, 'yan daudu and karuwai often dance in front of large crowds of male patrons and onlookers; such dancing is also a stereotypically feminine activity. 'Yan daudu are usually available in such venues to assist men who want to meet karuwai, and they expect from these men some sort of payment or "help" (taimako) in return. This explains 'yan daudu's widespread reputation as prostitutes' agents or "pimps" (kawalai). The crowds attending these nightclubs and outdoor festivities typically also include gay men who come to socialize with each other and to look for potential sex partners, especially, but not exclusively, among the 'yan daudu. The presence of female karuwai and their male patrons allows these men—whom 'yan daudu call fararen-hula (civilians), 'yan aras,[9] or simply maza (men, husbands)—to rendezvous without revealing their sexuality to outsiders. For its part, heterosexual Hausa society usually turns a blind eye to apparent or suspected connections between 'yan daudu's cross-gender behavior and their homosexuality. (One gay in-group term for a straight man is in fact makaho, blind man.) Nevertheless, gay Hausa men generally fear being exposed as homosexual; even 'yan daudu, who are unabashedly open in their adoption of womanlike behaviors, remain highly discreet when it comes to their sexual involvements with other men.

Despite the paucity of ethnographic evidence offered in most academic works referring to 'yan daudu, their alleged status as "transvestites" and "homosexuals" has attracted the attention of Western scholars writing on comparative constructions of homosexuality. In particular, academic references to 'yan daudu have been cited by scholars in discussions of male homosexual relationships in various cultures in which sexual partners assume distinctly masculine and feminine roles, for example, "husband" and "wife." Sociologist David Greenberg calls this phenomenon "transgenderal homosexuality" and cites the feminine behavior of "Hausa male prostitutes" as one example (1988: 60–61). Stephen Murray's discussion of the spiritual implications of "gender-defined" homosexuality in Latin America (particularly Haiti) refers to Hausa "homosexual transvestites" in the bori spirit-possession cult to support his assertion of possible cultural continuities between West Africa and diasporic African communities in the Americas (1987: 94). The characterization of homosexuality in Hausa society as "transgenderal" and "gender defined" accurately reflects the fact that the most commonly acknowledged sexual relationships among Hausa men have much in common with the customs of the dominant heterosexual society. Extreme gender segregation stands out as a major organizing principle—both socially and spatially—of most Hausa-speaking cities and towns. Married Hausa women of all but the poorest and wealthiest classes are usually veiled and secluded according to orthodox interpretations of Islamic law, and they are supposed to be dependent on their husbands for their sexual and material needs. Adult women who defy these expectations—by remaining unmarried, for example, or by going out of the house without a veil—run the risk of being labeled a *karuwa*.

This strict delineation of the male and female realms is partially reproduced among *masu harka*. *'Yan daudu*, who often refer to each other using feminine linguistic forms (such as women's names and feminine pronouns and adjectives), typically cast themselves in the role of "wife" (*mata*) or *karuwa* in discussing their relationships with their male sexual partners, whom they call *miji*, "husband," or *saurayi*, "young man/boyfriend." By employing heterosexual concepts to characterize their own sexual roles, *'yan daudu* and their masculine-identified partners reproduce some dominant ideologies of gender and power relations while challenging others. For, whereas the idea of a man who has a "husband" and calls himself a "wife" disrupts mainstream Hausa beliefs about gender and sexual identity as biologically based, the sexual, economic, and other expectations that *'yan daudu* and their boyfriends/husbands bring to their relationships follow mainstream norms governing how women and men should behave in heterosexual relationships. For example, the "civilian" or masculine-identified partner is expected to assume the insertive role during sexual intercourse and to give his *'dan daudu* "wife" presents, such as money, clothing, or travel, on a regular basis.

The ways in which *'yan daudu* exploit the gendered grammatical and semantic structure of the Hausa language to assume subject positions as "wives" and "girlfriends" reveal their awareness of what postmodernists call the role of discourse in the construction of gender identity. This awareness, however, typically coexists with a commitment to local religious and cultural ideologies that view gender as naturally and divinely determined; in fact, many if not most *'yan daudu* marry women and have children, fulfilling Hausa Muslim ideals regarding respectable adult male behavior. A number of scholars make the erroneous assumption that married *'yan daudu* are distinct from "homosexual" *'yan daudu* (e.g., Abdullahi 1984: 34; Pittin 1983: 298). The sexual experiences of many *'yan daudu* and other gay Hausa men, however, indicate that heterosexual marriage and homosexual behavior are in no way mutually exclusive in Hausaland. Like other Hausa men (gay and straight), married *'yan daudu* take seriously their responsibilities as husbands and fathers and expect their wives, children, and other dependent kinfolk to show them due respect.

In contrast, *'yan daudu* typically downplay their "feminine" practices, including dancing, joking, and having sex with men, by describing them in terms connoting frivolity or irresponsibility, such as *wasa* (play) or *iskanci* (craziness, vice), and therefore not real or serious. *'Yan daudu's* use of the term *play* in some ways parallels Western scholars' depictions of drag and other gender-bending practices as forms of cultural parody. For example, Judith Butler's (1990) celebration of the emancipatory implications of drag finds qualified support in *'yan daudu's* use of "womanlike" ways of speaking, which reveals an awareness of the instability and mutability of language and gender identity. For some segments of Hausa society, this awareness seems dangerous and subversive. In particular, conservative religious and political leaders periodically condemn *'yan daudu* as purveyors of sexual immorality and actively or tacitly encourage the abusive treatment, including arrest, extortion, and physical violence, that *'yan daudu* often face at the hands of police and young hooligans. Female *karuwai*, whose sexual and economic independence also threatens patriarchal norms, are likewise subject to such denunciations and abuse, whereas the masculine-identified male patrons of both *'yan daudu* and *karuwai* are only rarely accused, much less prosecuted. Yet, that *'yan daudu* outwardly discount the seriousness of their "feminine" activities and continue to enjoy a number of patriarchal privileges as husbands, fathers, and patrons complicates any attempt to cast them as agents of a postmodernist strategy for undermining gender binarism.

Although gender differences do appear to be a highly salient factor characterizing homosexuality in Hausa society, *'yan daudu* and other gay Hausa men also engage in sexual relationships in which other social factors, such as age and wealth, play an important role. These relationships conform in some ways to two ideal types of homosexuality that D. Greenberg offers as alternatives to the "transgenderal" model, namely "transgenerational" and "egalitarian" homosexuality.[10] "Transgenerational" relationships are said to entail an unequal distribution of power between sexual partners by virtue of age and, usually, wealth (1988: 26), while "egalitarian" relationships occur between partners who see themselves as social and economic equals (66). Homosexual relationships in Hausaland, like heterosexual ones, are frequently of the "transgenerational" type, although the age differential between partners need not span an entire generation. Typically, an older masculine-identified man will seek the sexual companionship of a younger man or boy and will make material gifts to the younger man in return.

In this case, the older, wealthier man is called *k'wazo* (which in standard usage means "diligence, hard work"), while the younger man, who may be a masculine-identified "civilian" or a feminine-identified *'dan daudu*, is known as the older man's *haja* (goods, merchandise). The sexual expectations attached to such a relationship—the *k'wazo* normatively takes the insertive role in anal intercourse, while the *haja* is receptive—parallel the gendered grammatical distinction between the two terms: *k'wazo* is a masculine noun; *haja* is feminine. Thus, even when both partners have conventionally masculine gender identities, the grammatical gender of the nouns used to refer to them reinforces dominant, heterosexual understandings of the gendered nature of power in sexual (and other) contexts.

Just as heterosexual norms are not always adhered to by heterosexuals, in the gay community norms related to status, wealth, and gender are sometimes subverted. Indeed, it is in the context of relationships that conforms less strictly to heterosexual models that gay Hausa men seem more likely to defy the economic and political expectations traditionally attached to sex. In some cases, conventional power relations are partially inverted such that the "female" partner exercises some degree of dominance over the "male" by virtue of "her" age or wealth. Thus, an older *'dan daudu* might offer cash and other material gifts to a younger "civilian" in exchange for the latter's sexual companionship; gay and straight Hausa men also report that similar relationships occur between older female *karuwai* and younger men. Such relationships confound normative expectations about sex and power to such an extent that no conventional discourse seems adequate to describe it. The masculine *saurayi* (boyfriend) or *miji* (husband) is also a *haja*, the feminine property of a *mata* (wife) who has assumed the powerful masculine role of *k'wazo*. The successful pursuit of a younger man by a *'dan daudu* demonstrates that contrary to the dominant belief that only "masculine" males have the prerogative to act on their sexual urges, feminine-identified individuals are also capable of accumulating the kind of socioeconomic capital that allows them to assert their own sexual desire. Of course, this logic in many ways preserves the conventional patriarchal view of sexuality as an exercise of power. Moreover, to the extent that this sort of coupling reproduces the traditional sexual roles of an insertive masculine partner and a receptive feminine one, the socioeconomically powerful *'dan daudu* will still be seen in many circles to have degraded himself by affirming his "feminine" desire to be sexually passive.[11]

A potentially greater challenge to patriarchal power arrangements is posed by gay Hausa relationships between partners who see each other as equals—D. Greenberg's "egalitarian" type. As feminine-identified men, *'yan daudu* often call each other *k'awaye* (girlfriends), referring to a special, supposedly nonsexual friendship traditionally developed between Hausa women or girls. Although sex between "girlfriends" is largely frowned on, it nevertheless does occur; when *'yan daudu* have sex with each other, they call it *kifi* (lesbianism).[12] Although some male "lesbians" (*'yan kifi*) establish relationships with one another that conform to the *k'wazo/haja* model, *'yan daudu* and other gay Hausa men usually use "lesbianism" to refer to sex between men who are social equals. I have even heard it used half-jokingly to apply to sex between two masculine-identified "civilians" of similar age and socioeconomic status. The notion of "lesbian" sex in a male context typically connotes that neither party insists on a particular sexual role; for example, partners are said to *yi canji*, "do an exchange"—that is, alternate between insertive and receptive roles. Sexual reciprocity is but one manifestation of a more general understanding of "lesbianism" among gay Hausa men as a relationship in which neither partner seeks to exercise a kind of unilateral power over the other by virtue of gender, age, or wealth.

The linguistic difficulties posed by the variety of ways in which gay Hausa men enact and challenge both dominant and subcultural norms of gender and sexuality echo the problems faced by feminist theorists who, in recent years, have debated the status of the body as the basis for gender identity. As scholars have documented the myriad ways in which femininity and masculinity are constructed and practiced in societies around the world, it has become increasingly unclear to what extent such basic analytical concepts as "woman" and "man" adequately represent the diversity of people's experiences of gender in different cultures. In North America, the stability of these categories has been challenged by queer and transgender activists, who refuse to see gender identity as fixed or natural; this cultural resistance is manifested in such cultural practices as cross-dressing, butch/femme role-playing, and transsexualism, which writers such as Butler have described as harbingers of the end of the binary sex/gender system. Others, however, treat such claims of cultural resistance and subversion with skepticism: the assumption by some men of a "feminine" status might equally reflect the greater power men have to employ dominant discourses of sex/gender in pursuit of their own interests, without implying any progressive change in the ability of women to do the same.

Butler makes particular rhetorical use of drag and other forms of gender parody practiced in the Western world to support her claim about the possibility of radical reconfigurations of gender and sexuality. Focusing on the way gender and sexuality distinctions are produced in discourse, she identifies and advocates these parodic practices as forms of discursive resistance to dominant cultural norms that could lead to an unfettered proliferation of cultural configurations of sex and gender: "When the constructed status of gender is theorized as radically independent of sex, gender itself becomes a free-floating artifice, with the consequence that *man* and *masculine* might just as easily signify a female body as a male one, and *woman* and *feminine* a male body as easily as a female one" (Butler 1990: 6). For Butler, drag and other types of gender-bending practices exploit and expose the constructedness of "natural" gender categories, opening the way for the ultimate rejection of such categories altogether (136ff.). The prevalence of such practices in gay and lesbian communities reflects the particular gender and sexual repression gay men and lesbians experience under the binary gender/sex regime.

Jacquelyn Zita (1992) accepts the argument that gender identity is discursively produced, but she questions whether gender is so easily trans-mutable. Focusing on "male lesbians"—biological males who claim to be lesbians—Zita challenges the claim that individuals have the capacity to use discourse to effect the kind of radical reconceptualization of the body and of gender identity that Butler describes. Grouping together lesbian-identified male-to-female transsexuals along with men who claim to be lesbians on behavioral or political grounds but make no effort to conceal or change their male anatomies (a practice she refers to as "genderfuck"), Zita rejects the idea that any biological male can ever become a "real" woman or lesbian. She locates "real" gender identity not simply in the material body but in what she calls the "historical gravity of the sexed body"—the history of cultural discourses that constructs the body as intrinsically sexed—which informs her pessimism regarding human beings' capacity ever to transcend these discourses. In particular, she asserts that no man can ever deny the patriarchal privileges with which all males are born and raised, regardless of his social position relative to other men or his effort to reject or disown those privileges: "What agency we have in this culture to move beyond these assigned categories, to become 'unstuck' from our constructed bodies, to travel transgendering and transsexing journeys of relocation, or to deconstruct sex binarism altogether are questions left uncomfortably unanswered in my thoughts. Perhaps all is 'drag' made up of cells, soma and style marked redundantly in memory and public readings" (125–26).

Whereas Butler focuses on the subversive and potentially liberating implications of drag, envisioning a discursive regime in which "woman" and "feminine" might signify a male body "as easily as" a female one, Zita remains doubtful. She insists that, for all its contingency, the sexedness of the body is hardly as "lightweight and detachable" as some postmodernists suggest.

Although Butler and Zita have very different perspectives on the subject of gender mutability, they have much in common when it comes to the cultural evidence that they focus on to bolster their arguments and that which they choose to ignore. For example, despite their professed interest in cultural practices that challenge gender norms, both Butler and Zita pay remarkably little attention to transsexualism, focusing instead on performative practices such as drag and "genderfuck," which do not generally entail physiological or anatomical transformations of the body. The reasons for this oversight undoubtedly stem from the theoretical complications that surgically mediated transsexualism raises for both historical-materialist and postmodernist theories of the body and gender identity. As the phrase "gender-reassignment surgery" implies, transsexualism perpetuates the dominant ideology that prescribes congruence between gender and anatomical sex and is therefore antithetical to Butler's goal of celebrating discursive resistance to that ideology. At the same time, the permanent consequences of surgical transsexualism and the extreme social stigma attached to it challenges Zita's assertion that the only "real" gender/sex identity is that which is based on the bodies we are born with. The failure to examine the philosophical and political implications of this phenomenon suggests an unwillingness on the part of both Zita and Butler to consider evidence that contradicts their basic arguments.

Another oversight common to Butler and Zita is particularly relevant to the subject matter of this essay: their almost exclusive reliance on cultural evidence from the Euro-Western world. Both writers' interest in such subaltern Western practices as drag and genderfuck reflect a growing fascination among cultural theorists with the political implications of performance and parody, especially those types of performance that have, themselves, become increasingly activist and politicized. This interplay between theory and activism often creates a positive and powerful synergy, but it also runs the risk of tying cultural criticism to the actions of particular social groups defined in terms of geographical location, ethnicity, nationality, class, language, education, and so forth. Gender theory, and the ultimate goal of widening the scope of human beings' options for self-expression and survival, thus stands to benefit from the consideration of practices that do not derive from the same political or philosophical framework as the theories themselves; this applies equally to the practices of middle-class transsexuals in Western societies and to other gender and sexual minorities around the world.

The discursive practices of Hausa "male lesbians" offer a particularly instructive perspective on Western scholars' theoretical debates. The acknowledged existence of "egalitarian" relationships between some gay Hausa men suggests the possibility of an alternative Hausa cultural system in which sex is not always associated with dominance. However, the fact that such relationships are construed in Hausa gay men's discourses as "lesbian," and therefore "feminine," reveals the normative strength of the idea that a valid sexual encounter involving a "real" man must entail a distinct power asymmetry. Many *masu harka*—including *'yan daudu*—deride or condemn "lesbian" sexual relations between *'yan daudu* as absurd or immoral. Yet, no such complaints are made against masculine-identified "civilians" who have sex with each other, since sex between such men is typically assumed to take the form of the hierarchical *k'wazo/haja* relationship. The fact that "lesbianism" is thus subject to particular disdain among *masu harka* reveals that sexist and heterosexist attitudes permeate the gay Hausa subculture as much as they do Hausa society in general. Hausa gay and straight men alike tend to view women as subordinate to men; "womanlike" men are in turn subordinate to "real" men. Although "lesbianism" represents a challenge to male dominance, in the gay context, the idea of a male "lesbian" in many ways reinforces traditional Hausa values that associate sexuality with relations of dominance and inequality. As long as gay Hausa men accept this patri-archal equation of sex and power, sex between equals is cast as something "feminine" and is therefore seen as mere play, less real and less consequential than sex between people of different social statuses.[13]

That many *'yan daudu* subvert conventional norms of gender and sexuality in a way that both titillates and disturbs other men demonstrates that the constructed nature of identity and power affords individuals some room to play (à la Butler) with and in discourse to enhance their own power and pleasure.[14] However, several factors cast doubt on the emanci-patory possibilities one might want to attribute to such play. For example, the fact that *'yan daudu's* gender "play" draws from and refers to idealized norms of femininity and masculinity and that it does not invalidate *'yan daudu's* male social identities, which, as Muslims, they see as part of God's plan, reflects their belief in a fundamentally "real" gender/sex identity that human beings cannot and perhaps should not change.[15] Indeed, the Hausa language makes no distinction between "gender" and "sex." The term *jinsi* refers to all the observable distinctions between women and men—biological, psychological, and cultural—and *'yan daudu's jinsi* is universally understood to be male (*namiji*). Though their performance of "womanlike" practices undeniably puts them in a subordinate and often vulnerable social position vis-à-vis other men, *'yan daudu's* continued insistence on claiming the social privileges accorded in principle to all men in Hausa society, including the right to preside over patriarchal family units, demonstrates that discursive challenges to established orders are always subject to the difficulty, if not impossibility, of subjects' transcending the boundaries of the discourses in which they live.

Notes

1. Cf. the southern Nigerian anthropologist Ifi Amadiume's indignant, dismissive, and homophobic rejection of the suggestion that lesbianism might characterize any Igbo woman-woman marriages (1987: 7).

2. All Hausa terms discussed in this paper are written according to standard Hausa orthography, which, unlike academic-pedagogical usage, does not indicate phonemic vowel length or tone. Because of technical limitations, the "hooked" Hausa letters representing glottalized 'd and k' and implosive 'b are rendered as shown, using apostrophes instead of the standard "hooks." The standard orthographic symbol 'y (as in 'yan daudu) represents a glottalized consonant distinct from the unglottalized semivowel y. Other letters in the Hausa alphabet are pronounced more or less like their English counterparts, with the exception of the letter c, which is always pronounced like English ch.

3. The fieldwork on which this essay is based was carried out over a period of 18 months in northern Nigeria in 1992–94, with the support of a Fulbright Junior Research grant administered by the Institute for International Exchange. Earlier versions of this essay were published, under the same title, in *SALSA III: Proceedings of the Third Annual Symposium about Language and Society–Austin* (Linguistics Department, University of Texas, Austin, 1995, 19–27), and under the title, "Unreal Women and the Men Who Love Them: Gay Gender Roles in Hausa Muslim Society," in *Socialist Review* 25(2) (1995): 121–36.

4. Nor do all North American gay men think alike on this subject. The generalizations I offer here are meant to facilitate discussion about differences and similarities between gay male communities in Hausaland and North America, not to obscure the diversity of perspectives on sexual identity that exists in those communities.

5. While standard Hausa has both formal/legal and colloquial terms for male homosexuality, most gay Hausa men avoid them, either because they carry an implicit negative moral judgment (e.g., *lu'du, luwa'di*, "sodomy") or because they are too wordy (e.g., *maza masu cin maza*, "men who fuck men"; *maza masu neman maza*, "men who seek men").

6. Men who choose to pursue extramarital sexual relations with both women and men are sometimes referred to as *mai cin wake da shinkafa*, "one who eats beans and rice." This term plays on the ambiguity of the word *ci*, which can mean either

"eat" or "fuck," as well as on the grammatical gender of the collective nouns *wake* (beans), which is masculine, and *shinkafa* (rice), which is feminine.

7. *Daudu* is an abstract noun referring to the phenomenon or practice of men who act like women. *'Dan daudu* (literally "son of daudu"; pl. *'yan daudu*) refers to the men themselves.

8. Christin Pittin calls *karuwai* "independent women," a direct translation of the phrase *mata masu zaman kansu*, which the women themselves tend to prefer. She rejects the terms "prostitute" and, to a lesser extent, "courtesan" as inaccurate and culturally inappropriate. My own field research confirms Pittin's findings in that although some *karuwai* do engage in commercialized, Western-style prostitution, many have long-term affairs with men that resemble Western lover/mistress relationships. Still others are businesswomen who are deemed *karuwai* simply because they are unmarried (usually divorced) and living on their own.

9. *Aras* is an in-group term, essentially synonymous with *harka*, denoting the practice of male homosexuality.

10. The same distinctions with slightly different labels were made earlier by Barry Adam (1986) and Murray (1984: 45–53).

11. Sexual passivity is conveyed linguistically through the use of so-called impersonal constructions such as *ana yi masa* (one does [it] to him, [it] is done to him) and *ana cinsa* (one fucks him, he gets fucked), while the insertive partner is described using syntactically active constructions such as *mai yi* (one who does) and *mai ci* (one who fucks). The insulting connotation of sexual passivity can be strengthened by referring to the receptive partner as feminine, thus, *ana cinta* (she gets fucked).

12. *Kifi*, literally "turn one thing over onto another," is an in-group term used in place of the standard Hausa *ma'digo* (lesbianism). My very limited contact with "real," self-identified Hausa lesbians (sing. *'yar kifi*, lit. "daughter of *kifi*," pl. *'yan kifi*) allows me to say only that (1) they exist; (2) some Hausa lesbians are acquainted with the terms discussed in this paper and make active use of at least some of them; and (3) many gay Hausa men claim that lesbians engage in the same types of relationships as they themselves do, that is, involving the exchange of material gifts and the attribution of roles such as *k'wazo* and *haja*.

13. Hausa men's derogatory and dismissive attitudes toward lesbianism resemble, in some respects, the ways lesbianism has been used as a signifier in the Western world (see Roof 1994).

14. Note that Butler's celebration of the emancipatory and pleasurable effects of gender play is somewhat mitigated in her later discussion of the "ambivalence" articulated in the gender performances of the poor black and Latino drag queens depicted in the movie *Paris Is Burning* (1993: 121–40).

15. Surgical transsexualism is not available in Nigeria and is unknown to many *'yan daudu*, except perhaps as a phenomenon that exists in Western countries. I never heard any *'yan daudu* discuss transsexualism as an option they would like to have available to them, even when I made a point of explaining the procedure to them.

West African Homoeroticism

West African Men Who Have Sex with Men

NII AJEN

There are many claims, from Edward Gibbon in *The Decline and Fall of the Roman Empire* to Richard Burton in his terminal essay to *A Thousand and One Nights* and right down to contemporary African and even gay publications, that deny homosexuality exists in sub-Saharan Africa. Even the Spartacus international gay guide claims that there is little or no homosexual life in Ghana or in other African countries. I shall attempt here to lift the thick veil of ignorance that has hitherto obscured people's perception of sexual realities in West Africa and in African societies in general, for that matter.

To begin with, it is important to know that in the entire region of West Africa and all over Africa, the issue of sex is not one that people feel comfortable discussing openly, as some in the West do. Let us take Ghanaians, for instance. They are naturally good-humored people. Teasing and joking are an important part of their popular culture. Nevertheless, it is only when they feel very comfortable with someone else that their jokes and talk border on sex. Even then, they frequently employ euphemisms in order not to sound bawdy. This is not at all to say that West Africans are not sexual people. Many reasons account for this "code of silence" regarding sex. They include Victorian, colonial, and Christian ideas of what is "prim and proper," which have had a great impact on the sense of decency of the average Ghanaian, to the extent that they scarcely discuss certain issues they consider unseemly. It is my contention, therefore, that this is the best explanation as to why sex and sexuality are not publicly highlighted in these regions.

In my experience, when West Africans decide to talk with friends about sex (including their own sexual experiences with persons of the same sex, if they have same-sex preferences) they tend to speak quite openly about its quality (as good, fantastic, and so forth), focusing more on the act than on the partner. Those who directly speak of their partners are considered "base." The point is that decent people seldom discuss their lovers, sex partners, or even their sex acts publicly. It should be no surprise, therefore, that very few studies have been done by West Africans (or other Africans) on sexuality in general, let alone on homosexuality.

To the average Ghanaian, however, the issue of homoeroticism is likely to arise when there is talk about androgynous characters (known as *kojobesia*, which can be translated "man-woman") or about boarding schools (especially single-sex schools). Because Ghana was a British colony (then officially named the Gold Coast), with an education system much the same as that of England's, homoeroticism in boarding schools resembles what Lilian Faderman describes in *Surpassing the Love of Men* (1981): strong bonds between members of the same sex are permissible, with the understanding that the senior partner in those circumstances will protect, help, and generally make the junior's life in school fulfilling. Everyone would admit that the reason for allowing this kind of pairing of students was laudable and that it did have many positive results. It cannot be denied that frequent homoerotic activities involving both males and females also took place and are to this day encouraged under this boarding school system. In Ghana, for instance, girls describe those to whom they have this strong attachment as their *supi*, which denotes a specially loved one. Stories circulated that *supis* participated in sexual activities in secrecy but, until one party decided to release the information (because of a disagreement), not much would be known. Moreover, in West Africa, as in other parts of the continent, females are permitted to publicly display their affection for other females without fear of being branded lesbian. Boys also have this practice, and various schools have had distinct terms for homoerotic activity. I have yet to hear of any boarding school without at least one story of homosexual activity occurring on its premise.

In contrast to most Western societies, in Ghana, Nigeria, Senegal, Burkina Faso, and the Côte d'Ivoire, the general attitudes toward those who openly declare themselves "gay" or "homosexual" are coldness and possible rejection. It is interesting to note, however, that while most Ghanaians may prefer not to have anything to do with an openly declared homosexual, they tend not to see anything bad about the same-sex holding of hands in public, as many do in the West. The experience of an African American brother in Ghana and Nigeria provides an interesting example of this. After emphasizing repeatedly that they should be very discreet, a young man to whom he had just been introduced immediately holds his hands and puts his arms around him in public. The African American brother had a hard time understanding what was happening, and he had to learn later that same-sex holding of hands in public is not stigmatized in Africa as it is in Western societies. In fact, in many discos across Africa, one sees people of the same sex dancing, which is not condemned nor interpreted as having any homosexual implication at all. It is seen as just an expression of brotherly warmth. Anyone who has a problem with that invariably has been influenced by Western stigmas. Because people do not want to be labeled by their sexual preferences or practices, categorically naming a club, newspaper, church, and so forth as "gay" has negative repercussions. Sexual behavior is considered private and not characteristic of one's personality and identity; it does not influence people's behavior in general or lead to a lifestyle. People are seen as people, and their sexual expression is considered their private choice. Provided they apply discretion in their sexual behavior, whether homoerotic or otherwise, there is really no issue.

Another difference that might be very striking to Westerners is that even the man you may have just done everything with sexually will say no if you ask him if he is "gay." And if you should ask that same man if there is homosexuality in Africa, a likely response will be, "No, there is nothing like that in Africa."

Professor Griff, of the rap group Public Enemy, claimed that "there's not a word in any African language which describes homosexual. . . . There are no such words. They didn't exist." Of course, his own speech is not African either. Nevertheless, homoeroticism and gender variance (and exchanging sex for material goods) are not phenomena alien to Africa, just as silence does not mean absence. A code of silence protects what happens among men from question or condemnation, as was true in the United States before WWII and the publication of the Kinsey data. Samuel M. Steward recalled that during

> the years from 1920 to 1950 . . . everyone stayed deep in the closet, save those who had been caught in flagrante delicto and been publicly disgraced or fired or disciplined in some way.

> Still, those of us who could maintain our secret lived under an extraordinary protective umbrella: the ignorance and naiveté of the American public. . . . Under the umbrella we lived and moved and made love and enjoyed our beddings, told our jokes and in general found life happy. . . . The publication of Kinsey's *Sexual Behavior in the Human Male* in 1948, although it did much good for our cause, also stripped away the last tatters of the silk, to leave only the metal ribs above us. (1982: ix, xii)

From my interviews with Africans, homoerotic activities seem to have either started or have been most common in both sexes around adolescence. Nearly all the men admitted to having played with other males at least at that stage in their life. Quite a number of them said it was a "phase" for them, and they very much enjoyed same-sex intimacy. Those same men pointed out that once they married, they tried to forget about "all that stuff." Late marriage is encouraged in West Africa, especially in the urban areas. Women, unlike the men, might be married off soon after puberty. Yet, for reasons such as bride-price, and sometimes simply because they want to achieve their educational goals, men are often encouraged not to marry until their late 20s or early 30s. They can therefore "play" with whomever they feel attracted to for many years beyond puberty without being considered "gay" (by themselves or by others). This is yet another striking aspect of African life, especially when compared with Western culture, with its general outright suspicion that single males older than 20 who do not talk of their girlfriends or marriage must be gay. There appears to be some allowance made for a homoerotic "stage" or "phase" (to use the words of those I interviewed) as boys attain manhood in West Africa. Some see such "playing about" as very positive, since it helps young men let off some steam while not posing a threat to girls' virginity. Apparently considering it a natural boyhood stage, most parents prefer not to discuss same-sex activities of their children even if they see or suspect them. Eventually, sons are expected to settle down and father children. It is when sons refuse to marry and perpetuate the family tree that parents generally step in and attempt to correct what they see as unacceptable "deviance."

In almost every town in West Africa, some men fail to marry, and they show no interest in the opposite sex, even after turning 30 years old. Socioculturally acceptable reasons, such as not being able to support a wife, are assumed to explain nonmarriage. I would hesitate to call such men "closeted," because West Africans generally do not label people "homosexual" or "heterosexual," and there are no gay institutions in Africa to "come out" into.

Along with the few men who do not marry are those who marry and still continue to have sex with men. This is very similar to practices in Muslim societies: "Sexual behavior is not so much determined by personal preferences or someone's personality, as by a person's role and circumstances in which he finds himself. Generally speaking, a person behaves . . . according to social role patterns. . . . Therefore, concepts of homo- and heterosexuality make no sense in cultures like these. . . . As long as he maintains his role in public, his private preferences and idiosyncrasies are nobody's business but his own, that is, if he is discrete [*sic*] about them, and harms no one" (Schild 1992: 184).

According to the *Spartacus Guide* (1993), such "bisexuality" plus "role versatility" is especially common in northern (that is, predominantly Hausa) Nigeria. This is the picture I see of men who love men throughout the continent of Africa; it is not restricted to northern Nigeria. Also, most European gay males who are attracted to African men generally support this view. For example, three white European gay males I interviewed who live in West Africa with their boyfriends spoke of their mixed feelings because of their lover's marriage and partial commitment to their relationship. All three of them admitted enjoying sex profoundly with their African men and only wished they could have had them to themselves. Interestingly, the three lovers they spoke of were said to be extremely versatile in their erotic behavior with their male partners and also in their social roles.

In a survey I conducted in London during 1994 of 15 men born and raised in West Africa who moved to Europe no later than 1990 and who have sex with men, the respondents regularly provided the following information. They were between the ages of 23 and 40. Of the 15 men, 4 were exclusively homosexual; the other 11 said they didn't mind sleeping with a woman. What was more striking was that 2 of the 11 said they have problems with sleeping with women, yet cannot think of living without a woman in their life. Also, only 2 of the 15 accepted the label "gay"—both were effeminate, exclusively homosexual, and exclusively receptive (that is, "bottoms"). The other 13 refused the label themselves outright, as they see "gay" as a Western, stigmatized label. This, again, is very similar to the attitude of the Arabs and Islamic people described in Arno Schmitt and Jehoeda Sofer (1992) and Murray and Roscoe (1997). Of the 15 men, 13 also had childhood sexual experiences with friends or schoolmates before puberty. Three of them were anally raped as children. The other 10 learned from friends, schoolmates, or caregivers. Eleven are versatile in their sexual roles now. The other 2 discovered sex long after puberty: 1 at age 22 and the

other at age 25. The 2 who had their first experiences in their 20s say they
are exclusively insertive ("tops"). Although they admit to enjoying same-sex
intimacy whenever they have it, these two men indicated that they do have
moments when they feel bad about going to bed with men.

When I asked whether they see that as a problem, and if so, what
kind of solutions they have considered, I received the following responses:
One man, who is a Pentecostal Christian, told me he wanted to be realis-
tic and that several fastings and prayers have not as yet taken that "bitter
cup" from him. He says that whenever the opportunity strikes, he has
resolved to assess, accept, and enjoy those moments without feeling guilty,
until the Lord takes those feelings away from him. He was determined to
continue loving and serving the Lord while he loves men, too. The other,
exclusively active man said he does feel bad about his inclination for men.
All 15 were comfortable speaking to a fellow African who loves men about
their enjoyment of sex with men, though nearly all of them did not want
their homosexual activities known in their natal communities (or, indeed,
anywhere outside their friendship circles). Most of them indicated that the
secrecy surrounding homosexuality in Africa made them feel bonded to
their same-sex partners in a very reassuring way.

Only 1 of the 15 men interviewed was married. The rest—from
Burkina Faso, Nigeria, Cote d'Ivoire, Mali, Ghana, and Senegal—said they
were not sure they would marry and that they preferred living in Europe,
because they were insulated from the pressure to marry from parents and
relatives. It sounds like a kind of "sentimental asylum," that all 15 of these
wonderful brothers would be romantic refugees! The one man who is married is from Ghana and is a choreographer, designer, and instructor. He is
polygamously married to two women and has a total of three children. He
was open about his sexual preference and claims his parents know about
it, as do his wives. He spoke proudly of countering homophobic attacks.
He cited an instance when he confronted a prominent woman at a major
social gathering after she had branded him "homosexual" (a word considered
derogatory in Ghana). He had attended the event flamboyantly dressed
and caused a scandal. In his response, he punctuated every phrase with the
proud assertion, "Yes, I am homosexual," while he enumerated the wealth
and influence his homosexual lifestyle has helped him acquire. He ended by
calling himself a "big bitch" when upset, but otherwise regarded himself as
a very nice person. According to him, his reaction made those present (and
those who heard about it) be careful about the subject of homosexuality,
and it stifled any homophobic remarks.

In West African countries, as in other parts of the continent, the common, Western methods of cruising are far from effective because the signals are as different as the various cultures. Yet, men who know how to find African men testify that there is probably as much homosexuality in Africa as elsewhere. The difference is that it comes with pure African flavors, not in any Western forms. Holding eye contact with strangers, for instance, isn't necessarily a signal. It is not interpreted as having sexual overtones at all. Loitering in or near certain parks is not likely to yield the same results as it would in the West. Aside from the extremely effeminate men, who are most often assumed to be homosexuals (even though they might well not be), it is difficult to tell who is and who is not available for same-sex activities from external appearances. Two men holding hands or with arms around each other does not necessarily evidence a homosexual connection to the average Ghanaian, for instance; it indicates only good friendship. Other countries in West Africa and throughout the continent similarly interpret displays of same-sex fondness. Nor does a same-sex pair dancing in a nightclub constitute stigmatized behavior.

One of the most effective ways that both African and non-African homosexuals meet partners for sex and ongoing relationships is by direct contacts from friends of friends. Among men in West Africa, many same-sex activities occur under the umbrella of friendship. There is nothing wrong in having as many male friends as one can handle, if only one knows how to maintain good friendships—that is the key. Friends and guests can sleep in the same room and even on the same bed without suspicion of any homosexual intimacy.

My experience when I visited a Ghanaian male friend one weekend in Cambridge, England, eloquently demonstrates the basic difference between African and Western perceptions. Two male friends, one from Nigeria and the other from Zimbabwe, had come over to my friend's place. The immediate reaction of his white roommates was, in a word, homophobic. Without talking to us or finding out who we were, they concluded that we were gay and were getting together to have sex—simply because they saw us hug warmly. The most outspoken one, a girl apparently in her mid-20s, addressed us and wished us good fun. Seeing their attitude and erroneous assumptions, we took that opportunity to educate them about some African values. When this story is told to other Africans, their immediate reaction is that people from the West have different values that warp their perceptions.

West Africans often tend to assume that men in "feminine" professions like hairdressing are homosexuals. As in other parts of the world, this is not always true, although there are disproportionate concentrations of effeminate men in such occupations.[1] It is worth noting that the gender associations of professions in this region differ from many Western conceptions. Chefs and secretaries, for example, are thought of as feminine, and therefore, there is a general suspicion that men in these occupations are homosexuals.

Moreover, there are intensely secret "friendship clubs" for men who love other men. These clubs are often as secretive as intelligence agencies. While on safe ground and among themselves, members can be as camp and flamboyant as they wish; almost all of them change their appearance and behavior when elsewhere to fit the traditional roles of men in society. They often have sociolects that nonmembers do not understand. Among such men, "trousers" or "pants" are "skirts," "shorts" are "hot pants," and "briefcases" are "handbags." It is amazing how members switch codes as soon as an unknown person appears!

There are no labeled "gay" bars or clubs or organizations in West Africa, but there definitely are certain places where gay clients often go. In my survey conducted in London, most respondents indicated they met their partners, aside from friends' introductions, at parties, on the beach, in restaurants and hotels, at church, and other everyday places. One could also speak of "hustlers" or "rent boys" in West Africa. Their main business grounds are hotel lounges, nightclubs, beaches, and other places where tourists especially are likely to go. One striking thing about them is that they tend to shy away from locals. A Dutch tourist told me that he had had four different guys, who, he said, were sexually versatile. Like hustlers everywhere, they were said to be too materialistic, and my informant would not say exactly what they required of him aside from the amount they agreed on. Most of them are said to be flexible about going back to the clients' hotel or home. One hustler actually required my informant to wear two condoms before he would play the anally receptive role. The boys did not seem to be enjoying their work; one of them was doing it to get money to marry a girl, and the others responded in the negative when my informant asked if they liked their work.

From the legal perspective, given that sodomy was not a crime under the Napoleonic code and was only decriminalized in England at the time the colonies were becoming independent, one would expect British laws on sodomy to remain on the books and not to be in the criminal codes of former French colonies. Paradoxically, former French colonies have more restrictive laws than former British colonies in West Africa. For instance, Burkina Faso's penal code section 331 makes contact (heterosexual or homosexual) with anyone younger than 21 years of age illegal. However, the 1995 International Lesbian and Gay Association's compendium the *Pink Book* describes homosexuality as ignored and unsupported in Cameroon and the Ivory Coast, while the attitude of people in Senegal, Togo, and Gabon is described as intolerant and hostile. As long as discretion is employed, the public does not pay attention to homosexuality in former British colonies such as Ghana, Nigeria, and Sierra Leone. The 1993 *Spartacus Guide* cites a 3-year penalty for sodomy in Gambia and asserts there is none for adult males in Burkina Faso, although claims of rape are taken seriously and may lead to years of imprisonment.

In conclusion, I will say that there is homoeroticism in West Africa and throughout the continent, even though the words to denote it are not those that Western culture uses. As David Halperin put it in his essay "Sex before Sexuality," " 'Heterosexuality' and 'homosexuality' do not properly name eternal aspects of the human psyche but represent, instead, a distinctively modern cultural production alien to the experience of the ancient Greeks [among others]" (1989: 48). Thus, when most Africans and Arabs reject these sexual labels, they are in effect proclaiming that they do not fit within Western concepts. If there are no terms to aptly denote same-gender loving people in these cultures, we must face this challenge and not force modern labels on them. I've only been able to say a little on lesbianism in Africa, but I believe it could be a rich area for research. On the whole, what this essay underscores is the need for more of us to undertake research on same-sex love in non-Western cultures.

Note

1. See Stephen Murray (1995a: 71–79, 1996a: 195–96).

Part III

Central Africa

Overview

Central Africa has the continent's densest forests and a climate of high temperatures and heavy rainfall. The prevalence of the tsetse fly precludes economies based on stock raising, and consequently most groups are agriculturalists, an exception being the Mbuti ("Pygmy") hunter-gatherers. Typically, men clear the forests, and women undertake the cultivation of various root crops. Bantu-speaking groups of the equatorial regions are patrilineal, patrilocal, and polygynous. They are largely egalitarian societies without elaborate political structures. In contrast, while pursuing a similar subsistence pattern, the Central Bantu in the Savannah zone to the south have matrilineal descent systems and created powerful kingdoms such as the Kongo and the Ndongo. They are part of a band of matrilineal Bantu societies extending across the continent from the Atlantic coast, through the Congo basin, to Tanzania and Mozambique. In Angola, where Nzinga's Mbundu kingdom flourished, matrilineal Bantu groups combined agriculture and cattle herding.

Equatorial Region and the Congo Basin

According to the early 20th-century German ethnographer Günther Tessman, homosexuality among male adolescents was accepted in the Cameroon town of Bafia, a region occupied by patrilineal Bantu-speakers (the Fia or Bafia) (and believed to be the original homeland of the Bantu-speaking peoples) (1921: 124–28). Older boys penetrated younger boys, or they engaged in reciprocal anal intercourse (*jigele ketön*). Tessman reported that this was common among boys too young to have intercourse with females. Once they reached the *ntu* age grade and could have sex with females, however, they were expected to give up homosexual relations—and certainly to do so by the time they became fathers (the *mbang* age grade). Tessman believed that not all did, but he did not know of any specific instances. A somewhat earlier report indicated that young Dualla (Duala) men in the Cameroons practiced mutual masturbation (Hammer 1909: 198).

Elsewhere, Tessman reported some unusual beliefs regarding homosexuality among the Bantu-speaking Fang (Pahouin, Pangwe)[1]—slash-and-burn farmers in the rainforests north of the Congo River (present-day Gabon and Cameroon). These groups believed that same-sex intercourse was a medicine for wealth, transmitted *from* the receptive partner *to* the penetrating partner by anal intercourse (1904: 23). At the same time, the disease yaws was believed to be the supernatural punishment for committing these acts. Nonetheless, according to Tessman, same-sex relations among peers and between adults and youths were fairly common: "It is frequently 'heard of' that young [Pangwe] people carry on homosexual relations with each other and even of older people who take boys, who as is well known 'have neither understanding nor shame' and readily console them by saying *biabo pfia'nga* (we are having fun, playing a game). . . . Adults are excused with the corresponding assertion: *a bele nnem e bango* = 'he has the heart (that is, the aspirations) of boys.' Such men were said to have a heart for boys: *bian nku'ma*" (1904: 131, Human Relations Area Files translation; Tessman's 1921 article and a Pangwe tale recorded by him follows). Tessman also reported the Pangwe claim that the Central Bantu Loango were major poisoners and pederasts. He personally observed how Loango male favorites were excused from carrying burdens when even the chief carried loads.

Especially interesting is Gustave Hulstaert's report that among the Nkundo (a patrilineal group of the Mongo nation in the curve of the Congo River), the younger partner penetrated the older one, a pattern contrary to the usual roles assumed in age-stratified homosexual relationships (1938a: 86–87). He also described how "the game of *gembankango* in which boys, imitating monkeys chase each other through the trees and creepers can—and does—result in reprehensible scenes" (73).

In the early 20th century, Emil Torday and Thomas Joyce noted "sterile" men, called *mokobo* and *tongo* among the Bambala (Mbala), a Central Bantu group in the Kwango River basin (1905: 420, 424). The same authors reported mutual masturbation among young men of the neighboring Bayaka (Yaka) agriculturalists (1906: 48). Somewhat earlier, Herman Soyaux reported sexual relations between men and boys among the matrilineal Bangala (Mbangala) in Angola, which occurred on lengthy business trips when men were unaccompanied by their wives (1879, 2:59).[2] John Weeks also reported that mutual masturbation was frequently practiced by Bangala men and that sodomy was "very common, and is regarded with little or no shame. It generally takes place when men are visiting strange towns or during the time they are fishing at camps away from their women" (1909: 448–49).

In west central Angola, missionary David Livingstone observed individuals who he termed *dandies* among the Temba (Tamba/Matamba). These men adorned their bodies with decorations and used so much grease in their hair that it drenched their shoulders (1857: 452). Livingstone did not hazard any comments about their sexual behavior, however.

In his extensive description of the Mukanda, or boys' circumcision rites, of the Ndembu in what is now northwestern Zambia, Victor Turner (1967) related that initiates mimed copulation with a senior male's penis. The rationale for the practice is reminiscent of those underlying actual same-sex contact between men and youth in Melanesian initiations: it was considered a way to strengthen the novice's penis. Similarly, among neighboring Central Bantu groups (the Luvale/Balovale, Chokwe, Luchazi, Lucho, and Lunda), throughout the first phase of initiation, boys remained nude while they recovered from their circumcision. At this time, they played with the penises of the *vilombola* (keeper of the initiation lodge) and *tulombolachika* (initiated assistants of the *vilombola*). According to one report, "This is considered to hasten healing; the novices also hope that by so doing, their own penes will grow large and strong. The same is done to visitors to the lodge" (White 1953: 49).

In the early 1980s, Karla Poewe described kinship terminology with cross-gender implications among the Central Bantu of the Luapula province in northwestern Zambia: "Dual sexuality, if such a designation is appropriate, refers to the fact that a person who is anatomically male, can play a female role. For example, a person's maternal uncle, specifically 'his/her maternal uncle,' is *nalume*. *Na* means mother of, *lume* means masculine gender" (1982: 172). Poewe did not indicate, however, whether such practices resulted in a social role based on "dual sexuality" or in any particular sexual practices. Forms of sexuality other than heterosexuality, on the rare occasions that they were mentioned, "call forth hilarity" (172).[3]

The anthropological popularizer Colin Turnbull wrote that male homosexuality was rare and regarded derisively by Mbuti hunting bands of the Ituri forest (1965: 122; 1986: 118). He later added "that when men sleep huddled together, sometimes one ejaculates, but he then ridicules himself for this 'accident,'" and "the Mbuti do not reject homosexuality so much as they favor procreation" (D. Greenberg 1988: 87).[4]

The Kitesha Role among the Basongye

North of the Central Bantu, in the present nation of Congo (formerly Zaire), are groups of the Luba nation, patrilineal societies that betray traces of former matrilineality. They include the Basongye (Basonge/Bala) of the Kasai Oriental Province, where Alan Merriam found that an alternative gender role, called *kitesha*, existed for both males and females. Although his account is somewhat confusing, the role, when occupied by males, clearly entailed systematic departures from men's conventional behavior (particularly in terms of dress and work), along with expectations of unconventional sexual behavior. Merriam's informants (two men and one *kitesha*) agreed that *bitesha* (pl.) did not like to work and, improperly for men, went about bare chested (1971: 97), but they did not agree on what sexual behavior typified the role—whether homosexuality, exhibitionistic heterosexuality, or asexuality.

The one self-acknowledged *kitesha* at the time of Merriam's research, Mulenda, was "married and says that he likes his wife and likes to have intercourse with her." He told Merriam, "I like women; I don't want to be without them" (1971: 95). While he denied that *kitesha* committed homosexual acts or that anyone suspected them of doing so, he also denied that it was shameful for him to be a *kitesha*, although he acknowledged that other men thought so (97). Merriam added that "others in the village swear to having been eyewitnesses" of Mulenda having intercourse with a female *kitesha* (96–97).

Similarly, a non-*kitesha* informant stated, "*Bitesha* like to expose their genitals in public, but they do not have homosexual relationships. They are not interested in women, and as for masturbation, who can tell? In a desperate situation, a *kitesha* may have public intercourse with a female *kitesha*. This is terribly shameful: no one would ever look at such a thing on purpose, but people cannot help seeing. Then they know he is a *kitesha* and they leave him alone. He does not have to work in the fields" (Merriam 1971: 94–95). Although this indicates social tolerance for gender nonconformity, the nature of *kitesha* involvement in heterosexual relations is unclear, and one is left to wonder what female *kitesha* do other than have sex with male *kitesha*.

Yet, another of Merriam's informants was "at no loss" to speak of "males who act like women" and reeled off a list of distinctive traits: "He doesn't want to work. He doesn't want to be with other men. He doesn't even have a concubine. He eats everywhere except at his own house. He doesn't do the things other men do. He never keeps a job. He has good luck. He acts like a woman, that is, rushes about hither and yon and wig-

gles his hips when he walks. He wears women's clothing, but not kerchiefs"
(1971: 94). This last detail underscores the unique nature of the *kitesha* role.
Although native descriptions of male *bitesha* emphasize their nonmasculine
and womanlike traits and behaviors, their incomplete cross-dressing (women's
clothes but not kerchiefs) ensures that they are not taken for women, while
other traits attributed to them (laziness, good luck) appear to be unique
to the *kitesha* role.

Merriam repeated much of this in his 1974 book on the Bala, with
some additional details regarding female *bitesha*. According to Mulenda,
"Female *bitesha* do not like men, prefer the company of women, but most
of all wish to be with male *bitesha*. They like to have sexual relations with
men, particularly male *bitesha,* and they do not like to wear men's clothing.
They do not like to cook or to do other female tasks save to gather wood
'because that is the easiest work'" (321). Merriam did not encounter any
female *bitesha*, so this statement could again reflect Mulenda's desire to assert
his own heterosexuality against the view of *bitesha* as homosexual.

A possible reconciliation of the contradictory views reported by Merriam
(that there is no homosexual behavior among Bala men, on the one hand,
and that *bitesha* are homosexuals, on the other) is that, because *bitesha* occupied a gender status distinct from that of both men and women, sex with
them was simply not viewed as homosexual, that is, as involving two men.[5]

Southern Congo and Angola

The lower reaches of the Congo River and adjacent coastal areas were home
to the Kongo kingdom, comprised of matrilineal Central Bantu groups.
According to the Italian missionary Biovanni Cavazzi, one of the supervising
priests of the Giagues (Jagas) was a male who wore women's clothes and
was referred to as "Grandmother" (see the chapter "Ganga-Ya-Chibanda,"
which follows) (Labat 1732: 195–99).[6] Additional evidence is provided by
testimony collected from a slave in Brazil originally from the Congo region,
which was recorded in the Inquisition's *Denunciations of Bahia, 1591–1593*:

> Francisco Manicongo, a cobbler's apprentice known among the
> slaves as a sodomite for "performing the duty of a female" and
> for "refusing to wear the men's clothes which the master gave
> him." Francisco's accuser added that "in Angola and the Congo
> in which he had wandered much and of which he had much

experience, it is customary among the pagan negros to wear a loincloth with the ends in front which leaves an opening in the rear . . . this custom being adopted by those sodomitic negros who serve as passive women in the abominable sin. These passives are called *jimbandaa* in the language of Angola and the Congo, which means passive sodomite. The accuser claimed to have seen Francisco Manicongo "wearing a loincloth such as passive sodomites wear in his land of the Congo and immediately rebuked him." (quoted by Trevisan 1986: 55; his ellipses)

Reports of an alternative gender status in Angola date back to the comments of the Englishman Andrew Battel, cited earlier, first published by Samuel Purchas in his 1625 collection of travel accounts. Purchas also published an account from the Portuguese Jesuit João dos Santos from the area of Luanda, within Queen Nzinga's kingdom. Dos Santos described "certayne *Chibadi*, which are Men attyred like Women, and behave themselves womanly, ashamed to be called men; are also married to men, and esteeme that unnatural damnation an honor" (Purchas 1625, vol. 2, bk. IX, chap. 12, sec. 5, p. 1558). The priests Gaspar Azevereduc and Antonius Sequerius also encountered men called *chibados*, who dressed, sat, and spoke like women and who married men "to unite in wrongful male lust with them." Even more shocking to them was the fact that these marriages were honored and prized (Jarric 1616: 482).

Similarly, in 1680, Antonio de Oliveira de Cardonega noted: "Sodomy is rampant among the people of Angola. They pursue their impudent and filthy practices dressed as women. Their own name for those [of the same sex] who have carnal relations with each other is *quimbanda*. Some *quimbandas* are powerful wizards, who are much esteemed by most Angolans" (1680: 86, translation by S. O. Murray). Clearly, *chibadi*, *chibanda*, *chibados*, *jimbandaa*, *kibamba*, and *quimbanda* are related terms. Given the participations of such individuals in the religious rites of the Kongo kingdom, it may be that the term (and the role) diffused with the expansion of that state.

More recent ethnographic reports indicate that the social status observed by the Portuguese in the 16th and 17th centuries survived into the 20th century. In the 1930s, Wilfred Hambly learned of gender-mixing medicine men among the (Ovi)Mbundu and a case of a boy who persisted in dressing in women's clothes and beating corn (women's work), despite punishment. His informant, Ngonga, explained, "There are men who want men, and women who want women. . . . A woman has been known to make an artificial penis for use with another woman" (1937: 426; 1934a: 181). Lack of approval did not prevent visibly gender-mixing homosexuals of either sex.

A gender-mixing religious role for males among the Ondonga, one of the Bantu-speaking Ambo groups in southern Angola and northern Namibia, was mentioned in the early 20th century by the Finnish missionary M. Rautanen.[7] According to Rautanen, both pederasts and men presenting themselves as women (*eshenga*) existed among the Ondonga and were detested by them. Most *eshenga* were also shamans (*oonganga*) (1903: 333–34).

This role was described in more detail by Carlos Estermann in the 1970s. According to Estermann, Ambo diviners are called *kimbanda*. The highest order, the *ovatikili*, are "recruited exclusively among men [who] are few and feared and their activity is surrounded by profound mystery" (1976: 197). Although Estermann did not say that all *ovatkili* are possessed by female spirits, he notes that a large number of the owners of a certain musical instrument called *omakola* (big gourd) were males called *omasenge*, who dressed as women, did women's work, and contracted marriage with other men (who might also have female wives). "In a general way," he suggests, "this aberration is to be interpreted by the spiritism or spiritist belief of these people. An *esenge* [sing. of *omasenge*] is essentially a man who has been possessed since childhood by a spirit of female sex, which has been drawing out of him, little by little, the taste for everything that is masculine and virile" (197).

More recently, Wolfram Hartmann, an historian at the University of Namibia, has reported that in the (Oshiw)Ambo language of the (Ov)Ambo, anally receptive males are called *eshengi* (pl. *ovashengi*), "he who is approached from behind." He also noted, "The *ovashengi* of the Unkwambi [Ukuambi], a subgroup of the Ovambo, are respected as healers, or *onganga*. Among another Ovambo subgroup, the Oukwanyama [Ovakuanyama], the *ovashengi* are not treated as well; however, they are the only Oukwanyama members entitled to play the *ekola*, a special music instrument" (in Jones 1996: 41).

Woman-Woman Patterns

In the 1930s, Hulstaert described relationships between Nkundó women in the Belgian Congo (now Zaire): "Nkundó girls play at 'husband and wife' and even adult married women engage in this vice. According to my informants, the causes are as follows: first, an intense and very intimate love

between two women, second and above all, the fact that wives of polyga-
mists find it difficult to satisfy their passions in a natural way. Often they
engage in this practice with co-wives of the same man" (1938a: 95–96). He
added that "in establishments where girls are too securely kept away from
the opposite sex, there has been an increase" in sexual relationships between
girls. "The latter often engage in sex with co-wives. A woman who presses
against another woman is called *yaikya bonsángo*" (96).

Notes

1. This group of peoples includes the Bene (Bane), Bulu (Boulou), Jaunde
(Yaunde), Mokuk, Mwelle (Mvele), and Ntum (Ntumu).

2. As Ferdinand Karsch-Haack long ago noted, this still does not explain
why the men chose boys for long-distance sexual relationships rather than women
(1911: 148).

3. Elsewhere, Poewe expresses hostility to Western male homosexuality even
as she claims "tolerance" for it (1982: 211).

4. On the insistence of anthropologists not to see homoeroticism in same-
sex behavior, see Stephen Murray (1995a: 264–73, 1997a).

5. William Bentley's Kongo dictionary lists *uzeze/zeze* for "effeminate man"
(1887: 746).

6. Rudi Bleys questions whether the phrase "foulest crimes" necessarily means
homosexuality (1995: 57, n. 101), although he reads another section (Labat 1732,
2:55–56) as providing "signs of incidental, disguised homoeroticism" (Bleys 1995: 33).

7. Like the Mbundu, the Ambo raise sorghum and millet as well as cows.
Unlike them (and most other African pastoralists), Ambo women share in caring
for the cattle and participate in pastoralist rituals.

Homosexuality among the Negroes of Cameroon and a Pangwe Tale (1921, 1911)

GÜNTHER TESSMANN

Translated by Bradley Rose

Generally, one must consider sexual phenomena not in isolation but always in the context of the entire social situation, and not just with regard to material but to spiritual domains as well.[1] This principle applies all the more to native peoples, whose customs present themselves to us as indeed incomprehensible and therefore silly, because we consider them entirely on their own, not in connection with their other customs and ways of seeing. Among the social customs that sexual practices significantly depend on, religion is by far the most decisive. Accordingly, it can be said: wherever a different religion appears in Africa, sexual activity is different as well. Consequently, before I describe homosexual life among the Negroes of Cameroon, I will identify the various religions and lay out the basic views contained in them.[2]

The colony of Cameroon is but a relatively small part of Africa. Yet, if all of Africa is often treated alike in circles of nonspecialists, then it is not surprising that the Negro tribes in Cameroon are believed to be similar to one another. This, however, is not the case. Linguistically, to be sure, one has to acknowledge two basically different divisions of the race, namely the Bantu, who occupy the coastal lands and the whole of the south, and the Sudans, who occupy the east. The cultural differences, however, are even greater, particularly in religion. Until recently, almost nothing was known

about the religion of these tribes. This difficult subject was first investigated
more closely in research by the author in the years 1904 to 1917 and was
reported in various essays and in unpublished studies.

According to my investigations, one has to distinguish two complexes
of cultures, religions, and worldviews among the Negro tribes of Cameroon,
which are not reflected in the linguistic divisions.

The first and apparently historically older element is the one I have
called Austral culture and religion, represented only by some small tribes in
central Cameroon (between Jabassi-on-Wuri and Jaunde), of which I would
mention in particular the Bafia [Fia]. The name "Austral culture" was chosen
because the worldview of these tribes is similar to that found in Australia,
which in Africa would exist in more or less pure form but only in vestiges,
yet nonetheless spread over the greatest part of Negro Africa. This hypothesis
suggests that we are dealing here with an earlier, widely dispersed race, which,
however, was almost completely absorbed by subsequent invading Negro
peoples. The present-day tribes that are included in this "Australian" racial
division belong linguistically to the Bantu but nevertheless occupy among
them a special position, which is revealed through certain idiosyncrasies, for
example, sound shifts in singulars and plurals.

The second, historically more recent, and therefore a higher-standing
element includes all the remaining Negro tribes, those that speak Bantu as
well as those speaking Sudan.

First, let us consider the Australian type in relationship to its religious
outlook. According to their myths, everything in the world developed from an
egg. They recognize basic masculine and feminine sexual forces as the primary
powers, symbolized by a mystical snake or vine (masculine) and a cave or
hollow tree (feminine). Through the interplay of these two elementary powers
the first people (man and woman) originated, and the man, as forefather,
was equipped with quite extraordinary powers, that is, magical powers. This
forefather, of course, died, and his memory lives on in the spells he gave to
his descendants. This religious view does not recognize a God. Consequently,
it recognizes no afterlife. At death, everything is over, the Bafia say.[3] The most
important thing to us, however, given this negative feature of the Bafia—no
God, no afterlife—is the fact that no moral evil is known. Where there is no
God, there is also no sin, and where there is no life after death, there is also
no punishment. Thus, in contrast to other Negroes, sexual relations among
the Bafia cannot be sinful or subject to punishment.

One result of this fundamental religious outlook is a conspicuous, and
significant, naïveté and freedom in sexual activity—a naïveté and freedom

that have made possible a marked proliferation of homosexuality reminiscent of the Greek period among this primitive and powerful tribe. From this fact the conclusion arises that homosexual desires are firmly established in human nature.

Before we move on to the description of homosexual activity among the Bafia, it must be noted that the Bafia recognize three stages of development. The first is that of *kiembe*, boys who have not had sexual relations with females; the second is that of *ntu*, boys or men without children who have had sexual relations with females; and finally is that of *mbäng*, men who have children. The corresponding stages among women are *ngon*, sexually inactive virgins; then *tsobo*, women without children; and third, *gib*, women with children.

Like all Negroes, the Bafia view the sexual activity of children differently from that of adults. It is looked on as play and is accordingly called by a different name than same-sex acts at a later time. As far as my investigations go, the sexual activity of Bafia children is hardly distinguished from that of other Negroes, though it would seem that they are initiated even earlier into the mysteries of sex.

Among them only the infant is completely innocent, that is, not forced into the mysteries of sexual relations and birth. So long as the infant cannot speak, "He doesn't even know the place where children come out; but if he can indeed speak, then he knows everything." Even if these words of one of my informants are somewhat exaggerated, it is certain that one of the first efforts of older siblings and other relatives is to enlighten the little one as soon as possible, particularly in the presence of the mother. Not only that—the parents, and especially the father, actually take pleasure in coaching the offspring in this respect: "Do you really know where you came out?" "Yes," says the child. "Out of the head?" "No!" "Out of the knee?" "No!" "Then show me where you came from." At that, the child points to the vagina of the mother. Then great joy reigns in the house, just as it does with us when the little child is able to distinguish his father from his baby bottle. Well, after this, we can hardly wonder, or wonder at all, that the child acquires even "more" (!) knowledge when, as my informant admitted, he can walk. At five, six, or seven years, there are no more secrets for the boys or the girls, and they now throw themselves whole-heartedly into the "special study" [of sexuality], with "practical exercises" and "demonstrations" by older siblings.

The sexual activity of the boy falls into two stages, which, however, occur in part simultaneously. The primary stage—somewhere up to the age of 15—seems to involve common promiscuity, which can be observed among the other Negro tribes as well and is also looked at as child's play. This prevailing promiscuity—partly in a purely playful, imitative form—consists in relationships between boys and girls, and boys with boys. It takes place mainly by day in the houses during the absence of the parents. Should adults chance upon them and reproach the boys somewhat, then the latter simply ask if they [the parents] didn't do the same thing when younger.

The second stage entails pure homosexual relations, which are looked upon as a "national custom."[4] Among adults, the love of friends is viewed no worse than the expression of heterosexuality. Apart from the above-mentioned liaisons of boys with boys in their earliest years, the Bafia boy of five or six years plays the passive role with an older brother, and then changes his acquired sexual drive through enticement to active practices with his brother or acquaintances. However, the friendship with one important older boy and a younger boy appears to be characteristic of the Bafia. Perhaps one reason for the homosexual activity of youth is that the common promiscuity gives the indeed already sensuous tendencies of the Bafia major encouragement. At the same time, the girls (to whom I will come to later) are strictly prohibited to the opposite sex, so that boys around puberty and for long time after—perhaps ordinarily until the 18th or 20th year—are compelled to satisfy their instincts in homosexual unions. To this end, older youths simply take for themselves a younger or contemporary boy from among their relatives, especially, of course, a brother with whom they sleep. Youths before the age of reason employ an entirely similar means as the Pangwe[5] and Mbum—and, so it seems, most of the Cameroon tribes—namely, the inquiry "by flowers" [by indirect means]. They show their chosen one a basketry plate of some earthnuts. If the other takes the fruit and eats it, then he consents, otherwise not. The metaphor in this silent mode of expression lies in the fact that the earthnut is a pleasantly "sweet" food that nevertheless is found in the filthy earth. Since the boys—as they say—don't hesitate to have intercourse with their fellows by day at home, it sometimes happens that the father will chance upon them. But he only laughs over it and in no way punishes his boy.

After puberty, therefore, the first stage consists of *kiembe* (youths who don't yet sexually associate with females). Girls of the same age, that is, before puberty, are kept from sexual activity. In case of a transgression, the youth is threatened with an extremely harsh punishment, namely, torture or even sale into slavery. With the sexually active maidens (*tsobo*), the youth at this stage is rarely successful, since there is much competition. In this difficult situation, the practice of homosexual intercourse proves very useful to him. If he hadn't previously tried it, then he is now wont to seek a younger or contemporary friend (*lexan*, "bosom buddy"), who is in the same situation, *a ji'gele keton* [?], that is, *cohabitat in anum* [anal intercourse]. Such friendly alliances are almost always involved in the customary sleeping together of youths. Later, the friends seek women together as well.

It seems to me that this feeling of sexual solidarity can be traced back to earlier homosexual circumstances, which took the form of two brothers sharing an abducted or married woman, a custom that is not at all as common among other Negro tribes and is nowhere so obvious as it is here—jealousy hinders even the living together of two brothers. Naming practices give us further evidence of the influence of homosexual relations on the customs and habits of the Bafia. In particular, the peculiar, original nickname for men must be mentioned, namely, "He who hunts for men." Quite unique, as well, is the custom of the father giving a newborn child, in remembrance of his "bosom buddy," the latter's name, even when the child is female. Since among the Bafia, as with us, there are separate names appropriate to males and females, it thus happens that a delicate lass runs about with a formidable male name like Buffalo or Man of Death. This circumstance, unheard of among the rest of the Negroes, again shows how little differentiated these people are in their consciousness.

At the second stage after puberty, the *ntu*, the youth generally turns away from his own sex and tries, as is the custom here, to abduct a female with whom he has sexual relations—not secretly, however, as among other Negroes, but together with the other young men of the same settlement, or—which is especially the case later on—together with his brother. This suggests the possibility that those who formerly engaged only in homosexual intercourse, aroused by the sight of their comrades, are thereby won over to heterosexual relations. There are a few, however, who, even into maturity, are only given to associate with the same sex, and these are the ones who can be labeled actual homosexuals [*eigentlichen Homosexuellen*]. I myself have not met any, but it was reported to me by natives that they are present and known by name. My belief is that the percentage of them is the same as among us.

Let us now consider the second, more recently evolved division of the Cameroon Negroes, to which almost all of the rest of the tribes belong. As different as they might be in linguistic and cultural respects, the main features of their worldviews and therefore of their character are the same. This worldview is based on the belief that there is a creator God of whom the sun is the chief manifestation. Because of the sin of mankind, God has removed himself to an unreachable remoteness—inaccessible to any kind of influence, accept perhaps by prayer. After death, the people return to him in another form, namely as souls, but only the righteous, who did God's Will (that is good) and avoided evil, which is sin. What is considered to be sin? First of all, sexual intercourse. From the belief in the wickedness of sexual intercourse comes the persecution of everything sexual. The tolerance of those relations practiced by the majority of the tribe in question is explained by a simple, social agreement. According to this, it is clear that normal sexual intercourse between a married man and his wife, although officially a sin, unofficially is indeed permitted and was most pleasant. But it may take place only at night—when the sun, the living manifestation of God, no longer stands in the sky—and totally in private. All other forms, including coitus by day, which otherwise would be acceptable, and peculiar forms of it, and above all homosexuality, remain "sin" par excellence.

With this "theory" of sin is a second, closely associated one, namely, the official innocence of youth until puberty. "In youth there is no sin," it is said, and even the 16- or 17-year-old Negro, when asked whether he already has had sexual relations, immediately responds: "How so? I am still a child!" The determination to firmly preserve this theory of the innocence of youth reveals itself unconsciously in several of their practices. First, there is the fact that only boys are taken to the consecration of holy figures, the cult figures, because they are pure (as among the Pangwe). Among the Baja, another of these tribes, there is a prohibition against children eating jackal meat, for otherwise they would become as carnal as that wild dog. Above all, there is the effort to represent youth as sexless, in which sexual wishes, urges, and practices are represented as play or as playful imitation. This effort goes so far that, during my ethnographic research among the Pangwe, I once elicited the names of native games, called *ebobane bongo*, along with the names for round dances, rope play, and hen-and-hawk [a hide-and-seek game that culminates with the hawk "mounting" the hen]. When I later requested that the lads demonstrate for me the previously named games, they became embarrassed about *ebobane bongo* and explained, laughing, that that was the name for the sexual experiments of children, which indeed mostly take place in connection with a game "Man and Wife" (among us, "Mother and Child"). These sexual experiments, which I already mentioned among the Bafia, consist of a kind of promiscuity, to the extent that the little boys carry out coital attempts with same-aged girls or boys. In the course of time, an actual sexual union takes place, which, in the last case, is homosexual. As the lads get older, they appear to incline to the same sex, perhaps because they have a greater preference for it or because the mother pays more attention to bigger girls, and they are drawn more to field and kitchen work.

In the case of the little affairs between boys, the practice is similar to that of the Bafia, in which the boys come to an agreement "by flowers." One of them gathers any sort of debris, dry stalks, dirt clods, so forth, from the village square, puts them in a leaf wrapping and gives them to his friend with the words: "Here is the food I cooked for you!" The other takes the bundle, opens it, and acts as if he were eating it, if he consents, or if he doesn't, throws it away (as among the Pangwe). That the Mbum, although they are reckoned among the Sudan Negroes, have this same custom only shows its age. After puberty, homosexual involvement is harshly judged. Among adults, such an acquaintance is looked on as something immoral and contrary to nature, simply unheard of. In reality, it is rather often "heard of" that young people cultivate relationships with one another and that even older people take boys for themselves—who "have neither understanding nor shame"—and they entice them easily with *bia bo pfianga*—let's have fun, joke, play. The latter are excused with the well-known statement whose deeper meaning is rarely understood properly: *bö ne bongo*, "they are ignorant, that is, they know not what they do," and the former with the corresponding *a bele nuem e bongo*, "he has the heart of a boy," which of course is not at all flattering.

Because of social ostracization, along with embarrassment about sexual matters and the prudery of the Negroes of this cultural type, it is extraordinarily difficult to learn anything about such cases. A casual traveler would get the impression that homosexuality generally does not exist among the unspoiled Negroes. But whoever stays long in the country and knows the land and people, knows under which heading homosexuality can be found. Among the Pangwe, it is called, for instance, "wealth medicine." With "wealth medicine" comes, along with many mystical instincts, urges for homosexual release. Through close union, which carries with it mystical powers to create, it is believed that the two partners become rich. This view no doubt originated from the observation that through close solidarity and mutual support between two friends, wealth could more easily be accumulated and amassed than when a man is on his own.

The religious view of homosexual love as a sin entails punishment by divine power or its cult representative, most especially the *Ngi*, which inflicts on the sinners a terrible illness. We hear, therefore, most of all among the

Pangwe, that the people who have taken the "riches medicine" together became sick with leprosy or yaws and die—so, too, in the peculiar tale of the two homosexuals that was communicated in my monograph on the Pangwe.[6]

Punishment through temporal justice exists among no tribe, since no one feels harmed by homosexual relations.

The frequency of homosexual relations among the Negro men—in contrast to the female sex—is shown in tales that repeatedly speak of a woman-hater. I hereby submit two such tales. The first comes from the Pangwe.[7]

The Woman-Hater

There once was a man named Malong me Ntona, and he was always hunting. He was always going into the bush and returning by evening with his catch. One day, however, he lost his way. He came to a stream and descended along it, always hoping to find the path, but he kept getting farther and farther into the bush. Thus he wandered lost for seven months, until he met a woman who was going upstream. Then he asked her: "Where have you come from?" She said: "Oh, I went fishing and—I don't know how it happened—I took the wrong course and got lost. I have been in the bush already seven months." Then the man responded: "Oh, same with me; let's go together so we can find a trail."

The two of them had not gone far when they suddenly saw a small path diverging from the river. They decided to take the path. They wandered a little bit when they heard voices, as if people were making a clearing in the forest: "Thus one clears the dense forest for a plantation, thus one clears the dense forest for a plantation!" And then they indeed saw a plantation in the forest. Then the voice called: "And thus one burns it,"[8] and already the plantation clearing was burnt. "And thus one plants." Then maize stalks were already standing in the clearing. "Thus a village is made," rang out, and then a pretty village appeared at the plantation.[9]

Then the man left the woman some distance behind and went on closer and heard voices that called out: "Oh, a man is coming." Then the man sat down in the meeting hall. The chieftain was very friendly and honored him with food. But Malong did not want to eat and only kept looking at the path. So his host asked him: "Why do you not eat? What do you seek on the path over there." The man replied: "I left a woman behind over there." The chieftain called the man to his side and said: "Right here are three beautiful girls, take them, marry them, and stay here!" Then the man said: "No thanks, you must take me for a fool!" At that, the chieftain took 6,000 speer (430 marks, or as much as a woman) and laid it out and repeated his demand. But the other said: "How am I supposed to marry the girls; I think you are out of your mind and take me for a fool." Then the chieftain called all the women into a house and said to Malong: "And these I would give to you, all." But Malong replied: "You are completely deranged and take me for a fool!" Then the chieftain walked to the village square and called loudly to the man: "Then what do you want, to stay here or to go away again?" But he didn't answer this time. Then suddenly again the voice is heard as before: "And thus I remove it." Hardly had the voice said that when the houses vanished along with the women and the meeting hall, and as he looked around in astonishment, the large plantation was also no longer, but everything was dense forest as before, and he was in it alone with the woman.

Both began again to wander on, but soon the woman complained, "Oh, my knee hurts." Not long afterward, they had to sit down, and the woman died. Then the man went on for two more days, until he suddenly became sick and died.

The second tale comes from the Baja[10] in East Cameroon.

The Story of the Man Who Didn't Love Women

Once there was a man who had three dogs, named Godongkela, Kils, and Gbara, and who helped him in all things. Since there were at the time many women who had no man, one of the women asked if this man didn't want to marry her. But he said: "I love no women, so what's to do? My dogs help me with everything."

The woman who was rejected planned her revenge. Once when the man had gone hunting with his dogs, and they had pursued a beast afar, she used the opportunity to carry out her purpose. She changed herself into a cannibal and went out in this form to kill the man. When he saw the woman coming, he took flight and finally escaped up a high tree. Then the woman began to chop the tree with her sex organ. She had already gone halfway through the tree when the toad, who had been a spectator of this business, came to help the man. It called: "Solo loe, solo loe"—"come back together again," at which the tree grew together again. When the woman saw that her work was interrupted, she stopped what she was doing to seek out the toad and strike it dead. But she could not find it since it had hidden itself in a bunch of leaves. Then she went back to the tree and again began to chop, more vigorously than before. There was just a little bit more to go and the tree would be felled. Then the toad again called: "sola loe, sola loe," and the tree again grew back together. But the woman didn't tire, she would not give up.

Meanwhile, the man had been calling his dogs to the tree, and they now heard the call, although they were a long way off. They came running in a hurry to help their master, charging at the woman. The first ripped the sex organ she had tried to fell the tree with; the others lacerated her face and body, so that she died. Then the man climbed back down from his tree and sought his rescuer, the toad, whom he took along to the village. There he showed it to all the people and told them how it had saved him when he was in need. He said: "From now on the toad can no longer be eaten." And thus it was, and no Baja will eat a toad. The man, however, never married. He had his trusty hounds, who always continued to help him. But some of the women changed themselves into men so that there were now not so many women without a man.

A still different conclusion must be made from that concerning the primitive Negroes in regards to the civilized and Christianized coastal Negroes. For them, there is no religious restraint anymore, and the social restraints are, as a result of the disintegrating influence of white culture, mostly so negligible that they aren't worth mentioning. Among these people, from whatever tribe they may have come from, homosexual inclinations are clearly more out in the open.

The Four Suitors: A Pangwe Tale

The story of Scho-bo-num-e-kub-b'ogbuale-ba-jem-e-kidi-a-lenne and Akúkedanga-be-bongo-be-ntúudumo.[11]

There was once named a man Bongo-be-ntúudumo, who had a daughter who was called Akúkedanga-be-bongo-be-ntúudumo and was very beautiful.

Once upon a time, four lovers met on a path who were all walking to their beloveds. When they asked each other, "To whom do you go?" it was answered on all sides, "To Akúkedanga!" Then said they, "Well then, let us go together and see whom the girl loves."

The lovers, all from different families, were called thus—the first Scho-bo-schua, the second Scho-bö-ngönne-ma-kö-make, the third Scho-bö-kaa-jem-bodscho-melang, and the fourth Scho-bo-num-e-kub-b'ogbuale-ba-jem-e-kidi-a-lenne.

So the four lovers came into the village where they sought the father of the girl. He said, "Oh! How is it that four men have arrived when there is but one girl! But we can indeed see that it is so."

The mother likewise said, "Oh! Four men! I know surely that this or that lover has come, and if the girl loved him, he slept with her; if she loved him not, then he went home again. But four men all at once?"

Then the young men said, "We will see whom the girl loves."

The girl loved only the Scho. . .lenne, while the father loved the Scho-bo-schua, the mother loved the Scho. . .make, and the brother of the girl loved the Scho. . .melang. So they all slept together in the cottage and the girl slept with the Scho. . .enne in bed. But when Scho. . .lenne wanted to embrace the girl, one of the other three from the other beds would say, "Oh! How lecherous this girl is! Immediately on the first day she lets her lover embrace her!"

Then the girl said, "Oh! How this man speaks! Stop, we must choose another day."

At night, however, the lover of the girl asked, "Don't you want to marry me?" The girl consented, but they decided that the lover should not steal her at night, since the other young men might notice this, but rather by day. They would say they were going bathing. And so it happened.

The husband went the next day ostensibly to the water, where the girl followed him. Then both walked to the village of the lovers.

When in the afternoon the two didn't come back, and it became obvious that Scho. . .lenne had abducted the girl, Scho. . .make addressed the mother, the one he liked, and reproached her. But the mother said, "Oh! What do I know of it? I don't occupy the skin of the girl!" Then Scho. . .make became angry, seized a bush-knife, and drove it into the mother. She died on the spot. Then he went straight home.

As Scho-bo-schua was unwilling to be satisfied with that, the father went to the lover who had abducted the girl and demanded from him a bride-price. Scho. . .lenne gave it to him, and the father took it back and said to Scho-bo-schua, "Here is the money; I will compensate you with it."

But Scho-bo-schua said, "No! I don't want it."

So then the father took one of his wives and the money and tried to offer them to Scho-bo-schua as compensation. But he would not take it, saying, "No! I don't want it; instead, we shall always be together. When you piss, I shall piss, as well; when you defecate, I shall be near; when you sleep, I shall sleep in the same bed with you."

Thus Scho-bo-schua did it, and both slept together. In the end, however, both became sick from framboise and died.[12] Scho. . .melang slept with the brother of the girl in one bed and both got leprosy and they, too, died.

Notes

1. Originally published as "Die Homosexualität bei den Negern Kameruns," *Jahrbuch für sexuelle Zwischenstufen unter besonderer Berücksichtigung der Homosexualität* 21 (1921): 121–38. Tessman's sources in the following notes are not included in the bibliography unless cited elsewhere in this work—B. Rose.

2. The Negro race occupies the largest part of Cameroon, especially the coast, of the south and east. The north, on the other hand, is mainly occupied by tribes of other races, namely Hamites (Fulbe) and Arabs.

3. The Bafia as always are representative of the whole Austral-Bantu group.

4. When the question is put to a Bafia as to whether he, too, engaged in homosexual relations, it is answered immediately in turn with the question: "Am I expected to give up my national custom?"

5. See Günther Tessmann on homosexual relations of the Pangwe in the work of Ferdinand Karsch-Haack (1911: 155).

6. Tessmann, 1904, 2:271. A translation of this tale follows.

7. Tessmann, *"Ajong's Erzählungen"* Kentaur Verlag, 1921, Berlin [n.d.]. [*Ajongs erzählungen: marchen der Fangneger*. Berlin: Pantheon-Verlag, 1921.]

8. The felled trees and bushes would be left to dry for some days in the sun and then set on fire.

9. At the establishment of a new settlement in the forest, the plantations are, first of all, laid out by people sent out ahead. Later, houses are built into which the inhabitants move.

10. Tessmann, "Die Baja," Völkerkundliche Monographie cines westafrikanischen Negerstammes. Manuscript.

11. Originally published in Karsch-Haack (1911: 152–54). See also Tessman, *The Fang Peoples: An Ethnographic Monograph on a West African Group*, trans. Richard Neuse (New Haven, CT: HRAF, 1959), 131–34. The characters, and Tessman's translation of their names, are Scho-bo-num-e-kub-b'ogbuale-ba-jem-e-kidi-a-lenne, father of Akúkedanga-be-bongo-be-ntúudumo, "One who is more beautiful than a snail," a young woman of marriageable age; Scho-bo-schua, not translated, the first of the four suitors, who ends up declaring his love for the girl's father; Scho-bö-ngönne-ma-kö-make, "I go out in order to come back," the second suitor; Scho-bö-kaa-jem-bodscho-melang, "He knows no wickedness," the third suitor;

Scho-bo-num-e-kub-b'ogbuale-ba-jem-e-kidi-a-lenne, "Hen and quail, they know when the morning starts," the fourth suitor. Because of the length of the names, they are abbreviated after their first use—W. Roscoe.

12. Frambosia or yaws is a disease spread by skin-to-skin contact and caused by the same spirochete as syphilis. This folktale seems to moralize a disease to make a statement against homosexuality, much as HIV has been exploited in recent years. Whether this is the attitude of the Fang people, however, or of Tessman is not clear—W. Roscoe.

Ganga-Ya-Chibanda (1687)

GIOVANNI ANTONIO CAVAZZI

Translated by Will Roscoe

Among the numbers of these *Ganga-Ya*, there is one, of whom my author excused himself from speaking, since accuracy does not demand it of him, were it not for the instruction of the missionaries who are going to be consecrated to the instruction of these peoples, which has been somewhat fruitless up to now.[1]

He is called *Ganga-Ya-Chibanda*—that is to say, the superintendent of that which concerns the Sacrifices. To fill this post, a shameless, impudent, lewd man is required, deceitful to the last, without honor. He dresses ordinarily as a woman and makes an honor of being called the Grandmother. Whatever bad action that he might commit, there is no point of law that might condemn him to death; also he is one of the very loyal Ministers of the Demon of impurity. The privileges of his character go so far that one is not able to say the outrages that he does to married persons—may be with their women, may be with their concubines. He penetrates into the better guarded seraglios, and there, he indulges his brutal passions, through indulging those women who, there, are enclosed, who hold the honor of having his company.

He is moreover a seller of sashes of great credit. They are made by him for all sorts of uses and for very infamous superstitions.

Whenever he finds himself at some Sacrifice, he puts on his costume, a skin of a lion, tiger, wolf, or other ferocious beast, and attaches to his sash a number of small bells called *Pambas*, which according to him have a

159

marvelous property of calling the divinities of peace and the spirits of the dead: the thing most necessary, so that the expense of the sacrifice might not be wasted by those who offer it.

It is there at the ceremonies where he puts around his loins a bit of linen, tissue of the leaves of the tree *Bonde*. He covers his face with flour, paints his body with diverse colors that disfigure him horribly, and in that equipage, he offers the sacrifice of three victims for himself. These three victims are a cock, a serpent, and a dog. When these victims are killed and cut up into pieces, certain of the assistants skillfully take the head of the dog and hide it beneath the earth in some place a little removed. The *Ganga* himself then appears and asks who has taken the head of his dog? When no one responds to him, I see well, says he, what has been hidden, but I go to you to show that there is not a trifle that it is hidden to me. I will know well to find it. Follow me. He leaves; one follows him, and as he is agreed with his confidant concerning the place where he buried it, he goes there directly, he finds it, he brings it back with all the other pieces of Sacrifice, and all the assistants remain convinced of his knowledge, and of the commerce that he has with the spirits that have so fortuitously guided his steps and have led him to find that which from him was carried off. It is then proclaimed to all that he is the most able, and for good cause, the chief and master of all the *Ganga-Ya-Chibanda*. It is by these means, unmannerly persons that they are and all full of deceits, that these ministers establish their reputations and oblige the people to resort to them and purchase at high price the trinkets that they sell to them.

When the *Ganga-Ya-Chibanda* dies, it falls to the oldest of his sect to convene the assembly that celebrates their funerals. They never do it at night, and the place that is chosen for the grave is always in the thick of the forest. The *Ganga* carry the body there, with very indecent and very sordid ceremonies, which would make the pages blush, if one sullied oneself in writing them down. One learns of them through the Negroes of that area, who are converted and who have made known these mysteries of iniquity and of turpitude. The old *Ganga* scoops out an extremely deep grave, and before lowering the body there, he commands that the stomach be opened, that the heart and the other major parts be pulled out, and that the fingers of the hand and the feet be cut off him. He seizes for himself all the pieces, guards them as precious relics, and sells them in little particles, and very dearly, to all those who are eager to come to buy them for wearing on themselves, as sure preventives against all sorts of maladies and misfortunes. The possession of these noble relics place and install him in the position of the deceased: he is recognized as the *Ganga-Ya-Chibanda*, and in that capacity, he is respected and honored in all the world.

These *Ganga* are in a very high repute and win for themselves so much credit in the state that no general officer, whether governor of province or village, does not have one among them, without the council and approbation of which he does not propose to undertake anything or to perform a single act of Jurisdiction.

Note

1. Translated from the French version published by J. B. Labat in *Relation historique de l'Ethiopie Occidentale: Contenant la description des royaumes de Congo, Angolle, & Matamba, traduite de l'Italien du P. Cavazzi* . . . , vol. 2 (Paris: Charles-Jean-Baptiste Delespine, 1732), 195–99. Cavazzi was an Italian Missionary, who arrived in the Congo in 1654. His original report was published in 1687. In the 17th century, the "Giagues" (Jagas or Imbangala) were the dominant power in the Mbundu region of Angola.

Same-Sex Life among a
Few Negro Tribes of Angola (1923)

KURT FALK

Translated by Bradley Rose

. . . I have found homosexual intercourse from Orange [South Africa] northward up to the Congo. Natives have indicated to me that it is generally widespread among South African natives.[1]

When it comes to the same-sex life of the Wawihé,[2] dwellers of the high plateau of Benguella, one can clearly distinguish between same-sex life on a bisexual basis from that due to homosexuality. Homosexuals, called *omututa*, who actively or passively practice *podicatio* [anal intercourse] are sneered at and punished, so they hide themselves. *Okulinga omututa* is the verb form. On the other hand *digitatio*, that is, mutual masturbation, is widely practiced by heterosexuals as well as by homosexuals. The pertinent word is *okulikoweka* and designates male-male as well as female-female intercourse.

The most frequent same-sex technique, however, is that of *coitus inter femora* [intracrural intercourse]. The practice is called *otjizenja*; the verb is *okulinga otjizenja*. The same terms designate *coitus inter femora* practiced by the man on the woman. *Okulinga otjizenja* is performed lying breast to breast, either simultaneously or one after the other. *Okukoweka*, solitary masturbatory, is looked at extremely disdainfully. The sleeping together of two persons, regardless of sex, without sexual activity is described as *okuzukata*.

Same-sex activity is today practiced mostly by the younger generation: by boys from 7 until 18 years and by girls of the same age. However, adult

163

males also gratify themselves in these ways, either with boys or with peers, whenever they are separated for a long time from their wives, without being condemned because of it. But it is to be noted that while the act is permitted, speaking about it is considered disgusting.

If one asks a young boy if he practices same-sex intercourse, he denies it at first. If one says to a native that, after all, others have done it as well, the typical answer is, "Yes, the others do it, but not I." Only when one is more familiar with him does he admit that he has homosexual intercourse, naming also his *eponji*, or lover—this term probably serves to distinguish him from the *mukuetu*, the comrade or nonsexual friend.

Usually, both *aponji* (plural of *eponji*) remain together a long time, and jealously guard that neither commits "infidelities." If one asks a young boy which intercourse he prefers, that with a boyfriend or that with a girlfriend, the usual answer is, "Either is equally good and beautiful!"

But while here, same-sex activity, although practiced by all, takes place in secret (at night on a common sleeping mat or in the day in the deserted bush), the basic picture changes when one comes to the Gangellas [possibly the Ovagandjera, an Ambo group] in the area east of the Wawihé. *Katumua k'ame* means literally "my girl" but is also applied to the lover and is regarded as a public designation. The *eponji* of the Wawihé is called among the Ovigangellas *m'uzonj'ame* and has a similar meaning as *katumua*.

Katumua, like *m'uzonj'ame*, are usually acquired in the following manner. A young, unmarried, circumcised male, around 18 years old, sees a boy of about 12 years who pleases him. He goes to the father and asks if he could receive the boy for a *katumua*. In return for a present—a cow, a piece of cloth, or about 40.50$00 [*sic*]—the father agrees, and the boy draws his older friend into his hut. They are now recognized as being in that "relation." If the older one later marries, this changes nothing in his relation to his *katumua*; he merely sleeps alternately with his wife and his boyfriend, until finally the boyfriend, growing up, wants to marry. Then the older one brings the younger one back to his father and pays the agreed price. The younger now, for his part, takes a boyfriend, while the older looks for a new *katumua*. So it comes to be that almost every man without exception, whether single or married, has his lover.

Whereas *podicatio* is regarded disdainfully by the Wawihé, the *podicator* even being punished with beatings, here the *podicator*, called *m'ndumbi*, as well as *podication*, prompts only a slight smirk and is not at all punishable.

The term *otjizenja* (coitus inter femora), which is equivalent to *m'ahanda* among the Ovigangellas, is also applied to coitus inter femora by the man on the woman. The term *kuzunda* refers to a manner of mutual masturbation in which the glans are rubbed against each other. Solitary masturbation is so unfamiliar among them that not a single word exists for it; in any case, I can offer no example of one.

Whereas among the Wawihé mutual masturbation by the women is common—practiced with an artificial penis—it does not occur among the women of the Ovigangellas (?). The woman stricken by sexual desires looks for a certain tree in the bush, whose pulverized wood they spread in the vagina to suppress sexual attraction.

Undoubtedly, the spread of the M'gonge association, which only circumcised men can join, also serves to accommodate homosexual urges among the Ovigangellas. The M'gonge has significant social influence, possesses a secret language known only to the higher members, and has its own songs and dances. Its parties are celebrated at night in the middle of the forest by those who ought not to get drunk. The various pairs of lovers, aroused by the dance, then lie in the hut of the lover who is closest.

Whether homosexuality is practiced at the time of circumcision, for boys as well girls, is doubtful, at least nothing is indicated in the description of the circumcision rite.

In any case, however, it is quite clear that same-sex love and intercourse are an integral component of the sex life of both of the African tribes mentioned. Homosexuality or pseudo-homosexuality definitely belongs to the sex life of other tribes, as well.

Thus my boy, a Swahili who had been a soldier for a year in Loanda in the hinterlands and in the Cabinda enclave, told me the following: The Nginé [Nguni?], because of their sodomitical attacks upon their bed partners, are feared by the surrounding tribes. Consequently, Nginé who serve as soldiers are shunned by other soldiers, at night at least. My informant told me a revealing episode. A Nginé made a sexual attack on a fellow soldier, who was asleep. He fought back, making considerable noise, and complained to the on-duty white sergeant. The next morning, the wrongdoer was punished with a beating. To the complaint of the Sergeant as to why he didn't procure a woman, he replied: "Doesn't the Sergeant know that are there men who from youth on desire women, and others, who are attracted only to men? Why then should he be punished now? After all, he knows not why God created him like this—that he can only love men!"

The Colubengue or Cabiri [possibly the Kalukembe/Caluquembe, an Mbundu group] are also credited with engaging in overt same-sex intercourse. And therein may lie the problem's solution: when same-sex intercourse is customary among a tribe, or generally permissible, then that tribe is viewed by others as especially tainted with homosexuality, even though among those tribes that would condemn homosexual acts, they are practiced secretly to exactly the same extent.

Notes

1. Originally published as "Gleichgeschlechtliches Leben bei einigen Neg-erstämme Angolas," *Archiv für Anthropologie* n.s. 20 (1923): 42–45.

2. Possibly the Viye/Bie/Bihe, an Mbundu group, although Karsch-Haack discusses the "Wahehe" under the heading of Bantu-speaking North Kaffirs (that is, Xhosa) (1911): 137—B. Rose.

Part IV

Southern Africa

Overview

Most societies in southern Africa are based on a combination of cattle herding and the cultivation of grain crops. In southeast Africa, extensive population shifts have occurred over the past 1,500 years, as patrilineal Bantu pastoralists and farmers pushed southward from the Congo and East Africa. States such as that of the Bemba in Zambia and the Tswana of South Africa absorbed surrounding peoples. The matrilineal Central Bantu belt extends across the northern part of this region.

The Kalahari Desert

As early as 1719, Peter Kolb (1719: 362) mentioned Khoi-Khoin males, called *koetsire*, who were sexually receptive with other males. In the 1920s, Kurt Falk reported that homosexuality among Khoisan speakers was fairly common, especially among young married women. He described a practice among the Naman ("Hottentots") whereby two individuals, either of the same or of opposite sex, enter into a specially intimate bond of friendship called *soregus* (see the translation that follows and Karsch-Haack 1911: 132–33; Schapera 1930: 242–43; Schultze 1907: 319). As a rule, the relationship implies deep friendship and mutual assistance, especially in economic matters but, according to Falk, was also used as a means of establishing a homosexual relationship, especially by boys, who jealously watched over each other.

According to Falk, the usual homosexual practice for both men and women was mutual masturbation. Anal intercourse between men and the use of an artificial penis between women also occurred, but more rarely. Falk mentioned three cases known to him of men who were confirmed sexual "inverts." However, he reported no concrete data regarding the public attitude toward such men or toward homosexual relations in general. As far as can be gathered from his brief account, they were regarded as routine.

Among the Herero—semi-matrilineal Bantu agriculturalists and pastoralists—Falk noted that special friendships (*oupanga*) included anal sex (*okutunduka vanena*), as well as mutual masturbation (1925–26: 205–6). Some years earlier, the missionary Johann Irle, in denouncing Herero morality, cited Romans (1:18–31) (about men forsaking the natural use of women and burning with desire for each other) to indicate their sexual transgressions (1906: 58–59). When he challenged their sexual practices, the Herero blithely replied that they had grown from childhood in their own natural way.

Southeastern Africa

Monica Wilson's 1951 book, based on her fieldwork in the 1930s among the Bantu-speaking Nyakyusa, agriculturalists northwest of Lake Nyasa (in present-day Tanzania), is a fascinating description of a society in which age-grading is the central organizing principle. The inhabitants of each village contained only one generation of males, spanning five to eight years (1951: 32).[1] Of course, for unmarried male contemporaries to dwell together in temporary villages or in men's houses (especially during initiation) was common in "traditional" Africa. But as Wilson observed:

> The peculiarity of the Nyakyusa consists in the fact that contemporaries live together permanently through life, not merely as bachelors. . . . The Nyakyusa themselves associate living in age-villages with decency in sex life—the separation of the sex activities of successive generations, and the avoidance of incest. . . . The emphasis on the separation of parents and children is matched by the value laid on good fellowship (*ukwangala*) between contemporaries. . . . The value of good fellowship with equals is constantly talked about by the Nyakyusa, and it is dinned into boys from childhood that enjoyment and morality alike consist in eating and drinking, in talking and learning, in the company of contemporaries. (159, 162–63)

Despite this extreme gender segregation, an "exceptionally reliable informant" told Wilson that a man "never dreams of making love to another man" and that "not many cases of grown men having intercourse together come to light, but only of boys together or of a man and a boy."

When a boy sleeps with his friend they sleep together; it is not forbidden. Everyone thinks it all right. Sometimes when boys sleep together each may have an emission on the other (*bitundanila*). If they are great friends there is no wrong done. . . . Boys sometimes agree to dance together (*ukukina*) and work their evil together and that also is no wrong.[2] . . . Boys do this when they are out herding; then they begin to dance together and to have intercourse together. . . . To force a fellow thus this is witchcraft (*bo bulosi*); he is not a woman. But when they have agreed and dance together, then even if people find them, they say it is adolescence (*lukulilo*), all children are like that. And they say that sleeping together and dancing is also adolescence. (196)

According to this informant, interfemoral intercourse was "what boys mostly do," but anal and oral sex also occurred. He was aware of and disapproving of "some, during intercourse, work[ing] in the mouth of their friend, and hav[ing] an orgasm. . . . [Intercourse] of the mouth people do very rarely when they dance together" (Wilson 1951: 196).

Egalitarian/reciprocal sex between adolescent friends seems to have been most common, although some age-stratification also occurred: "When out herding, some of the older boys do evil with the young ones, the older persuade the little one to lie down with them and to do what is forbidden with them between the legs. Sometimes two older boys who are friends do it together, one gets on top of his fellow, then he gets off and the other one mounts" (Wilson 1951: 196–97). Two other informants agreed that homosexuality occurred frequently in boys' villages: "A boy has intercourse with his fellow, but a grown man? No, never, we've never heard of it. They always want women; only when a man cannot get a women he does this, only in youth. A few men do not marry but they are half-wits who have no kind of intercourse at all" (197). Wilson was also told that "to force a fellow to have homosexual intercourse against his will was a serious offence, comparable to witchcraft" (88, 196).

Wilson reported that "lesbian practices are said to exist, but we have no certain evidence of this" (1951: 88). She speculated that such relations were "much more likely to be among the older wives of chiefs and other polygynists than among the girls, who have so much attention from young men." This reflects her logic, however, not an actual report by the Nyakyusa. She also mentioned that "a case was also quoted of a doctor in Tukuyu who 'is a woman; she has borne children, now her body has grown the sexual organs of a man and her feelings have changed also; but she keeps it very secret, she is spoken of as a woman' " (197). Whether the new male organs were used sexually, and with whom, Wilson did not indicate.

In southern Zambia, along the border with Zimbabwe, live the Ila, an agricultural, matrilineal Bantu-speaking group. In the early 20th century, Edwin Smith and Andrew Dale observed an Ila-speaking man who dressed as a woman, did women's work, and lived and slept with, but did not have sex with, women (1920, 2:74). The Ila called such individuals, *mwaami*, translated as "prophet." They also claimed that "pederasty was not rare" but was considered dangerous because the boy might become pregnant (2:436).

In what is now southwestern Zimbabwe, David Livingstone speculated that the monopolization of women by elderly chiefs was responsible for the "immorality" of younger men (1865: 284).

The southernmost Bantu-speaking groups in Africa are patrilineal societies that combined sedentary agriculture and pastoralism and were organized into complex states. Among the Zulu, there appears to have been occasional substitution of boys for women in establishing the potency of men seeking recognition as adult warriors (E. Krige 1965: 276–77; Morris 1965: 36, 52).[3] Gender-crossing diviners also have been documented, although not all men-women engaged in spirit mediumship. According to Absolom Vilakazi, such males were called *inkosi ygbatfazi*, "chief of the women" (1962: 204).

Donald Morris has suggested (based on hearsay) that the great warrior Shaka, who forged a kingdom in southern Africa prior to European incursions, was homosexual (1965: 46). He had no wives, sired no children, and preferred the company of the uFasimba, a regiment of the youngest bachelors (Morris 1965: 36). His soldiers, he declared, "must not be enervated by matrimony and softened by family ties" until "the advance of years which, while unfitting him for soldiering, won him permission to marry" (Ferguson 1917: 206).[4]

The case of Shaka was not unique. In the 1890s, a time of violent dislocation of black South Africans, a Zulu man named Nongoloza Mathebula (who took the name Jan Note) became leader of a group of rebel bandits operating south of Johannesburg. Called "King of Nineveh" by the whites, he ordered his troops (mostly non-Zulus) to abstain from physical contact with females: "Instead, the older men of marriageable status within the regiment—the *ikhela*—were to take younger male initiates—the *abafana*—and keep them as *izinkotshane*, 'boy wives' " (van Onselen 1984: 15). In 1900, Nongoloza was captured, but his organization extended from townships to mining camps to prisons, in all of which the sex ratio was very skewed, and men were concerned about venereal disease among the few available women. Nongoloza testified that homosexuality among warriors (*hlabonga*) "has always existed. Even when we were free on the hills south of Johannesburg some of us had women and others had young men for sexual purposes" (Director of Prisons Report, quoted by Achmat 1993: 99). As South African activist Zackie Achmat argues in castigating social historians (van Onselen in particular) for eliding local understandings, "Nongoloza did not apologise for the fact that some of the Nineveites 'had young boys for sexual purposes.' He did not try to justify its existence by referring to venereal disease or tradition. Instead, he justified it in terms of sexual desire" (1993: 100).[5]

In modern Zimbabwe, the official history is that male homosexuality diffused from South Africa during the 1950s. Nonetheless, Marc Epprecht has found court cases involving homosexuality from the beginning of the colonial period. As he reports in his chapter in this book, the balance of black and white defendants was proportional to that of the population as a whole, although whites convicted of sodomy or indecent assault generally received more severe sentences. Of course, as Epprecht notes, what came to the attention of the courts was far from a random sample of sexual behavior in the colony: most consensual relations in private did not provoke the attention of colonial authorities.

"Wives of the Mines" in South Africa

Same-sex relations among peers and among men of different ages were common in many southern African societies. In 1883, the Basotho chief Moshesh testified that there were no punishments under customary law for "unnatural crimes" (which he also claimed were rare; Botha and Cameron 1997: 13). While the European colonialists ostensibly sought to repress and criminalize such relations, some of the conditions they introduced actually fostered them. This occurred among migratory workers in South Africa, especially miners. By the beginning of the 20th century, the English had become aware of widespread homosexuality in gender-segregated work settings. According to the 1907 H. M. Taberer report:

> It appears to have become a well-recognized custom among the mine natives recruited from the East Coast to select from the youths and younger men what are termed *amankotshane* or *izinkotshane*. An *inkotshane* may be described as a fag and is utilised for satisfying the passions. Any objections on the part

of the youth to becoming an *inkotshane* are apparently without
very much difficulty overcome by lavishing money and presents
upon him. . . . An *inkotshane*'s duty appears to be to fetch
water, cook food and do any odd work or run messages for his
master and at night time to be available as bedfellow. In return
for these services the *inkotshane* is well fed and paid; presents
and luxuries are lavished upon him. (p. 2, quoted in Moodie
et al. 1988: 234)

An old Mpondo added that *tinkonkana* "were boys who looked like women—
fat and attractive" (Moodie et al. 1988: 232).

In 1912, the Swiss Presbyterian missionary Henri Junod described
elaborately organized homosexual relationships among miners from the Tsonga
(Thonga) of southern Mozambique. The *nkhonsthana*, or "boy-wife,"[6] was
"used to satisfy the lust" of the *nima*, "husband."[7] He received a wedding
feast, and his elder brother received bride-price. Junod mentioned that some
of the "boys" were older than 20, and he described a dance in which the
nkhontshana donned wooden or cloth breasts, which they removed when
paid to do so by their *nima* ([1912] 1927: 492–93, 294).

An aged Tsonga named Philemon related to Mpande wa Sibuyi how
the "wives" of the mine (*tinkonkana*) were expected to perform domestic
chores for their "husbands": "Each of these *xibonda* [room representatives]
would propose a boy for himself, not only for the sake of washing his dishes,
because in the evening the boy would have to go and join the *xibonda* on
his bed. In that way he had become a wife. The husband . . . would make
love with him. The husband would penetrate his manhood between the
boy's thighs" (Sibuyi [1987] 1993: 53). Fidelity was expected, and jealousy
on occasion led to violence. Philemon was very explicit that "some men
enjoyed 'penetrating the thighs' more than they did the real thing [that is,
vaginas]" (54). Moreover, agency was not always a monopoly of the older
partner. Philemon mentioned the consequences of "when a boy decided to
fall in love with a man" (54) and related how male couples "would quarrel
just as husbands and wives do. Some quarrels would also lead to divorce"
(58). When Sibuyi asked Philemon whether the boy *wishes* to become
someone's wife, he replied, "Yes: for the sake of security, for the acquisition
of property and for the fun itself" (62). Grateful husbands bought presents
for their wives, including clothes, blankets, and bicycles.

The elderly Pondo miner Themba, whom Vivienne Ndatshe interviewed
in 1982, told her that "most of the miners agreed to be 'girls of the mines.'

Some wanted to pay *lobola* [bridewealth—for the boys] once they had returned to their homes," and he stressed the domestic duties of cooking, washing, and cleaning that went with the role. According to Themba, the boys would say, "Why should we worry since we can't get pregnant." Themba himself had evaded "a boss boy [who] was after him because he was young and fat." He also recalled "men dressed like women," most of whom were clerks, and how "miners proposed love to them" (Ndatshe [1982] 1993: 49, 51).

During the 1950s, in Mkhumbane, a black settlement adjacent to Durban, male-male weddings occurred at the rate of about one a month. According to Ronald Louw (1996), each celebration lasted a whole weekend. Some "brides" wore Zulu dress; some wore Western bridal white and had bridesmaids in attendance. The pair might live together, with the "wife" doing domestic work, or live separately (as did many male-female couples). Some of the men involved in these relationships already had female wives, who treated the new bride as an ideal junior wife—one who would not produce children that might rival her own. Louw suggested that the term for the female-gendered homosexual men *skesana* might be a cognate to *zenana*—a Hindu term for cross-dressing male prostitutes.[8] Their masculine partners were called *iqgenge*.

In the Bantu-speaking groups of South Africa, intracrural intercourse "is typical of a form of sexual play among adolescent Nguni [Ngoni] boys and girls called *metsha* among Xhosa-speakers and *hlobongo* by the Zulu. These young 'boys' of the miners are not merely sexual partners, but are also 'wives' in other ways, providing domestic services for their 'husbands' in exchange for substantial remuneration." According to Dunbar Moodie, homosexual dyads occurred "almost exclusively between senior men (men with power in the mine structure) and young boys. There is in fact an entire set of rules, an *mteto*, governing these types of relationships, whose parameters are well-known and enforced by black mine authorities" (1988: 231).

As Philemon explained, proper "wifely" behavior did not include ejaculation by the youth or any kind of sexual reciprocity:

> The boys would never make the mistake of "breathing out" [ejaculating] into the hubby. It was taboo. Only the hubby could "breathe out" into the boy's legs. . . . [Another] thing that a *nkonkana* had to do was either to cover his beard with cloth, or cut it completely off. He was now so-and-so's wife. How would it sound if a couple looked identical? There had to be differences, and for a *nkonkana* to stay clean-shaven was

one of them. Once the nkonkana became a "grown-up," he
could then keep his beard to indicate his maturity, which would
be demonstrated by him acquiring a boy. . . . When the boy
thought he was old enough he would tell the husband that he
also wished to get himself a wife, and that would be the end.
Therefore the husband would have to get himself another boy.
(Sibuyi [1987] 1993: 58, 57, 55)

Sources do not discuss (because observers apparently did not ask) whether
the same asymmetry of roles occurred among boys involved in sex play with
each other in the home villages, or whether certain individuals specialized
in sexual receptivity and were regarded as effeminate.

Despite the terminology, cross-dressing does not appear to have been a
requisite of the wife role. As in ancient Greece, however, appearance of leg
and facial hair indicated that a boy had become a man and was no longer
an appropriate sex object for other men but was now a competitor for boys.

Junod vacillated between attributing homosexuality among Tsonga
laborers to the unavailability of women or to a preexisting, indigenous
homosexual preference ([1912] 1927: 492–93, 294). Moodie interpreted
the institution partly as a resistance to proletarianization—one young man
in 1940 consented to be a *tinkonkana* because he wanted to accumulate
money to meet traditional bride-price requirements back home. Thus, in
some cases "men became 'wives' in the mines in order to become husbands
and therefore full 'men' more rapidly at home" (Moodie et al. 1988: 240).
Those playing the wife role could accumulate money (bridewealth and gifts),
while the husbands not only received domestic and sexual service but also
spent less than they would have in dance halls with women prostitutes:
"Although these relationships for the Mpondo seldom extended beyond
one contract and were never brought home, and although men preferred
to conceal these liaisons from their home fellows, everyone knew that such
affairs existed and joked with each other about them. . . . According to
Philemon, among the Tsonga 'mine marriages' were accepted, indeed taken
for granted by women (including wives) and elders at home, and relationships might extend beyond a single [work] contract" (233). Thus, according
to Philemon, when one partner finished his contract before the other, the
husband might go to their boy-wives' homes or boy-wives might go to their
husband's homes. They would be "warmly welcomed," everyone knowing
"that once a man was on the mines, he had a boy or was turned into a
wife himself" (Sibuyi [1987] 1993: 56, 57).

Neither Moodie nor Charles van Onselen (1976) appears to have considered that some of the older men who continued to return to the mines
may have preferred young male "wives."[9] Preoccupied with the economic
aspects of these relationships, most observers have been unwilling to take
seriously statements such as, "We loved them better [than our girlfriends]"
(Moodie et al. 1989: 410). Similarly, although the "wife of the miner" role
developed under conditions of migration to capitalist enterprises owned and
operated by white Europeans, there is no evidence of such relationships being
imposed or suggested by white Europeans.[10] (Although some, attempting
to claim local purity, have contended that homosexuality was introduced
by "foreign" Shangaan workers from Mozambique, who were reputed to be
the most frequent and enthusiastic participants in *bukhontxana* [*inkoshana*]
[Harries 1990: 327].)[11] As an adaptation to the conditions of prolonged
sex segregation, these practices drew on conceptions of what a Tsonga wife
should be and on sexual acts (intracrural intercourse) within the repertoire
of rural adolescents. The available sources do not discuss whether the same
asymmetry of roles occurred among boys involved in sex play with each
other in the home villages or whether certain individuals specialized in
sexual receptivity and were regarded as effeminate.

In recent years, migrant labor has become less common, and the "wife
of the mine" role has declined, if not disappeared. With the breakdown of
rural society, wives accompany or follow their husbands and live as squat-
ters near the work sites. Moodie concluded, "It is precisely because mine
marriages were isomorphic with marriages at home that they are breaking
down as the home system collapses. . . . The old arrangements represented
accommodations to migration and at the same time resistance to prole-
tarianisation. . . . The contemporary turn to 'town women' and squatter
families represents accommodation to the exigencies of stable wage-earning"
(1988: 255).

Woman-Woman Patterns

Unfortunately, Dudley Kidd was not specific about the "indecencies,"
"degradations," and "obscenities" involved in Southern Bantu female initiations, which, he claimed, demoralized their womanhood forever (1904:
209).[12] Falk, however, reported that same-sex relations were common among
Hottenot (Nama) young married women (1925–26: 209–10). To the east,
Tswana women formed homosexual relationships while their husbands were

away working in mines. According to Isaac Schapera, "Lesbian practices are apparently fairly common among the older girls and young women, without being regarded in any way reprehensible" (1938: 278). Elizabeth Colson (1958: 139–40) mentioned a possible "man-woman" and a possible "woman-man" among the Tsonga of what is now Zimbabwe.

Judith Gay has offered a more detailed account of institutionalized friendships among the women in Lesotho, who remain in their villages while men migrate to South Africa to work. According to Gay, "Young girls in the modern schools develop close relationships, called 'mummy-baby' with slightly older girls. Sexual intimacy is an important part of these relationships. Mummy-baby relationships not only provide emotional support prior to marriage, but also a network of support for married and unmarried women in new towns or schools, either replacing or accompanying heterosexual bonds" (1985: 97). These relationships "are always initiated voluntarily by one girl who takes a liking to another and simply asks her to be her mummy or her baby, depending on their relative age" (102). Gay adds, "The most frequently given reason for initiating a particular relationship was that one girl felt attracted to the other by her looks, her clothes, or her actions." A "mummy" might have more than one "baby," but according to Gay, the "baby" can only have one "mummy"—although one woman might be both a "baby" and a "mummy" in simultaneous relationships (108). All three of Gay's cases, however, involved, over time, more than one "mummy." When the women marry, their same-sex relationships are "transformed, but do not cease altogether" (110).

Gay argues that the use of English-language terms ("mummy" and "baby") indicates that such relationships developed since the 1950s (1985: 100). (She does not, however, consider the possibility that while the terms may be recent, the practices might be traditional.) In fact, the patrilineal, patrilocal Lovedu of Lesotho were unusual in being ruled by queens who had wives, indeed, a harem (see Krige and Krige 1947: 165–75). These queens were assisted in their role by "the mothers of the kingdom." The prestige of the 19th-century queen Mujaji I seems to have legitimated queens in the neighboring Bantu groups of Khaha, Mamaila, Letswalo (Narene), and Mahlo (Krige and Krige 1947: 310–11; Krige 1938).

Gay interprets mummy-baby relations alternately as preparations for "the dynamics of heterosexual relations"—even "explicit opportunities for initiation into heterosexual relations"—and as substitutes for relations in the absence of men who are working in South African mines (1985: 109). Marriage resistance may be another motive: Gay contrasts the autonomy of "mummies" with the constraints on Sesotho wives (107, 109, 110).

Although traditional Sesotho initiation for girls is no longer practiced in lowland villages, where more than half the nation's population lives, girls continue to lengthen their own or each other's labia minora in the belief that it will later enhance sexual pleasure (Gay 1985: 99). The procedure is done alone or in small groups. Gay states that "the process is said to heighten *mocheso* (heat) and appears to provide opportunities for auto-eroticism and mutual stimulation between girls" (101). These contacts are not regarded as emotionally significant, "whereas falling in love with a girl and simply caressing her is" (112).

In the 1970s, Martha Mueller described similar relationships in two Lesotho villages (1977), and some years earlier John Blacking reported fictive kinship relationships among Venda and Zulu schoolgirls (1959, 1978). All of this is strong evidence that "age-stratified" is a pattern of female as well as male homosexuality. Age differences need not be great, however. In the 11 instances in which Gay specified the age of both, the mean difference was 4.8 years and the median difference was 5. (The range was from 1 to 12.) Those playing the "baby" role ranged in age from 8 to 24, and "mummies" from 15 to 35 (1985: 114–15).

According to Deborah Green, an African American medical student who formed a relationship with a white woman in the Shangaan homeland town of Gazankulu in the northern Transvaal, "There are some stories from Venda (a nearby tribe) about lesbian-type people—I mean, women that lived together and raised families together. But the Shangaan had no concept of a lesbian relationship, no preconception about it. They just know that I came along and started living with Tessa, and then Tessa was much happier. So they thought it was a good thing" (Hartman 1992: 16).

In some accounts of traditional society, same-sex sexuality has been associated with spirituality. "Forms of overt homosexual behavior between women are described by female *isanuses* [chief diviners]." Moreover, homosexuality is widely ascribed to women who are in the process of becoming *isanuses* (Laubscher 1937: 31). Use of artificial penises has been reported among Ila and Naman women of South Africa (Schapera 1930: 243; Smith and Dale 1920: 181).

Notes

1. The discussion of the Nyakyusa here, in the context of the region of southern Africa, is arbitrary as Tanzania is generally considered part of the eastern African culture zone. There are, nonetheless, some affinities between Tanzanian cul-

tures and those of southern Africa, including Bantu languages, the cattle complex, and historical migration.

2. If correctly transcribed, one has to wonder what was translated as "working evil."

3. Yrjö Hirn (1900: 247–48) interpreted Gustav Fritsch (1872: 140) as describing pederastic male initiation rites.

4. On the other hand, the journalist John Gunther contrasted "tribes like the Zulus [who are] sternly upright and moral for the most part and tribes greatly addicted to homosexuality, like the Pondos [Mpondo]" (1955: 523)—whatever *addicted* may mean.

5. As a political prisoner in 1978, Achmat personally experienced such allocation of young prisoners for sex to Ninevite leaders, who then undertook their protection.

6. Junod glossed the term as "girlfriend" (1927: 492). It "apparently corresponds to the Xhosa *intombi*, which is used for the junior partner in love affairs, whether biologically female, at home or in town, or male, on the mines" (Moodie et al. 1988: 237).

7. *Nkhonsthana* is etymologically distinct from *nsati* (wife) although this latter term is also sometimes used for the boy-wife.

8. See Nauman Naqvi and Hasan Mujtaba (1996). The Durban area had many South Asians. However, the term probably derives from the earlier-attested Tsonga term *nkhonsthana*; the role-complement term *iqgenge* might also be related to the earlier-attested *ikhela*.

9. Mark Gevisser summarized South African critiques of Moodie's assumptions: that men's motivations for remaining in the mines were exclusively economic, that husbands found boy-wives an inferior substitute for "the real thing," and that the normative restriction of sex practices to intercrural intercourse was always observed (1995: 71–72). Junod (1927) at least considered black agency as a part of the phenomenon (on Junod, see Harries 1990, 1993; Achmat 1993).

10. Adolf Bastian provided some basis for suspecting that before the mines developed, at least among the "Basuto" (Lesotho), there were men who did women's work and adopted all-female manners and expressions (1872: 173 n. 1).

11. Shangaans lived in the Transvaal as well as in the then-Portuguese colony of Mozambique. And in the mine compounds, "Each tribe lives separately to others, and so compounds housed only Pondos, Xhosas, etc. People only mixed at work," although "boss boys" had greater mobility, according to the Pondo former "boss boy" Daniel interviewed in 1982 (published in Ndatshe and Mpande 1993: 46). In 1916, a compound manager, while assuring the Transvaal Native Affairs Department that intracrural intercourse (he used the Zulu term *hlbongo*) was more common than sodomy, also reported that heavily perfumed young Mozambicans attended dances wearing imitation breasts and had noticeably greased crotches (cited by Moodie et al. 1988: 231).

12. "The customs observed when girls enter the period of womanhood vary very much in detail in different tribes; yet in practice the various tribes seem to vie with one another in the matter of obscenity. As Theal has pointed out, the very last traces of decency are stamped from a girl's mind by the customs she has to go through, and her womanhood is demoralised for ever. In Pondoland the natives seem to have sunk to the lowest possible depths of degradation in these matters, and I have heard Natal Kafirs, who were traveling through that country, express utter astonishment that such practices should be tolerated" (Kidd 1904: 209; he was similarly horrified but vague about male initiation in the preceding two pages).

Homosexuality among the Natives of Southwest Africa (1925–1926)

KURT FALK

Translated by Bradley Rose and Will Roscoe

For a better understanding of the following remarks, I would like to note that I include under "homosexuality" same-sex life [*gleichgeschlechtliche Leben*], the same-sex activity of bisexuals, and pseudo-homosexuals, but under "homoerotic," I include same-sex life with respect to the same-sex activity of genuine, innate homosexuals [*richtigen, geborenen Homosexuellen*].[1]

The native tribes of the former beautiful colony of German Southwest Africa, which was taken from us by the enemy, are the following (going north to south): the Ovambos; the Ovahimbas [Ovashimbas] to the west of them; and to the east and somewhat south of the Ovambos, various Bushmen tribes. Adjacent to the middle of the country come the formerly very powerful, cattle-rich people of the Ovahereros, Hereros for short. From the prefix *ova-*, one can already recognize the connection of the Ovambos, the Ovahimbas, and the Ovahereros, who are all counted among the Bantus, a language that has one common structure. Then follow, taking in the whole south, the interesting and wholly isolated people of the Hottentots [a derogatory name for Khoisan-speakers who had adopted herding] , . . . Situated among the Hottentots are various Bushmen bands.

In considering homosexuality in these various tribes, we will begin with the Ovambos and move from north to south.

The homosexuality of the Ovambos, one of the most exceptionally powerful Bantu tribes, is, one might almost say, proverbial in this country.

183

This is due to the unfortunate sexual relations at the diamond fields at
Lüderitzbucht, where the Ovambos compose the chief contingent of workers.
However, even in the Ovambo areas that are closed to whites, homosexual
intercourse occurs.

And indeed there are *ovashengi* (sing.: *eshengi*), effeminate men who
submit to passive *coitus in anum* for income. They are usually fat, large persons who go about in female clothing and are employed mainly in women's
work. They bedeck themselves with female jewelry and try to arouse the
attention of men through flirting. Since among some tribes there, the young
maidens enjoy no freedom at all, the *ovashengi* are in great demand by the
young, unmarried men. These passive effeminates always stay within their
tribal boundaries and never go out for employment.

If one sees a train of Ovambos, who have been enlisted by the Ovambo
recruiters, headed for the first, northernmost station in order to go from there
by railway to Lüderitzbucht, one frequently notices among them small lads
of 10 to 12 years who, being too young for work, were not tolerated at all
by the police. Should one then ask the Ovambos where these young fellows
are being taken, one usually gets the answer that they are going along as
"kitchen boys," as helpers with the cooking, to be used to fetch wood and
water, and for similar work. But this answer is only half of it; for although
these boys do perform these duties, the real reason for their accompanying
the grown-ups is essentially something else. That is, they serve the others
as passive pederasts on the journey and during the term of service at the
[mine]fields. Indeed—and this is the remarkable thing about it—these boys
are given to the young men usually by their wives or betrothed "to keep
the men faithful," as was explained to me by an old Ovambo, to whom I
am much indebted for this information.

Obviously, we are dealing here primarily with pseudo-homosexuality,
which is clear from the fact that these same men, who make use of those
boys while in the fields, are in part already married or betrothed, and truly
of heterosexual natures. Naturally, single ones are found among them who
are actual homosexuals.

Whereas in the case of these boys we are dealing with, so to speak,
forced passive pederasts, the above-mentioned *ovashengi*, are born homosexuals. And, indeed, as the virile homosexuals attract little attention, it is
especially the highly effeminate men who voluntarily place themselves in
the role of the *ovashengi*.

The type of intercourse engaged in by pseudo-homosexuals among
the Ovambos is *podicatio* [anal intercourse], while true homoerotics, it was

confessed to me, use mutual masturbation. Probably it is constrained this way everywhere: a small portion of innate homosexuals (homoerotics [*Homoeroten*]) and the large majority of pseudo-homosexuals employ *podicatio*, while the remaining portion of homoerotics choose *digitatio*.

As the Ovambos very much indulge in same-sex intercourse at the [mine]fields, a mine physician told me that an Ovambo once came to him with a totally ripped, bleeding anus. He had in one night consorted with no fewer, I declare, than 45 men. But it had suited his taste, since, as he told the inquiring doctor, he had demanded and received from each man not less than £1 (then equal to 20 Mk). In that night, he thus earned approximately 900 Mk. The fact that, incidentally, not only the Ovambos but also the other coloreds (and, it is rumored, the whites as well) surrender themselves to these passive pederasts should be obvious, given the lack of women in that place. Thus, there should also be many Cape-boys engaged in passive pederasty, according to the head visitor of the Ovambos. However, in Ovamboland and in the rest of the Southwest, the Ovambos indulge the most in same-sex intercourse, which is can be explained in terms of habitual tribal custom. One could claim quietly that nearly every Ovambo has consorted with the same sex and, therefore, has engaged in homosexual intercourse.

However, not every Ovambo chief will permit the above-mentioned *ovashengi* in his region. Thus, the Ovambo chief Epumbo will shoot down by his own hand with his Browning every *eshengi* that he meets in his tribe.

Although among the Ovambos 2 percent innate homosexuals are found, I encountered among the many Ovambos with whom I made contact during my 10-year stay in the Southwest only three true homosexuals. Unfortunately, I failed to inquire into the corresponding expressions in the Ovambo language, because I conversed with them nearly always in the Herero language, which nearly all Ovambos master. I will mention the words concerned when discussing the Hereros.

We turn now to the western neighbors of the Ovambos, the Ovahimbas, who are also called Ovashimbas. I must note, however, that different ethnologists do not view this tribe as separate, but rather, they look at them only as impoverished and detached Hereros—although they speak another dialect—and not the pure Herero.

Among them, I found a true invert, who was active as a wizard and medicine man. Moreover, the single wizard that I met among them was simultaneously inverted. He, who seems a somewhat effeminate and cunning old man, had confessed same-sex inclinations to the whole tribe and the neighboring natives. When I asked him if he was married, he winked at me slyly, and the other natives laughed heartily and subsequently declared to me that he does not love women, but only men. He nonetheless enjoyed no low status in his tribe. Thus, I found here, confirmed for the first time, Edward Carpenter's theory that homosexuality often coincides with priest-craft and wizardry.[2]

That exhausts all that I could find out about homosexuality among the tribe of the Ovashimbas.

East and south from the Ovambos live, as mentioned above, various Bushmen tribes. Small and slight, with their more or less yellow color, they stand out very much from the large, sturdy, dark-brown Ovambos. Among them there are said to be, according to a declaration of police officials who were active for years in the Bushman region and knew the Bushmen well, quite a few inverts.

I have encountered only a few true homoerotics. However, most of the Bushmen who I questioned about this matter admitted to me after a little hesitancy, then willingly, that in the absence of women, they gratified themselves with each other mutually. Solitary onanism is also practiced by many of them, which is notable because this kind of gratification is looked down on by the other native tribes of the Southwest. However, podication also occurs among the Bushmen, although likewise only *faute de mieux* [for want of something better]. Digitation, however, in contrast to the prevalent podication of the Ovambos, prevails among these little yellow people.

Whereas I could find out nothing about *tribadie* [lesbianism] among the Ovambos and Ovashimbas, I heard here that the married Bushmen women are said to be very devoted to it. In fact, it is practiced by mutual *digiti*, or with an artificial penis. Innate homoeroticism among the Bushmen I cannot recall.

South of Ovamboland, reaching up to the middle of the country, extends Damaraland, which was formerly occupied by the Ovahereros alone. Its southern border could be described by a line from Swakopmund to Wind-huk and more easterly. The Hereros, to describe briefly, clearly distinguish between nonerotic and sexual friendship. Whereas the nonerotic friend, the comrade, is called *omukuetu*, "lover" is *epanga*, and the erotic friendship is *oupanga*.[3] This term applies to a female friend as well as a male friend, that is, to the homosexuality of men as well as the *tribadie* of women. Therefore, Professor Dr. G. Fritsch is mistaken when he specifies the words for tribadic intercourse among the Hottentot women [in Karsch-Haack (1911) 1975: 472]. The terms he reports are, as related above, Otjiherero, and not from the Namaqua language. The Hottentot women naturally would make use of their mother tongue, that is, Namaqua. In sum, the position that Fritsch states refers to a well-known myth of the Hereros and not the Namans.

The Hereros did not formerly have a punishment for homosexuality. Doubtless, if caught by surprise, they would be subject to the ridicule and laughter of others. Moreover, it mainly seems to have involved the podication of boys, as the expression used for it suggests, *okutunduka vanena*, which literally means "mounts boys." *Okutunduka* is otherwise used only in reference to the mounting of bulls, while other verbs for sexual intercourse by men are available.

In general, two boys ordinarily form an *oupanga*, which is strictly and jealously guarded on both sides so that neither engages in any escapades. If the young lads subsequently marry, which seems to occur at quite an early age, they turn naturally to heterosexual intercourse; this can also occur after puberty and before marriage, which often coincides with their circumcision (if the boy had not already been circumcised at birth, which was often the case). Anyway, uncircumcised boys in general have little success with girls. In the meantime, whenever adult and married men go on "Pad," that is, make a long tour with the ox-wagon on which they cannot take their women, they provide for it instead by going preferably with their former *epanga*, or they bring a friendly contemporary with whom they have sexual intercourse on the way. They primarily practice mutual masturbation.

In fact, if one asks about sexual intercourse among contemporaries, adult Hereros naturally deny it and reply that only boys did this, that this was only child's play, but as adults they no longer did it. However, if one more closely befriends an Herero and speaks his language, he will admit that this was a well-known thing among them, practiced by every adult man in the absence of women, without it being given any importance. (Presently, because of the spread of Christianity, many Hereros no longer allow themselves to be circumcised; also, heterosexual intercourse by the young boys naturally no longer closely follows their circumcision.)

Mention must be made of the rules of decorum that ban speaking about sexual doings, particularly if a member of another generation is present: "The act is allowed but speaking about it forbidden." And when, in the evening perhaps, two young boys leave the collective circle around the fire, supposedly to lock up a calf that is not yet in the corral, quick grins might fly across the faces of those remaining behind, but it will occur to no one to follow or watch them. That would contravene all norms of decorum. And if one encounters two such young chaps in the bush, one looks away and sees nothing.

Because the Herero is free to gratify his desire, the question of "how" [they do it] is unimportant; only the question "if at all" is of concern. So even the adult Hereros see nothing in pseudo-homosexual activity, so long as it does not occur too publicly.

To exactly the same extent that homosexual activity occurs among the men, *tribadie* is common among the Herero women. In fact, exactly the same expressions apply to it—*epanga, omukuetu, oupanga*—as to male homosexual intercourse. The mode of intercourse the women engage in is either *fricatrices*, or they use mutual manual manipulations or an artificial penis. This latter is made from the root of a certain tree. Only an elderly man no longer sexually active himself is allowed to carve this penis. It is kept concealed from the fearful eyes of the men, so that, despite promises of high payment, I was not able to catch a glimpse of an artificial penis that I knew was present in our shipyard.

One might guess that the tribades were old women, no longer visited by men, or women without husbands, but almost the opposite is the case: only the newly married, younger wives, who could not complain over the lack of heterosexual intercourse, practice same-sex intercourse with each other almost insatiably.

Among the many Hereros that I became acquainted with during 10 years in the Southwest, I encountered only three or four homoerotics. I became acquainted with not a single inborn tribades, which is even more surprising, since there are unmarried women among the Hereros.

The terms are as follows: "to commit solitary onanism," *okurikuatisa* ("they beget themselves; they produce offspring themselves"); *okuripikapikisa* and *okutirahi*, "to commit mutual onanism;" *okutjanda omuzu, okukara omuzu, okurareka 'mukuao* ("sleeps together with another"). These terms apply equally to female-female as well as male-male intercourse.

Among the Hottentots, homosexuality, like homoeroticism, also occurs widely. Consequently, I cannot share the opinion of Fritsch when he writes, "About pederasty among South African natives I have altogether nothing in experience to bring and am convinced that, at that time at least, it was hardly to be found. I therefore view aversion to perversity as corresponding to the natural state" [in Karsch-Haack (1911) 1975: 133]. To the contrary, I have found precisely this perversity among the Hereros. Also, I believe that this perversion is no rarer among the yellow than among the black. Similarly, as with the Hereros, two boys here often unite themselves and watch each other jealously. If one grown-up Hottentot wants to invite another for same-sex intercourse, he does so by serving the "Sore-drink," which is also mentioned in Karsch-Haack [(1911) 1975: 132–33]. If a Hottentot wants another to enter into homosexual relations, he gives him a cup, filled with coffee or, in an emergency, water, while simultaneously saying: *Sore-gamsa are!* (Drink yet the Sore-water) or *Sore-gamsa ure!* (Take yet the Sore-water!). If willing to engage in the intended intercourse, the other takes it, in case of refusal, they do not. Ordinarily, from this Sore affair, an intimate, dear friendship then develops within which an extensive comradeship prevails.

Ordinarily, mutual onanism is practiced; rarely, on the other hand, actual podication. If, therefore, a Hottentot is offered the Sore-water, it is assumed that mutual onanism is meant. If one invites a Hottentot to homosexual intercourse, he will likely refuse it at first because he thinks specifically of podication. When one clarifies that only mutual onanism is meant, he nearly always willingly consents with the words: "Yes we natives know that as well—we all do it!"

I have encountered among the Hottentots three innate homoerotics, of whom one, by a twist of fate, was a police servant, who would be punished immediately by the German court if he confessed his sexual relations. On the other hand, among the natives, it was generally acknowledged that this very police servant, Fritz, never consorted with women but had a young Hottentot with whom he shared house, food, and camp.

Just as among Herero wives, tribadie is committed in licentious dimensions by Hottentot women, specifically by newly married wives. The typical practice is the same as that of the Herero women.

Only the Klippkaffirs, Kaffirs for short, remain to be discussed. (Concerning mixed-bloods residing in the Southwest, I will say nothing, since I know nothing about their sex life.)

But first a short ethnological aside is in order. The barely studied Kaffirs [members of a southern Nguni (Ngoni) group also called Xhosa] were probably the original people of the Southwest. They have completely forgotten their own language and accepted the language of the conquering Hottentot. That Namaqua, the language of the Hottentots, is not their mother tongue is apparent from the fact that Kaffirs fail to correctly speak Namaqua, making crude blunders in it that a Hottentot would never commit [. . . .] In taking over the language of their conquerors, the Kaffir also adopted their manners. Consequently, the same-sex life of the Kaffirs is organized according to the same customs and figures of speech current among the Hottentots, which we have already met, such as the Sore-drinking. They also employ the same words for homosexual intercourse. They are as follows: "to commit solitary onanism" is called *gûi-gûisen* ("makes himself stiff") and "to commit *tsora*-mutual masturbation" [i.e., within a Sore relationship] is called *ôa-/huru*, or also simply */huru*; and "to commit tribadie" is */goe-ugu*.

We find with the Kaffir, as already mentioned, exactly the same manners respecting tribadie as with the Hottentots, except that because of the extremely low morals among them, homosexuality is also widely practiced, as with the remaining tribes of the country. Even homosexual incest (as well as heterosexual incest) is not rare among the Kaffirs, in that not only brothers (which one finds in other tribes) but even father and son, and mother and daughter, gratify themselves homosexually—a fact that one encounters with no other tribe and evokes the utmost abhorrence.

As far as I can remember, I have encountered three homoerotic Klippkaffirs, paired off among them, who for years had a relationship and, as man and wife, lived together and only accepted work together. How low and lax the morals of the Kaffirs are one can see from the following incident, of which I was an eyewitness: Between two adult Kaffir women sat a boy approximately seven years old crying pitifully. To soothe him, a woman picked him up and masturbated him, indifferent to our presence— we being two Europeans and three natives. This certainly evoked the most active indignation by our natives.

So we have spoken of all the native tribes of the Southwest and found that active, same-sex intercourse is engaged in by all [. . . .] Thus, the fear [expressed in some German publications] that "the morality of the natives thereby is done harm" [by contact with white homosexuals] is baseless. It would be more correct to say that the harm is to the whites by their proximity to the natives. But then, sexual intercourse between whites and coloreds is completely prohibited and untolerated and, indeed, is penalized [. . . .] In any case, given the present circumstances, this fear is unsubstantiated, because to the natives, having sex is as normal as eating and drinking and, by all means, tobacco smoking. They understand it as something wholly natural, that whites also require and seek. And so, they see nothing special in same-sex intercourse, provided only it is kept secret. As long as this happens, all is in order. Because they view homosexual intercourse with unbiased eyes and find nothing monstrous there, they have known and practiced it the same way from time immemorial. In this sense, the native judges more naturally than most whites, who, because of their ignorance based in old superstitions, are embarrassed.

Every alert observer to come upon the sex life of the natives, as evident from the articles at issue, as well as from my essay appearing in *Archiv für Anthropologie* [Falk 1923, reprinted in part III of this book], concludes that bisexuality, or anyway the ability to be able to consort sexually with both sexes, is substantially widespread, as with the white races. Or might this ability have been originally present and repressed only by convention, morality, and up-to-date or customary viewpoints? One sees the same picture among those people for whom same-sex traffic is (or was) allowed or even a national custom. Quoting examples of it, in my opinion, is unnecessary. Anyway, I am very inclined to assume, based on my experiences, which arise from a 12-year residence as a sexologist among the natives, that the percentage of bisexuals is far higher than Hirschfeld was able to conclude from his research. My opinion is that the percentage among the natives able to consort with both sexes and (according to the evidence of many natives questioned about it) who feel the same desire with both is around 90 percent. On the other hand, however, 2 percent homoerotics seems to me somewhat too low, while 23 percent, as Dr. v. Römer in his essay, "Nogmalls het derde geslacht," states, is too high. Based on my experience with the natives, I accept 3.5 percent.

Everyone who has worked as a sexologist among natives must instinctively shake his head when certain representatives and supporters of the ominous paragraph 175 want to deny the inborn nature of the homoerotic, especially seeing what Ferdinand Karsch-Haack has shown through his great compilation, *Das gleichgeschlechtliche Leben der Naturvölker*—that in the absence of repressive laws, homoeroticism manifests very strongly in certain individuals, while the rest are in no way seduced to homoeroticism, but always, as soon as they are allowed, go back to women, seeking homosexuality only *faute de mieux*. Anyone denying innate homosexuality should without prejudice make inquiries hereabout with the natives, and he soon will have another opinion.

Notes

1. Originally published as "Homosexualität bei den Eingeborenen in Südwest-Afrika," *Archiv für Menschenkunde* 1 (1925–26): 202–14—B. Rose and W. Roscoe

2. See Edward Carpenter 1914—B. Rose and W. Roscoe

3. Cf. the terms *mukueta* and *aponji*, which Falk reports for the Wawihé in his 1921 article reprinted in part III of this book—B. Rose and W. Roscoe

"Good God Almighty, What's This!"

Homosexual "Crime" in Early Colonial Zimbabwe

MARC EPPRECHT

Missionaries, anthropologists, native commissioners, novelists, and psychologists throughout southern Africa observed and described homosexual relationships, rituals, and other "queer" behavior among African men many decades ago.[1] In some cases, such relationships and behaviors were recognized as eccentricities that predated colonialism. In most cases, however, African homosexual behavior was linked to the specific conditions created by colonial rule and racial capitalism. In the mining compounds that arose in South Africa's industrial centers in the late 19th century, homosexual "mine marriages" came to be regarded as common. Prisons and mission schools were also reputed to have given rise to expressions of sexuality that had customarily been rare or unknown. Some "tribes" purportedly even became "addicted" to "unnatural vice" in these circumstances, notably the Shangaans and Pondos (Gunther 1955: 513).[2] These men were regarded as spreading the contagion to other peoples—and indeed many regional languages now contain borrowed words that denote "copulation between male persons." Local idioms also reflect the changing nature of masculine sexuality over the course of the colonial era.[3] The original mining boomtown and center of migrant labor in the region (Kimberly), for example, is still recalled in Basotho oral tradition as "Sotoma" (Sodom) (Coplan 1994: 68).[4]

All of this is entirely in keeping with recent research from elsewhere in the world that shows human sexuality is far more historical (that is, socially constructed and contingent) than formerly imagined.[5] Yet until very recently, historians in southern Africa have been slow to grasp the implications of such research. Indeed, they have been tacitly and, in some cases, actively complicit in denying the existence of homosexuality among "real" Africans (those not corrupted by decadent Western culture). For example, a recent history dissertation asserts flatly that male homosexuality was "an impossibility for most if not all Basotho migrants (Maloka 1995: 306). John Caldwell and colleagues' (1989) sweeping overview of African sexuality is similarly striking in its refusal to acknowledge even the possibility of homosexual or bisexual relationships. A recent review of two books that give prominent attention to the phenomenon of "mine marriages" in South Africa simply does not mention the dread concept (Phimister 1996).[6]

Zimbabwe is no exception to this type of discursive denial or blindness—the topic of male homosexual behavior was not broached in a scholarly way until 1976. In that year, Charles van Onselen's *Chibaro* conceded in passing that African men did have sex with African men in the mining compounds from at least the 1910s (see van Onselen 1976: 174–75, 307, n. 91). They did so, he opined, for the same reasons and with the same frequency that they did bestiality, a crime of implicitly identical perversion. Such perversion was "forced" on the men by the conditions they faced in the mining compounds—crowded housing, poverty, shared blankets, and a justifiable fear of poxy prostitutes.[7]

By characterizing male homosexuality as a pathology that was created by and was useful to capital, van Onselen in effect apologized for behavior he himself judged unbecoming of men. The anthropologist Michael Gelfand, meanwhile, although hinting that homosexuality may have taken place at the mines, claimed that it was virtually nonexistent in Shona tradition. Despite a strikingly low level of inquiry, Gelfand's definitive tone invited closure of the discussion (1979: 201–2).

Subsequent historians of Zimbabwe have proven quite obliging in accepting that invitation—Ian Phimister's "social history" of the mines is entirely mute about men's sex lives. Even Diana Jeater's study, which is specifically focused on changing sexualities in an urban context, relegates homosexuality to a single paragraph. Most recently, Timothy Scarnecchia's study of colonial Highfields carries on this historiographic tradition with the scantiest of evidence. The practices of the *magube* (those who stayed too long? tricksters?) were, he suggests, essentially alien and confined to the migrant hostels (Jeater 1993: 194–95; Phimister 1988; Scarnecchia 1993: 65–78).

Whatever the reasons for such de facto denial, the fact is that it helps perpetuate the dangerous myth that "real" Africans are exclusively heterosexual by nature. One consequence of allowing this myth to stand can be seen in the chauvinistic assertions of Zimbabwean leaders (that homosexuality is a "white man's disease" or is spread by inferior "tribes" like the MaBlantyre, the MaNyasa, the MaZambezi, and so on). Since 1994, there have been periodic rhetorical campaigns that incite violence to rid the country of this supposed scourge (see pp. 242–49 below).[8]

The obvious bigotry behind Zimbabwe's "anti-homo" campaigns, as well as a wealth of new scholarship from elsewhere in the region, demand a revisit to the history of homosexual practices among the African people of Zimbabwe. Zackie Achmat, for example, has not only accused van Onselen and other social historians of heterosexist blind spots and bias, he even suggests that van Onselen actually suppressed evidence to sustain his homosexuality-as-pathology or function-of-capital thesis (1993: 99).[9] Achmat argues, by contrast, that African men and women entered into homosexual relationships for positive, sensual reasons in the past just as they do in the present.[10] That view is eloquently expressed in Zimbabwe in the publications of Gays and Lesbians of Zimbabwe (GALZ), a predominantly black male association administered by an indigenous black lesbian.[11]

This chapter seeks to test the validity of the various assertions that have been made about homosexuality through a calm investigation of its history in early colonial Zimbabwe. It inquires: Are there any indications that homosexuality existed in Zimbabwe prior to the coming of European rule? Did Europeans or other Africans introduce or abet the "perversion" of indigenous sexuality? Was homosexuality among African men confined to the migrant labor hostels and prisons? Is it explainable by the conditions of accommodation or the geography of urban areas? Was it contagious? Was it a "function" of racial capitalism, which served to perpetuate profitable patriarchal relations among Africans? And did African men regard sex with men as a sickness to be fought or phase to be grown out of? This chapter is part of an ongoing research project and represents only the preliminary findings.

The intuition that homosexual practices and feelings were known among black Zimbabweans prior to the coming of whites—just as they have been found in virtually every other society in the world—is supported by a variety of historical sources. The ancient San, first of all, had the indiscretion to record their "egregious sexual practices" for posterity in their rock paintings—group anal or intracrural sex dating from as far back as several thousand years (Garlake 1995: 28).

The Bantu-speaking peoples who have predominated on the plateau for the past millennium were more circumspect. No representations or oral tradition remember such activities. Indeed, even the most thorough ethnographic accounts and descriptions of customary law deny the existence of homosexuality through their almost studious silence. Yet when pressed, experts on custom will concede that homosexual relations were frowned on and hushed up but did sometimes occur. According to some, these were customarily "actually expected" among male youths as "experimental" at the age of puberty (see also Bourdillon 1995).[12]

Rare admissions in colonial court documents also suggest that male homosexual behavior existed in traditional society. In 1921, a Mazoe headman (Zezuru) told a Bindura magistrate that "native custom" dictated a fine of one beast for attempted sodomy.[13] Such a fine bespeaks of a fairly common misdemeanor rather than a serious felony.[14] This would appear to be the case also from the testimony of an Ndebele man Tayisa tried in 1917. When charged with indecent assault, Tayisa said simply, "I admit the offence. I did not know it was a crime."[15] Bantu migrants from other countries at the very onset of colonial rule also commonly used the notion of custom to defend their behavior. As for cross-dressing or mixed-gender identity, this appears to have been an extremely rare but accepted eccentricity.[16] The testimony of one father whose adult son was discovered posing as a female nurse and wearing female clothes (including underwear and high heels) is quite telling in that regard: "I have never noticed anything peculiar about Accd [accused, *sic*]. I have always thought him sound in his mind. . . . At the kraal Accd used always to dress in female clothes. He has always worked as a nurse. He associated mostly with girls at the kraal. My son has been wearing dresses ever since he was a baby. He has never discarded them although I have often given him males' clothes but he has refused to wear them. I have never thought him mentally affected."[17]

We cannot know how ancient or widespread these "customs" actually were. Indeed, like many other "customs" that were codified in the early colonial era, these could well have been self-serving inventions of the men who asserted them. The linguistic evidence is also inconclusive. The word currently used to denote homosexuality in chiShona—*ngochani*—for example, can be documented as established in the language as early as 1907, less than two decades into the colonial era. At that time, it was linked to the "Zambezis," a generic term for people of the lower Zambezi valley, including the Sena, Chikunda, and Tonga.[18] The latter was an indigenous minority group, but the others hailed from an area of long-standing Portuguese and

"Arab" (or Islamicized African) presence. The "oriental" connection is also suggested by the Taberer report of 1907 in South Africa, which posits that the word *izinkotshane* emanated from the Shangaan, the people occupying an area between Beira and modern-day Maputo. If, however, as my own informants tend to think, the word *ngochani* originally derives from siNdebele or chiNdau, then it could date as far back as the 1840s, when these languages were introduced to the country by invading offshoots of the Zulu and Ngoni peoples. A former chief native commissioner, Charles Bullock, also surmised that "sodomy," being less rare among the Ndebele than among the Shona, could have had its origins in the sexual edicts of Shaka of the Zulu in the 1820s.[19] Early colonial court records do refer to *jiga*, *jigger*, and *chikile*, which may be "Kitchen Kaffir" or may stem from a siNdebele word meaning "to turn and twist."[20]

Whatever the origins of these terms, the fact that chiShona has no indigenous word for same-sex sex does not prove that the latter did not take place—in cultures throughout the world, specific sexual acts are commonly denoted by exotic words. In chiShona, delicacy on these matters appears to have been preserved by the use of ambiguous or harmless euphemisms: *shamwari* (friend), *kurinda* (to fuck, not specifying who or what), and *kutamba chete* (just playing).

"Just playing" among Shona adults in the normal circumstances of precolonial life was almost certainly very rare, highly disapproved of, and almost never talked about. Indeed, homosexuality in adults (as opposed to adolescents) seems to have been regarded as a form of witchcraft, an otherwise inexplicable exception to the normal moral order. Children were sternly warned to stay away from men rumored to do such things (although absolutely not told why).[21] That women could be sexually attracted to women was even less admissible. The only possibility for women to avoid heterosexual marriage leading to childbirth was to become a "healer" or "prophetess." We may therefore probably safely accept the testimony of one GALZ member who tells of older women who believe they have been bewitched or cursed because they have a longing to love their own sex. They marry, derive no satisfaction from sex, have children, and endure rituals of purification, but the longing is still there.[22]

The reasons for the inadmissibility of homosexuality can easily be explained without essentialist arguments about African nature. In precolonial Zimbabwe, as throughout the region, wealth was primarily measured in people. Shortage of people (labor power) was one of the principal constraints on production. Children were thus valued as crucial economic and political assets, not merely little bundles of joy. Furthermore, producing children was the defining characteristic of social adulthood for both women and men. To remain childless or to be impotent was to remain a perpetual child oneself. Heterosexual marriage resulting in successful pregnancy was thus the vocation that children were taught from their earliest years. It was also virtually the only sensible path to a relatively secure old age. Numerous offspring were insurance against poverty and could even provide "income" in the form of bride-price (*lobola*) received for daughters. For a man or woman to choose to forgo all this and at the same time to elicit universal condemnation of family and community for the love of another man or woman was an absurd and dangerous life choice.[23]

That ambiguous sexual feelings existed among Africans prior to the coming of whites is strongly suggested by the appearance of homosexual "crimes" in the first full year of operation of the colonial courts. The British South Africa Company (BSAC) occupied Mashonaland in 1890 but only established the first two magistrates' courts late the next year. In 1892, five cases of sodomy and indecent assault by men upon men or boys were tried in Salisbury (Harare) and Umtali (Mutare). None of these involved a white man. Rather, the accused were a "Hottentot," a "Matibili," a "Zambizi," and the rest unspecified "natives," presumably local Shona.[24]

The frequency of the crime as it was perceived and prosecuted by the new administration also suggests that it was not new to the country with the arrival of white settlers. Homosexual crimes amounted to 1.5 percent of all criminal court cases in 1892. This compares to zero for bestiality and heterosexual crimes such as rape, indecent assault, and *crimen injuria*. In other words, of all the "perversions" that plagued polite society at the moment of birth of colonialism, male homosexuality was the most visible. Considering that this later changed dramatically (homosexual crimes declining in proportion and heterosexual crimes increasing), it seems fair to conclude that the first colonial magistrates—in their naïveté—were bearing witness to existing practices that shocked their sensibilities.

Before analyzing the magistrate court records, the principal source of data attesting to queer behavior in early colonial Zimbabwe, I will note some of the difficulties that render this source unreliable for making definitive conclusions. First, people who love each other or who have made satisfactory monetary arrangements do not normally bring their sexual relations before the public eye, particularly when those relations are considered illicit. As a result, with the exception of a small number of cases in which the accused were caught *in flagrante delicto*, most of the cases on record stem from a complaint lodged with the police by "the victim." The latter clearly had a vested interest in characterizing homosexuality as violent or mercenary. As a result, this source provides only the barest hints of the existence of consensual homosexual relationships.

Court records also understate the prevalence of nonconsensual relationships. As with heterosexual rape, shame and fear of retribution were powerful constraints on victims coming forward to lodge a complaint. Even today, with "majority rule" and years of "feminist" propaganda, police estimate that only 5 percent of heterosexual rapes actually make it to court. This would have been all the more true in the context of BSAC rule, under which colonial courts represented to Africans one institutional face of a racist, occupying, and notoriously unjust power. It often took considerable courage to risk both the shame of a public admission of victimhood and the unpredictable whims of the *varungu* (whites). Reported homosexual crimes must therefore be regarded as the tip of an iceberg whose size can never be known but was, we may safely assume, much larger than the visible portion.

Second, homosexuality was punishable under the crime of unnatural offenses. These were defined in such a way that renders lesbianism or lesbian-like behavior utterly invisible. As Oliver Phillips points out, not a single case of lesbian sex appears ever to have been tried in either Rhodesia or the Cape Colony/Province (whence the law originated) (1997b: 8). This source is utterly useless in attempting to detect the provenance of lesbianism.

To this male bias must be added an ethnic bias stemming from the nature of the colonial judicial systems and the dualistic economy. Throughout the period of company rule, most indigenous people continued to live in what are now termed *communal* areas, formerly known as "tribal homelands" or "reserves." Here, they retained "traditional" chiefs and headmen who continued to exercise residual powers. Although typically appointed by the colonial administration and theoretically subject to the authority of the local native commissioners (NCs), these chiefs, in practice, dealt with most minor infractions of law among indigenous people. As such, matters like indecent assault tended to be invisible to the eyes of NCs, who were generally swamped by more serious crimes and a host of other administrative duties. The documentary evidence thus almost certainly understates the existence of homosexual crime in the reserves.

The invisibility of indigenous queers was even greater for urban-based magistrates and the police force. From the onset of BSAC rule, the majority of the population of the areas administered by the magistrates consisted of "alien natives"—mostly migrants from Nyasaland, northern Rhodesia, and Portuguese East Africa. Europeans, Asians, and people of mixed race were also both disproportionately found in the urban areas.[25] Moreover, by virtue of their relative affluence, these exotic groups were disproportionately the target of false accusations and blackmail attempts. In other words, the relatively low numbers of Shona among the accused do not conclusively demonstrate that the Shona were immune to illicit activities. Rather, it reflects the fact that while the Shona were the majority of Africans in the colony as a whole, they were a minority in the places where their illicit behavior stood to be caught and recorded. The same bias overstating the criminality of "aliens" is found in almost all other types of crime as well.

The reliability of forensic evidence in the case of colonial Zimbabwe also suffers from the fact that at least two translations stand between the researcher and the testimony of African men. The first translation is from the vernacular into English, with all its potential for misrepresentation. The second translation is from English into a type of legalese that not only homogenizes the acts committed but also equates them with bestiality. Euphemisms such as "have connection," "fundamental orifice," and "obtained his purpose" combine with a phlegmatic, business-like tone to erase nuance and emotions. Moreover, while the accused was allowed to cross-examine his accuser and other witnesses, this cross-examination was not recorded for posterity. One can only guess from the reactions of the complainants how the accused specifically sought to defend himself. One can also only guess at the validity of the verdict. Were the men actually guilty of the crimes for which they were tried and convicted? Or was the magistrate—in his haste, in his racist prejudice, or perhaps even in his prurient interest—prepared to entertain the feeblest, concocted evidence? We cannot know with certainty.

Bearing all these provisos in mind, the evidence of the criminal courts nonetheless raises compelling questions. Between 1892 and 1923, approximately 300 cases of homosexual crimes came before the magistrates. Records of these cases provide a rich database including the age, "tribe," place of birth, employment, and previous convictions of the accused and complainants. They also generally contain an often-detailed description of the offense, testimony of witnesses, medical opinion, comments by the magistrate or attorney general, and finally, the sentence. The documents also record the testimony of the accused both directly, in the form of their sworn statements in defense, and indirectly, in the form of police accounts of comments the men made at the time of their arrest. Through these documents, we can actually hear the voices of the ancestors of Zimbabwe's nascent gay community.

The numbers alone give cause to suspect the prevailing stereotypes of homosexuality as a "white man's disease" or as a pathological spin-off of racial capitalism. Were this a white man's disease, how would one explain that nearly 90% of all cases of homosexual crime involved African men "assaulting" other African men or boys? As noted above, in the first year in which such cases were recorded, no whites were involved at all. In first 30 years of colonial rule, only 26 whites were ever tried (8.7 percent of the total), at least one-third of whom appear to have been the victims of false accusations.[26] Asians and people of mixed race were an even smaller fraction of cases (11 or just over 3 percent of the total, with an equally high proportion of apparent blackmail attempts).

Statistical analysis also shows that among Africans, no one ethnic group appears to have had a special affinity for homosexual relationships. On the contrary, bearing in mind the bias of the courts, the cases are remarkably well distributed among the many ethnic groups in the country. "Alien natives" account for about two-thirds of the identifiable total of accused. The majority of these came from various "tribes" in Mozambique (about 19 percent of the total), Nyasaland (9 percent), and Northern Rhodesia (mainly BaLozi, 6 percent)—the territories that supplied the majority of migrant laborers. Interestingly, while there is a small indigenous population of Shangaans who were already notorious in South Africa in the first decade of the century, they are notably rare among the accused in cases of homosexual crime in Zimbabwe (3 percent of the total). Similarly rare are other migrants from the more industrialized south ("Hottentot," Xhosa, Basotho, and Zulu). Among indigenous peoples, the Ndebele and related groups account for about 16 percent of the total cases, and the Shona about 17 percent.

Whatever their ethnicity, the overwhelming majority of the accused and complainants alike were men and boys who were far from home and either employed or imprisoned in colonial institutions. By no means, however, was homosexual crime confined to the mines and jails. In fact, the majority of cases occurred in other urban contexts—hotels, police camps, industrial compounds, hospitals, the veldt between working and drinking places, private homes, and even in the African townships (28 percent). The mines (22 percent) and jail (17 percent) were only slightly ahead of commercial farms, woodlots, rural kraals, and other rural areas (17 percent) in the frequency with which they were the site of allegations of homosexual impropriety.

In line with the above, the cases are remarkably distributed geograph-ically. This again confounds stereotypes. For example, Hartley (modern Chegutu) was a small town with large mines around it and a large migrant population. As one might expect, it was a veritable den of iniquity, with 42 cases of homosexual crime in 17 years. Yet, just down the road, the even larger mining center of Gatooma (Kadoma) recorded less than half that number of cases, while Selukwe (Shurugwi) recorded no cases at all. Cases are meanwhile recorded from even small agricultural centers such as Odzi and Marondellas (Marondera), while some of the largest urban centers produced almost no cases. In 31 years of the operation of magistrate's court in Fort Victoria (Masvingo), for example, only a single case is recorded, while Gwelo (Gweru) had but 4. Nor can the preponderance of cases from the two main cities (Salisbury and Bulawayo, at around 60 cases each) be interpreted as proving the stereotypical link between homosexuality and urbanization. The jurisdiction of these urban courts in fact extended over a wide swath of commercial farms, compounds dotted along the railway lines, and even kraals in the surrounding reserves.

Considering the numbers over time, the evidence similarly defies easy stereotypes about male homosexuality. For instance, were it the case that male sexuality was transformed by the declining ability of African men to afford proper wives (as van Onselen and Jeater maintain), one would expect a steady increase in the frequency of the crime as real wages declined. In fact, from a busy year in 1892 (5 cases), there were none again until 1895. In absolute numbers, the peak year was 1912, with 20 cases recorded throughout the country. The numbers declined unsteadily to only 8 in 1920, then rose again to 18 in 1923. In relative terms, the frequency of the crime declined even more precipitously, from 3 out of a total of 228 criminal cases in Salisbury in 1892 (1.3 percent of all crimes) to 4 out of approximately 5,000 cases in 1923 (0.08 percent). Yet, while homosexual crimes became rarer, heterosexual crimes increased. By the time of acute economic crisis in the early 1930s, cases of rape of girls and women outnumbered homosexual assaults in the High Court by at least 20 to 1. Clearly, we must look for other factors to explain the vagaries in the statistics.

Finally, a quantitative analysis of cases of homosexual crime in early colonial Zimbabwe calls into question one of the key assertions of T. Dunbar Moodie and Patrick Harries in their studies of mine marriages in South Africa—the rigid formality and absolute conformity to set rules. Certainly, intracrural sex (that is, ejaculation between the thighs) by one partner on a supine "wife" was the predominant form of sexual practice recorded. Oral sex and mutual masturbation were exceedingly rare, with only two cases of the former ever alleged in the whole period of company rule.[27] Yet, anal sex was not "almost unheard of" among African men. On the contrary, nearly one-third of all cases beginning from 1892 involved accusations of sodomy. Cases where actual anal penetration seem in fact to have taken place account for about one in six of the total number of cases. Homosexual practices among African men were clearly more varied than prevailing stereotypes assert.

A close qualitative analysis of the court records reveals further, often surprising, evidence. Among the most striking discoveries are that reciprocal, relatively long-term, and apparently loving relationships actually did exist in an atmosphere that so utterly militated against them; cash was able to transform gender identities at a personal level with such relative ease; and Zimbabweans of yore could be so phlegmatic about an issue that today causes outrage.

To begin with, evidence from trials for homosexual crimes in early colonial Zimbabwe makes it clear that homosexual liaisons were the active preference of many of the accused. Unlike in South Africa, where migrant laborers were mostly housed in huge single-sex hostels, in Zimbabwe, they tended to be left to their own devices. The men erected huts of their own or to share with two to three others in the vicinity of work. Cases certainly did occur in which physical proximity in crowded quarters or snuggling under a shared blanket caused "accidents" to happen. More commonly, however, the accused traveled from his own hut (or bed) to that of the complainant. In some cases, this involved a walk of several hundred meters, strongly indicating premeditation. In one Umtali (Mutare) case, a man traveled all the way from Penhalonga (more than 30 kilometers) to be with a former "room-mate" who had moved to the city.[28] In a startling number of such cases, the traveler or guest took his satisfaction while the complainant was asleep, a variant on the Shona custom of heterosexual *kuruvhurera*. Even at the mines, the fact that the offences did not always take place in cramped quarters (but also at the back of wagons, in the veldt, and even in underground shafts) rather undermines the "they-were-forced-to-do-it" thesis.

That said, in some of the isolated wood-cutting and railway camps, sexual frustration arising from the absence of women did indeed appear to be a factor encouraging the men to take their satisfaction on a sleeping comrade. Yet, scarcity of women cannot be taken as a general explanatory factor. Again, unlike South Africa, where women were excluded from the

migrant hostels and could only be found in distant and dangerous townships, in Zimbabwe, women were fairly readily available to migrant men.
Some mining compounds were veritable villages, with wives, children, and
"prostitutes" mingled among the workers' accommodations.[29] Indeed, a
common lament in the testimony of complainants and witnesses is that
they asked the accused at the time of the assault or proposition, "If you
want a woman, I will fetch one for you," or "Why do you not get yourself
a woman instead of doing it to this boy?"[30] Several defendants scoffed at
their accusers in a similar vein: "If I wanted to have a woman, I can get
plenty in the location," or "there are plenty of women," or "I could not
have had connections with the picannin. I have my own wife."[31] Several of
the accused were locally married men with children.[32] In one unusual case
from Dawn Mine, Hartley district, the accused surreptitiously entered the
hut where the complainant was actually sleeping together with his wife—and
fucked the man![33]

The accused in most of these cases seemed to have considered themselves normal, heterosexual men and, in some cases, expressed shame or
repugnance at the accusations brought against them. A large number did
not even attempt a defense beyond the barest (or barefaced) denial. Among
those who tried to offer a rational defense, however, several factors were
cited to explain why they chose to have sex with males. These included the
inability to afford a female prostitute or proper wife, the correct belief that
intracrural sex with young boys was safer healthwise than vaginal sex with
female prostitutes, and being so "staggeringly drunk" that they did not in
fact know what they were doing. Others simply passed the buck: Satan or
the "Supreme Diety" made them do it.

Yet, it also appears that there was a "gay-affirmative" ambience at
some of the native locations that made the option of homosexual relations
relatively socially acceptable. This allowed men to express feelings of sexual
attraction to males that, in the past, they would have repressed or denied.
Homosexuality was reportedly a "common practice on the mines" as early
as 1907.[34] The accused in some cases also pleaded that they had only done
it after being advised to do so by their superiors or seeing it practiced by
others.[35] One defendant justified his actions by explaining that "in Beira
[Mozambique] the big boys always had connection with the piccanins and
paid them for it." Ergo, why shouldn't I try it?[36]

Homoerotic dancing—with genitals exposed and garishly painted—
was also by the 1920s at least commonplace at some mines and even in
townships among "mine boys."[37] These dances were attended by the wider

community, suggesting that people may have disapproved in theory but, in practice, enjoyed a good show. Similarly, in practice, it appears that open homosexuals could win widespread respect in the broader community for their other qualities as people. According to Scarnecchia, one particularly flamboyant homosexual known as Dhuri came to be regarded as a virtual folk hero in 1930s Highfields for his strength and daring vis-à-vis the police (1993: 78–92).

The often-uninterested attitude of potential witnesses against homosexual assailants seems to suggest a fairly tolerant, if not blasé attitude as well. Indeed, a frequent difficulty encountered by complainants was the inability to rouse co-workers in their defense at the time of the alleged assault. One complainant, Jim, found this out to his dismay after being awakened one night with the penis of a certain Mwangala between his buttocks. "I was very cross," he told the court. But when one of his companions shouted for assistance, "The natives in the next room laughed and told him to shut up."[38]

The appearance before the courts of a small number of repeat offenders points to the existence of men who were "gay" in the sense of liking sex with other males for sensual reasons. Simonas, alias Bye-Bye, made this quite clear to one of his many "victims" in a case from "Salisbury township" (probably Highfields) in 1923. Simonas allegedly told Mapanda that "he preferred piccanins to girls."[39] This preference entailed anal sex on a daily basis. In several other cases, the innocence of the "victims" was called into question by medical testimony: "I am of the opinion as the result of my examination that the act of sodomy has been committed by both parties consenting thereto," "sodomy might have been committed frequently previous to this," or "habitually," to cite three different doctors.[40]

Manwere (alias Antonio, alias Joe or Jonas) certainly deserves honorary mention as the most frequent guest of colonial hospitality for this tendency. A Sena originally from Tete in Mozambique, Manwere first appeared as a precocious "victim" in Umtali in 1900. On a commercial farm in the Salisbury area the next year, and still apparently in his preteens, he had graduated to the status of accused and was found guilty of sodomizing a co-worker. Over the next 16 years, Manwere found himself before the courts on similar charges no less than seven more times in various locales around the country. On every occasion, he denied the charge.[41]

Such repeat offenders were in fact quite rare. It seems that a stint or two in the lockup with lashes and spare diet was a significant deterrent, at least to carelessness in allowing oneself to be caught. One way to avoid the latter was to ensure that the "victim" was properly compensated. Few

committed the error of Pickin (alias Sifumo) more than once, who was
hauled before the court, that is, on account of failing to pay the agreed
amount to his "victim."[42]

The issue of money goes to the heart of the fragility of gender identity in the colonial context and exposes the sometimes tenuous connection
between biological sex and social gender. Formerly, boys attained a recognized status of social manhood by the acquisition of a wife, children, and
land under the approving gaze of their family and wider community. With
the advent of colonial rule, however, African men became permanently
"boys"—no matter how old or how many children they may have had, they
remained less than men to their white masters: boss boy, cook boy, herd
boy, what-have-you. Also, migrant labor removed "boys" from the gaze of
the community, which defined manhood in traditional terms. Social boys
could in this context more easily make tactical sexual decisions than in the
past. They could, for example, engage in predatory or conquest-style sex with
women or girls without the need to consider marital commitments. They
could also become "women" (that is, people upon whom semen is spent)[43]
without fear of permanently compromising their masculine dignity. Indeed,
in the context of urban areas and labor camps, it proved to be surprisingly
easy for social boys to become social women. The switch could be made
for as little as a few pence, a bar of soap, a pen knife, or a ratty blanket.

"Women" or "wives" in this sense could rest assured that no permanent signifiers of the gender change would remain. Social manhood could
be regained as soon as sufficient cash was available. As Moodie and Harries
have argued, social womanhood for young men may even have been a step
to attain or ensure eventual social manhood, that is, to the extent that
it allowed "boys" to husband their resources in town toward the goal of
acquiring land and a female wife back home in the village.

For migrant workers in town, the difficulties of becoming social men
were compounded by the ethnic chauvinism of the local blacks. "MaZambezi,"
for example, were condescended by the Shona of colonial Salisbury and
disproportionately left to the dirtiest jobs—brown collar workers, if you
will. An apparent reflection of this is that chiShona today has incorporated
the term *matanyero*, meaning latrine cleaner or scavenger, from chiChewa.
By 1926, at least, *matanyero* had also come to have another meaning: "for
one male to have connection with another male between the thighs."[44] The
colonial state abetted this by lending its power to keeping alien African men
and indigenous women apart. The Native Adultery Ordinance of 1916 was

specifically directed at migrants who interfered with the wives and daughters of Shona patriarchs.

Yet, indigenous African men also increasingly lost the wherewithal to attain social manhood in similar ways to foreign Africans. Whereas many Shona had initially been able to prosper as farmers from the growth of urban demand for their produce, by the late 1910s the reserves were already becoming exhausted and eroded, precipitating a sudden rise in internal migration. The forensic evidence suggests that indigenes turned to many of the same "perversions" as foreign migrants when exposed to the same "unmanning" circumstances of colonial rule. Hence, in 1921, Shona for the first time actually constituted a majority of the accused in homosexual crimes countrywide. This is not to suggest that homosexual liaisons among Shona men were purely a function of rural impoverishment. Rural impoverishment, however, made it harder for them to pass as "real men." For that minority who were attracted by the possibilities of alternative sexualities, this was a strong incentive and opportunity to experiment.[45]

The dominant type of homosexual "perversion" echoed the heterosexual type of temporary marriage known in chiShona as *mapoto*. In these, the "wife" or *ngotshana* was usually a (real) boy ranging in age from as young as seven to the late teens. The boy "was used" for domestic and sexual tasks just as a female wife would be, including cooking and fetching wood and water. In return, "she" was supposed to receive protection by an older man in the essentially hostile and alienating environment of the location or labor camp, as well as gifts such as blankets, cigarettes, trousers, and petty cash. As with *mapoto* marriages, *ngotshana* marriages were generally transient affairs, typically ending as the boy grew older and confident enough to seek his independence or his own "wife." In some cases, *ngotshana* marriages ended when the boy found a new, more generous or loving protector. In others, the "wife" was sent away for demanding too many gifts. Of all those cases that came to court, the most durable *ngotshana* marriages were never longer than a year; more commonly, they ended in a matter of weeks.

As was typically the case with heterosexual marriage, these relationships were characterized by an abiding contempt for the feelings of the "wife" on the part of the husband. "I have emitted semen on you and it does not matter because you are only lad," explained Bisamu to his unhappy *ngotshana* Lindunda. Other men justified sometimes horrific acts of violence, including anal rape resulting in bloody internal damage, with the casual defense, "I was only playing." This contempt stemmed from the discrepancy in power between the partners, a discrepancy of which "husbands" were often all too willing to remind their "wives." Very commonly, the boys put up with virtual slave labor and demeaning, painful sex because of fear. They feared either the physical violence that their "husbands" could inflict or the "husband's" ability to hurt them financially. A servant could be dismissed (backpay withheld), a "boss boy" could refuse to sign an employee's work ticket, and an employer could refuse to condone the pass that every African needed to remain in town.[46]

Another type of homosexual relationship was closer to prostitution in the form of servicing another man's immediate desire for sexual release for a negotiated price. This appeared in the court records of Salisbury as early as 1908 and in Bulawayo possibly even earlier.[47] The price asked for individual acts of sex normally ranged from 5 to 10 shillings, precisely the amount most commonly demanded by female prostitutes for the same service (Barnes 1993: 364). Interestingly, this price was significantly below the level of fines traditionally levied as "damages" for sexual misbehavior. Yet in the minds of many of the men who came to court, the two concepts were often virtually indistinguishable. Indeed, in many cases, the accused only offered to pay "compensation" after having taken his gratification (rather than negotiating the amount beforehand). Some men demanded sex in lieu of unpaid debts. This sense of economic entitlement could entail the most extraordinary logic: "I admit the offence, I slept with Shilling because I had given money to Tom and a friend of Shilling had killed a dog of mine some time ago."[48] In other instances, cases came to court because of failure to pay "damages" (rather than grievance against the assault itself). As Tshakusamba quite frankly (and to the prejudice of his case) told the magistrate in Hartley: "If the accused had paid me the money I should not have reported the matter. I considered I was entitled to damages because he had treated me as a woman and had spent on my legs."[49]

The price for a single act of "connection" could earn the equivalent or more than traditional damages if fear of public exposure was an issue for the accused. A complainant could make as much as 10 pounds by threatening to report the case, an amount equal to several months' wages as a general servant. It is worth noting here that the practice of blackmail, which besets the gay and lesbian community in contemporary Zimbabwe, has a long history. As early as 1900, clearly spurious charges were brought against "boss boys," whites, and Indians (that is, men with relatively good incomes and professional or social status). Boys and young men also lodged patently spurious accusations, often in concert with one another, to exact revenge on their superiors for unpopular decisions at work or out of "tribal" animosity.[50]

Criminal court records by definition principally involve cases of violence, extortion, insult, exploitation, or threats. Given the oppressive and exploitative nature of many heterosexual marriages, there is no reason to doubt that this was not also the dominant tendency in homosexual relationships, whether *ngotshana* marriages or outright prostitution. Yet in some cases, and against all apparent odds, real ties of affection did develop to bind the partners together. Some "husbands" even sought to establish a kind of marital stability in line with heterosexual custom. In one case from Kanyemba mine near Gatooma in 1915, the "husband" (Singame) appears to have actually negotiated with his "father-in-law" for *lobola* for his "wife." The marriage came to court because the "wife" (possibly instigated by his father) wanted more—10 pounds—which Singame refused to pay.[51]

In another case from Victoria Falls, an affair in jail led Siamasari to pledge *lobola* in more customary terms—a cow. According to one Mutambo, "He [also] said that when we returned to Wankies [*sic*] I should stay with him as 'his' wife and he would give me many things."[52] In several other cases, "husbands" who were brought to court by unhappy "wives" expressed real surprise and the kind of hurt or disappointment one associates with deep emotional attachment. "He was my friend," Sitwala plaintively told the court after his betrayal by Mumbera. "I called the piccanin my friend."[53]

Also, contrary to expectation and to the assertions of Harries in particular, cases of consensual, reciprocal homosexual play or love did come to court. The accused in these cases had typically been caught in the act of having sex by their accusers. Also, typically, such cases took place in prison or in isolated labor camps where it truly could be said that neither women, piccanins, nor cash were available. In such cases, "damages" could only be paid by returning the favor. Yet, by no means were these favors strictly functional or entirely lacking in joie de vivre. On the contrary, it appears that fun was sometimes had for one and all. As one prisoner complained to the Bulawayo magistrate about two of his cellmates: "They were both lying on their side laughing and wriggling and making a noise and Mbwana told them if they went on like that he would call the guard."[54]

Of all the cases that came to court in the history of BSAC rule, none more poignantly illustrates the humanity of African homosexuals than that of Mashumba and Njebe. The husband in this case, Mashumba, was BaSili (a Bushman) living in a peasant community near Wankie. He was widowed during the influenza epidemic of 1919 and claimed to have been unable to remarry. "I want to say that it was the need I was in through not being able to get a woman that tempted my heart and I made the boy Njebe agree to become a woman for me."[55] For his part, the 16-year-old Njebe explained simply, "We loved one another." For three years, he had played the role of a wife, including penetrative sex three times a week. "Every time accd [accused] had connection with me he allowed me to do the same to him. We did it in the hut and also in the veld. . . . I never objected to accd doing what he did before because it was not painful and I did it to him."

As he matured, Njebe began to have doubts and specifically to wonder if he were not in danger of becoming pregnant. The lovers separated amicably on these grounds. They later quarreled, however, when Mashumba proposed to have another go. According to Njebe, "I struck accd because he said, 'Come on, let us mount one another as before.'" After this, Mashumba took the matter to the local headman, who ultimately sent the case to the local magistrate. Remarkably, the headman claimed that in all those years that a homosexual marriage had been taking place under his very nose, he never noticed anything "abnormal."[56]

What was the attitude of the state toward the emergence of new and at least potentially subversive sexual practices? Scholars who have investigated this question suggest that the European officials in southern Africa regarded homosexual crime as morally disgusting but actually preferable to the other more dangerous "perversions" to which African men were purportedly prone (having sex with white women or organizing trade unions). As a result, white bosses tended to turn a blind eye to African men's homosexual practices—if it keeps the men quiet and free from the clap, then what business is it of ours? The infrequent stiff sentences administered by the colonial courts were more to appease tiresome missionaries than out of true homophobic conviction.

The evidence from early colonial Zimbabwe does not fully support such a conclusion. Neither the police and doctors who testified nor the judges who passed sentence on homosexual crimes left more than the most phlegmatic of observations. The severity of the sentences must therefore speak for themselves. These ranged from as little as three days to as much as five years in prison with hard labor or one year with 100 lashes. The latter was severe by the standard of the day compared to other crimes involving violence, including culpable homicide. In the context of a chronic shortage of African labor, even the more typical sentences of three to nine months were fairly heavy—it was not an insignificant inconvenience to capital to lose five to eight sometimes senior workers ("boss boys") for such a period every year. Nor do the sentences appear light or token in relation to the sentences meted out for heterosexual crimes among Africans. In an era when wife battery leading to death could earn an African man as little as three months' imprisonment, six months for nonviolently emitting semen onto another man's legs seems disproportionately severe.[57]

Such relatively heavy sentences probably indicate a reflexive defense of patriarchal, heterosexual masculinity by the homophobic representatives of the colonial state. Men getting physically intimate and perhaps emotional with other men was simply too viscerally threatening to the dominant ideology of male control, self-containedness, and self-discipline for the representatives of order to bear. This appears to be particularly so in cases involving white men, in whose bodies and sexuality the imperatives of imperial masculinity were most at stake. Hence, while very few Africans ever received sentences harsher than a year in jail, and this only in cases where there was pederastic violence, few whites received sentences of less than a year. This applied even when the arrangement had clearly initially been consensual. In other words, whereas homosexual relations came to be almost expected of Africans in certain contexts, whites doing it deeply offended the magistrates' sense of racial dignity. The sentences they meted were designed to register that disapproval.[58]

Peer pressure also seems to have been a significant factor in restraining white men from joining in the generalized debauchery at some mines. One exchange between two white miners captures both the shock and disgust on the part of the witness and the desperate sense of shame of the accused. The former in this case, William Roe, left for his shift one afternoon at Cam and Motor mine near Gatooma. On the way to work, he remembered something he had left in his room and returned to fetch it. When he got there, he found his co-worker on top of his servant on his bed in his pajamas. Roe testified, "I said, 'Good God Almighty, what's this!' You said, 'I'm not fucking him, I am whispering in his ear.'" Neither Roe nor the magistrate were convinced.[59]

African men's own testimony also shows that they generally expected and often feared the stern disapproval of whites and sought, for that reason, to keep their homosexual practices secret. "Husbands" could use it to cow their naïve *ngotshana*. Mafillio, for example, was alleged to have told Matenza that the whites would beat him if he so much as complained.[60] As late as 1921, Zaza's defense against the accusation of indecent assault was simply that "my heart would not let me sleep with that boy, I am frightened of what the Government would do to me if I had slept with that boy."[61]

On the other hand, the colonial state was not a monolith nor was there any official policy to guide magistrates in their dispensation of justice on this matter. As a result, individual magistrates were able to develop and express increasingly liberal views over time. These included the ability to distinguish between consensual and nonconsensual sex. As early as the 1910s, some courts began to differentiate between cases involving violence and those in which the "victim" either enjoyed or profited from the act. If the latter were demonstrated to have been the case, the charge was usually downgraded (from sodomy or attempted sodomy to indecent assault). Sentences were also reduced for men whose "victims" were not entirely guiltless, even in cases in which the victims suffered grievous violence. Nyambe, for example, was found guilty of having anally raped 12-year-old Sagauchimba no less than five times. Yet, the court seemed to accept as a mitigating factor his "defense" that Sagauchimba had agreed to sex for money. Nyambe's sentence was accordingly relatively light given the gravity of the accusations.[62]

Some magistrates began to dismiss cases altogether as soon as they suspected prior consent. "It seems to me no offense has been committed," ruled L. F. H. Roberts in 1913, in dismissing a case in which the complainant had repeatedly accepted payment for intracrural sex but came to court after the accused had attempted anal penetration.[63] The attorney general simply declined to prosecute another case of consensual sex in 1915: "As complainant was old enough to appreciate what was being done, and consented, no crime was committed."[64] The solicitor general Clarkson Tredgold overturned a conviction for indecent assault in a local court because, as he phrased it in 1922, the evidence "points almost directly to a case of consent."[65] Tredgold also reduced the sentence levied by the NC of Gutu on a court messenger accused of sodomy. The "whole affair was so trivial" he ruled, that it should never have come to court in the first place.[66]

That African men observed this liberalizing tendency, and so progressively stopped bringing their more routine cases to court, is implied in some of their testimony. One *ngotshana* defended his tardiness in reporting an assault as arising from his belief that the police no longer cared: "I did not report it because they said the white people know these things we are doing."[67] The overall decline in the number of court cases after 1912 suggests the same. How else can the virtual disappearance of the crime from Hartley be explained?[68] From an average of a case every two months in the mid-1910s, the number coming to court dwindled in the late 1920s. A single case involving the allegation of sodomy between 1928 and 1931 was discharged, while in the first three years of the 1940s, not even indecent assault charges were laid. Had African men found virtue? More likely, they found that lodging a complaint on such matters was becoming a waste of time. Those who were truly aggrieved by homosexual assault or solicitation therefore seem instead to have turned increasingly to private avenues of redress. As one such "victim" explained when reluctantly brought before a Salisbury judge in 1931, he had not initially reported the indecent assault but "decided to get up a gang to give accused a hiding."[69] Homosexuality as a crime receded from the public gaze.

Conclusion

Notwithstanding the evident shortcomings of colonial documents on this topic, they do allow us to draw several tentative conclusions about the history and nature of homosexual relations among African men in Zimbabwe.

First, colonial records do not support the contention that African men either required or received more than minimal "instruction" by Europeans, Indians, Arabs, Portuguese, people of mixed race, or any other supposedly decadent and morally degraded people. "Unnatural crimes" occurred overwhelmingly between African men and boys.

If the coincidence of the arrival of Europeans and the emergence of "unnatural crimes" among Africans cannot be accounted for by European "immorality," it can be linked to urbanization and the revolutionary transformation of the economy, which the Europeans so quickly stimulated, as scholars such as Moodie and colleagues have cogently argued. Homosexual behavior was rare before colonial rule and was common after, at least in certain contexts. The evidence from Zimbabwe, however, suggests that Moodie and other historians are almost certainly wrong to identify homosexual behavior among African men so closely with mining compounds. In fact, homosexual crimes were committed throughout the country—on rural commercial farms, in the administrative and agricultural centers, in police camps and prisons, in urban households, in hospitals, and even (albeit rarely) in native kraals. Although prisoners and "alien natives" do comprise a disproportionate number of the accused in cases of homosexual crime, indigenous men and boys were a significant and generally increasing minority. Almost all of these were internal migrants. Yet, a sufficient number of cases of men with (female) wives nearby exist to call into question the "sexual frustration" explanation for men turning to men for sexual release.

Similarly, African men's sexual attraction to men cannot be explained simply by the conditions of accommodation. As van Onselen has described, this may indeed have been the case in many instances (1976: 175; 1982: 179 passim). In cramped huts or workers' quarters, men's and boys' naked bodies were often pressed together in the most intimate contact. The common defense that "I was only dreaming" is surely plausible under such conditions. Yet, cases of men traveling some distance seeking sex from a specific person are also found throughout the record. These men had their own quarters, their own beds, and their own blankets. They clearly were not forced or even unconsciously enticed to commit "indecent acts." They chose to do so.

This element of agency is brought forward by Moodie, Harries, and other recent scholars. Yet in doing so, Moodie and colleagues assert that homosexual relations were rigidly structured, hierarchical, and, at root, functional for the maintenance of both patriarchy in the rural areas and profits for the big corporations. The evidence from Zimbabwe is quite ambiguous on this. Certainly, cases of older men preying on "piccanins" are the most common type of homosexual crime. In these cases, the men may well have had some of the motivations stereotypically ascribed to them: fear of town women or the desire to pass the humiliations structured into their work experience down the social hierarchy. Yet, many other cases bear witness to the existence of homosexual relationships that simply cannot be categorized in strictly functionalist terms. These include relationships between men and adolescents of rough parity in age and employment status. Actual sexual practices also varied to an extent that forces us to question the dominance of a strictly rule-bound sexuality. There is testimony as well to mutual consent and enjoyment and to emotions such as love and friendship. That these emotions can be discerned even through so opaque a mirror as court records suggest that they were quite powerful.

Finally, the role of the state in policing male homosexual crime was ambivalent. In the absence of any clear-cut policy, magistrates adjudicated cases according to their own prejudices and on an ad hoc basis. This evolved over the period to witness a growing tolerance of consensual homosexual relations. Although the courts continued to be exceedingly intolerant of interracial homosexual relations (just as they were of interracial heterosexual relations), magistrates were increasingly inclined to turn a blind eye to nonviolent sexual affairs between African males.

We cannot know how common such affairs were, nor how enduring were the emotions that they involved. We can safely conclude, however, that a much more significant proportion of Zimbabwe's black male population historically engaged in sexual relations with other men than has hitherto been acknowledged. What relationship this fact may have to the rise of homophobia in contemporary Zimbabwe remains to be investigated.

Notes

1. See, for example, H. M. Taberer (1907; cited in van Onselen 1982), Henry Junod ([1912] 1927), Peter Lanham and A. S. Mopeli-Paulus (1953), Ethelreda Lewis ([1934] 1984), Barend Laubscher (1937), Monica Wilson (1951: 196–97; based on field research carried out in the 1930s), Percival Kirby (1942), Charles Bullock (1950), and Elizabeth Colson (1958). My use of the word *queer*, I should add, is deliberate. Although its meaning at the time was equivalent to "odd" and did not imply homosexuality, it later became a derogatory term and to some extent remains so here in Zimbabwe. Nevertheless, since the 1970s, it has also been defiantly embraced by gay rights activists in the West for reasons that make sense to me. In particular, I admire its vagueness and its potential to bring together people with different sexualities (viz., who is not queer to some extent?). For the politics of language around this issue, see Rosemary Hennessy (1995).

2. John Gunther, admittedly not a scholarly source, was drawing on the "common knowledge" of his mainly missionary and colonial administration informants.

3. As one dictionary so discreetly phrases it (Dent and Nyembezi 1969: 434). For example, the Zulu word *inkoshana* may be related linguistically to *bukhontxana* in Shangaan and the Shona *ngochane*. Other terms, like *hlabongo* in Zulu, *intombi* in Xhosa, *ukumetsha* among the Mpondo, and *maotana* in Sesotho today imply male homosexual sex but may have been co-opted from words that formerly denoted nonpenetrative heterosexual sex play.

4. Recent scholarly treatments of "mine marriages" can be found in Moodie et al. (1988, 1994), Harries (1990: 318–36; 1994), and Vivienne Ndatshe and Mpande wa Sibuyi ([1982] 1993). See also Don Edkins (director), *The Color of Gold* (New York: Icarus Films, 1991). For a rare study of the appearance of lesbian-like relationships in the colonial era, see Judith Gay (1985).

5. A large literature exists exploring this insight, much of which owes its primary intellectual debt to Michel Foucault ([1978] 1981). I review this literature as it pertains to southern Africa in Marc Epprecht (1996), but see also Ann Stoler (1995) as well as, of course, the other essays in this book.

6. See my rebuttal (Epprecht 1997).

7. Van Onselen later applied the same type of analysis to the Ninevites, a gang in the Rand area reputed for both their violence and their fondness for

homosex (1982: 98; 1984: 15). For a trenchant critique of this interpretation of African men's homosexuality, see Achmat (1993).

8. President Mugabe's "anti-homo" campaigns since 1995 are discussed in Iden Wetherell (1995b, 1996) and Chris Dunton and Mai Palmberg (1996). On the history of the construction of homosexuality as a European phenomenon, see Oliver Phillips 1997a.

9. A close reading of *Chibaro* supports this. At the very least, it must be noted that van Onselen relies on an inappropriate source (criminal court records) to conclude (1) that consensual homosexual relations were less frequent than heterosexual rape and (2) that "victims" were "reluctant." Yet, since courts by their very nature do not record most consensual relationships, how can such general assertions be made? Likewise, a close reading of Jeater (1993) and Scarnecchia (1993) shows that their conclusions are extrapolated from secondary sources elsewhere (Moodie, above all) rather than serious interrogations of local sources.

10. Among a growing number of other scholars and activists in the region making similar claims, see Matthew Krouse and Kim Berman (1993), Mark Gevisser and Edwin Cameron (1994), Desmond Tutu (1996), papers of the First Gays and Lesbian Studies Colloquium, Cape Town, October 1995, and papers of the Gays and Lesbians in African Studies caucus at the African Studies Association conference, San Francisco, California, November 1996.

11. See, for example, the undated pamphlets by Derek Matyszak, "Gay and Lesbian Rights, Human Rights, and the Law," and GALZ, "Homosexuality/Ngochane," as well as *GALZ Newsletter*. Scholars interested in pursuing these sources may contact GALZ directly at Private Bag A6131, Avondale, Harare, Zimbabwe.

12. Interview with G. M. Chavunduka, cited in Phillips 1997a; Solomon Mutsvairo cited in Anon (1996: 17). It should be noted that oral testimony is unusually unreliable on this topic. Homosexuality is now regarded as so shameful and dangerous in popular culture that it simply cannot be admitted, sometimes even by men and women who engage in same-sex relations (yet continue to marry and have children). Moreover, among the very few Zimbabwean gays and lesbians who have come out, knowledge of history is significantly "colonized" by the dominant heterosexist ideology. I have found, for example, that many gays and lesbians accept the view that homosexual practices were introduced into Zimbabwe from South Africa as late as the 1950s. As will be seen, this is patently false.

13. Mbata, testifying in Rex vs. Jenwa, case 149 of 1921, Zimbabwe National Archives [ZNA] D3/10/2.

14. This compares to a fine of 3 cattle for breaking off an engagement without justification, 6 cattle for incest, and up to 11 beasts for committing adultery with another man's wife (Holleman 1969: 89, 225–28).

15. ZNA D3/26/2 (Fort Usher, Matobo), case 247 of 26.11.1917.

16. See, for example, D3/6/42, case 995 of 22.4.1907, referring to "Zambesi" custom, and to D3/7/32, case 409 of 7.6.1915, referring to Achewa. As Kamtengo

expressed it in the latter, "I do not [illegible] deny the charge. In my country it is the custom to commit Sodomy when we are unable to get a woman."

17. High Court case 3838A of 10.1.1927 (Rex vs. Nomxadana @ Maggie).

18. D3/6/42 (Bulawayo), case 995 of 22.4.1907.

19. Bullock 1950: 254–55.

20. D3/6/17 (Bulawayo), case 644 of 14.8.1900.

21. Gelfand 1979: 201–2; Bourdillon 1995; interview with "Baba Itai," August 30, 1996. Witchcraft as a defense is also alluded to in some of the court cases discussed below. See 1540 of 1913 (Bulawayo, D3/6/69) and 311 of 1923 (Wankie, D3/37/8).

22. Pam, quoted in Sayagues 1996.

23. Universal heterosexual marriage does not, it must be emphasized, necessarily denote universal heterosexual orientation. African cultures in Zimbabwe actually provided mechanisms to ensure that sterile marriages could still appear to be fruitful. Hence, a man who felt queer in orientation and was repulsed by the very thought of sex with his wife could invite her to take her own lovers (if she had not done so already in frustration or at her family's insistence). *Lobola* ensured that any offspring would be socially recognized as his, and fictions about his own social manhood, with all the economic and political benefits that accrued to it, could be maintained regardless of his actual sexual feelings. In chiShona, this practice was known as *kupindira* or *kusikira rudzi*, "raising seed" (Holleman 1969: 217–19). On precolonial Shona gender relations, see also Elizabeth Schmidt (1992).

24. Criminal registers of Salisbury and Umtali, D4/3/1 and D4/7/1. Note that these tribal designations must be taken with a large grain of salt. Moreover, "Matabele" and "MaShona" tended to be more narrowly defined in the period under discussion than at present. In accordance with contemporary practice, I lump together their many constituent "tribes" (the Ndebele, which include the groups Kalanga, Basotho, Venda, and Mnyai; and the Shona, which include the groups Zezuru, Korekore, Manyika, and Karanga).

25. As late as 1956, nearly two-thirds of the African population of Salisbury originated from outside the colony (Raftopolous 1995: 82).

26. It could, of course, be argued that the small number of cases of European men indicted for unnatural crimes actually reflects a cover-up of European perversion by embarrassed court officials or by perpetrators able to buy silence from their victims. The case against BSAC officer Edgar Baker, for example, does seem to have been discharged with suspicious disregard for incriminating evidence against him (D3/5/21, 1221 of 1908); likewise that against Leslie Wilson, an Australian touring the world on foot who may, in fact, have been Zimbabwe's first "sex tourist" (D3/26/1, 233 of 26.7.1911). The conspiracy theory, however, is entirely implausible as a general thesis. The courts were actually quite willing to try Europeans for other forms of "perversion" that called racial dignity into question (incest and rape, for example). When one recalls that the settlers came from intensely homophobic societies and

that they had compelling political reasons to maintain social distance from African men, the relative lack of interest in sex with African men that the court record implies is hardly surprising. For the record, in 30 years of court documents, there is but a single example each of repeat offenders who are described as Indian (Abdul Karim of Bulawayo) or European (Raphael Gabriel Benatar, in fact, a Turkish Jew). The stark singularity of the latter—a violent and predatory man (see, for example, 116 of 7.4.08, Mazoe, D3/15/1)—again strongly belies the anti-white rhetoric of some of Zimbabwe's contemporary homophobes.

27. Case 147 of 14.2.1902 (Bulawayo, D3/6/22) and 1509 of 8.8.1918 (Mount Pleasant, D3/5/46).

28. Case 696 of 12.1.1903 (Umtali, D3/7/9).

29. Teresa Barnes maintains that by the 1930s, there were "often just as many women and children in the larger compounds" as men. One police report from 1929 Bulawayo maintained that "most males are living with women in the location," and in Que Que, "All [men] have a woman" (1995: 100; 1993: 75). Barnes is referring to the very end of or after the period I am considering here. The frequency of court cases involving women in the urban locations between the late 1890s and 1923 (including rape, liquor violations, infanticide, abortion, and so on) supports her contention that women were a significant presence in and around the towns from as early as the turn of the century.

30. D3/21/3 (Hartley, 10.3.1910), D3/6/37 (Bulawayo, 465 of 1906).

31. D3/6/55 (Bulawayo, 15 of 1910), D3/18/3 (Gatooma, 778 of 1912), D3/2/15 (Sinoia, 30.4.1918).

32. See, for example, the fairly clear-cut case of consensual anal intercourse, 546 of 1906 (Salisbury D3/5/15) or 561 of 1907 (Old Nick Mine, Bulawayo district, D3/6/42).

33. D3/21/17 (Hartley, 383 of 14.9.1916)

34. D3/6/42 (testimony of Bisamu, a 40-year-old Tonka "boss boy" at Bush Tick Mine, 995 of 22.4.1907).

35. Testimony of Jonas of Lewanika's of Giant Mine, Hartley (D3/21/1, 184 of 19.9.1905) and Munalula of Barotseland at Letombo labor camp, Salisbury (D3/5/46, 2045 of 11.10.1918).

36. D3/31/1 (Penhalonga, 155 of 5.9.1923).

37. 3320 of 12.1.17 (a charge of public indecency, Bulawayo, D3/6/85); interview with "Sekuru Tendai" recalling Jumbo Mine near Mazoe; Scarnecchia 1993: 78.

38. 3433 of 22.12.1919 (Bulawayo, D3/6/101).

39. 3060 of 21.9.1923 (Salisbury, D3/5/60). Simonas was a 35-year-old mattress maker originally from northern Rhodesia. The four complainants in this case were all his former employees.

40. D3/5/15 (Salisbury, 546 of 14.8.1906), D3/7/11 (Umtali, 349 of 1904); D3/6/63 (Bulawayo, 731 of 1.4.1912).

41. D3/7/4 (102 of 1900), D3/5/6 (751 of 1901), D3/5/21 (713 of 1908—two counts), D3/5/29 (394 and 808 of 1912), D3/5/43 (726 of 1917), and D3/18/9 (172 of 1917, which also refers to a previous conviction in Umtali in 1913, file destroyed). Interestingly, after disappearing from the colonial gaze for a few years, Manwere reappeared in 1919, in a "native kraal" near Mvuma. By this time he was married, or at least shared a hut with a young woman. Although the charge against him in this case was stock theft, doubt about his sexuality is hinted at in the testimony of the five-year-old boy who hesitantly called him "father." D3/36/7 (Mvuma, 757 of 11.9.1919). Of course, it is possible there were multiple Manweres.

42. D3/34/1 (Gwanda, 186 of 7.6.1921).

43. Time and time again, in cases ranging from anal rape to wet dreams, men who were the victims of indecent assaults describe themselves as having been "made into a woman" or "wife" (the word in chiShona is the same for both). This phraseology does more than shed light on homophobia in traditional culture. It seems to me to express an even greater contempt for women in Shona society than some feminist scholars have described. In the men's minds, it clearly was not necessary to be fertile to be a woman, let alone have intelligence or domestic skills. One merely had to be on the receiving end of a man's ejaculate to qualify. Conversely, manhood is implicitly understood as the right to spend semen on or in somebody else. This low qualification could explain the relative ease with which the men in these cases switched between being wives, boys, and men.

44. D3/5/72 (Salisbury, 1787 of 23.6.1926).

45. An even more explicit connection was also attested by the clerk to the NC of Sinoia in 1915: "I know that Zambezi natives habitually go in for sodomy and it is common for them to keep small boys for the purpose. Sodomy is very common thing among them" (D3/2/6, 137 of 16.4.1915). Scarnecchia's Shona informants, recalling the 1940s, asserted the same (1993: 65).

46. See 777 and 791 of 1912 (Gatooma D3/18/3). In the latter case, 12-year-old Mumbera put up with over a month of relentless use by Sitwala out of fear of not getting paid. "I consented because I saw another boy whose ticket was not marked because he refused to go to the accused's hut."

47. 1453 of 19.11.1908 (D3/5/22); 561 of 12.3.1907 (D3/6/42).

48. Rex vs. Manswa, Sinoia (D3/2/7, 1.4.1913).

49. 36.656 of 5.1.1904 (D3/21/1).

50. See, for example, 247 of 9.12.1900 (Salisbury, D3/5/2), 147 of 14.2.1902 (Bulawayo, D3/6/22), 349 of 1904 (Umtali, D3/7/11), and 12 of 16.1.1916 (Sinoia, D3/2/11).

51. D3/18/6, Rex vs. Singane, case 1162 of 1915.

52. 34 of 4.2.1910 (D3/37/1).

53. 791 of 20.11.12 (Gatooma, D3/18/3).

54. 469 of 18.6.1900 (D3/6/17).

55. Rex vs. Mashumba, 311 of 1.11.1923 (D3/37/8).

56. Rex vs. Mashumba, 311 of 1.11.1923 (D3/37/8).

57. The double standard in this respect is best captured in the person of Assistant Magistrate T. P. van Broembsen, whose court sat in Wankie in the mid-1920s (D3/37/12). In his sentencing, this man also tacitly condoned the view that emitting semen on boys was less serious than doing so on grown men, even when the former involved violence. Contrast, for example, the four-month sentence for Lukumba's virtual rape of nine-year-old Siamakoma (208 of 29.7.1926) with six months given to Kapata for having a wet dream on a fellow prisoner (42 of 31.1.1926, D3/37/12).

58. The most extreme sentence ever handed down against a white man was in Umtali in 1916. George Burgess, a 47-year-old blacksmith at the railway shop, received five years in prison with hard labor for raping an African man at knifepoint (725 of 23.10.1916, D3/7/35). All of the cases involving white male adults, incidentally, involved them as the seducer/rapist. Given that black men could be sent away for 10 or 12 years for even touching a white woman on the arm, we may safely assume that no African was ever foolish enough to force his sexual attentions on an unwilling white man. The possibility remains, of course, that powerful white men may have led surreptitious lives as "passive" homosexual partners of African men (as has sometimes been implied about the founder of the country, Cecil John Rhodes). The courts, obviously, are silent about such matters.

59. Rex vs. Ernest Coles-Jex, 537 of 3.9.1912 (D3/18/2).

60. 247 of 9.12.1900 (D3/5/2).

61. 224 of 5.7.21 (Marondellas, D3/24/3).

62. Eight months' imprisonment with hard labor and 15 cuts with a cane—2043 of 5.12.1913 (Bulawayo, D3/6/70).

63. 406 of 10.11.1913 (Hartley, D3/21/10).

64. 1162 of 12.11.1915 (Gatooma, D3/18/6).

65. 637 of 12.7.22 (Gatooma, D3/18/19).

66. D3/46/10, 40 of 18.2.1921.

67. 791 of 20.11.12 (Gatooma, D3/18/3).

68. Hartley Criminal Registers, S546, S1030.

69. D3/5/109 case 4203 of 8.10.1931. This particular case involved white men only, but other cases of violent retribution involving Africans abound. See, for example, D3/6/143 82 of 1927, where the accused in an indecent assault case suffered a broken collarbone.

"When a Woman Loves a Woman" in Lesotho

Love, Sex, and the (Western) Construction of Homophobia

KENDALL

My search for lesbians in Lesotho began in 1992, when I arrived in that small, impoverished southern African country and went looking for my own kind.[1] That was before the president of nearby Zimbabwe, Robert Mugabe, himself mission educated, declared moral war on homosexuality and insisted that homosexuality was a "Western" phenomenon imported to Africa by the European colonists.[2] When I left Lesotho two and a half years later, I hadn't found a single Mosotho[3] who identified herself as a lesbian. However, I had found widespread, apparently normative erotic relationships among the Basotho women I knew, in conjunction with the absence of a concept of this behavior as "sexual" or as something that might have a name. I learned not to look for unconventionality or visible performance of sex-role rejection as indicators of "queerness," for most Basotho women grow up in environments in which it is impossible for them to learn, purchase, or display symbols of gay visibility, where passionate relationships between women are as conventional as (heterosexual) marriage and where women who love women usually perform as conventional wives and mothers. I've had to look again at how female sexualities express themselves, how privilege and lesbianism intersect (or don't), and whether what women have or make together—in Lesotho or anywhere else—should be called "sex" at all. I have concluded that love between women is as native to southern Africa as the soil itself, but that homophobia, like Mugabe's Christianity, is a Western import.

Background: Lesotho and Its History

Surrounded on all sides by South Africa, with no natural resources except population, Lesotho squirms in an ever-tightening vise. Only 10 percent of the land in Lesotho is arable, but 86 percent of its population of more than two million engage in subsistence agriculture (1996 CIA Factbook). Most Basotho have no source of cash income at all, while a few are wealthy even by US standards; under these circumstances, "mean national income per household member" means little, but in 1994, it was M56.57[4] per month (about $13) (Gay and Hall 1994: 20). The conclusion of international experts is that Lesotho is experiencing a "permanent crisis" (9) exacerbated by unemployment, population growth, decline in arable land, reduction in soil fertility, desertification, and hopelessness.

Lesotho acquired independence from British "protection" in 1966, but it is still mostly "rural," meaning that the population is scattered through mountainous areas with no roads, electricity, or telephone lines; few commercial outlets and towns; and relatively little contact with the so-called global village. Although information about Lesotho is available on the Internet, most Basotho have never even seen a computer, and net-surfing is restricted to a few computers at the National University and in the capital city, Maseru. Urban sprawl is confined to the lowlands near Maseru, and there are a few good-sized towns, where "modernization" makes an impact on culture in the form of Kentucky Fried Chicken stands, South African fashions, newspapers, and TV. There is a national radio station that broadcasts most of every day and a national television station that operates a few hours a day. There are all the "contrasts" that have long been clichés of ministries of tourism in Africa, but Lesotho is mostly a nation of villages full of destitute people. Most men are jobless and illiterate. Although in 1976, up to 48 percent of men worked as laborers in South African mines, now only 25 percent have mine employment, and by 2001, it is estimated that only about 17 percent will be so employed (Gay et al. 1995: 170). Home beer-brewing keeps the little cash there is, in circulation in the villages, but it also contributes to the problem of alcoholism. Some studies show that as many as 50 percent of families experience problems resulting from alcoholism (Gay et al. 1995: 75). Some young men till small gardens or fields; some guard diminishing herds of sheep on overgrazed, open land. First-world pastimes aren't available; only 2 percent of households have electricity (Gill 1992: 2). There is precious little for men to do in Lesotho but drink, develop social and sexual relationships, and hang out.

The situation for girls and women is different from that for men. Owing to social custom reinforced by Christian missionaries, girls and women have plenty to do. They haul water, often from distances as far as an hour away (Gill 1992: 13), gather firewood from increasingly deforested hillsides, wash and mend clothing (though often there is no soap and no thread), tend children, gather "wild vegetables" (known in other countries as weeds), cook, clean, sweep, and decorate their houses. Lesotho is unlike most of Africa in that Basotho women are more likely to be literate than Basotho men. (Because census figures are old, outdated, and questionable at best, no reliable literacy figures exist.)

Women's legal status is nil. All women are legally "minors" in Lesotho under customary law; under common law, women are minors till age 21, but they revert to minor status if they marry, attaining majority status only if single or widowed (Gill 1992: 5). Women cannot hold property; have no custody rights in the case of divorce; cannot inherit property if they have sons; cannot borrow money; cannot own or run property or businesses; cannot sign contracts; or buy and sell livestock, land, or "unnecessary" goods. Nor can a woman obtain a passport without a husband's or father's consent (5). The franchise is one of the few areas in which women have gained legal rights since independence in 1966, so women do now vote. A few well-educated, middle-class women are fighting for greater equity. The Federation of Women Lawyers has "mounted an awareness campaign on the rights of women" and is trying to secure legal rights for women. However, the fact that there are three legal codes (customary law based on tradition and the chieftaincy, common law based on the Roman-Dutch system of South Africa, and constitutional law), which often contradict each other, makes the going difficult, to say the least, for Basotho feminists (Thai 1996: 17).

Social stratification by education, religion, income, occupation, and mobility in Lesotho means that there is no social hegemony; it also means it is difficult to define class in this African nation by the standard indicators used in Western countries. The "Lesotho" of a bilingual woman who is a government or university administrator educated abroad is very different from the "Lesotho" of a woman in a mud-and-thatch hut on a dirt track in the rural mountains, educated for a few years in a mission school, who has perhaps twice been to the capital city by bus. Their "Lesothos" are also different from that of a woman in the Roma Valley who cleans house for a succession of expatriates whose clothes, books, and memories speak of distant and more prosperous ways of life. None of them, not even the white-collar government worker, enjoys enough income or other privileges to qualify as "middle class" by American standards. The government worker may have electricity in her home (or she may not), and she probably has no telephone and car, but she may have a domestic servant who regards her as privileged.

A final but important aspect of the background of this study is that women in Lesotho endure physical abuse almost universally. Marriage is compulsory by custom, and divorce is very expensive; for this reason, the divorce rate is only 1 percent (Gill 1992: 5). However, women manage up to 60 percent of the households on their own, in small part because of male migrant labor but in larger part because of de facto separation and divorce occasioned by couples never having been married and then separating, by male abandonment, or by women leaving abusive mates (21).

In the two years I lived in Lesotho, I only met one woman who said she had never been beaten by a husband or boyfriend, and she said she was the only woman she knew who had been so fortunate. According to precolonial tradition, a man claimed a woman as a wife by raping her, and this custom is still common in the mountain areas. One scholar notes the "apparent tolerance of a man's unbridled right to exploit women sexually" (Epprecht 1995: 48), and it is in this context that I was not surprised to find a great many women seeking primary emotional and what could be called sexual relationships with other women.

Problematizing the Author

I cannot claim to have conducted an objective scientific study of Basotho women and sexuality, nor would I want to make such a claim. In every respect, what I see or understand of Basotho women's experience is filtered through my own range of perceptions and beliefs and is colored by my own experience of what is sexual, what is affectional, and what is possible between women. My experience as a lesbian shapes my interpretation of behavior I perceive as being "erotic" or "lesbian-like."[5] My experience as a white, working-class woman who has made it into academe and thereby lost her class connections and identity shapes my understanding of privilege and its relationship to "lesbianism" as a lifestyle. I have now been "out" for 21 years, but I prefer not to share a household with my partner and resent definitions of lesbianism that reify the tidy domestic arrangement that features two middle-class women under one roof, so popular in lesbian communities in the United States. My personal experience strongly influences my perception of the intersections of class privilege (or its lack) and sexual choices in Lesotho. My informants were all black women, Basotho friends, neighbors, and acquaintances, mostly residents of the Roma Valley, an area of Lesotho steeped in and named for the Roman Catholic religion.[6] Although many of the women with whom I discussed women's sexuality had migrated to the Roma Valley from the mountains and can tell about rural women's lives firsthand, there is a distance, a separation, of their experiences from those of mountain women who have not migrated. The very fact that they were talking to a white woman about bodily functions sets them apart from women in the mountains who have never done so. Their lenses, like mine, are particular and not a random sample of Basotho women. I speak Sesotho, but not fluently, and I am not an anthropologist. Much of what I've learned about women, class, and sexuality in Lesotho has come to me fortuitously.

I got to Lesotho by accident. I'd been chosen as a Senior Fulbright Scholar in performance studies on the strength of my application to do research and teaching in Nigeria. When I found I was allergic to malaria preventives, I was hastily reassigned to Lesotho, and in two weeks I found myself living in a country about which I knew virtually nothing. My search for information on Lesotho during those two weeks turned up little more than its being one of the 15 poorest countries in the world. I found it on a map: a tiny island of basaltic mountains surrounded on all sides by South Africa. I stumbled across a line in a guidebook averring that the "mountain kingdom in the sky" is "a nation of women and children," because most able-bodied Basotho men work in the mines and factories of South Africa. Although I was soon to learn that the myth of the absent miner was outdated and had never been accurate, it piqued my interest, because as a theater historian specializing in lesbian dramatic literature in Queen Anne's England, I had come to the conclusion that women in homosocial environments are likely to explore homosexual expression (Kendall 1986, 1990, 1993). This notion is reinforced by others who have studied homosocial societies (cf. Shepherd 1987: 249–50). I imagined that a "nation of women and children" might be very attractive from my point of view, and I looked forward to further discoveries with considerable hope and enthusiasm.

Women in Lesotho

Probably the most important accident in my quest for lesbians in Lesotho was that on my arrival at the university, I was housed at the guest house, where I befriended 'M'e[7] Mpho Nthunya, the cleaning woman. Before long, I learned that 'M'e Mpho had actually, in a sense, married another woman (see below). When I asked her if she knew of any women-loving-women in Lesotho, she was puzzled. "Many of us love each other," she said, laughing. Thinking she had misunderstood me, I explained that I meant not just affectionate loving, but, as I stammered, "Women who share the blankets with each other," that being the euphemism in Lesotho for having sex.

'M'e Mpho found that uproariously funny. "It's *impossible* for two women to share the blankets," she said. "You can't have sex unless somebody has a *koai* [penis]." This concise, simple observation led me to two different but related trains of thought.

First, 'M'e Mpho's "impossible" brought to mind one of David Greenberg's remarks in *The Construction of Homosexuality,* to wit, "The kinds of sexual acts *it is thought possible to perform,* and the social identities that come to be attached to those who perform them, vary from one society to another" (1988: 3; italics mine). Greenberg points out:

> Homosexuality is not a conceptual category everywhere. To us, it connotes symmetry between male-male and female-female relationships. . . . When used to characterize individuals, it implies that erotic attraction originates in a relatively stable, more or less exclusive attribute of the individual. Usually it connotes an exclusive orientation: the homosexual is not also heterosexual; the heterosexual is not also homosexual. Most non-Western societies make few of these assumptions. Distinctions of age, gender, and social status loom larger. The sexes are not necessarily conceived symmetrically. (4)

Lesotho is one such non-Western society, and Basotho society has not constructed a social category *lesbian.* Obviously, in Lesotho the sexes are not conceived symmetrically. Nor is "exclusive orientation" economically feasible for most Basotho women. There is no tradition in Lesotho that permits or condones women or men remaining single; single persons are regarded as anomalous and tragic, unless they have joined celibate religious orders. Thus, women have no identity apart from that of the men to whom they are related; only comparatively wealthy divorced or widowed women could set up housekeeping alone or with each other. As in many other African societies, including that of Swahili-speaking people in Mombasa, Kenya, "A respectable adult is a married adult" (Shepherd 1987: 243). However, there is much less wealth in Lesotho than in Mombasa; the lesbian unions Shepherd describes as common and "open" among married and formerly married women in Mombasa are based, as she notes, on the constructions of rank and gender in that society, as well as on the existence of a considerable number of women with sufficient economic power to support other women (262–65). Even more important, women in Mombasa have a concept of the possibility of sexual activity between women, according to Gill Shepherd. In Swahili, the word for lesbian is *msagaji*, which means "a grinder" and has obvious descriptive meanings for at least one variety of lesbian sexual activity. Although I found no evidence of any comparable use of words in the Sesotho language, what is more significant is that Basotho women define sexual activity in such a way that makes lesbianism linguistically inconceivable—not that "grinding" doesn't take place, but it isn't considered "sexual."

The second train of thought 'M'e Mpho Nthunya's "impossible" led me to is the great mass of scientific sex studies. From Kraft-Ebbing, through Kinsey and Hite, and on up to the present, these studies repeatedly show that lesbians "have sex" less frequently than heterosexuals or gay men.[8] Marilyn Frye cites one study by Blumstein and Schwartz that shows that "47 percent of lesbians in long term relationships 'had sex' once a month or less, while among heterosexual married couples only 15 percent had sex once a month or less" (1992: 110). Frye is amused by how the sexperts count how many times people have sex. She notes that the question "how many times" they "had sex" is a source of merriment for lesbians. For what constitutes "a time"? Frye continues, "What 85 percent of long-term heterosexual married couples do more than once a month takes on the average eight minutes to do" (110). In contrast, what lesbians do so much less frequently takes anything from half an hour to half a day to do and can take even longer if circumstances allow. Frye concludes: "My own view is that lesbian couples . . . don't 'have sex' at all. By the criteria that I'm betting most of the heterosexual people used in reporting the frequency with which they have sex, lesbians don't have sex. There is no male partner whose orgasm and ejaculation can be the criterion for counting 'times'" (113).

Or as 'M'e Mpho Nthunya put it, no *koai*, no sex. On a similar tack, Diane Richardson notes, "How do you know you've had sex with a woman? Is it sex only if you have an orgasm? What if she comes and you

don't? . . . What if what you did wasn't genital, say you stroked each other
and kissed and caressed, would you later say you'd had sex with that woman?
And would she say the same? The answer, of course, is that it depends; it
would depend on how you and she interpreted what happened" (1992: 188).

Because among liberated Western lesbians it is difficult to determine
when one has had "sex" with a woman, it is not at all surprising that in
Roman Catholic circles in Lesotho, "sex" is impossible without a *koai*. Among
Basotho people, as among those surveyed in numerous studies in the United
States and the United Kingdom, sex is what men have—with women, or
with each other. The notion of "sex" or "the sex act" is so clearly defined
by male sexual function that 'M'e Mpho Nthunya's view of it should not
surprise any of us. However, women in Lesotho do, as 'M'e Mpho said,
love each other. And in expressing that love, they have *something*.

Judith Gay documents the custom among boarding-school girls in
Lesotho of forming same-sex couples composed of a slightly more "dominant" partner, called a "Mummy," and a slightly more "passive" partner,
called a "Baby" (1985). The girls do not describe these relationships as
sexual, although they include kissing, body rubbing, possessiveness and
monogamy, the exchange of gifts and promises, and sometimes, genital
contact.[9] Gay also describes the custom among Basotho girls of lengthening
the labia minora, which is done "alone or in small groups" and "appears
to provide opportunities for auto-eroticism and mutual stimulation among
girls" (1985: 101). Certainly, there are ample opportunities for Basotho
women of various ages to touch each other, fondle each other, and enjoy
each other physically. The fact that these activities are not considered to
be "sexual" grants Basotho women the freedom to enjoy them without
restraint, embarrassment, or the "identity crises" experienced by women in
homophobic cultures like those of the United States and Europe. Margaret
Jackson writes convincingly that the valorization of heterosexuality and the
"increasing sexualization of Western women [by sexologists] which has taken
place since the nineteenth century should not be seen as 'liberating' but
rather as an attempt to eroticize women's oppression" (1987: 58).

I have observed Basotho women—domestic workers, university students,
and secretaries (but not university lecturers)—kissing each other on the mouth
with great tenderness, exploring each other's mouths with tongues, and for
periods of time in excess of 60 seconds, as a "normal," even daily, expression of affection. The longest kisses usually take place out of view of men
and children, so I presume that Basotho women are aware of the eroticism
of these kisses and are protective of their intimacy, yet never have I heard

any Mosotho woman describe these encounters as "sexual." When I called attention to this activity by naming it to a Mosotho professional researcher who was educated abroad, she told me, "Yes, in Lesotho, women like to kiss each other. And it's nothing except—." She seemed at a loss for words and did not finish the sentence but skipped, with some obvious nervousness, to "Sometimes . . . I—I—I—don't like it myself, but sometimes I just do it."

It is difficult to discuss women's sexuality in Lesotho because of the social taboos (both precolonial and postcolonial) against talking about it. Even now, it is socially taboo in Lesotho for a woman who has borne children to discuss sex with girls or women who have not. (Fortunately for my research, I have borne children; a childless American colleague also doing research in Lesotho found it difficult to have discussions about sexuality with adult Basotho women.) My Basotho women friends would not dream of explaining menstruation to their daughters; rather, they expect girls to learn the mysteries of their developing bodies and of sexual practices from other girls, perhaps a year or two older than themselves. Like everything else in Lesotho, this is changing—very slowly in more remote rural areas and rather quickly in the towns. Sex education two or three generations ago took place in "initiation schools" for boys and girls, but these traditional schools were a major target of missionary disapproval and have now just about disappeared in all but the most remote areas. The taboo on talking about sex certainly hampered the efforts of family planning advocates to institute sex education from the 1970s, and the Roman Catholic Church did little to change that, but as a result of concerted efforts of a number of nongovernmental agencies and of the Lesotho government itself, birth control information, drugs, and other pregnancy-prevention techniques are now widely available in health clinics. For the most part, the church now seems to look the other way when women line up at the clinics for pills, IUDs, and injections to prevent pregnancy. More recently, government-sponsored AIDS education workers have been at pains to dispel dangerous myths kept alive by groups of prepubescent teenagers, to popularize the use of condoms, and to encourage young people to learn about and talk about "safe sex." This may in time have profound and lasting effects on sexual behavior in Lesotho.

A number of difficulties remain. The Sesotho language was first written down by missionaries, who compiled the first Sesotho-English and Sesotho-French dictionaries. Not surprisingly, these dictionaries include few words to describe sexuality or sex acts. If there ever were words for "cunnilingus," "g-spot," or "Do you prefer clitoral or vaginal orgasm?" in Sesotho, they certainly did not make it into the written records of the language, nor do translations of these terms appear in phrase books or dictionaries.

My attempts to "come out" to rural woman and domestic workers were laughable; they couldn't understand what I was talking about, and if I persisted, they only shook their heads in puzzlement. Despite this, I had some long conversations with Basotho women, especially older university students and domestic workers, who formed my social cohort in Lesotho and who trusted me enough to describe their encounters in as much detail as I requested. From these, I learned of fairly common instances of triba-dism or rubbing, fondling, and cunnilingus between Basotho women, with and without digital penetration. They initially described this as "loving each other," "staying together nicely," "holding each other," or "having a nice time together." But not as having sex. No *koai*, no sex.

Lillian Faderman's observation that "a narrower interpretation of what constitutes eroticism permitted a broader expression of erotic behavior [in the 18th century], since it was not considered inconsistent with virtue" makes sense here (1981: 191). If these long, sweet Basotho women's kisses or incidences of genital contact were defined as "sexual" in Lesotho, they could be subject to censure both by outside observers, who seem to disapprove of sex generally (nuns, visiting teachers, traveling social workers), or by the very women who so enjoy them but seek to be morally upright and to do the right thing.[10] If the mummy-baby relationships between boarding-school girls were defined as "sexual," they would no doubt be subject to the kind of repression "particular friendships" have suffered among nuns.

Since "sex" outside of marriage in Roman Catholic terms is a sin, then it is fortunate for women in this mostly Catholic country that what women do with women in Lesotho cannot possibly be sexual. No *koai*, no sex means that women's ways of expressing love, lust, passion, or joy in each other are neither immoral nor suspect. This may have been the point of view of the 19th-century missionaries who so energetically penetrated Lesotho and who must have found women-loving-women there when they arrived. Judith Lorber notes, "Nineteenth-century women were supposed to be passionless but arousable by love of a man; therefore, two women together could not possibly be sexual" (1994: 61).

Nthunya dictated her entire autobiography to me over the two years I lived in Lesotho, published as *Singing Away the Hunger: Stories of a Life in Lesotho* (1996; reissued in the United States by Indiana University Press in 1997 as *Singing Away the Hunger: The Autobiography of an African Woman*). In it she describes, in addition to a loving and affectionate (though compulsory) heterosexual marriage, a kind of marriage to a woman that included an erotic dimension. According to Judith Gay, these female marriages were common among women of Nthunya's generation. She writes, "elderly informants told me that special affective and gift exchange partnerships among girls and women existed 'in the old days' of their youth" (1985: 101). The chapter of Nthunya's autobiography that is most pertinent here is "When a Woman Loves a Woman," first published as " 'M'alineo Chooses Me," in the anthology *Basali! Stories by and about Women in Lesotho* (1995).

Nthunya describes how the woman she calls 'M'alineo chose her as her *motsoalle* (special friend) with a kiss: "It's like when a man chooses you for a wife, except when a man chooses, it's because he wants to share the blankets with you. The woman chooses you the same way, but she wants love only. When a woman loves another woman, you see, she can love with her whole heart" (1997: 69).

Nthunya describes the process of their relationship, the desire that characterized it, the kisses they shared, their hand-holding in church, and their meetings at the local café. And she describes the two ritual feasts observed by themselves and their husbands, recognizing their relationship. These feasts, held one year apart, involved the ritual presentation and slaughter of sheep, as well as eating, drinking, dancing, singing, and exchanging gifts, as well as the general merriment and validation of the commitment they made to each other by all the people they knew. "It was like a wedding," Nthunya writes (1997: 70). This ritual, which she describes as taking place around 1958, was widespread and well-known in the mountains where she lived. She describes the aftermath of her feast this way:

> So in the morning there were still some people drinking outside and inside, jiving and dancing and having a good time.
>
> Alexis [my husband] says to them, "Oh, you must go to your houses now. The *joala* [home-made beer] is finished."
>
> They said, "We want meat."
>
> He gave them the empty pot to show them the meat is all gone. But the ladies who were drinking didn't care. They said, "We are not here to see you; we are coming to see [your wife]."
>
> They sleep, they sing, they dance. Some of them are *motsoalle* together with each other. (71)

It would appear from Nthunya's story that long-term loving, intimate, and erotic relationships between women were normative in rural Lesotho at that

time and were publicly acknowledged and honored. Judith Gay describes
an occasion when she was discussing women's relationships with three older
women and a 24-year-old daughter-in-law interrupted the discussion by
clapping her hands. "'Why are you clapping so?' asked the straightforward
ninety-seven-year-old woman. 'Haven't you ever fallen in love with another
girl?'" (1985: 102).

The celebration of *motsoalle* relationships with gift-giving and feasting
bears a striking similarity to the celebration of *bagburu* relationships among
the Azande women of the Sudan as described to Edward Evans-Pritchard
(1970) by male Azande informants in 1962 and 1963. However, since
Evans-Pritchard was unable to converse with Azande women involved in
such relationships, one can only speculate about what the Azande women's
relationships really involved and whether or not they were similar to *motsoalle*
relationships. Evans-Pritchard's secondhand information is full of the same
sort of male fantasies about lesbian love-making that European males indulge
in. (See John Cleland's *Fanny Hill* [1749], for example, for the assumption
that women need to acquire and indeed strap on penis substitutes to give
each other sexual pleasure.) What is most interesting to me about Evans-
Pritchard's work is that one of his informants, who clearly believed that the
Azande *bagburu* relationships included sexual activities resembling male-female
intercourse, reported, "Once a woman has started homosexual intercourse
she is likely to continue it because *she is then her own master* and may have
gratification when she pleases and not just when a man cares to give it to
her" (1970: 1432; italics mine). This may be merely male conjecture about
what women feel, but it does unself-consciously spell out a man's perception of connections between lesbianism and personal agency and between
heterosexuality and the domination of women. Jackson develops this line
of thought very provocatively: "Although individual women, and different
groups and classes of women, will experience heterosexuality as more or less
coercive according to their specific circumstances, in terms of the production
and reproduction of male supremacy it is absolutely crucial that the vast
majority [of women] be structured into the system of hetero-relations which
lies at the very base of that supremacy" (1987: 77).

There is no indication in Nthunya's account, however, that she
viewed her relationship with her *motsoalle* as an alternative or a threat to
her marriage. She says that her husband and her *motsoalle*'s husband were
both supportive of the relationship; she and her *motsoalle* enjoyed kissing
and touching (but she says nothing about genital touching); and in her
own case, the heterosexual marriages outlasted the *motsoalle* relationship.

Whether Evans-Pritchard's informants were right or not about what Azande women did in bed, it is clear that Nthunya's husband would have had no justification for sharing Azande men's fears about women in acknowledged special relationships with each other.

The Sexuality Debates

After 'M'e Mpho Nthunya told me her story, I tried several times to get more detailed information from her about her *motsoalle* relationship. I asked her to describe what she and 'M'e Malineo did in detail, and on these occasions, she avoided making eye contact with me and said that kisses and hand-holding were the extent of it. As I stumbled over words on these occasions, trying to translate her answers into English and my questions into Sesotho, I felt the same kind of embarrassment I would have felt had I asked such questions of my own grandmother. Why, I wondered, do I think I need to know her answers to these questions? Why does it matter to me what 'M'e Mpho and 'M'e 'M'alineo did in 1958? Why does it feel important to me to know whether there are or were women in Lesotho who might be called lesbian? Why do I care what women did in bed in Queen Anne's England or in Lesotho at any time and how they thought about or named what they did?

After all, constructing or recovering lesbian history is, in a way, an act of legitimation that presumes illegitimacy. If, in Lesotho, love between women was (and still is) perfectly legitimate—not limited to "sexual" behavior but rather viewed as an activity or a feeling as ubiquitous as air—my prying questions become irrelevant, and the laughter that most often greeted those questions when I put them to Basotho women becomes understandable. Judith Roof explains that legitimation is not about "power or authorization, but anxiety and emptiness" (1994: 64). The need for legitimacy only arises in cultures (like my own) in which love between women had been pathologized or made illegitimate. I might examine, instead of lesbian history, the history of heterosexist social institutions. I might ask, as Shane Phelan suggests, "Why is homophobia virulent in some societies and mild or nonexistent in others?" (1993: 771). She suggests that lesbian scholars avoid "constructions of lesbianism that trap us" into prying into our foremothers' bedrooms, because these constructions reify the notion that there is a "natural, or an authentic lesbian identity, by which we can measure and justify our existence."

It is partly because I identify as something that has been socially constructed (in Western cultures) as monstrous, that I go looking for others like me. It is also partly because I have been targeted for abuse in my own culture that I feel this "anxiety or emptiness" Roof describes and that I seek support and recognition from others who might be like me. It is also, of course, because I enjoy the company of other women who find women emotionally and physically attractive that I seek out other lesbians. Among them, I don't have to pretend to be what I am not or to have interests or attractions I do not have. Among lesbians, I am not presumed to be heterosexual; I do not have to explain myself or my personal life, and that, for me, is a great relief.

My discovery of lesbian or lesbian-like behavior among Basotho women, and my perception of its similarity to behavior among privileged women in Queen Anne's England, has clarified my thinking about homophobia and women's ways of loving each other. In addition, it may offer a way out of the realist/essentialist vs. nominalist/social constructionist controversy in gay and lesbian studies. The classical exchange in this debate pits a realist/essentialist, who believes that lesbians have existed in most cultures and throughout history, against a nominalist/social constructionist, who believes that lesbians only appear where and when there is the socially constructed concept "lesbian." The situation in Lesotho suggests that women can and do develop strong affectional and erotic ties with other women in a culture where there is no concept or social construction equivalent to "lesbian" nor is there a concept of erotic exchanges among women as being "sexual" at all. And yet, partly because of the "no concept" issue and in part because women have difficulty supporting themselves without men in Lesotho, a lesbian lifestyle option is not available to Basotho women. Lesbian or lesbian-like behavior has been commonplace, conventional, but it has not been viewed as "sexual" nor as an alternative to heterosexual marriage, which is both a sexual and an economic part of the culture.

The situation in Lesotho might be evidence that the realist/essentialists are right (or one step closer to being right) in supposing that women will love women anywhere and in any culture and will express that love erotically when it occurs to them to do so, even if there are no words to describe it.[11] The social constructionists are also right that the idea of having a sexual identity, the possibility that what women do together could be called "sex," and the notion that "lesbian" is an identity that one might claim and celebrate are culturally specific.

It should not be surprising that the Nigerian scholar Ifi Amadiume finds "shocking and offensive" the assertions made by some African American lesbians that some of their ancestors in the motherland were lesbian (1987: 7). Amadiume, through the lenses of her virulent homophobia, sees African American lesbians as legitimizing themselves at the expense of African women's reputations; she claims, "These priorities of the West are of course totally removed from, and alien to the concerns of the mass of African women" (9). If by "priorities of the West" Amadiume means cultural expressions such as self-conscious and defiant lesbian costuming, lesbian literature, and lesbian families, she is probably justified in claiming they are removed from the concerns of the mass of African women. However, it would be insulting and essentializing in the extreme to suggest that the bonds of love and loyalty among Basotho women are in any way "Western" or that the erotic expression of those bonds is "alien" to the women who enjoy them. The evidence seems to me to lead to the conclusion that homophobia is a priority of the West that is removed from and alien to the concerns of the mass of African women.

If there has been a tendency on the part of black heterosexist cultural observers to insist that lesbianism is a "white" or a "Western" construct, there has also been a tendency on the part of white Western lesbians to attribute their own cultural issues to lesbians or women who express lesbian-like behavior in other parts of the world. Queer theory, based on queer people's performances of themselves as nonconformists in gendered societies, privileges both nonconformity and the visible.[12]

The Basotho domestic workers I met who love each other do not perform themselves as "queer." They marry men and conform, or appear to conform, to gender expectations. Most will bear and tend the culture's children, carry those children on their backs, fetch firewood and water that they will then carry on their heads, cook, work for wages if they can find wage work, manage their households, and cater for the physical needs of their husbands or boyfriends. There seem to be simply no other choices available to poor Basotho women, culturally or economically. I found no models of other ways to be, and despite close and sometimes erotic relationships occurring between many of the women I knew, I found no women in Lesotho choosing to live in same-sex couple relationships or to defy heterosexual expectations by choosing female lovers exclusively.[13]

In examining the question of options or choices, it may be useful to clarify to what extent women in Lesotho have social or sexual options. Five years before Judith Gay wrote her article on "Mummies" and "Babies" for the *Journal of Homosexuality*, she completed a PhD dissertation at Cambridge, "Basotho Women's Options: A Study of Marital Careers in Rural Lesotho" (1980). There she examined the lives of married women whose husbands are migrant workers and those whose husbands remain at home, of widows, and of separated or divorced women. She did not even mention the possibility of single, independent women living alone nor of lesbianism as an option for Basotho women. Instead, she stated, "Marriage is the principal means whereby these women attain adult status and gain access to the productive resources and cash flows which are essential to them and their dependents" (299). She accurately predicted growing unemployment among men in Lesotho and conjectured, "It is possible also that the resulting marital conflict and economic difficulties will lead to increasing numbers of independent women who become both heads of matrifocal families and links in matrilateral chains of women and children" (312). That is certainly happening, and perhaps in another decade, the lesbian option, as it is experienced in the northern hemisphere (or "the West"), will have come to Lesotho. If it does, it will no doubt come with its shadow, homophobia.

'M'e Mpho Nthunya concluded the first version of the story of her "marriage" to 'M'e Malineo as follows: "In the old days [note that here she refers to a period up to the late 1950s] celebrations of friendship were very beautiful—men friends and women friends. Now this custom is gone. People now don't love like they did long ago" (1995: 7). As Nthunya and I were preparing her autobiography for press, I asked her if she could add something to the conclusion of that chapter, perhaps to explain why people don't love like they did long ago. She added the following: "Today the young girls only want men friends; they don't know how to choose women friends. Maybe these girls just want money. Women never have money, so young girls, who want money more than love, get AIDS from these men at the same time they get the money" (1997: 72). Perhaps that is all there is to it, though I would have thought that women in the "old days" needed money, too.

I believe that one pressure leading toward the demise of the celebration of *batsoalle*[14] is the increasing Westernization of Lesotho and the arrival, at least in urban or semi-urban areas and in the middle class, of the social construction "homophobia"—with and without its name. Judith Gay noted in her study of lesbian-like relationships in Lesotho that women who live "near the main road and the South African border" were "no longer involved in intimate female friendships" (1985: 102). Living near a "main road" or a South African border would expose a woman to imported ("Western") ideas and values, as would formal education. Women in rural areas would be less likely to suffer the pollution of homophobia.

By scrutinizing homophobia as the "queer" thing it is, given examples of healthy lesbian activity in indigenous cultures in Lesotho and elsewhere, we might conclude that homophobia is an "unnatural" vice, that homophobia is far more likely to qualify as "un-African" (if it weren't essentialist to use such a word) than homosexuality, and that homophobia is the product of peculiar (western or northern hemisphere) cultures.

As Michel Foucault wrote in his groundbreaking *History of Sexuality*, it is useful to view sexuality not as a drive, but "as an especially dense transfer point for relations of power" ([1978] 1981: 103). No *koai*, no sex. In that case, the loving and egalitarian erotic friendships of Basotho women would not be "sexual" at all, which is exactly what Basotho women have been saying whenever anyone asked them. The freedom, enjoyment, and mutual respect of Basotho women's ways of loving each other, occurring in a context in which what women do together is not defined as "sexual," suggests a need to look freshly at the way Western constructions of sexuality and of homophobia are used to limit and oppress women. Having a (sexualized) "lesbian option" may not be as liberating as many of us have thought.

Notes

1. An earlier version of this paper appeared in *NUL Journal of Research* 6 (1996), though I have never seen it, and a different discussion of the same phenomenon will appear in *Women's Studies Quarterly* (1998).

2. Mugabe was quoted in the South African newspaper *Mail and Guardian* declaring homosexuality "immoral," "repulsive," and "an 'abhorrent' Western import" (Iden Wetherell 1995a: 15).

3. Lesotho is the country; Sesotho is the language. One person from Lesotho is a Mosotho; two or more are Basotho.

4. *M* stands for the unit of currency in Lesotho called the maloti. It is pegged to and therefore equal in value to the South African rand, which fluctuated in 1996 at around 4.5 to the dollar.

5. If by *lesbian* we mean an identity that emerged in the 20th century in certain Western cultures, then by definition, the word cannot be applied to the Basotho situation; some scholars are using the term *lesbian-like* to describe erotic and deeply affectional relationships among women who don't have the option of identifying themselves as lesbian. See, among other sources, Martha Vicinus (1994: 58) and Valerie Jenness (1992).

6. The particular form of Roman Catholicism that prospers in Lesotho is strongly influenced by Basotho customary beliefs and has incorporated much of the African religion that was well developed when the missionaries arrived.

7. 'M'e is the honorific or Sesotho term of address for a mature woman; literally, it means "mother." It is used with the woman's first name, and it is an insult to speak of her without the honorific or to speak of her by her surname only. In submission to Western academic custom, I sometimes refer to 'M'e Mpho as "Nthunya" in this paper, but I would never address her in that form. One Mosotho woman said to me, "To speak of a grown woman without using 'M'e is the same as stripping off all her clothes."

8. These studies have so much cachet that they are widely believed by even the most unlikely sources. For example, the US Centers for Disease Control had not carried out any research on woman-to-woman transmission of the HIV virus in 1992, because, in the words of one official, "Lesbians don't have much sex" (Smith quoted in Richardson 1992: 207).

9. Interestingly, John Blacking (1978) reports an almost identical custom among schoolgirls in Venda and Zulu schools in South Africa.

10. There are two words for *pervert* in the *English-Sotho Vocabulary* (ed. A. Casalis, 11th rev. ed., 1989): one is *mokhelohi*, which literally means "one who goes the wrong way," and the other is *mokoenihi*, "one who changes his mind." These words are apparently not in common use. When I asked people if they had ever known a *mokhelohi* or a *mokoenihi*, I got only puzzled stares and incomprehension.

11. One might argue that the existence of *motsoalle* relationships and the visibility of women expressing affection for each other in erotic ways constitute the construction of a "lesbian" way of being in Lesotho, but to do that, one would have to construct a nonsexual definition of "lesbian" which, in my opinion, begs the question.

12. See Phelan (1993: 774) and Judith Butler (1990) for enunciations of "queer theory" in lesbian contexts and Vicinus (1994) for a criticism of privileging the visible.

13. On this issue, I would be glad to be proved wrong. No doubt there are exceptions; I heard but was unable to confirm that some prostitutes in the capital city live as same-sex couples, some of which are "lesbian." In mountain villages, there are bound to be widows or single women who have established long-term unions that may also feature erotic expression; it would be astonishing if there were not. There may even have been lesbian relationships flourishing in Roma, where I lived and studied, among women to whom I had no social access. My point does not rest on the presence or absence of some defiant or closeted lesbians but on the absence of exclusive unions among the women I did know who openly expressed physical affection and attraction for each other and among whom erotic exchanges were commonplace.

14. Plural of *motsoalle*, special friend.

Sexual Politics in Contemporary Southern Africa

Stephen O. Murray

South Africa

A public black gay subculture has been identifiable in Cape Town since at least 1950 (Gevisser 1995: 72). In the 1990s, Dhianaraj Chetty interviewed three "moffie" performers who had been photographed and discussed in publications for black audiences for four decades (Chetty 1995). All three were hairdressers. Two came from devout Muslim families, and the third had been sent to Christian mission schools. Nonetheless, they all reported family support for their homosexuality and cross-dressing from an early age. One of them had had a relationship lasting 10 years with a man who also had a wife and children.

The general southern African derogative term for homosexuals, *moffie*, derives from *hermaphrodite*. According to Zackie Achmat, a black South African activist, "Moffies were men who dressed like women or who dressed in high style. Moffies were men who were really women in spirit. They spoke like women, flirted openly with men and kept men." He recalled that in the Salt River of his youth in the early 1970s, "The moffie hairdressers were also places where 'straight' men could go for a 'regular blow job' " (Achmat 1995: 335).

Officially, "sodomy" was a punishable offense under the apartheid regime's laws. Sex between women, however, was not criminalized, although, as part of the 1968 sex panic in South Africa, a law was added banning the manufacture, sale, or supply of any article "intended to be used to perform an unnatural sex act" (Immorality Amendment Act §2, quoted in Botha and Cameron 1997: 23). In fact, according to Oliver Phillips, "There is no record of any case, in either South Africa or Zimbabwe, where two women have been prosecuted for committing an 'unnatural offense' " (1997c: 46). (Now, as in the era studied by Marc Epprecht, the majority of "unnatural offense" cases that reach courts involve dispute over payment or resistance to blackmail. Phillips explains that "because of their economic power, white men are considerably more vulnerable to extortion than black men, with the result that they find themselves prosecuted more often for what were consensual acts. Second, they can more easily afford legal representation and so are more likely to appeal against a conviction or sentence, thus taking the case into the higher courts, the findings of which are recorded in the law reports" [49].)

By the 1980s, men and women who pursued same-sex relations became increasingly visible in South Africa. In the late 1980s, for example, a discotheque in Salt River, near the Cape Town suburb of Woodstock, occasionally hosted drag competitions for so-called colored gays. Many families of the participants attended and helped their sons prepare their costumes and make up (Isaacs and McKendrick 1992: 110).[1] In Cape Town, the African Gay Association (AGA) had an active membership of 70, and a bar in the city center provided a venue for "colored" gay women and men. At the same time, Soweto was reported to have 15 small "shebeens," or music halls catering exclusively to gays (100). In the early 1990s, an interracial gay liberation movement mobilized in the largest cities (see Bull 1990; Gevisser and Cameron 1995; Miller 1992). In October 1990, 800 people participated in Africa's first Gay Pride Parade in Johannesburg. An estimated 30 percent of the participants were black (*Bay Area Reporter*, November 1, 1990).

By the 1990s, even black townships had organizations of lesbians and gay men. Neil Miller attended a party sponsored by the Gays and Lesbians of the Witwatersrand (GLOW) and reported, "The 40 or so guests were mostly men, all quite young and very campy. They referred to their boy-friends as wives and barked orders at them. The boyfriends were deferen-tial. . . . GLOW attracted younger black men who, traditionally deprived of many social outlets, saw the organization as a place to have fun" (1992: 4, 8). Linda Ngcobo, a male founder of the group who later died of AIDS, described township gay culture to Miller as being centered on cross-dressing and role-playing. According to Miller, "No one, including gay men, seemed to be quite sure what 'gay' meant—were gay men really women? men? or something in between? This confusion was compounded by the fact that sex education was extremely limited in the townships; moreover, among some tribes, talking about sex at all was taboo. . . . Some, like Linda, were treated as women by their families [his parents expected him to do 'women's work,' including washing, ironing, and baking] and seemed to believe that deep down they actually were females"[2] (14, 17).

Linda also recounted the belief of a boyfriend and his family that Linda could bear a child. Miller notes:

> I wouldn't have lent much credence to this story except for an article about township gay life I had read in the *Weekly Mail* newspaper. In the article, the reporter asked a member of a gay male couple if he practiced safe sex. The man said he was "scared" of condoms, because, "if I used them I won't be able to have a baby. I am throwing my sperm away." The reporter pressed him: By sleeping with a man, wasn't he throwing his sperm away as it was? "No," the man replied. "One day my 'wife' and I hope to have children like any normal couple," (1992: 15)

According to Simon Nkoli, a black gay activist, in the Soweto townships, "People use the Sesotho *wor sitabane* to describe gay people. It means a person who has got two organs—sexual organs—a vagina and a penis. . . . We never really saw people with two organs. But if you are a feminine man, many will say you are a *sitabane*. And if you happen to be over twenty years old and you don't have a girlfriend, many will presume you are gay . . . [even though] in the black community, people don't know what gay is" (1993: 22).

Nkoli's siblings were asked, "Is it true that your brother has got two sexual organs?" and fellow students would ask to examine his genitalia. Because he had only a male organ, Nkoli's stepfather was certain that he must be normal (1993: 23–24). A lesbian born in Soweto in 1974 (17 years after Nkoli) encountered the same belief that "gays have two genitals," and for a time thought, "I can't be gay because I have to have two things" (Mamaki 1993: 3).

Male pregnancy is not the only "exotic" belief about homosexuality in contemporary South Africa. Miller talked to a 32-year-old man named Robert who had left his 20-year-old male wife along with a female wife and child in the diamond-mining center of Kimberley. Robert told him that if his parents found out about his homosexuality, they "will think I am bewitched and will take me to a witch doctor" (1992: 54). Nkoli's mother took him to four *sangomas* (traditional healers), three of whom suggested different persons as his bewitcher (1995: 251–52). The fourth, on the other hand, said he was fine as he was. (He was sent to a priest and a psychiatrist, too. The latter also declared him to be fine as he was [Nkoli 1993: 23, 26].)

Whether traditional cultures conceived of two or three genders, same-sex relationships in the homelands today are organized according to husband-wife roles. The relationships also seem to be marked by age differences as well.

South Africa's interim constitution, enacted in 1994 following the end of apartheid and the ascension to power of the African National Congress, included a clause prohibiting discrimination on the basis of sexual orientation in its bill of rights (section 8, part 2). The major opposition party in South Africa, the Inkatha Freedom Party, also included sexual orientation in its proposed constitution (Gevisser and Cameron 1995: 96). In 1996, this provision was incorporated into section 9, part 3 of the new constitution with the approval of an overwhelming majority of the parliament and the endorsement of the African National Congress, the Pan-African Congress, the National Party, and Archbishop Desmond Tutu, making South Africa the first nation in the world to ban in its constitution discrimination based on sexual orientation.

Eugene Patron has suggested that "perhaps it is because the South African liberation struggle lasted so long that the liberation movement was able to achieve a level of maturity that recognized the necessity of full and genuine inclusion of all minorities in society" (1995: 22). The inclusion also reflected the years of involvement of lesbian and gay activists in the anti-apartheid struggle and the intensive lobbying efforts of the National Coalition for Lesbian and Gay Equality.

President Robert Mugabe and Zimbabwe International Book Fairs

South African developments stand in sharp contrast to those in neighboring Zimbabwe.

In the traditional laws of the Shona and Ndebele people, homosexual behavior was not sanctioned. According to the journalist Bart Luirink, until July 1994, "Gays and lesbians in Zimbabwe lived relatively undisturbed lives" (*Johannesburg Weekly Mail and Guardian*, September 22, 1995). The gay activist Mike Coutinho noted that "older gay men tell tales of dodging the police while cruising Salisbury's Cecil Square (now Africa Unity Square in Harare) as far back as the early 1950s. Older black gay men recall tales of romance and hardship on the other side of town in the single-sex hostels for migrant labors" and also in prison (1993: 63).

From its founding in 1989 until 1994, Gays and Lesbians of Zimbabwe (GALZ) "had lived a quiet life as a support group and social club for the small but growing gay and lesbian community in Zimbabwe" (Dunton and Palmberg 1996: 8). In the early 1990s, Coutinho wrote that "with its limited and apolitical agenda, GALZ is treading a cautious path designed to break down isolation without drawing unwanted attention from the police," adding that in the townships "small networks of gay men are emerging" (1993: 65, 64).[3] At least some lesbians have connected with these networks as well, and "if they are lucky, they are able to link up with other lesbians in the townships" (64).

In January 1994, when GALZ placed an advertisement for its counseling service in the *Daily Gazette,* it set off the nation's first public debate about homosexuality. The heated discussion raged for some months then completely ceased when "rumor had it that the government had placed an embargo on all gay related subjects" (Dunton and Palmberg 1996: 8).

With the theme of the 1995 Zimbabwe International Book Fair (ZIBF) being "human rights and justice," GALZ applied for a small booth space to exhibit and advertise its literature on legal and constitutional aspects of lesbigay rights. The Publishers Association of South Africa supported GALZ participation,[4] and the application was accepted in March of that year. A week before the fair, however, Zimbabwe's director of information Bornwell Chakaodza sent ZIBF executive director Trish Mbanga a stinging letter:

> The government is dismayed and shocked by the decision of the Book Fair Trustees to allow the so called Gays and Lesbians of Zimbabwe (GALZ) to participate in the Zimbabwe International Book Fair (ZIBF) which will be officially opened by the President of the Republic of Zimbabwe, His Excellency Cde. R. G. Mugabe. The Government strongly objects to the presence of the GALZ stand at the Book Fair which has the effect of giving acceptance and legitimacy to GALZ.
>
> Whilst acknowledging the dynamic nature of culture, the fact still remains that both Zimbabwean society and government do not accept the public display of homosexual literature and material. The Trustees of the Book Fair should not, therefore,

force the values of gays and lesbians onto Zimbabwean culture.

In the interest of continued cooperation with the government, please withdraw the participation of GALZ at this public event. (July 24, 1995, letter, quoted by Dunton and Palmberg 1996: 9)

ZIBF trustees asked GALZ to withdraw, which GALZ leaders refused to do. Claiming "greatest regret" and that "its decision in no way compromises its commitment to freedom of expression," ZIBF withdrew GALZ's registration. (Two of the 18-member ZIBF board resigned in protest.) The contradiction between the fair's theme and the suppression of GALZ by fair trustees was not lost on Africans (including Nobel Prize winners Nelson Mandela, Desmond Tutu, Nadine Gordimer, and Wole Soyinka). Non-Africans also condemned the ban in a resolution approved at a pre-fair "Indaba on Human Rights and Freedom of Expression" in July.

President Mugabe subsequently opened the fair on August 1 with a denunciation of "rights to have sex in public." He went on to state, "I find it extremely outrageous and repugnant to my human conscience that such immoral and repulsive organisations, like those of homosexuals who offend both against the law of nature and the morals of religious beliefs espoused by our society, should have any advocates in our midst and elsewhere in the world" (Dunton and Palmberg 1996: 9). At a press conference following his speech, he added, "I don't believe they should have any rights at all."

Amnesty International and the Publishers' Association of South Africa issued statements condemning the ban on GALZ participation the same day. Various human rights advocates in South Africa and the rest of the world added their condemnation, and even the Catholic Commission for Justice and Peace in Zimbabwe weighed in for a right to privacy extending to homosexuals. The international attention, almost entirely critical, by no means fazed Mugabe. Two weeks later, he departed from his prepared speech on Heroes' Day to comment: "What we are being persuaded to accept is sub-animal behaviour and we will never allow it here. If you see people parading themselves as lesbians and gays, arrest them and hand them over to the police" (quoted by Dunton and Palmberg 1996: 12–13). A week later he told a crowd that "homosexuality is prevalent in jails where there are mad people and criminals, but, outside, we shall never accept it" (Inter Press Service Africa, August 21, 1995, hereafter cited as IPS).

Speculating about the reasons for Mugabe's high-profile attacks, Luirink has commented that "maybe the economic misery and the approaching presidential elections next year created a need for a new scapegoat. Maybe the South African winds of change shook nerves in Harare's presidential offices." According to Luirink, "Evelyn," a GALZ spokeswoman, "suspects that Mugabe himself, when he underwent a 12-year prison sentence under Ian Smith, may have been sexually abused. 'It happens all the time in our prisons. Moreover, his white adversaries once smeared him as a "moffie.'" It is because of the absence of any dialogue on the issue, Evelyn believes, that many Zimbabweans associate homosexuality with sexual abuse (1995). Challenging the common assertion that same-sex relations are not part of "traditional" African cultures, Evelyn added, "There are no Shona words for genitals or orgasm. There is, however, a Shona word meaning gay—*ngochane*. That proves that our sexual preferences are not 'alien' to black culture" (1995).

In the ensuing months, a number of Mugabe supporters elaborated on his condemnations.[5] On November 7, 1995, in an interview on the US National Public Radio program *All Things Considered*, Dr. Marvelous Mhloyi, a University of Zimbabwe AIDS researcher, explained that she refuses to ask male participants in her studies if they have sex with men, because "homosexuality is foreign to the African tradition." Her rationale was not unlike one commonly heard in conservative religious circles in the United States: asking research participants questions about same-sex sexual contact would interest them in it, and this would inevitably result in African culture being "corrupted."[6]

As the controversy unfolded, a number of those who joined GALZ for social reasons dropped out. As a precaution, the organization's leaders moved its records from its office to a safe house.

Before the 1996 fair, ZIBF trustees "reiterated its commitment to freedom of expression and the fullest dissemination of information," claiming that "no government pressure will be submitted to by the Trust" and that it would fight government objection to participation of any organisation in court" (press releases quoted in Dunton and Palmberg 1996: 16–17). How-ever, when the Zimbabwe government again strongly condemned GALZ's presence at the 1996 fair (which could have come as a surprise to no one), fair organizers again closed GALZ's stand. Four members of the ZIBF's board of trustees resigned in protest. Director of Information Chakaodza claimed that the move was "not a question of contravening the laws of Zimbabwe or the country's own Declaration of Rights. It is an issue of guaranteeing the cultural health of Zimbabwe" (IPS, August 7, 1997).

In early 1997, as police were investigating charges of homosexual rape against Mugabe's mentor, ex-president Canaan Banana, Michael Mawema, a former Zimbabwean nationalist leader, launched a campaign to persuade the government to punish homosexuality with castration and public whipping. Mawema claimed that "these crimes are on the increase and Zimbabwean laws against sexual perverts [specifically the maximum penalty of 7-year incarceration] are too soft." He also asserted that both Christianity and Zimbabwe's traditional African culture were unequivocally against "these perverts" (Cris Chinaka, March 5, 1997, Reuters).

As of this writing, the trial of Banana for raping a bodyguard who later killed a man who taunted him about it is ongoing.[7] At the 1997 Zimbabwe International Book Fair, the theme of which was "libraries and access to information," GALZ did not apply to be an official exhibitor but distributed its literature as part of a joint human rights stand that included women's organizations, human rights groups, universities, and a host of other organizations. Information distributed at the booth included how to get in touch with other gay people in Zimbabwe, discussion of personal identity problems and family issues, how to practice safe sex, and HIV education. In an interview, GALZ members stated:

> This is not about recruitment of people to become gay. You cannot recruit a "homo," because he is born like that, a GALZ member told an Inter Press Service reporter. "People are scared to come out in the open, so we want to help them learn to live with what they are through counseling. . . . A lot of people have shied away because of President Mugabe's statements, but in a way it has worked out in our favor, because it started something. It got people to talk about it." (IPS, August 7, 1997)

Mugabe's interventions certainly brought both the book fair and GALZ far more publicity, local and international, than they would have otherwise. Indeed, the attempt to suppress GALZ has inadvertently increased its size, strength, and visibility. According to Phillips:

> While previously, GALZ had found it difficult to negotiate many of the social, economic, and racial barriers that exist so endemically in Zimbabwe, homosexual men and women in Zimbabwe now found themselves asserting a common identity regardless of their backgrounds. Black men and women who identified themselves as gay or lesbian "came out" to insist that they did exist. making themselves publicly visible on an unprecedented

scale. Many Zimbabwean same-sex lovers and transgendered people who had previously not heard of GALZ or had not considered membership now contacted and joined the organization. Members who previously resisted using GALZ for anything other than social purposes now became politically motivated, leading to its rapid transformation into a much more politically directed organization. GALZ received a large number of new offers of support and alliance from many different nongovernmental and international organizations. (1997c: 53)

Namibia

During the fall of 1995, while the controversy over Mugabe's denunciations of homosexuality raged in Zimbabwe, government officials on the opposite side of southern Africa flaunted their ignorance of both history and human biology.

Namibia's finance minister, Helmut Angula, warned that homosexuality had recently infiltrated Namibia and that homosexuals' antisocial lives not only "are sources of deadly communicable diseases" but also lead to "social disorder."[8] Hadino Hishongwa, deputy minister for Lands, Resettlement and Rehabilitation, echoed the claim that homosexuality was un-African and recommended that homosexuals be given surgery "to remove unnatural hormones." The Clinical Psychological Association of Namibia issued a stinging reply, calling Hishongwa's comment "a foolish statement that reflects total ignorance of medical, surgical and psychological treatment techniques." The association's chair was quoted as saying that such statements could be "extremely harmful to the harmony and general well-being of the Namibian society" (quoted in Dunton and Palmberg 1996: 23).

Prime Minister Hage Geingob reportedly assured Namibia's homosexual citizens of their rights under Article 10.2 of the constitution at the time of Namibia's independence in 1990 (after 75 years of occupation by the Union of South Africa).[9] However, at the opening of the South-West Africa People's Organization (SWAPO) Women's Council Congress on December 6, 1996, President Sam Nujoma departed from the prepared text of his speech to assert that "all necessary steps must be taken to combat influences that are influencing us and our children in a negative way. Homosexuals must be condemned and rejected in our society." Other SWAPO public figures followed their leader's denunciations. Namibian gays and lesbians responded by forming the Rainbow Project to "answer them and start actively fighting for our rights." According to Nico Kisting:

> We formed a movement to fight for gay and lesbian rights and to address other issues in the gay and lesbian community. We named the movement the "Rainbow Project," on the one hand because the name celebrates the positiveness of diversity and on the other hand because the rainbow is an international gay rights symbol.
>
> We have formulated a Constitution and are now in the process of getting legal opinion on it. Once we have it adopted at our general monthly meeting, that would enable us to open a bank account and raise funds in the name of the organisation. At present we are making use of the infrastructure of "Sister Namibia," a women's organisation with a strong lesbian agenda.
>
> We have furthermore formed three working groups, a Legal Lobby Group to lobby lawmakers for legal change, a Cultural Group to raise awareness and educate the gay and lesbian community as well as the wider society on issues regarding homosexuality and a Counseling Group to provide counseling to gays and lesbians, to act as a homosexual referral service for the counseling mainstream and also to raise awareness about homosexuals and homosexuality in the counseling and social welfare community. . . . We have been very active in the last few months after many decades of hiding in the closet and suffering in silence.
>
> The response from the wider society has been very positive and supportive and even the politicians have softened their tone somewhat (although they still seem to deem it necessary to now and then denounce us publicly).
>
> Our big battle will be to decriminalise sodomy and to get the age of consent equalised with that of heterosexuals. Then of course we will also fight for other equal rights regarding spouses, adoption, etc.
>
> Our Labour Code interestingly enough already explicitly prohibits discrimination in the work place on the grounds of sexual orientation. (Kisting, e-mail posting, January 28, 1997)

Botswana

The debate triggered by Mugabe spilled over to neighboring Botswana. Thlaodi, a member of the ruling Botswana Democratic Party, echoed Mugabe's claim that homosexuality is foreign to "traditional African society." His comments have been challenged by other politicians, and in the course of the debate, Botswana gays and lesbians began telling their own stories in the country's press for the first time (Dunton and Palmberg 1996: 26).

It would appear that Mugabe's antigay campaign has had an opposite effect to the one he intended. As the debate has spread across southern Africa, lesbians and gay men have become more vocal and visible, offering living proof to counter claims about the un-Africanness of homosexuality. Meanwhile, South Africa, the nation once viewed around the world as epitomizing racist ideology and state oppression, is now a world leader in the recognition of lesbian and gay humanity. Whether its example of pluralism and nonvindictiveness will influence its immediate neighbors seems possible but has yet to be seen.

Notes

1. "The writers believe in the importance of narrating these events, for they contradict some of the more widely held myths that homosexual behaviour is 'forbidden' and 'non-expressed' in the so-called 'coloured' communities" (Isaacs and McKendrick 1992: 110; see Louw [1996] on same-sex heterogender marriages during the 1950s in Mkumbani, near Durban).

2. Mark Gevisser described the mix of gay liberationists and black Christian fundamentalists at Ngcobo's funeral on February 13, 1993 (1995: 14–17).

3. "In the slums she [Elizabeth, the heroine of Bessie Head's 1974 novel, *A Question of Power*] had grown up in in South Africa . . . homosexuals were laughingly accepted as one of the oddities of life, but they were never unduly disturbed people. Perhaps totally normal people don't think about it at all because it isn't their problem" (1974: 117).

4. South African publishers are second in number only to Zimbabwean publishers at the ZIBF (Dunton and Palmberg 1996: 11).

5. See Chris Dunton and Mai Palmberg for some examples, including Chief Mangwende's call to "see what pleasures women get in marrying each other" (1996: 13–14).

6. She is far from the only one who apparently believes that homosexual sex is irresistible, so that anyone who learns of its possibility will be impelled to try it and then to abandon heterosexuality.

7. Banana was found guilty in 1999 of 11 counts of sodomy. He was released from prison in 2001 and died in 2003 (*The Guardian*, November 10, 2003)—W. Roscoe.

8. Namibia is twice the size of California but has a population of only 1.7 million people (of whom 70,000 are government employees). According to Donald McNeil, "The president's credibility from 23 years as a guerrilla leader is seen as balancing competing factions. Black-white relations are peaceful, but those between the Ovambo-speaking people, who dominate his party, and the Hereros and Namas are tense" (*New York Times*, November 16, 1997).

9. Article 10.2 of the Namibian constitution states that "no person may be discriminated against on the grounds of sex, race, colour, ethnic origin, religion, creed or social or economic status." The growing international trend is to interpret "other status" to include sexual orientation, as Prime Minister Geingob seemed to do.

Part V

Conclusions

Woman-Woman Marriage in Africa

JOSEPH M. CARRIER AND STEPHEN O. MURRAY

Woman-woman marriage—in which one woman pays bride-price to acquire a husband's rights to another woman—has been documented in more than 30 African populations (O'Brien 1977: 109), including at least 10 Bantu-speaking groups in present-day southern Africa and Botswana—Sotho, Koni, Tawana, Hurutshe, Pedi, Venda, Lovedu, Phalaborwa, Narene, and Zulu. In these groups, female political leaders are also common.[1] These women chiefs rarely have male husbands (whether or not they had wives). Indeed, among the Lovedu, the queen was prohibited from having a male husband and was required instead to have a wife (Krige 1974). (George Murdock referred to Lovedu monarchs as *female kings* rather than *queens*, "because they very consciously play a male role" [1959: 389].)

In East Africa, female husbands have been mentioned among the Kuria, Iregi, Kenye, Suba, Simbiti, Ngoreme, Gusii, Kipsigis, Nandi, Kikuyu, and Luo. In Sudan, they occurred among the Nuer, Dinka, and Shilluk; in West Africa (particularly Nigeria), they existed among the Dahomean Fon, as well as the Yoruba, Ibo, Ekiti, Bunu, Akoko, Yagba, Nupe, Ijaw (O'Brien 1977: 110; Seligman and Seligman 1932: 164–65), the Nzema (Grottanelli 1988: 210), and the Ganagana/Dibo (Meek 1925, 1:204–10). In her survey of Kenya and South Africa, Denise O'Brien verified the continued existence of such roles among the Kuria, Kikuyu, Kipsigis, Nandi, and other southern Bantu populations, including the Venda. Eileen Krige and Sandra Barnes, respectively, told her that such marriages continue to exist among the Lovedu and the Yoruba (O'Brien 1977: 122).[2]

Edward Evans-Pritchard described woman-woman marriages among the Nuer in some detail:

> What seems to us, but not at all to Nuer, a somewhat strange union is that in which a woman marries another woman and counts as the pater of the children born of the wife. Such marriages are by no means uncommon in Nuerland, and they must be regarded as a form of simple legal marriage, for the woman-husband marries her wife in exactly the same way as a man marries a woman. When the marriage rites have been completed the husband gets a male kinsman or friend or neighbour, sometimes a poor Dinka, to beget children by her wife and to assist, regularly or when assistance is particularly required, in those tasks of the home for the carrying out of which a man is necessary. When the daughters of the marriage are married he will received for each a "cow of the begetting" and more beasts if he has played any considerable part in the maintenance of the home. (1951: 108)

Similarly, Max Gluckman reported:

> As among the Nuer, a rich and important Zulu woman can marry another woman by giving marriage-cattle for her, and she is the pater of her wife's children begotten by some male kinsman of the female husband. They belong to the latter's agnatic lineage as if she were a man. If a man dies leaving only daughters and no son, the eldest daughter should take his cattle and marry wives for her father to produce sons for him. This and the preceding forms of marriage [including ghost marriage] are weighty customs enforced by ancestral wrath, and they arise from the importance of continuing the agnatic line. (1950: 184)

George Huntingford described comparable practices among the Kenyan Nandi:

> A Nandi widow who had no children but possessed cattle could marry a young woman and become her *manong'otiot* ("husband") by paying the current rate of bridewealth, whereupon the young woman became her "wife." This gave both women the legal and social status of husband and wife respectively. There was no les-

bianism involved here, for the female husband could have her own men friends and the wife could have intercourse with any man of whom her "husband" approved. If she had children, not the man, but the female "husband" of the young man was the sociological father. (Huntingford 1973: 412)

Gretha Kershaw similarly described woman-woman marriages as a way for a childless woman to acquire offspring by the Kikuyu as well. These children were considered the female father's child because her descent group provided the bridewealth for her "wife" (1973: 55). In South Africa, Venda women who had male husbands could acquire their own wives by paying bride-price (*lobola*, a term borrowed from the Zulu) in cattle, just as men did. According to Hugh Stayt:

> Women in a position of authority, such as petty chiefs or witch-doctors, who have been able to accumulate the necessary wealth, often obtain wives in this way, even though they may be themselves married in the ordinary way. A woman may bring three wives to live with her at her own home. . . . These women are really in the position of servants and are obliged to do all the menial work; they may be given to different men for the purpose of obtaining children, but these men, not having paid the *lobola* for them, have no legal rights over them or their children. (1931: 143–44)

Inheritance of the female father's goods are the same as they would be for a male father's (170–71).

O'Brien also interprets female husbands as "social males" (1977). In the Sudan, "a Shilluk princess may become a husband (Farran 1963), or she may take lovers, but she should not give birth" (O'Brien 1977: 120)—that is, while she can have sex with men, she herself must be a genealogical dead end. Shilluk female shamans (*ajuago*) could also have lovers but not marry (123, n. 4, citing Seligman and Seligman 1932).

The Gender of the Female Husband

In her survey of the status of women, Niara Sudarkasa argues that there is a general de-emphasis on gender in "traditional" African societies and a corresponding emphasis on status ("personal standing"), which is usually, but not always, determined by wealth (1986: 97). Claire Robertson also argues that age and lineage override gender in traditional African societies (1987: 111), while Lorand Matory distinguishes "gender" from "sex" and stresses (in reference to the Yoruba) that "far stronger than the ideology of male superiority to the female is the ideology of senior's superiority to junior" (1994: 108). In the title of her 1980 article on woman-woman marriage among the Nandi, Regina Smith Oboler poses the question, "Is the female husband a man?" Evans-Pritchard (some years earlier) had already answered the question in the affirmative:

> A woman who marries in this way [i.e., takes a wife] is generally barren, and for this reason counts in some respects as a man. She acquires cattle through the marriage of kinswomen, including some of those due to uncles on the marriage of a niece, or by inheritance, since she counts as a man in these matters. A barren woman also often practices as a magician or diviner and thereby acquires further cattle; and if she is rich she may marry several wives. She is their legal husband and can demand damages if they have relations with men without her consent. She is also the pater of their children and on marriages of their daughters she receives "the cattle of the father," and her brothers and sisters receive the other cattle which go to the father's side in the distribution of bridewealth. Her children are called after her, as though she were a man, and I was told they address her as "father." She administers her home and herd as a man would do, being treated by her wives and children with the deference they would show a male husband and father. (1951: 108–9)

P. G. Rivière added: "It is clear that one finds in numerous societies women acting out male roles, including that of taking a wife" (1971: 68). Thus, an Efik-Ibibio (Nigerian) woman who grew up during the 19th century (and whose husband had 11 other wives) recalled: "I had a woman friend to whom I revealed my secrets. She was very fond of keeping secrets to herself. We acted as husband and wife. We always moved hand in glove and my husband and hers knew about our relationship. The village nicknamed us twin sister" (in Andreski 1970: 131). In other words, African marriages are between individuals in male and female *roles*, not necessarily between biological males and females.

The very possibility of a formal status for female husbands reflects the divergence between gender and sex in African societies. The exact nature of this status, however, is still the subject of debate.[3] Krige, for example, argues that Lovedu female husbands are neuter, neither masculine nor feminine within the terms of a binary gender system (1974: 32–33). At the same time, she offers no evidence that this status amounted to an intermediate or distinct third-gender role, involving special dress, social roles, or religious functions. The view of the societies she considers (southern Bantu groups) appears to be that the female husband becomes a "social male" within a system of binary genders—which are, however, not homologous with biological sex.

In Nigeria, John McCall interviewed an elderly Ohafia Igbo *dike-nwami* (brave-woman) named Nne Uko. Early on, she told McCall, she "was interested in manly activities" and felt that she "was meant to be a man"[4] and so "went as my nature was given to me—to behave as a man" (1996: 129).[5] She was initiated as a woman, but after being married for a time and producing no children, she was divorced. She subsequently farmed and hunted while dressed as a man, was initiated into various men's societies (including the most exclusive one), and took two wives of her own. She did not, however, take her wives to bed (130).[6] Her wives' children (who were sired by her brother) referred to her as "grandmother." At the time she was interviewed, she was no longer active in men's societies, having "risen to a position as a priestess of her matrilineage's ududu shrine, offering sacrifices to the ancestresses in her maternal line" (131). According to Nn Uko, upon her death she will join those ancestresses to whom sacrifices are made in the *ududu* shrine by those seeking good crops and children. In other words, despite her departures as an *adike-nwami* from the conventional role for women, she remained a woman in the view of the Ohafia Igbo. As McCall concludes, "Throughout her life Nne Uko was recognized in her community as a woman, socially and otherwise" (131).

Oboler argues that among the Nandi of Kenya, "The key to the question of the female husband's gender lies in her relationship to the property that is transmitted through her to the sons of her wife." The Nandi believe that the most significant property and primary means of production should be held and managed exclusively by men. Thus, a female husband is categorized as a man—"promoted" to male status (*kagotogosta komostab murenik,* literally "she has gone up to the side of the men") (1985: 131). According to to Oboler, this "frequently reiterated public dogma" is "unanimous." Her informants insisted "that a woman who takes a wife becomes a man and (except for the absence of sexual intercourse with her wife) behaves in all social contexts exactly as would any ordinary man" (1980: 69, 70).

Nonetheless, Oboler found that such women do not easily or automatically assume male roles in all spheres. The female husband, at least in the past, adopted the dress and adornments of men "to some extent"—which suggests that gender-mixing rather than gender-crossing was the actual pattern. Similarly, although female husbands ceased doing "women's work," being old, they did not undertake a lot of heavy male work either. "Informants make it a point to argue that female husbands are doing the work of men when they are in fact doing work that is equally appropriate to men or women" (1980: 84). They attend male initiations and have the right to "participate in public meetings and political discussions but admit they have never done so" (85). Finally, while female husbands say they converse with men rather than women, Oboler's observations did not confirm this (84–85).

The sexuality of the female husband does not appear to have been a factor in defining her role. Female husbands were expected to discontinue sex with men and, indeed, abstain from sexual intercourse with either gender, because if "she should conceive, both the issue of inheritance and the dogma that she is a man would be too thoroughly confounded to be withstood" (Oboler 1980: 85). Female husbands' most strenuous attempts to conform to male behavior occur "in contexts that are closely connected with the management of the heirship to the family estate" (86).

Oboler characterizes the Nandi female husband as "a woman of advanced age who has failed to bear a son" (1980: 69). Since the purpose of the union is to provide a male heir, the wife of the female husband has a male consort whose sole function in the relationship is to serve as the progenitor. Oboler suggests several motivations for females marrying female husbands: (1) the somewhat higher bridewealth paid by female husbands; (2) greater and more casual companionship; (3) somewhat greater participation in household decisions; (4) sexual autonomy; (5) less quarreling with and physical violence than with male husbands; (6) and a dislike of men (76, 78).

In her 1980 article, Oboler concluded that the Nandi wives are under the control of their female husbands and are not promiscuous. In her 1985 book (based on the same 1976–77 fieldwork), however, she wrote that the wife of a female husband "is free to engage in sexual liaisons with men of her own choosing" and suggested that this represented a change from earlier practice: "Formerly, it is said, it was the right of the female husband to arrange a regular consort for her wife. . . . Today, sexual freedom is cited as one of the advantages of marriage to a female husband" (132; see also 1980: 76). On the other hand, some women were reluctant to become female husbands, since they were expected to forgo sexual intercourse. However, Oboler does not report any data about the actual sexual conduct of Nandi females, and she acknowledges that at least some Nandi claims regarding their sexual restraint reflect ideal rather than actual behavior.[7] In any case, the institution is still flourishing—10 of the 286 households in the community she studied in the 1970s had female husbands. However, Oboler anticipates that Christian disapproval and the spread of bilateral inheritance will eventually undermine the institution.

   Although the coding of the female husband as a man is widespread, not all woman-woman relationships in Africa are conceptualized as those of a husband and wife. Hugo Huber has reported that among the Simiti (a Bantu-speaking group on the eastern shore of Lake Victoria), "Neither in the view of the people, nor in the terminology, nor in the wedding ritual itself is there any suggestion that a woman assumes the role of a husband in relation to another woman. Rather, the two main persons concerned are related as mother-in-law and daughter-in-law." Huber translates the usual expression for the relationship, *okoteta mokamona wa nyumba ntobu*, as "to give cattle for a daughter-in-law on behalf of a poor house"—a "poor house" being one that has produced no male offspring (or none that reached child-producing age) (1968: 746).

Marriage without Sex?

Anthropologists and Africans alike have been almost unanimous in denying the possibility that woman-woman marriages include sex or even emotional attachment. (See, for example, the comments of Ifi Amadiume [1987: 7] quoted by Kendall earlier in this book.) Krige (1974), Christine Obbo (1976), Sudarkasa (1986: 97), and others have all warned against assuming that women who married each other, even when they slept together, had sex. Few of these denials, however, are based on actual inquiries with or observations of the individuals involved—and certainly not observations of sexual behavior.[8] (Most ethnographic accounts do not even report where or with whom the partners usually slept.)

   O'Brien, for example, argues that "a female husband does not engage in sexual interaction with her wife; indeed, nowhere do the African data suggest any homosexual connotation in such marriages." Her rationale, however, is that "if homosexual behavior were a regular component of female-husband marriages, the association would have been noted in the ethnographic record" (1977: 109, 123, n. 1). Such an assumption attributes more acuity to anthropologists on sexual matters than is warranted, overlooks the fact that sexual behavior is generally invisible to outsiders (especially hostile ones), and ignores the history of enforced silence on homosexuality in Western discourse.[9]

Even ethnographers not hostile to the phenomenon may overlook it. Robert Brain, for example, spent two years doing fieldwork among the Bangwa of Cameroon (1976: 31). His "best woman friend in Bangwa was Mafwa, the chief's titled sister," with whom he often traveled to distant rites and with whom he spent many happy hours drinking and talking (55). Nonetheless, "it was not until some months after I first knew Mafwa that I found out that my rather androgynous princess had her own wife" (56). In fact, she had inherited two wives when her father died. Aside from accumulating bridewealth when her (wives') daughters married, Brain concluded that Mafwa had become a female husband "to have her own compound, with a wife to cook for her and her own children around, without the overbearing or annoying presence of a husband" (57). Once he became aware of the relationship between Mafwa and her co-resident wife (whose daughter called Mafwa "father"), Brain observed "their obvious satisfaction in each other's company." He took this as "evidence of a perfect alliance between two mature women who felt no need of the presence of a male husband" (58).

Brain correctly notes that cross-culturally the "rights of sexual access and domestic companionship are only some of the aspects involved in marriage. . . . 'Husband and wife' are joined in marriage for many purposes—not merely to enjoy sexual intercourse, companionship, or even have children" (1976: 58). The latter two are clearly part of the Bangwa "bundle of marital rights" in marriages between men and women as well as woman-woman marriages.

Some have questioned ethnographic reports that indicate (or simply allow the possibility of) a sexual dimension to woman-woman marriages. Feminist anthropologists Krige and Obbo, for example, criticized Melville Herskovits, whose 1937 and 1938 reports on "woman marriage" in Dahomey suggested that homosexuality might be involved. Krige complained that "Herskovits (1938) imputed to it sexual overtones that are foreign to the institution when, after stating quite definitely that such marriage did not imply a homosexual relationship, he went on to add 'although it is not to be doubted that occasionally homosexual women who have inherited wealth . . . utilize this relationship to the women they marry to satisfy themselves' (Herskovits 1937b: 338). He made no attempt to substantiate his statement" (Krige 1974: 11).

Obbo echoes Krige's criticisms:

> She [Krige] questions Herskovits' unexplained, unelaborated assumption that such a marriage was a homosexual relationship. Krige asserts that homosexuality is foreign to the marriage as practiced among the Lovedu today. . . . Herskovits seems to imply that mutual masturbation is necessarily homosexuality (1938: 289) and that there was no doubt that prosperous female "husbands" utilize the relationship in which they stand to the women they marry to satisfy themselves (1937b: 338). His passing remarks cannot be taken as conclusive evidence, and therefore we cannot know whether the Dahomean women who practiced woman-to-woman marriage were lesbians or whether it was a slip of Herskovits' pen. (1976: 372)

In a note to this passage, Obbo adds, "While no one can categorically dismiss the possibility that a woman-to-woman marriage may involve a homosexual relationship, there is no excuse for assuming it" (1976: 385, n. 4). She does not explain, however, what might be "heterosexual" in female-female mutual masturbation, a practice that does not seem to involve gendered roles.

A careful reading of Herskovits, however, shows that Krige, O'Brien, and Obbo exaggerate his remarks. (Moreover, Obbo misrepresents Krige, as well as Herskovits, in her criticisms.) Herskovits carefully outlined aspects of the institution of woman-woman marriage, explicitly noting it does not necessarily imply a homosexual relationship between the "husband" and the "wife" and concluded: "The motivating drive behind it—the desire for prestige and economic power—reflects the dominant Dahomean patterns of thought and the fundamental forces that underly Dahomean patterns of thought and behavior in all aspects of life" (1937b: 340).

In his 1938 work on the Dahomeans, Herskovits presented a detailed discussion of the sex education and sex experience of females (and males) (1938: 277–90). He reported that between the time of puberty and marriage, when the young girls have been withdrawn from the boys of their age, "Homosexuality is found among women as well as men; by some it is claimed that it exists among women to a greater extent" (289). He also noted that prior to the onset of puberty, because of the value attached to thickened vaginal lips in that society, "girls between the ages of 9 and 11 are assembled by compounds in groups of eight or more . . . and these engage in the practice known as *axoti*, which consists of massaging and enlarging the lips of the vagina" (282). An older woman, "whose most desired qualification is an age not too far removed from that of the girls so that she will not have forgotten her own experiences when undergoing this regimen," assists in the task, which Herskovits described as follows:

> With a shaped piece of wood, this woman manipulates the lips of the vagina of each girl, pulling at them, stretching them, and lightly puncturing the vaginal tissues in several places. This she does eight or nine times for each of her charges during the first year of instruction, and during the next year the girls do this for each other. . . . For two years at the very least this is continued, and in addition there is the outer massaging of these "lips" to cause thickening and muscular development, for "thin-lipped" women are considered lacking in comeliness. (282)

The end product of this practice is the "enhancement of pleasure in sex play . . . the roughened surface of the inner vagina lips heightens pleasure during coitus, since the scarifications are not unlike the body cicatrizations" (Herskovits 1938: 282–83).

One final bit of information provided by Herskovits on the sex experience of Dahomean girls is of interest. When the sex education of the girls begins, "they no longer go about the compound naked but are given small cloths to wear" (1938: 283). They are also warned to avoid hidden play with boys and told not to allow the boys to approach them sexually. Herskovits noted that at this stage, "When the girls find themselves with others who have been given small cloths to wear, and with those older than themselves, they compare sex organs, each boasting of the size of the lips of her own. When none of the older people are about, the girls may indulge in mutual masturbation" (285). Males may also be involved in long-term homosexual relationships:

> One situation which arises in the sex life of the boys during middle adolescence deserves some consideration, for it is at this time of life, when the young girls have been withdrawn from the boys of their age, that any tendencies to homosexuality develop;

when, indeed, according to one account, homosexuality, which is ordinarily looked upon by the Dahomeans with distaste, is recognized as normal. Once the games between boys and girls are stopped, the boys no longer have the opportunity for companionship with the girls, and the sex drive finds satisfaction in close friendships between boys of the same group. (289)

Given the broader context of Dahomean sexual behavior, no great leap of the imagination is required to suggest, as did Herskovits, that some of the females involved in woman-woman marriage in Dahomey might also use the relationship as a means of obtaining sexual satisfaction.

Which touches are "sexual" and which are not varies from person to person, and "sex" (as an activity) is not a clearly bounded domain with universally agreed-upon criteria even in one society, let alone cross-culturally. Our assumption is that people who sleep together tend to touch each other and touches that are experienced by some as erotic are not experienced as erotic by others. Of course, there are economic bases and economic motivations for woman-woman marriages as there are for man-woman marriages in Africa—and elsewhere. Yet, no one questions whether men and women in mandatory, arranged marriages have or desire sex with each other or, indeed, even "prefer" the opposite sex in general. The practice of mandatory marriage does not require it. At the same time, alliances that are arranged, as well as alliances contracted for reasons other than love and sexual attraction, may eventually result in erotic attraction and sex. This would seem to be especially likely for those not having sex with other partners. And this is a category that is shaped at least to some degree by individual desires.

Notes

1. The discussion of Oboler and Obbo and their readings of Herskovits by Joseph Carrier originally appeared in *Anthropology Research Group Newsletter* 2(3): 2–4, in autumn 1980. Supplemental material has been added by Murray. We are grateful to McCall for prompt and helpful answers to queries about his Igbo research.

2. Matory considers that *all* Oyo Yoruba " 'women' are husbands to somebody and simultaneously wives to multiple others" (1994: 2). See also Amadiume (1987).

3. See Stephen Murray's (1994) critique of the dominance of gender as an analytical category in contemporary anthropology (what he calls "the empire of gender").

4. McCall adds:

> I tried to get Nne Uko to go into more detail about what she meant when she said she was supposed to have been a man. I wanted to find out if it concurred with notions I had previously encountered in other interviews pertaining to reincarnation or prenatal agreements. While she readily asserted that she believed in reincarnation, she did not identify with particular ancestors. Nor did she elaborate her case in relation to a specific cosmological model. She preferred to leave it on the level of the manifestly apparent: her proclivity to move in the masculine domain was evidence of a prenatal disposition that diverged from her biological endowment. (1996: 132)

5. Although Nne Uko's "disposition" was evident before she gave birth to children, nothing in the evidence McCall presents supports his suggestion that Igbo viewed such a disposition as "biological" or believed that its timing was "prenatal."

6. "Women go to their husband's bed for sexual relations and may subsequently sleep there, but otherwise they sleep in their own beds. Hence 'take to bed' implies sexual activity" (McCall, personal communication to S. O. Murray, March 28, 1996).

7. Oboler did report the expectation that girls had sex with boys before their initiation and marriage (1985: 86, 94).

8. Nne Uko anticipated questions about her sexuality from McCall, and if she herself denied having sex with her wives, she does not seem to have found the idea shocking or inconceivable.

9. See Murray (1997a). British social anthropologists (notably the contributors to Fortes and Evans-Pritchard 1940) were preoccupied with formal jural relations; little interested in messy, actual behavior; and totally uninterested in psychological motivations.

Diversity and Identity

The Challenge of African Homosexualities

The contributions to this book unequivocally refute claims that African societies lacked homosexual patterns and had no words for those who desire their own sex. Evidence of same-sex patterns in some 50 African societies has been reported or reviewed in this book. All of these societies had words—many words, with many meanings—for these practices. Furthermore, these societies are found within every region of the continent, and they represent every language family, social and kinship organization, and subsistence pattern. There is substantial evidence that same-sex practices and patterns were "traditional" and "indigenous." Although contact between Africans and non-Africans has sometimes influenced both groups' sexual patterns, there is no evidence that one group ever "introduced" homosexuality to another. Since anthropologists and other observers have rarely inquired systematically into the presence of homosexuality in Africa (or elsewhere),[1] absence of evidence cannot be assumed to be evidence of absence. Considering that this book represents the first serious study of the subject, undoubtedly future research will identify many other groups with distinct patterns of homosexuality and gender difference.

Diversity of Same-Sex Patterns

African same-sex patterns are not only widespread but also diverse. In fact, they are more diverse than those found in other parts of the world.[2] The three most common patterns are gender-differentiated roles, age-differentiated roles, and (more or less) egalitarian or mutual relations, examples of which can be found for both males and females. (Age and gender in general are key bases for social organization, not just homosexuality, throughout Africa.)

The most often-reported pattern is that of a social status for males and sometimes females who engage in varying degrees of cross- and mixed-gendered behavior. It must be remembered that males who do not dress like other men or who do not perform typical men's work are more visible to observers—insiders as well as outsiders. It is literally easier to observe cross- or mixed-gender dress and hairstyles than to monitor sexual behavior, which is usually performed in private and in the dark. However, the apparent predominance of the gender pattern is almost certainly not an artifact of superficial observation. Sexually receptive males who dressed or wore their hair partially or completely in female ways have been noted throughout Africa. In several cases, they are also spirit mediums in possession religions or shamans.

Unfortunately, most ethnographies are unhelpful in establishing whether African cultures conceived gender as dualistic (male and non-male, with those who don't procreate being categorized as social nonpersons)[3] or multiple (male, female, and other kinds of adults). Donald Donham's report quoting an *ashtime* describing himself as neither male nor female is an all-too-rare glimpse into a native sexual cosmology in which a third-gender role appears to have existed (1990: 92). It is still possible in some cases (for example, among the Hausa or the Mombasans) to ask the questions that would clarify this issue—for example, how many genders are there? Is so-and-so a kind of man (or woman or other)?

Age-stratified relations are the second most commonly reported same-sex pattern. Examples range from the institutionalized relations of the Zande and Mossi, to societies in which such relationships occur but are not formally organized or sanctioned. In several cases, age-differentiated male homosexuality occurred in settings in which women were excluded or absent. These have included indigenous African courts, warrior camps, and trading parties, as well as colonial mining compounds and plantations. In some cases, the relationships were governed by complex conventions, such as the payment of bride-price to the boys' families (Azande, Ovigangellas).[4] While reports exist of reciprocal sex between partners of different ages (the Anyin) and of a younger partner penetrating the older (Nkundu), asymmetry is more common: the older partner generally penetrates the younger.

Although sexual contact between youths and adult men occurred during the circumcision rites of the Ndembu of Zambia and in neighboring groups, youths being sexually penetrated as a necessary part of their initiation—the Melanesian pattern—has not been reported anywhere in Africa. Although Zande boy-wives grew up to be warriors like their husbands, their adolescent service was not considered masculinizing as it was for some Melanesian initiates. The opposite was more often the case: the younger partner took on wifely roles and feminine behavior in addition to a receptive sexual role, so that the idioms of gender and age overlap.

The category of egalitarian homosexuality is more amorphous. There is difficulty in distinguishing reports of incidental homosexual behavior between individuals of the same age and institutionalized peer relations. The difference is between adolescents spontaneously engaging in homosexual relations and the organized homosexuality that often develops in sex-segregated settings, such as boarding schools (see Kamau's account in part I). In the case of the latter, peer relations are expected, and a variety of conventions and special terminology govern them. Kurt Falk describes such formalized same-sex relationships among the Herero and the Nama.

Almost all reports of mutual homosexual relations between men during colonial times involve lower-status males. Examples include sex between Bambara slaves and Nandi bachelors and between youth among the Ba-Yaka, Dualla, Iteso, Kru, Naman, Nyakyusa, and Pahouin groups. Given that none of these reports approach thick description, it would be incautious to assume that there was no structuring by age or gender within these relations, despite the relative equality of the partner's social status.

Aside from Falk's description of "special friendships" among the Herero and the Nama, the only others reports of egalitarian homosexuality for marriage-aged adults are John Week's 1909 account of Bangala men engaging in reciprocal sex when away from women (on fishing or trading expeditions) (448–49; cf. Soyaux 1879, 2: 59) and Malidoma Somé's recent characterization of some Dagara gatekeepers as "gay" (1993). Long-running primary sexual relationships between adult males in "traditional" societies have been little reported. (One exception is Jacobus X's [1893: 258] mention of "a Black Castor-and-Pollux pair" of Bambara archers.) Of course, this does not mean that such relationships did not occur.

Contributions to this book also provide evidence of a wide range of beliefs about, attitudes toward, and judgments of same-sex behavior—from South African miners who declared that they loved their boy-wives better than their girlfriends, to the Wawihé who told Falk that "either [sex] is equally good and beautiful," to the Ovambo chief who reportedly shot *ovashengi* on sight (with, significantly, his European rifle). At the same time, there are no examples of traditional African belief systems that singled out same-sex relations as sinful or linked them to concepts of disease or mental health—except where Christianity and Islam have been adopted. The Pangwe,

according to Günther Tessman, considered sexual intercourse—both heterosexual and homosexual—a sin, but by unspoken social agreement, sexual
relations were not sanctioned when they occurred in private and at night.
Further, the sexual behavior of children was exempt from this sanction,
because "in youth there is no sin." In other cases, punishments have been
reported for individuals who engage in same-sex relations, but these are
relatively mild in the context of other infractions.

The Pangwe provide a good example of how beliefs that superficially
seem similar to those of Western societies are in fact based on distinctly
African worldviews. According to Tessman, while they viewed intercourse as
sinful, they also believed that the power to acquire wealth could be trans-
ferred from one man to another through anal intercourse.[5] This benefit of
same-sex intercourse was offset by the belief that illicit sex (heterosexual and
homosexual) was punished by a cult figure who inflicted a disease on the
offenders. Unfortunately, Tessman did not inquire further into what must
have been a well-developed set of beliefs concerning supernatural power and
the physiology of the body and sexual intercourse.

Native explanations for homosexual behavior and individuals are also
diverse. According to the Fanti, individuals with heavy souls, whatever their
biological sex, desired women, while those with light souls desired men.
Hence, some males with light souls and some women with heavy ones desired
the same sex (Christensen 1954: 92–93, 143)—again one longs for a fuller
explication. The Bantu of north Kavirondo believed that a disposition for
the "impurity" (*luswa*) of homosexuality was in the blood, but not visible
(Wagner 1949 1:108–9). Other African explanations for homosexuality are
less esoteric. Falk quoted a Nginé soldier who was punished for attempting
to have sex with a fellow soldier: "Doesn't the Sergeant know that there are
men who from youth on desire women, and others, who are attracted only
to men? Why then should he be punished now? After all, he knows not
why God created him like this—that he can only love men!" (in "Same-Sex
Life among a Few Negro Tribes of Angola," part III). In this book, several
examples of native statements concerning the naturalness, normality, and
even banality of same-sex relations have been quoted.

Identities and Roles

We assume that homosexual *behavior* in some form occurs in all human
groups. Indeed, the ethnographic literature on Africa includes many reports

of casual same-sex contact. In some societies, however, same-sex patterns were formalized, and named social roles existed for individuals who engaged in them. These terms and roles were the basis for social identities incorporating sexual and gender difference, some stigmatized, some not. This is significant, because many recent historical and cultural studies of sexuality have claimed a unique status for Western sexual identities, especially "gay" or "homosexual," as constructs produced by social and historical factors specific to Western societies. Not only is it claimed that Western homosexual identity has no counterparts historically or cross-culturally, it is also often stated (or implied) that the very notion of social identities is uniquely Western.[6]

However, the chapters by Ruldoph Gaudio on the Hausa and Deborah Amory on coastal East Africa show how individuals in named social roles for nonmasculine males and (occasionally) nonfeminine females employ those labels to define and understand themselves. Furthermore, they participate in organized sexual subcultures, albeit those whose boundaries are drawn differently than those of Western gay subcultures. There appears to have been little Western influence in how these subcultures and identities have been conceptualized and organized. Even the "wife of the mine" status drew on existing African patterns of age-based and gender-defined homosexuality, although the conditions for its emergence—segregation of miners from women—were imposed by white employers.

In most cases, alternative gender statuses constituted lifelong identities. In contrast, roles in age-differentiated same-sex relations were temporary, at least for the younger partners, who eventually graduated to adult status and to the active role in same-sex intercourse. Even so, the role of the younger partner—and in some places the older partner—was labeled with a distinct term, and relationships sometimes persisted well into the adult years of the younger partner. Boy-wives in traditional Azande culture were called *ndongo-techi-la*, while in southern Africa they were called *tinkonkana*, *nkhonsthana*, and *nkonkana*. In contemporary Lesotho, older and young women in same-sex relationships are called "mummy" and "baby." These labels provide the basis of a social identity. To refer to oneself by one of them was to indicate both one's involvement in same-sex relationships and one's role (sexual and social) within them. While identities based on age-differentiated relations are certainly different from contemporary "gay" identity, which entails a political stance as well as a social identity, their existence problematizes the claim that sexual identities are uniquely Western or modern.

What is missing from this inventory of "traditional" African same-sex patterns is an identity and lifestyle in which homosexual relationships are primary and *not* based on gender difference (and on bisexual behavior on the part of the masculine partner or of both partners). This is the dominant, modern Western model of homosexuality, which defines individuals solely on the basis of sexual object choice. In Africa, however, heterosexual marriage and procreation—but not necessarily heterosexual desire, orientation, or monogamy—are universal expectations. Few men and even fewer women do not marry and have children. Only males in alternative gender roles might escape the requirement. But as Gaudio found among the Hausa and Gill Shepherd in Mombasa, even males defined as "not-men" sometimes marry women and have children (or wish to do so). Nor were roles for "brave women" and female husbands exclusive of heterosexual marriage and childbearing.

In contrast to the homophobia Western homosexuals confront, the social pressure on Africans who desire same-sex relations is not concerned with their masculinity or femininity, their mental health, their sexual object preference and its causes, or the moral status of their sexual preference—but primarily with their production of children, especially eligible heirs, and the maintenance of a conventional image of married life. This social code does not require that an individual suppress same-sex desires or behavior but that she or he never allow such desires to overshadow or supplant procreation. This is a less drastic social contract than the one offered to Western gays—to either repress same-sex desires and behaviors altogether or to accept a social outlaw status. At the same time, it largely forestalls homosexual identity construction, stigmatization, and subculture formation.[7] The "sexual subcultures" in which Hausa *'yan daudu* and Mombasa *mashoga* move encompass diverse kinds of illicit sexuality, both heterosexual (in the form of prostitution) and homosexual (commercial and noncommercial).

Social Correlates

To what extent are these different patterns linked to various features of social organization and culture? To answer that question, the societies with same-sex patterns considered in this book were cross-classified with language groups, subsistence patterns, division of labor, premarital sexuality, and other factors. The results of the analysis are presented in Appendix 2.

Little distinguishes societies with different same-sex patterns in terms of their subsistence—on average, the societies in the sample rely mostly on agriculture, although societies with egalitarian same-sex relations rely slightly more on animal husbandry. More significant relationships are found with kinship patterns. Among societies with a codable pattern of homosexuality, gender-defined and age-differentiated patterns are disproportionately frequent among matrilineal groups. In contrast, all the societies with female same-sex patterns in the sample follow patrilineal inheritance. These correlations do not necessarily correspond to findings from other culture areas. In North America, alternative gender statuses occur among groups with all types of kinship systems, and age-stratified homosexuality is absent. At the same time, the best-known examples of age-based homosexuality come from patrilineal societies—classical Greece, medieval Japan, and Melanesia. In short, the African data do little to clarify the relationship between homosexuality and kinship systems except to suggest that some relationship exists.

There is also an association between women's contributions to subsistence and the presence of egalitarian and age-differentiated homosexuality. Like the high frequency of matrilineality among groups with same-sex patterns, this might reflect the higher status of women in such groups. These results might be interpreted as indicating that societies in which women have higher status are conducive to the presence of same-sex patterns.

Equally significant is the finding that where boys are freest to engage in sex with girls, they are also relatively free to have sex with each other. This is the opposite of what one would expect if homosexuality was "caused" by the absence or lack of access to women.

Another interesting association revealed by the analysis involves gender-defined same-sex patterns and urbanization. Societies with gender-defined homosexual roles are more urbanized than those with either age or egalitarian patterns. Such roles are the only same-sex pattern reported for class-based societies in Africa. Societies with egalitarian homosexuality are much more likely to lack aristocracies and classes than are those with other same-sex patterns. This correlation suggests that as societies become more complex, so do organizations of homosexuality—to the extent that alternative gender statuses, involving named, lifelong identities with distinctive work roles, social statuses, religious functions, ways of dress, and so forth, can be said to be more complex than the roles of individuals in (often short-term) age-differentiated or egalitarian relationships.

The frequency of urban societies among those with alternative gender statuses offers some support to Will Roscoe's hypothesis (1996, 1997, 1998) regarding the diversification of gender roles as a means of accommodating growth in social specialization. At the same time, there are few examples of what Roscoe has termed "state third gender"—in which certain civic and religious roles are defined as alternative gender statuses—based on examples from the

Near East (where there is much greater time depth to the written record). One example might be the Ganga-Ya-Chibanda described by Giovanni Cavazzi, who was regularly consulted by tribal leaders (see part III). Other roles combining state functions and alternative gender status include the "eunuchs" (*lagredis*) in the Dahomey court and *soronés*, or "pages," in the Mossi court—roles that may reflect the influence of Muslim contact. The religious leadership role of *mugawe* among the Meru of Kenya also might be included here.

Traditional approaches to homosexuality invariably seek its cause—what distinct factors in this family, this community, this society cause homosexuality to be present. However, none of the associations uncovered in the statistical analysis can be interpreted as causal. The statistical correlation of female-female sexuality with societies in which women are the primary producers, for example, does not mean that this division of labor "causes" lesbianism—it could just as easily be the case that this kind of social system simply fails to prevent such behavior from occurring. In any case, female homosexuality has not been reported for many societies with this division of labor.

A similar issue of causality relates to the motivation for entering an alternative gender status. Is it because one's economic and social interests are of the opposite sex or because one has a different gender identity than that normally assigned to his or her sex? Or is it to fulfill sexual desires—to be able to form a socially accepted relationship with a member of the same sex or engage in sexual acts not possible with the opposite sex? There is an important issue here. In cultures with belief systems that recognize only two genders, is the gender of individuals in roles for nonmasculine men and nonfeminine women adjusted to match their sexual preference, in which case sexual object choice is their primary motivation, or is their sexual orientation determined by their gender identity, in which case gender preferences are primary and sexuality adjusted to match them? From a purely functionalist, perspective society does not need men to be masculine, but it does need them to procreate, and in this sense, sexual behavior is more important than gender-role behavior. Throughout Africa, gender roles shift, and men and women exceed normal bounds in various ways, temporarily or permanently, but almost no one is exempt from the requirement to procreate.

Woman-Woman Relations

Although egalitarian relationships between women certainly existed in "traditional" black Africa, the limited data suggest that the most common culturally marked form of female homosexuality is a role for a woman who becomes a sort of husband to another woman and claims some of the prerogatives of a man. In other words, gender is the major idiom of homosexuality in Africa for *both* men and women. One exception is the Lesotho mummy-baby relationship, in which the partners are differentiated by age, while remaining categorized as women. Similarly, among the Simiti, the roles in formal relations between women were conceptualized as those of mother-in-law and daughter-in-law. In other cases, the idioms of gender and age are combined—"female husbands," for example, appear almost always to be older than their wives.

Although female husbands often take on the parental, kinship, and work roles of men, they do not generally cross-dress. Another distinction between the role of female husbands and alternative gender statuses for males is that the latter are often lifelong identities assumed in childhood or youth. The careers of female husbands, on the other hand, sometimes include heterosexual marriage, with the adoption of female husband status occurring later in life.

The statistical analysis suggests that patterns of female homosexuality are most common in societies in which women make the greatest contribution to subsistence, even in patrilineal societies.[8] This correlation is stronger than any of the relationships between male homosexual patterns and social organization. In other words, whereas women's higher status may be an enabling but not a necessary factor in the presence of organized male homosexuality, it may be a necessary factor in the case of same-sex patterns involving women.

The Future of African Homosexualities

Despite the social, economic, and cultural upheavals related to European conquest and colonization, and the no less dramatic changes following decolonization, many large African societies—some organized into urbanized states long before European contact—have retained substantial aspects of their precontact language and culture. This cultural heritage includes same-sex relations. As the reports from Hausa, Mombasa, Dakar, and elsewhere show, roles for nonmasculine males (and in Mombasa for lesbians) that flourish today cannot be attributed to Western introduction (although Western influences are becoming apparent). At the same time, as Ajen and "Kamau" describe, much same-sex activity is occurring in the absence of public roles, subcultures, identities, or social acceptance, in a manner similar to gay life in Western societies before the emergence of a lesbian/gay political movement. In southern Africa, it is possible to identify not only "traditional" and "Western" patterns of homosexuality but also colonial and postcolonial forms—identities like that of the *moffie*, which hybridize traditional beliefs and cross-gendering practices with Western labels and constructions, and function within social spaces specific to the colonial period and its aftermath.

It appears that gender-differentiated same-sex patterns have fared better in the 20th century than age-differentiated homosexuality. There is little trace today of "boy-wives" or the pages of traditional African courts (although same-sex activity was reported in the Rwandan court as late the 1960s, and there are indications that some African elite males still maintain young male consorts, for example, in the trial of Zimbabwe ex-president Banana [Appiah 1996; see also part I, Stephen Murray, the oral history of Kamau].) Such practices were singled out by European colonialists and missionaries and suppressed when possible. In Uganda, when missionaries succeeded in converting pages in the court of the Baganda leader, Mwanga (ruled 1884–97), the boys began to refuse the king's sexual advances. When his favorite page resisted him, Mwanga killed him and, in a rage, many others—they were dubbed the Martyrs of Budanga (Faupel 1962: 82–83). In contrast, alternative gender statuses, including those first described by the Portuguese some four centuries ago, continue to exist in Angola, Namibia, Hausa, Kenya, and elsewhere.

Recent developments in southern Africa suggest a sharper break between past and present same-sex patterns. Antigay advocates vehemently deny the presence of homosexuality in traditional culture. While South African lesbians and gays have achieved unprecedented political recognition and legal protection, the rationale for these developments appears to draw more on Western ideals of social justice and human rights than on claims about traditional acceptance and social roles for same-sex patterns. This book, however, shows that such claims are viable.

South Africa now stands as an exemplar of a multiethnic, multiracial African society seeking to include sexual minorities in its body politic. Nonetheless, the opposite scenario is a real possibility elsewhere: religious fundamentalism married to nationalism, wielding the apparatus of the modern state to persecute (and murder) homosexuals. Exactly this scenario unfolded in Iran in the 1970s and 1980s. As Kevan Botha and Edwin Cameron observe, South Africa's constitutional protection of gays "is no doubt the product of our peculiar history, where institutionalized discrimination against people on the ground of race was perfected through the legal system. The racial legacy has given the majority of South Africans a repugnance for the use of legal processes for irrational discrimination. Gays and lesbians have been among the direct beneficiaries. For all South Africans, however, the problem now is to reconcile constitutional promises with daily practices" (1997: 37). The future of African homosexualities is certainly one of greater visibility, greater dialogue—and greater risks.

Notes

1. An exception was the cultural element survey of tribes in the American West, directed by Alfred Kroeber (see W. Roscoe 1998: 261, n. 98).

2. In North America, a gender-defined pattern is dominant, and no instances of institutionalized age-based homosexual relationships north of Mexico have been documented.

3. Local (or emic) definitions of the "non-male" category may include females, unfledged males (boys), eunuchs (with genitalia partially or totally excised), and failed males (uninitiated and/or unmarried and/or childless adults, even though they may still have fully developed male genitalia and have sex exclusively with women).

4. Whether the same constraint on wife selection applied for boys to be inseminated as for girls to be impregnated is not specified. It did among peoples in other parts of the world, with a boy sometimes being supplied to a family or clan who was "owed" a daughter that was too young or nonexistent (see Murray 1992a: 3–12 on Australia and Melanesia, and Murray 1995a: 264–73 on Amazonia). Similarly, the criteria for levies of pages for African royal courts have not been specified in published accounts.

5. Cf. the beliefs reported among contemporary male sex workers in urban Nigeria (Aina 1991: 88).

6. Melford Spiro (1993) vigorously challenges this shibboleth.

7. Murray (1995a: 33–70; 1997c: 14–21) and Badruddin Khan (1997) make similar arguments for other familialistic societies in which invisibility is the price of "tolerance."

8. W. Roscoe also finds an association between egalitarian societies in which women make substantial contributions to subsistence and the presence of female berdache roles in North America (1998: 91–92).

Appendix 1

African Groups with Same-Sex Patterns

Ethnonym[1]	Region	Language group	Terms
Akan (Ashante)	II	Niger-Congo	
Ambo/Ovambo (Wanyama)	III	Bantu	*kimbanda*, diviners; *esenge* (pl. *omasenge*), man possessed by female spirit; *eshengi* (pl. *ovashengi*), "he who is approached from behind"
Amhara (Amharic)	I	Afro-Asiatic	*wändarwäräd*, "male-female"; *wändawände*, "mannish women"
Anyi/Anyin	II	Niger-Congo	
Bafia (Fia)	III		*jigele ketön*, reciprocal anal intercourse
Bagishu/Bageshu, Gisu	I	Bantu	*mzili* (pl. *inzili*); *buyazi*
Bala/Basongye/Basonge/ Songe	III	Bantu	*kitesha* (pl. *bitesha*), male and female
Bambala/Mbala	III	Bantu	*mokobo, tongo*, sterile men
Bambara	II	Niger-Congo	
Bangala/Mbangala	III	Bantu	
Dagaari/Dagara	II	Niger-Congo	
Dahomey (Fon)	II	Niger-Congo	*akho'si, lagredis*, court eunuch; *gaglgo*, homosexuality

continued on next page

Ethnonym[1]	Region	Language group	Terms
Duala	III	Bantu (trade language)	
Eritrean (various)	I	Afro-Asiatic	
Fanti/Fante (Akan)	II	Niger-Congo	
Gangella/Ovigangella	III	Bantu	*m'uzonj'ame katumua*, male lover; *m'ndumbi*, "podicator"
Gikuyu/Kikuyu	I	Bantu	*onek*, active male
Gisu (Masaba)	I	Bantu	
Hausa	II	Afro-Asiatic	*'dan daudu* (pl. *'yan daudu*); *k'wazo/baja*, older/younger men; *kifi*, lesbianism
Herero (Damara)	IV	Bantu	*okutunduka vanena*, anal intercourse; *epanga*, lover; *oupanga*, erotic friendship (male or female)
Ila	III	Bantu	*mwaami*, "prophet"
Iteso/Teso	I	Nilo-Saharan	
Kongo	III	Bantu	
Konso	I	Afro-Asiatic	*sagoda*
Krongo/Korongo/ Kurungo	I	Kordofanian	*londo*, nonmasculine males
Kru	II	Niger-Congo	
Lango	I	Nilo-Saharan	*mudoko dako*
Maale/Male/Maalia	I	Afro-Asiatic	*ashtime*
Maragoli/Logooli	I	Bantu	*kiziri*
Meru	I	Bantu	*mugawe*
Mesakin (Ngile)	I	Kordofanian	*tubele*, nonmasculine males
Mombasa (Swahili)	I	Bantu	*mke-si-mume*, "woman, not man," male and female homosexuals; *mashoga* (sing. *shoga*), male; *basha* (pl. *mabasha*), partner of *mashoga*; *msagaji, msago* (pl. *wasagaji, misago*), "grinders," lesbians

Ethnonym[1]	Region	Language group	Terms
Mossi (More)	II	Niger-Congo	*soronés*, pages
Mpondo/Pondo (Pana)	IV	Niger-Congo	*tinkonkana*, boy wives
Naman/"Hottentot"	IV	Khoisan	*koetsire*, sexually receptive males; *soregus*, friendship bond; *ôa-/huru, /huru*, mutual masturbation; */goe-ugu*, "trabadie"
Nandi	I	Bantu	
Ndembu (Lunda)	III	Bantu	
Nkundu/Lonkundo (Mongo-Nkundu)	III	Bantu	
Nuer	IV	Nilo-Saharan	
Nyakyusa-Ngonde	IV	Bantu	
Nyoro	I	Bantu	
Nzema	II	Niger-Congo	*agyale*, "friendship marriages" (sex denied)
Ondonga (Ndonga)	IV	Bantu	*eshenga*, gender-mixing male shamans
Otoro	I	Kordofanian	
Pangwe/Pahouian (Fang)	III	Bantu	*a bele nnem e bango*, "he has the heart [aspirations] of boys"
Rwanda/Ruanda (spoken by Hutus and Tutsis)	I	Bantu	*umuswezi, umukonotsi*, "sodomite"; *kuswerana nk'imbwa, kunonoka, kwitomba, kuranana inyuma, ku'nyo*, male homosexuality; *ikihindu* and *ikimaze* (Mirundi), "hermaphrodite" priests
Tsonga (Thonga)	IV	Bantu	*nkhonsthana, tinkonkana, nkonkana*, boy-wife; *nima*, husband
Umbundu/Mbunda/ Ovimbundu	III	Bantu	*chibadi, chibanda, chibados, jimbandaa, kibamba, quimanda*

continued on next page

Ethnonym[1]	Region	Language group	Terms
Wawihé/Viye	III	Bantu	*omututa*, (male) homosexuals; *eponji*, "lovers"
Wolof/Woloff	II	Niger-Congo	*gor-digen*, men-women; *yauss*, insertors; *oubi*, "open," insertees
!Xun	IV	Khoisan	
Yaka/Ba-Yaka	III	Bantu	
Yoruba	II	Niger-Congo	
Zande/Azande/Sandeh	I	Niger Congo	*ndongo-techi-la*, boy-wives
Zulu	IV	Bantu	*inkosi ygbatfazi*, "chief of the women" (diviners); *amankotshane, izinkotshane, inkotshane*, boy-wife; *skesana*, cross-gender males; *iqgenge*, masculine partners

1. Most ethnonyms in the historical and ethnographic literature are names of languages (that is, glossonyms). In the case of names that are not glossonyms (for example, Dahomey), the language spoken appears in parentheses. Common variants of group names are separated by slashes. Roman numerals under Region correspond to the geographical organization of the book: I. Horn of Africa, Sudan, and East Africa; II. West Africa; III. Central Africa; IV. Southern Africa. Entries under Language Family identify the general group to which the language has been assigned. Bantu is a subdivision of Niger-Congo, which, together with Kordofanian languages, constitutes the Niger-Kordofanian macrofamily. Literal translations of terms appear in quotes.

Appendix 2

Organizations of Homosexuality and Other Social Structures in Sub-Saharan Africa

STEPHEN O. MURRAY

For the societies in which there is sufficient discussion of male homosexuality to code the presence of gender-stratified, age-stratified, or nonstratified organizations,[1] it is possible to correlate the occurrence of each of these types to other parts of culture and social structure, as these have been coded in the Human Relations Area Files (HRAF) organized by George Peter Murdock, and to cross-classify the presence of particular social and cultural structures with types of homosexuality. Table A2.1 lists the societies with discernible patterns of male-male sexuality by type.

This analysis shows correlations between organizations of homosexuality in "traditional" African societies and other social patterns. I recognize that in postmodern nihilism confidence that anything can be known or compared has shriveled, so that current fashion is to write about the ethnographer, with the people she or he visits occasionally impinging, or hyperparticularized "local history." I am well aware that this discussion will be castigated for considering patterns across most of a continent and, indeed, for suggesting that there *are* patterns, even statistical patterns, in a single time and place. So be it. I would be the first to welcome more detailed ethnography examining homosexuality and how it fits with other aspects of social structure in specific local contexts, but at present (and in the foreseeable future),

Table A2.1. Organizations of Male Homosexual Relationships in
African Societies

Gender-Structured Relationships

    Akan, Ambo, Amhara, Baigishu, Bambara, Dahomey, Fanti, Gisu, Hausa, Ila,
Iteso, Kongo/Nquiti, Konso, Krongo, Lango, Maale, Margoli (Wanga), Mbala,
Meru, Mesakin, Mombasan, Nuer, Nyoro, Ondonga, Otoro, Rwandan,
Umbundu, Wolof, Yoruba, Zulu

Age-Structured Relationships

    Anyin, Bafia, Bangala, Eritrean, Gangella, Ila, Krongo, Mesakin, Mossi,
Ndembu, Nkundu, Nyakyusa-Ngonde, Nyoro, Nzema, Ondonga, Pangwe/
Pahouian, Rwandan, Tsonga, "wives of the mine" (Mpondo, etc.), Zande,
Zulu; possibly also Hausa

Relationships Not Structured by Age or by Gender

    Bafia, Bambara (among slaves), Bangala, Dagaari, Duala, Herero, Iteso, Kru,
Naman, Nandi, Nyakyusa-Ngonde, Pangwe/Pahouian, Wawhihé/Viye, !Xun,
Yaka

---

ethnologists have very little to work with, except the record compiled by
early European travelers and ethnographers working under the protection
of colonial regimes.

    Most purported "social constructionism" consists of idiosyncratic inter-
pretations of a few European or North American texts (mostly printed) with,
perhaps, a claimed link to "capitalism" or to "professional dominance." In
the absence of influence of forensic medical (particularly psychiatric) texts,
the special (discursive) creation of "the homosexual" could not (or, at least,
theoretically should not) have occurred in "traditional" African societies.
This orthodoxy provides no claims or hypotheses about the organization of
homosexuality in "tribal" societies, because it does not expect there to be
any—and allegedly "social" constructionists rarely bother to compare even
as many as two societies.

    More a guiding hunch than an explicit hypothesis in my own work has
been that the elaboration and acceptance of male and of female homosexual
relations is more likely where females have relatively greater economic independence and (therefore, in my Weberian expectation) higher status. Having
significant responsibilities in the major production activities is intuitively

an avenue to status for women (if not always control of the resources they produce or help produce). Matrilineal inheritance, similarly, might seem to make male roles less highly valued than where inheritance is patrilineal,[2] so that we might expect the development of female homosexual roles (however organized) and of male homosexual roles organized by gender to be more common where there is matrilineal inheritance.

A recurrent explanation for homosexual relations is the unavailability of heterosexual relations. HRAF codings of "free love" and of the length of postpartum sex taboos provide indicators of male "deprivation" from sexual access to females. Those who view homosexuality as "situational" would expect it to be more likely to occur where there are longer postpartum taboos and for it not to occur where there is "free love," that is, lack of sanctions against heterosexual sex.

Anticonstructionist historian John Boswell (1980) asserted a relationship in medieval Europe between urbanization and repression of homosexuality, while constructionists (e.g., Adam 1986; Greenberg 1988) have related urbanization (at least in a capitalist context) to the development of "modern homosexuality." These conflicting expectations make it interesting to look at class stratification and urbanity in relation to organizations of homosexuality.

For distinguishing the social structural correlates of the three basic organizations of homosexuality, there is no theory beyond the quasi-evolutionary progression from age structuring to gender structuring to egalitarian homosexuality (with the last found only in industrial and postindustrial societies). The foray of this analysis is, then, more hypothesis generating than hypothesis testing.

The tables in this chapter provide cross-classifications of distributions of various social-structural variables in the societies with an attested organization of homosexuality (male first, then female). Table A2.2, however, relates organizations of homosexuality to a cultural pattern—language family. Before getting to that, some cautions about interpreting these numbers are in order.

Correlational claims should not be misinterpreted as causal ones, and the existence of counterinstances does not invalidate a statistical relationship. The associations between sociocultural phenomena that are examined below are tendencies (statistical relations) not exceptionless. While devoid of the functionalist optimism that everything fits together to produce stable equilibrium, I do think that the co-occurrences are often recursive, that is, rather than A causing B, A bolsters B, which bolsters A. Alas, the data to sort out the historical priority of organization(s) of homosexualities to that of other sociocultural features in "traditional" African societies are not available.

Harder to grasp, even for those who are comfortable thinking statistically, is that rather than being a single trichotomized dependent variable, the occurrence of each type is a distinct dependent variable. There are societies in which more than one type has been recorded. This reduces the apparent differentiation (between columns) of (other) social structural patterns and types of homosexuality. Even a comparison between a column for one type of homosexuality to the column for the pan-African sample involves some of the same societies being in both, so that tests of statistical significance of differences cannot validly be made. If I had the certainty to identify a single, dominant organization of homosexuality for each of these societies, differences would be more striking than they are in these tables.

Language

Although not immediately obvious, there does seem to be some geographical patterning of the occurrences of the three patterns of homosexuality across sub-Saharan African.[3] Table A2.2 shows that stratification by gender roles is the most commonly reported kind among the historically more northern of sub-Saharan African peoples (speakers of Nilotic, Semitic, and Chadic languages), whereas stratification by age roles is more common than by gender roles in West Africa and nearly as common among Bantu-speaking societies in central and southern Africa. Homosexuality not stratified by age or gender is more common in the south than in other parts of Africa, but it is not the most frequent organization in any of the four geohistorical clusters of languages.

Linguistic affiliations have been the favored means for making inferences about shared ancestry and prehistoric population movements. The southeastward spread of Bantu languages is particularly well accepted.[4] Cultural elements (and even complexes), including languages, can spread without the DNA of those originating the cultural element or speaking the protolanguage; how much "borrowing" of words and of grammatical patterns occurs remains controversial among linguistics, as is even the assumption of a steady rate of divergence from a protolanguage. But whether shared criterial features of language primarily derive from common origins or from conquest and other kinds of contact between human groups, they definitely are indications of cultural connections.

Table A2.2. Same-Sex Patterns and Language Macrofamily

	Gender-stratified (%)	Age-stratified (%)	Non-stratified (%)	No.
Language family Nilo-Saharan (Nilotic)+ Afro-Asiatic (Semitic, Chadic)	56	22	22	9
Niger-Congo (non-Bantu)	40	45	15	20
Niger-Congo/Bantu	38	35	26	34
Khoisan	33	33	33	3

Inheritance

In Murdock's sample of world cultures, there are 3.22 patrilineal sub-Saharan African societies for every matrilineal one. Among the societies in which the dominant organization of homosexuality is described in sufficient detail to code it (as gender stratified, age stratified, or not status stratified), the ratio of patrilineal to matrilineal societies is substantially lower: 1.9 patrilineal societies for each matrilineal one. The ratio is lowest for societies with age-stratified homosexuality (1.2:1). Gender-stratified homosexuality or relatively egalitarian homosexuality among the young appears more than twice as often in patrilineal as in matrilineal societies (2.4:1).[5]

Organizations of homosexuality—especially age-stratified—have been disproportionately noted within matrilineal societies. However, as Table A2.3 shows, matrilinearity does not cause one pattern of homosexuality rather than

Table A2.3. Inheritance Pattern by Same-Sex Pattern: Observed Value (Expected Value)* and Odds of Patrilineal:Matrilineal Inheritance

	Patrilineal	Matrilineal	P:M Odds
Gender-stratified	17 (15)	8 (4.7)	2.1 (3.2)
Age-stratified	11 (15)	9 (4.7)	1.2 (3.2)
Non-stratified	10 (15)	4 (4.7)	2.5 (3.2)

*Expected values are Murdock's patrilineal:matrilineal ratio of 3:2 for Africa, between columns, and equal frequencies for rows.

another. There are almost as many matrilineal societies with age-stratified as with gender-stratified homosexuality.

Subsistence Activities

Societies with gender-stratified homosexuality depend on animal husbandry for about 26 percent and agriculture for about 56 percent of their subsistence. For societies with age-stratified homosexuality, the means are 18 and 58 percent, and for societies with nonstratified homosexuality, 27 and 44 percent. These differences are not very dramatic, and it is perhaps more interesting to note that the only two societies in this sample that rely on animal husbandry for less than 5 percent of subsistence (Nkundu and Zande) are those with age-stratified homosexuality, and the three that do not engage in agriculture (Herero, Nama, and !Xun) have nonstratified homosexuality. In George Murdock's (1981:132) sample, 4.5 percent of African societies were hunter-gatherers and 7.2 percent pastoralists (the rest being tillers of fields).

Sexual Division of Labor

As the rightmost column in Table A2.4 shows, about one-third of "traditional" African societies relied more on male than on female labor for producing subsistence, one-third relied on greater female than male labor, and one-third relied on roughly equivalent amounts of labor (not necessarily shared

Table A2.4. Same-Sex Pattern and Involvement in Subsistence by Sex

	Gender-stratified (%)	Age-stratified (%)	Non-stratified (%)	Pan-African sample (%)
Involvement in subsistence				
Greater male involvement	33	29	27	35
Greater female involvement	38	53	27	34
Equivalent involvement	29	18	45	31
No. (%)	21 (100)	17 (100)	11 (100)	116 (100)

tasks). Rather than being evenly split, there are modal types of the sexual division of labor for each of the three major types of organization of male homosexuality. Greater female involvement, a presumptive indicator for (and basis of) higher female status, is somewhat more commonly the mode for societies with gender-stratified—and considerably more so for societies with age-stratified—male homosexuality than it is for societies with nonstratified male homosexuality or for the pan-African HRAF sample.[6] The societies with nonstratified male homosexuality are proportionately much more likely to be those in which there are equivalent roles for males and females in production (that is, those without a marked sexual division of labor). As in the "modern West," (relative) egalitarianism in (homo)sex correlates with egalitarianism in productive labor.

Lack of Male Sexual Access to Females

Although male sexual access to unmarried females is a category for which "missing data" is particularly common in HRAF coding (specifically, Murdock 1967), there is some indication in Table A2.5 that where boys are freest to engage in sex with girls, they also more freely (or at least more visibly) have sex with each other. Conversely, there is also some evidence

Table A2.5. Same-Sex Pattern and Permissiveness for Female Premarital Intercourse

	Gender-stratified (%)	Age-stratified (%)	Non-stratified (%)	Pan-African sample (%)
Permissiveness for female premarital intercourse				
Virginity necessary for brides	50	25	—	30
Weak negative sanctions	25	—	—	13
Allowed (barring pregnancy)	25	75	100	56
No. (%)	8 (100)	8 (100)	2 (100)	67 (100)

that the societies that are most concerned about premarital female chastity are the same in which male homosexuality involves nonmasculine sexually receptive males as substitutes. However, even if the codings are valid and the lack of information is random in regard to the true distribution of values of permissiveness, data are not available for most societies (and especially missing for those with nonstratified homosexuality).

Another cultural practice that keeps females away from male penetration (and often from any direct contact) is postpartum sexual taboos. These taboos are ubiquitous, and they last a year or more in more than two-thirds of the societies in each column of Table A2.6. Societies with gender-stratified homosexuality are somewhat more likely to have postpartum taboos of two or more years than the pan-African sample, whereas societies with age-stratified and nonstratified male homosexuality tend to have somewhat shorter taboos than the pan-African sample.

Taken together, these tenuous data suggest that organized male homosexuality is not particularly related to lack of male access to sex with females. They could better be marshaled to argue that organization of male homosexuality (particularly nonstratified male homosexuality) is more likely to develop in cultures that are "sex positive" for male-female relations.

Table A2.6. Same-Sex Pattern and Length of Postpartum Sexual Taboos

| | Percent of societies with same-sex pattern | | | |
	Gender-stratified (%)	Age-stratified (%)	Non-stratified (%)	Pan-African sample (%)
Length of taboo				
No taboo	0	0	0	0
<1 month	0	17	0	5
1–6 months	0	0	22	17
6–12 months	20	0	0	11
1–2 years	30	50	55	28
>2 years	50	33	22	38
No. (%)	10 (100)	6 (100)	8 (100)	77 (100)

Male Circumcision and Adolescent Male Isolation

Table A2.7 cross-tabulates same-sex pattern by male experiences of (1) circumcision at varying ages and (2) adolescent extrusion from the childhood home. In more than three-quarters of the African societies with nonstratified

Table A2.7. Same-Sex Patterns, Male Genital Mutilation, and Isolation of Adolescent Males

	Gender-stratified (%)	Age-stratified (%)	Non-stratified (%)	Pan-African sample (%)
Age of mutilation/ circumcision				
None	47	43	20	39
<2	6	—	—	7
2–5	6	—	—	4
6–10	—	29	40	11
11–15	24	29	20	24
16–25	6	—	—	5
25+	12	—	—	—
Present but age unspecified	—	—	20	10
No. (%)	17 (100)	14 (100)	11 (100)	251 (100)
Adolescent male segregation				
None	23	21	43	17
Sleep apart from family	31	28	29	40
Live apart from nuclear family with relatives	31	28	—	18
Live apart from nuclear family with agemates	15	14	29	23
No. (%)	13 (100)	13 (100)	7 (100)	166 (100)

male homosexuality, male genitals were mutilated.[7] In contrast, there was no male genital alteration in 43 percent of societies with age-stratified and 53 percent of societies with gender-stratified same-sex patterns. For societies with male genital alteration and age- or gender-stratified male homosexuality, the age range at which it was done was narrower for the age-stratified, the age being somewhat older for those with gender-stratified homosexuality.

Extrusion of male adolescents is less common in societies with documented organizations of homosexuality than in those without,[8] which constitutes evidence against homosexuality being "bred" in same-sex environments. Differences among societies with different organizations of homosexuality pale in comparison to this difference, although it might be noted that those with age-stratified homosexuality are only half as likely to have young males segregated and concentrated for "picking" by adult males.

Class and Urbanization

Table A2.8 shows that the (colonial-era) societies with gender-stratified homosexuality were more urbanized than the societies with nonstratified or (especially) age-stratified organizations of homosexuality and more urbanized than most African "traditional" societies. In that more populous societies

Table A2.8. Settlement Size and Same-Sex Pattern

	Gender-stratified (%)	Age-stratified (%)	Non-stratified (%)	Pan-African sample (%)
Percent of societies with largest indigenous towns <4,999	24	50	41	51
Percent of societies with largest indigenous towns 5,000–50,000	38	50	59	45
Percent of societies with largest indigenous towns 50,000+	38	0	0	4.5
No.	8	10	7	111

are more likely to have been studied, it may be that the difference is a function of the scantier records about the societies with smaller and more atomized populations, rather than there being any real relationship between organization of homosexuality and settlement size. The HRAF coding "mean size of local community" has five categories for societies whose aggregations are less than 1,000 persons but shifts to noting the largest aggregation for societies with settlements of 1,000 or more persons. Most of the African societies included in Murdock's (1967) survey are in the 50–1,000 range. The societies with age-stratified homosexuality have a median "mean size" of 5,000, whereas most of those with gender-stratified and nonstratified homosexuality have aggregates of more than 5,000.

Another indicator of societal complexity is the crystallization of classes: "complex stratification into social classes correlated in large measure with extensive differentiation of occupational statuses" is the category in Murdock (1967: 57). As can been seen in Table A2.9, gender-stratified male homosexuality is the only kind that has been reported in indigenous African class-based societies, whereas nonstratified homosexuality is considerably more common in classless societies than either of the other two organizations of male homosexuality. That is, the relatively egalitarian societies seem more likely to have relatively egalitarian homosexual relations.

Table A2.9. Same-Sex Pattern and Socioeconomic Stratification

	Stratification System				
	Gender-stratified (%)	Age-stratified (%)	Non-stratified (%)	Pan-African sample (%)	World sample (%)
Classless	11	13	36	37	45
Wealth distinctions	28	27	45	13	19
Land-holding elite vs. propertyless	6	7	0	1	2
Hereditary nobles vs. commoners	39	53	18	43	22
Social classes	17	0	0	6	11
No.	18	15	11	107	549

Summary

Compared with those with the other two types, societies with gender-stratified male homosexuality are more northeastern, more urban, more patrilineal (though less than the African average), less dependent on herding animals, and more concerned with female premarital chastity. With the possible exception of Hausa having both age- and gender-stratified homosexuality, gender-stratified homosexuality is the only kind occurring in African class societies.

Nonstratified male homosexuality tends to occur in societies in which there is equivalent male and female involvement in major production, "free love," and lack of significant differences in wealth. These societies are as patrilineal as societies with gender-stratified homosexuality and only somewhat less agrarian. Males in societies with egalitarian homosexuality are more than twice as likely to be circumcised as males in societies with the other two types.

Societies with age-stratified male homosexuality are more likely to be matrilineal, more likely to rest on greater female than male economic involvement, less likely to isolate adolescent males with their agemates, less urban, and somewhat less pastoralist than societies with the other two types.

Socioeconomic Structures of Societies with Female-Female Sexuality

The passing references to female-female sexuality rarely provide enough information to code its organization. The brevity of this section in comparison to the correlations of male homosexuality should not be interpreted as its being an "afterthought" or "symbolic" of any lack of interest in female-female relations[9] but rather *entirely* as a function of the scantiness of the ethnographic record on which these analyses are based and of the lack of variance in explanatory (social structural) variables for the few cases about which there is sufficient information to allow codings of patterns of female-female sexual roles.[10]

In all but two of the societies for which an organization of female-female sexuality can be provisionally coded, raising plants (agriculture) is more important than raising animals (animal husbandry), and the bulk of agricultural work is done by females in all of these societies (except in the two pastoralist societies in which there is equal responsibility for the animals).[11] In that greater female than male involvement in the prime subsistence activity is evidenced in only one-third of African societies, this is a marked difference. Patrilineal inheritance is also a feature in all of the societies for which an organization of female-female sexuality can be provisionally coded, although patrilineal inheritance is distinctly less common in societies with attested male homosexual roles than the African average (as shown in Table A2.3 above).

The reports of gender-stratified female homosexuality come from heavily urbanized, highly stratified societies (Mombasa, Dahomey, Hausa, Tsonga), while those of age-stratified and egalitarian homosexuality come from less urbanized societies that are, nonetheless, distinctly stratified between a hereditary aristocracy and commoners (age: Sotho, Kaguru, and possibly Cape Bantu; egalitarian: Zande, Wawhihé, and possibly Akan) or at least have wealth distinctions (e.g., Kurt Falk reported mutual female-female sexual relations among the pastoralist Herero and Nama).

Of the 10 societies with female-female sexuality reported with sufficient detail to classify it in one of the three types and in which Murdock (1967) was able to code norms of premarital sexual behavior, only 2 (Dahomey and Mombasa) insisted on premarital female virginity.[12] The others are among those coded as "free love" or "premarital sex relations allowed and not sanctioned unless pregnancy results," so it appears that female-female sex (particularly age-stratified and status-unstratified relationships) develops in societies with relatively freer premarital male-female sex, that is, not where repression was most acute. Generally, where boys could play sexually with girls, boys could play sexually with boys (see Table A2.5), and girls could play sexually with girls.

Although the sample is small, the African cases show a strong relationship between patterned female homosexual relationships and predominant female involvement in production, despite the patrilineality of the societies.

Notes

1. "Nonstratified" is not deployed as a residual category for places in which there is not information about organization. There must be positive indications that partners were of the same status (generally, unmarried/young males) and/or practiced sexual reciprocity. "Homosexuality" is used throughout this chapter as a shorthand for "same-sex sexual relationships."

2. In a sense, males become "sex objects" exchanged by matrilines, as women are in patrilineal societies.

3. North of the Sahara, the dominant idiom is pederastic, but boys are feminized and some adult pathics coexist with the valorization of pederasty (see Murray 1997a: 45–48).

4. Not that the spread of Bantu languages and associated cultural traits was solely a result of population movement, any more than the spread of Islam (southward in Africa and eastward in Asia and across the Indian Ocean) depended only on repopulating regions with Arabs.

5. It is conceivable that sexuality has been examined more carefully in societies in which the "aberration" of matrilineal inheritance appears. If this were so, the relationship here would be artifactual.

6. Many would expect gender-crossing or -mixing roles to occur more commonly in societies with greater female involvement in the main economic activity, on the presumption that there is less male status to lose where women are more involved in production (see Greenberg 1988: 47–48). However, based on a HRAF world sample, Robert Munroe and Ruth Munroe (1977: 307–8) coded 24 out of 24 societies with male transvestites as relying on males for more than half the contribution to subsistence, along with 32 of 49 societies without male transvestites. (Only 23 percent of the societies rely more on female labor, whereas Murdock [1981: 141] codes 35 percent of a world sample of 424 societies with agriculture relying more on female than on male labor.) There is a report of male transvestism in at least one of the six African cultures Munroe et al. (1969) coded as lacking the institution of male transvestites (see Smith and Dale 1920, 2: 74). The Ila are also a society in which females do appreciably more than males in agriculture. (Amhara and Hausa are the two African societies they coded as having male transvestitism.)

7. This is Murdock's category for what others call "circumcision" or "alteration."

8. Some Freudians might take this as evidencing a relationship between homosexuality and close male bonding to mothers. Against this interpretation, I would note that (1) there is no evidence of greater frequency of involvement in male-male sex in these societies, and (2), following Gilbert Herdt (1999), it may be that societies with particularly intensive bonding of male children to their mothers extrude the young males from the household with greater force after early childhood.

9. Such criticisms of placement and relative length have been made of other ethnological volumes focused on homosexuality (see Murray 1997a). The search for material on female-female sexuality has been, if anything, more diligent than that for material on male-male sexuality, and a higher proportion of what could be found about female relations is included in this book than what could be found about males. That is, the disproportion by sex in the ethnographic literature about homosexuality in Africa is even greater than the disproportion of discussions herein.

10. For example, Judith Brown's (1963: 840–41) cross-tabulation of postmarital residence patterns to the presence or absence of female initiation rites includes only two African societies (Dahomean and Naman) for which female-female sexual roles have been described that have female initiation rites and one that lacks them

(Zande). All three are patrilocal, as are most African "traditional" societies; Zande and Fon have male rites that include both genital operation and seclusion, whereas Nama only had partial seclusion.

11. The mean share of subsistence from animal husbandry in these societies is 18 percent, while agriculture accounts for 58 percent.

12. Female virginity is also "essential at marriage" in Mombasa (Porter 1995: 138).

Bibliography

Several of the following references are taken, with his generous permission, from Wayne Dynes's 1983 compilation. Some passing references not discussed elsewhere in this volume are included herein, in which case relevant page numbers appear in parentheses at the end of the citation.

Abdullahi, Salisu A. 1984. "A sociological analysis of the institution of 'dan daudu in Hausa society." Unpublished PhD dissertation, Bayero University, Kano, Nigeria. (See Kleis and Abdullahi 1983.)

Aberle, David F. 1961. "Matrilineal descent in cross-cultural perspective." In *Matrilineal kinship*, eds. David M. Schneider and Kathleen Gough, 655–727. Berkeley: University of California Press.

Abu-Lughod, Lila. 1986. *Veiled sentiments*. Berkeley: University of California Press.

Achmat, Zackie. 1993. " 'Apostles of civilised vice': 'Immoral practices' and 'unnatural vice' in South African prisons and compounds, 1890–1920." *Social Dynamics* 19(2): 92–110.

———. 1995. "My childhood as an adult molester: A Salt River moffie." In *Defiant desire: Gay and lesbian lives in South Africa*, eds. Mark Gevisser and Edwin Cameron, 324–41. New York: Routledge.

Adam, Barry D. 1986. "Age, structure and sexuality." *Journal of Homosexuality* 11: 19–33.

Aina, Tade Akin. 1991. "Patterns of bisexuality in Sub-Saharan Africa." In *Bisexuality & HIV/AIDS*, eds. R. Tielman, M. Carballo, and A. Hendriks, 81–90. Buffalo, NY: Prometheus Books.

Allen, James de Vere. 1981. "Ngoma: Music and dance." In *The customs of the Swahili people*, ed. J. de V. Allen, 233–46. Berkeley: University of California Press.

Alpers, Edward A. 1984. " 'Ordinary household chores': Ritual and power in a 19th-century Swahili women's possession cult." *International Journal of African Historical Studies* 17(4): 677–702.

Amadiume, Ifi. 1987. *Male daughters, female husbands: Gender and sex in an African society* [Nigerian Igbo]. Atlantic Highlands, NJ: Zed Books.

Ambrogetti, Paolo. 1900. *La vita sessuale nell'Eritrea*. Rome.

Amory, Deborah P. 1994. "Identity politics in Zanzibar." PhD dissertation, Department of Anthropology, Stanford University.

———. 1996. "Woman-woman marriage on the Swahili coast." Paper presented at the African Studies Association annual meeting, San Francisco, CA.

_____. 1997. "'Homosexuality' in Africa: Issues and Debates." *Issue* 25(1): 5–10.

_____. 2017. "Queering African Studies: Institutions and social networks," Paper presented at the African Studies Association annual meeting, Chicago, IL.

———. 2019. "LGBTIQ rights in Kenya: On artivism and social change." *Georgetown Journal of International Affairs*, May 14, 2019. https://www.georgetownjournalofinternationalaffairs.org/online-edition/2019/5/9/lgbtiq-rights-in-kenya-on-artivism-and-social-change. Accessed April 22, 2020.

Amselle, Jean-Loup. 1978. "Migration and neo-traditional society: The Bambara of Jitumu [Mali]." *Cahiers d'Études Africaines* 18: 487–502.

Andreski, Iris. 1970. *Old wives' tales: Life stories of African women*. New York: Schocken.

Anon. 1996. "Whose culture is it?" *WomanPlus* 1–2 (May–August): 17.

Anzaldua, Gloria. 1987. *Borderlands/La frontera: The new mestiza*. San Francisco, CA: Aunt Lute.

Appiah, K[wame] Anthony. 1996. "The pool." In *Shade: An anthology of fiction by gay men of African descent*, eds. B. Morrow and C. Rowell, 103–16. New York: Avon.

Argyle, W. J. 1966. *The Fan of Dahomey*. Oxford: Clarendon Press. (Refers to men "performing the intimate services associated with the king's person" [63–65].)

Asad, Talal. 1973. *Anthropology and the colonial encounter*. London: Ithaca Press.

Askew, Kelly. 1992a. "Female circles and male lines: The dynamics of Swahili musical performance and gender relations." MA thesis, Department of Anthropology, Harvard University.

———. 1992b. "Unity through performance: Swahili musical performance in the context of Tanzanian state-building." PhD thesis prospectus, Department of Anthropology, Harvard University.

Barnes, T. 1993. "'We women worked so hard': Gender, labour and social reproduction in colonial Harare, 1930–56." PhD dissertation, University of Zimbabwe.

———. 1995. "'So that a labourer could live with his family': Overlooked factors in social and economic strife in urban colonial Zimbabwe." *Journal of Southern African Studies* 21(1): 95–113.

Barth, Heinrich. 1857–58. Vol. 2, *Reisen und entdeckungen in Nord- und Central-Afrika in den jahren 1849 bi 1855*. Gotha: J. Perthes. Translated as *Travels and Discoveries in North and Central Africa*. New York: Harper and Bros, 1857. Reprint. London: F. Cass, 1965. (Mentions sodomy in Bornú, southeast of Lake Chad [2:39].)

Barret, Paul Marie Victor. 1888. Vol. 1, *Senegambie et Guinee, la region gabonaise, L'Afrique occidentale*. Paris: Challamel. (166).

Bastian, Adolf. 1860. Vol. 3, *Der Mensch in der Geschichte*. Leipzig: O. Wigand. (305 on Dahomey.)

———. 1872. *Die Rechtsverhältnisse bei verschiedenen Völkern der Erde*. Berlin: G. Reimer.

———. 1879. *Die deutsche Expedition an der Loango-Küste*. 3 vols. Jena: G. Fischer.

Baumann, Hermann. 1955. *Das doppelte Geschlect: Ethnologische Studien zur Bisexualität in Ritus und Mythos*. Berlin: Dietrich Reimer.

Baumann, Oskar. [1894] 1963. *Ngorongoro's first visitor: Being an annotated and illustrated translation from Dr. O. Baumann's Durch Mas[s]ailand zur Nilquelle*. Kampala: East African Literature Bureau.

Beattie, John. 1961. "Group aspects of the Nyoro spirit mediumship cult." *Rhodes-Livingston Journal* 30: 11–38.

———, and John Middleton. 1969. Introduction to *Spirit Mediumship and Society in Africa*. London: Routledge and Kegan Paul. (Suggests a relationship between spirit possession and male homosexuality among the Lugbara of Uganda, although this is not discussed in Middleton's chapter in the volume [xxv].)

Beidelman, Thomas O. 1973. "The Kaguru of central Tanzania." In *Cultural source materials for population planning in East Africa: Beliefs and practices*, ed. Angela Molnos, 262–73. Nairobi: East African Publishing House. ("The Kaguru consider male homosexuality very wrong, though it seems that it does occur among those who have worked on the coast or who have been employed by Arabs and Europeans. The Kaguru were more amused than shocked by such inquiries" [269].)

———. 1997. *The Cool Knife: Imagery of gender, sexuality, and moral education in Kaguru initiation ritual*. Washington, DC: Smithsonian Institution Press. (Relates that after seven years' acquaintance, some [Tanzania] Kaguru acknowledged that some Kaguru men were "homosexual," though this is a "secret pattern. This would not deter men from marrying and fathering children. . . . For Kaguru, marriage is so important that sexual proclivity would not be a decisive factor in preventing it." His male informants also conceded that at girls' initiation, women might teach initiates how copulation takes place by simulating it, either with an initiate or with each other while an initiate watches [273, n. 16].)

Bentley, William Holman. [1887] 1967. *Dictionary and grammar of the Kongo language as spoken at San Salvador, the ancient capital of the old Kongo empire, West Africa*. Reprint. Farnborough: Gregg. London: Baptist Missionary Society, the Trubner.

Besmer, Fremont E. 1983. *Horses, musicians, and gods: The Hausa possession trance*. South Hadley, MA.: Bergin and Garvey.

Beyrer, Chris et al. 2011. *The global HIV epidemics among men who have sex with men*. Washington, DC: World Bank.

Bieber, Friedrich J. 1909. "Brieflicher bericht uber Erhebungen unter äthiopischen Völkerschaften." *Anthropophyteia* 6: 402–5.

————. 1910–1911. "Neue Forschungen über das eschlechtsleben in Äthiopien." *Anthropophyteia* 7: 227–32; 8: 184–93.

————. 1920. *Kaffa, ein altkuschitisches volkstum in Inner-Afrika.* . . . Munster: W. Aschendroff.

Biersteker, Ann. 1996. *Kujibizana: Questions of language and power in nineteenth and twentieth century poetry in Kiswahili.* East Lansing: Michigan State University Press.

Blacking, John. 1959. "Fictitious kinship amongst girls of the Venda of the Northern Transvaal." *Man* 59: 255–58.

————. 1978. "Uses of the kinship idiom in friendships at some Venda and Zulu schools." In *Social system and tradition in southern Africa*, eds. J. Argyle and E. Preston-Whyte, 101–17. New York: Oxford University Press.

Blackwood, Evelyn. 1996. "Reading sexuality across cultures: Lesbian studies in anthropology since 1980." Paper presented at the American Anthropological Association annual meeting, San Francisco, CA.

Bleys, Rudi C. 1995. *The geography of perversion: Male-to-male sexual behavior outside the west and the ethnographic imagination, 1750–1918.* New York: New York University Press.

Boddy, Janice Patricia. 1989. *Wombs and alien spirits: Women, men, and the Zar cult in northern Sudan.* Madison: University of Wisconsin Press.

Boswell, John. 1980. Christianity, social tolerance, and homosexuality: Gay people in Western Europe from the beginning of the Christian Era to the fourteenth century. Chicago and London: University of Chicago Press.

Botha, Kevan, and Edwin Cameron. 1997. "South Africa." In *Sociolegal control of homosexuality: A multi-national comparison*, eds. Donald West and Richard Green, 5–42. New York: Plenum.

Bourdillon, M. F. C. 1995. *Where are the ancestors?: Changing culture in Zimbabwe.* Harare: University of Zimbabwe Publications.

Brain, Robert. 1976. *Friends and lovers.* New York: Basic Books.

Braiterman, Jared. 1992. "Beauty in flight: Rio and beyond." *Whorezine* 15: 9–11.

————. 1996. "Beat it: An anthropology oddity." PhD dissertation, Department of Anthropology, Stanford University.

Brincker, P. H. 1900. "Character, Sitten und Gebräuche speciell der Bantu Deutsch-Südwestafrikas." *Mitteilungen des Seminars für orientalische Sprachen an der Kaiser Friedrich-Wilhelms-Universität zu Berlin* 3: 66–99.

Brown, Judith K. 1963. "Cross-cultural study of female initiation rites." *American Anthropologist* 65: 837–53.

Browne, W. G. 1806. *Travels in Africa, Egypt and Syria from the Year 1792 to 1798.* London: T. Cadell and W. Davies. ("Pæderasty, so common in Asia and the north of Africa, is in the Soudân [Darfur] little known or practiced" [336].)

Bryk, Felix. [1928] 1939. *Neger-eros: Ethnologische studien uber das sexualleben bei negern.* Berlin: A. Marcus and E. Weber. Quoted from the 1939 English edition, *Dark rapture: The sex-life of the African Negro.* New York: Walden. Reprint. New York: AMS Press, 1975. The same material was published in *Voodoo-Eros: Ethnological studies in the sex life of the African aborigine* privately in New York in 1933 (p. 152) and by the United Book Guild in 1964 (p. 228).

―――. 1934. *Circumcision in man and woman: Its history, psychology, and ethnology.* New York: American Ethnological Press.

Bujra, Janet. 1975. "Production, property, prostitution: Sexual politics in Atu." *Cahiers d'études Africaines* 12: 13–39.

Bull, Chris. 1990. "No easy walk to freedom: South African gay activist Simon Nkoli fights oppression at home and abroad." *The Advocate* 542 (January 1): 44–47.

Bullock, Charles. 1950. *The Mashona and the Matabele.* Cape Town: Juta.

Bullough, Vern L. 1976. *Sexual variance in society and history.* New York: Wiley.

Burgt, Joannes Michael M. van der. 1903. *Un grand peuple de l'Afrique equatoriale: Elements d'une monographie sur l'Urundi et les Warundi.* Bois-le-Duc, Netherlands: Société "L'illustration catholique."

―――. 1904. *Dictionnaire Français-Kirundi.* Bois-le-Duc, Netherlands: Société "L'illustration catholique."

Burckhardt, John Lewis. 1822. Vol. 1, *Travels in Nubia.* London: John Murray. ("The Kashefs and their relations endeavour to imitate the Mamelouks in every thing, even in their most detestable vices," whereas Nubians generally abhorred "the execrable propensities which the Mamelouks have rendered so common in Egypt" [364].)

Burton, John W. 1981. "Ethnicity on the hoof: On the economics of Nuer identity." *Ethnology* 20: 157–62.

―――. 1988. "Shadows at twilight: A note on history and the ethnographic present." *Proceedings of the American Philosophical Society* 132: 420–33.

Burton, Richard Francis. 1864. *Mission to Gelele, King of Dahome.* 2 vols. London: Tinsley Brothers.

―――. [1865] 1924. "Notes on the Dahoman." In *Selected Papers on Anthropology, Travel & Exploration,* ed. N. M. Penzer, 109–133. London: A. M. Philpot.

―――. 1872. *Zanzibar.* London: Tinsley Brothers.

―――. [1903–04?] Vol. 10, *The book of the thousand nights and a night.* N.p.: Burton Club.

Butler, Judith. 1990. *Gender trouble: Feminism and the subversion of identity.* New York: Routledge.

―――. 1993. *Bodies that matter: On the discursive limits of "sex."* New York: Routledge.

Butt-Thompson, Frederick William. 1929. *West African secret societies: Their organisations, officials, and teaching.* London: H. F. and G. Witherby.

Buxton, Jean. 1963. "Mandari witchcraft." In *Witchcraft and society in East Africa,* eds. J. Middleton and W. Winter, 99–121. New York: Praeger.

―――. 1973. *Religion and healing in Mandari.* Oxford: Clarendon Press. (209, 220–21).

Calamé-Griaule, Geneviève. 1986. *Words and the Dogon world*. Philadelphia, PA: ISHI.

Caldwell, John C., Pat Caldwell, and I. O. Orubuloye. 1992. "The family and sexual networking in sub-Saharan Africa: Historical regional differences and present-day implications." *Population Studies* 46: 385–410.

Caldwell, John C., Pat Caldwell, and Pat Quiggin. 1989. "The social context of AIDS in sub-Saharan Africa." *Population and Development Review* 15(2): 185–234.

———, I. O. Orubuloye, and Pat Caldwell. 1992. "Underreaction to AIDS in sub-Saharan Africa." *Social Science and Medicine* 34: 1169–82.

Caplan, Pat [A. P.]. 1975. *Choice and constraint in Swahili society*. Oxford: Oxford University Press.

———. 1982. "Gender, ideology, and modes of production on the coast of East Africa." *Paideuma* 28: 29–43.

Carbutt, E. G. 1880. "Some minor superstitions and customs of the Zulus." *Folklore Journal* 2: 12–13.

Cardonega, Antonio de Oliveira de. [1680] 1940. *Historia general das guerras Angolanas*. Lisbon: Divisão de publicacoes e biblioteca, Agencia general das colonias.

Carpenter, Edward. 1914. *Intermediate types among primitive folk: A study in social evolution*. London: George Allen.

Carrier, Joseph M. 1980. "The Omani *xanith* controversy." *Man* 15: 541–42.

Cavazzi, Giovanni Antonio. 1694. *Historische Beschreibung . . . Congo, Matamba un Angola. . . .* Munich. (French and Portuguese translations are more readily available; the original Italian version was printed in Bologna in 1687.)

Cerulli, Enrico. 1923. "Note sul movimento musulamano della Somalia." *Rivista Studies Orientales* 10: 1–36.

Chan Sam, Tanya. 1993. "Coloured school days." In *The invisible ghetto: Lesbian and gay writing from South Africa*, eds. Matthew Krouse and Kim Berman, 155–63. Johannesburg: Cosaw.

———. 1995. "Five women: Black lesbian life on the reef." In *Defiant desire: Gay and lesbian lives in South Africa*, eds. Mark Gevisser and Edwin Cameron, 186–92. New York: Routledge.

Chapman, Catherine. 2016. " 'Pigs & dogs': British play highlights west's role in African homophobia." *NBC Out*, August 5, 2016. https://www.nbcnews.com/feature/nbc-out/pigs-dogs-british-production-highlights-west-s-role-african-homophobia-n623771. Accessed May 23, 2018.

Chauncey, George, Jr. 1982. "From sexual inversion to homosexuality." *Salmagundi* 58: 114–46.

———. 1994. *Gay New York: Gender, urban culture, and the making of the gay male world, 1890–1940*. New York: Basic Books.

Chetty, Dhianaraj. 1995. "A drag at Madame Costello's: Cape moffie life and the popular press in the 1950s and 1960s." In *Defiant desire: Gay and lesbian lives in South Africa*, eds. Mark Gevisser and Edwin Cameron, 115–27. New York: Routledge.

Chiang, Howard. 2019. *Global Encyclopedia of lesbian, gay, bisexual, transgender, and queer history*. Farmington Hills, MI: Charles Scribner's Sons.

Chirimuuta, Richard C., and Rosalind J. Chirimuuta. 1987. *AIDS, Africa, and racism*. Derbyshire: Bretby House.

Christensen, James B. 1954. *Double descent among the Fanti*. New Haven, CT: Human Relations Area Files.

Clark, Carolyn Martin. 1975. "Kinship morality in the interaction pattern of some Kikuyu families." PhD dissertation, Michigan State University.

Cleland, John. 1749. *Memoirs of a woman of pleasure* [Fanny Hill]. London: Fenton.

Collier, Jane F., and Sylvia J. Yanagisako, eds. 1987. *Gender and kinship: Essays toward a unified analysis*. Stanford: Stanford University Press.

Colson, Elizabeth. 1958. *Marriage and the family among the plateau Tonga of northern Rhodesia*. Manchester: Manchester University Press.

Coly, Ayo A. 2019. "Literature, African (Francophone)." In *Global encyclopedia of lesbian, gay, bisexual, transgender, and queer history*, eds. Howard Chiang et al., 964–71. Farmington Hills, MI: Charles Scribner's Sons.

Comaroff, John L. 1984. "The closed society and its critics: Historical transformations in African ethnography." *American Ethnologist* 11: 571–83.

———, and Simon Roberts. 1977. "Marriage and extra-marital sexuality: The dialectics of legal change among the Kgatla." *Journal of African Law* 21: 97–123.

Combier, F. 1890. Vol. 1, *Missions en Chine et au Congo*. Brussels: Congregation du Couer immacule.

Conner, Randy P. 1987. "In the land of Laddo: Gay people and the Yoruba spiritual tradition." *The Advocate* 467 (March 3): 28–31.

———. 1993. *Blossom of bone: Reclaiming the connections between homoeroticism and the sacred*. San Francisco: HarperSanFrancisco.

Constantinides, Pamela. 1977. " 'Ill at ease and sick at heart': Symbolic behaviour in a Sudanese healing cult." In *Symbols and Sentiments*, ed. I. M. Lewis, 61–84. San Francisco: Academic Press.

Coplan, David B. 1994. *In the time of cannibals: The word music of South Africa's Basotho migrants*. Chicago: University of Chicago Press.

Corre, A. 1894. *L'ethnographie criminelle d'après les observations et les statistiques judiciares receuillies dans les colonies françaises*. Paris: C. Reinwald.

Coutinho, Mike. 1993. "Lesbian and gay life in Zimbabwe." *The third pink book: A global view of lesbian and gay liberation and oppression*, eds. A. Hendriks, R. Tielman, and E. van der Veen, 62–65. Buffalo, NY: Prometheus.

Crowder, Michael. 1959. *Pagans and politicians*. London: Hutchinson.

Cureau, Adolphe Louis. 1904. "Essai sur la psychologie des races nègres de l'Afrique Tropicale." *Revue générale des sciences pures et appliquées* 15: 638–95.

———. 1912. *Les sociétés primitives de l'Afrique equatoriale*. Paris: A. Colin. Translated by E. Andrews, *Savage man in central Africa: A study of primitive races in the French Congo*. London: T. F. Unwin, 1915.

Czekanowski, Jan. 1909. "Die anthropologisch-ethnographiscen Arbeiten." *Zeitschift
    für Ethnologie* 41: 591–615.
———. 1924. *Wissenschaftliche Ergebnisse der deutschen Zentral-Afrika-Expedition,
    1907–1908.* Leipzig: Klinkhardt und Biermann. (Azande court pederasty [56].)
Damberger, Christian Frederick. 1801. *Travels through the interior of Africa.* . . . Charles-
    ton, MA: Etheridge. (Damberger was propositioned and assaulted by the son-
    in-law of the chief of the Muhotians in the vicinity of the Lorenzo River.
    When he complained, "The chief laughed and seemed to consider it nothing
    uncommon. This made me more attentive, and I now discovered that the
    contention at my first arrival at the kraal arose from every one's wishing to
    obtain possession of me for the same abominable purpose; and indeed, other
    attempts were afterwards made to seduce me." Damberger further averred that
    the Muhotians fought Kamtorians to their northeast, both groups seeking to
    use the other for the "gratification of their diabolical lusts" [158–59].)
Dannert, Eduard. 1906. *Zom Rechte der Herero, insbesondere uber ihr Familien- und
    Erbrecht.* Berlin: D. Reimer.
Dapper, Olfert. 1670. *Umbständliche und eigentliche Beschreibung von Agrika.*
    Amsterdam: von Meurs.
Davidson, Arnold I. 1990. "Closing up the corpses: Diseases of sexuality and the
    emergence of the psychiatric style of reasoning." *Meaning and method: Essays
    in honor of Hilary Putnam,* ed. George Boolos, 295–325. Cambridge: Cam-
    bridge University Press.
Davidson, Michael. [1970] 1988. *Some boys.* London: Gay Men's Press. (181–96,
    205–16.)
Degrapandré, Louis. 1801. *Voyage à la côte d'Afrique.* Paris: Dentu.
Delafosse, Marcel. 1912. Vol. 3, *Haut-Senegal, Niger, Soudan francaise.* Paris: Larose.
    (Reports humorous contempt with no attempt to punish homosexuality in
    the Sudan [92].)
Dent, R., and C. L. S. Nyembezi. 1969. *A scholar's Zulu dictionary.* Pietermaritz-
    burg: Shuter and Shooter.
Devisch, Renaat. 1985. "Self-production, production, and reproduction: Divination
    and politics among the Yaka of Zaire." *Social Compass* 32: 111–31.
Diop, Cheikh Anta. [1962] 1978. *The cultural unity of Black Africa:* Chicago: Third
    World.
Donham, Donald L. 1990. *History, power, ideology: Central issues in Marxism and
    anthropology.* New York: Cambridge University Press.
Driberg, Jack Herbert. 1923. *The Lango.* London: Thorner Coryndon.
Duarte de Carvalho, Ruy. 1995. "Has the future already begun?: Political transitions
    and identity affirmation among the Kuvale [Herero] cattle breeders of South-
    West Angola." *Lusotopie* 1: 221–37.
Dunton, Chris. 1989. " 'Wheyting be dat?': The treatment of homosexuality in
    African literature." *Research in African Literatures* 20: 422–48.

————, and Mai Palmberg. 1996. *Human rights and homosexuality in southern Africa.* Uppsala: Nordiska Afrikainstituet.

Duran, Khalid. 1993. "Homosexuality and Islam." In *Homosexuality and world religions,* ed. Arlene Swidler, 181–98. Valley Forge, PA: Trinity Press.

Dynes, Wayne R. 1983. "Homosexuality in sub-Saharan Africa." *Gay Books Bulletin* 9: 20–21. Reprinted in W. Dynes and S. Donaldson, *Ethnographic Studies of Homosexuality,* 166–67. New York: Garland, 1992.

Edel, May Mandelbaum. 1957. *The Chigu of western Uganda.* New York: Oxford University Press.

Edgerton, Robert B. 1964. "Pokot intersexuality." *American Anthropologist* 66: 1288–99.

Ekine, Sokari, and Hakima Abbas, eds. 2013. *Queer African reader.* Oxford: Fahamu Books.

Ellenberger, D. Frederic. [1833] 1912. *History of the Basuto, ancient and modern.* London: Caxton.

Ellis, Alfred B. [1890] 1965. *The Ewe-speaking peoples of the Slave Coast of West Africa.* London: Chapman and Hall. Reprint, Chicago: Benin Press, 1965.

Epprecht, Marc. 1995. "Women's 'conservatism' and the politics of gender in late colonial Lesotho." *Journal of African History* 36: 29–56.

————. 1996. "Culture, history, and homophobia." *SAPEM* 9(3): 33–38.

————. 1997. "Manliness in the mines." *Zimbabwe Review* 3(3): 20–22.

————. 2004. *Hungochani: The history of a dissident sexuality in southern Africa.* Montreal: McGill-Queen's University Press.

————. 2008. *Heterosexual Africa? The History of an idea from the age of exploration to the age of AIDS.* Athens: Ohio University Press.

————, et al. 2018. *"Boy Wives, Female Husbands* twenty years on: Reflections of scholarly activism and the struggle for human and sexual rights." *Canadian Journal of African Studies,* 52(3): 349–364. doi: 10.1080/00083968.2018.1546604. Accessed May 13, 2020.

————. 2020. "Sexualities in Africa." *Oxford Bibliographies: African Studies.* doi: 10.1093/obo/9780199846733-0215. Accessed May 13, 2020.

Estermann, Carlos. 1976. *The ethnography of southwest Angola.* New York: Africana.

Evans-Pritchard, Edward E. 1932. "Heredity and gestation as the Zande see them." *Sociologus* 7: 400–13.

————. 1937. *Witchcraft, oracles and magic among the Zande.* Oxford: Oxford University Press.

————. 1940. *The Nuer.* Oxford: Oxford University Press.

————. 1945. *Some aspects of marriage and family among the Nuer. Rhodes-Livingstone Papers* 11. (Mentions some obscure forms of "vicarious marriages by women or on behalf of women" socially reckoned as men [12].)

————. 1951. *Kinship and marriage among the Nuer.* Oxford: Clarendon Press.

————. 1957. "The Zande Royal court." *Zaire* 11: 379–80.

———. 1970. "Sexual inversion among the Azande." *American Anthropologist* 72: 1428–34.

———. 1971. *The Azande*. Oxford: Clarendon Press.

———. 1973. "Some notes on Zande sex habits." *American Anthropologist* 75: 171–75.

Evens, T. M. S. 1989a. "An illusory illusion: Nuer agnation and first principles." *Comparative Social Research* 11: 301–18.

———. 1989b. "The Nuer incest prohibition and the nature of kinship: Alterlogical reckoning." *Cultural Anthropology* 4: 323–46.

Faderman, Lillian. 1981. *Surpassing the love of men*. New York: Morrow.

Falk, Kurt. 1923. "Gleichgeschlechtliches Leben bei einigen Negerstämme Angolas." *Archiv für Anthropologie* n.s. 20: 42–45.

———. 1925–26. "Homosexualität bei den Eingeborenen in Südwest-Afrika." *Archiv für Menschenkunde* 1: 202–14 (also *Geschlecht und Gesselschaft* 13: 209–11).

Farran, Charles. 1963. *Matrimonial laws of the Sudan*. London: Butterworth.

Faupel, John Francis. 1962. *African holocaust: The story of the Uganda martyrs*. New York: P. J. Kennedy.

Felkin, R. W. 1884. "Notes on the Wganda tribe of Central Africa." *Proceedings of the Royal Society of Edinburgh* 13: 699–770.

Ferguson, W. S. 1917. "The Zulus and the Spartans: A comparative analysis of their military systems." *Harvard African Studies* 2: 197–234.

Fluehr-Lobban, Carolyn. 1977. "Agitation for change in the Sudan." In *Sexual stratification: A cross-cultural view*, ed. Alice Schlegel, 127–43. New York: Columbia University Press.

Forbes, Frederick Edwyn. 1851. *Dahomey and the Dahomans: Being the journals of two missions to the King of Dahomey, and residence at his capital in the years 1849 and 1850*. 2 vols. London: Longman, Brown, Green, and Longmans.

Forde, Cyril Daryll, ed. 1954. *African worlds: Studies in the cosmological ideas and social values of African peoples*. New York: Oxford University Press.

Fortes, Meyer, and E. E. Evans-Pritchard. 1940. *African political systems*. New York: Oxford University Press.

Foucault, Michel. [1978] 1981. *A history of sexuality*. New York: Vintage.

France, Hector. 1900. *Musk, hashish and blood*. London. Printed for subscribers only.

Freimark, Hans. 1911. Vol. 3, *Das Sexualleben der Afrikaner*. Leipzig: Leipziger Verlag. (273–80.)

Fritsch, Gustav. 1872. Die Eingeborenen Süd-Afrika's: Ethnographisch und Anatomisch Beschrieben. Vol. 1. (Breslau: Ferdinand Hirt).

Froelich, J. P. 1949. "Les sociétés d'initiation chez les Moba et les Fourma du Nord-Togo." *Journal de la Société des Africanistes* 19: 99–141.

Frye, Marilyn. 1992. "Lesbian 'sex.'" In *Willful virgin: Essays in feminism 1976–1992*, 109–19. Freedom, CA: Crossing Press.

Gadelrab, Sherry Sayed. 2016. *Medicine and morality in Egypt: Gender and sexuality in the nineteenth and early twentieth centuries*. London: Bloomsbury

Gamble, David P. 1957. *The Wolof of Senegambia*. London: International African Institute.

Gamst, Frederick C. 1967. Review of Levine (1965). *Journal of Developing Areas* 1: 545.

———. 1969. *The Qemant: A pagan-Hebraic peasantry of Ethiopia*. New York: Holt.

Gardner, Lyn. 2016. "Pigs and dogs review – a short, sharp response." *The Guardian*, July 24, 2016. https://www.theguardian.com/stage/2016/jul/24/pigs-and-dogs-review-caryl-churchill-royal-court-uganda-lgbt. Accessed May 23, 2018.

Garlake, Peter. 1995. *The hunter's vision*. London: British Museum.

Gaudio, Rudolf P. 1996a. "Man marries man in Northern Nigeria?" Paper presented at the African Studies Association annual meeting, San Francisco.

———. 1996b. "Unreal women and the men who love them." *Socialist Review* 95(2): 121–36.

———. 1997. "Not talking straight in Hausa." In *Queerly phrased: Language, gender, and sexuality*, eds. Anna Livia and Kira Hall, 416–28. New York: Oxford University Press.

———. 2009. *Allah Made Us: Sexual Outlaws in an Islamic African City*. Hoboken, NJ: Wiley-Blackwell.

———. 2014. "Trans-Saharan Trade: The Routes Of 'African Sexuality.'" *The Journal of African History*, 55(3): 317–330. doi:10.1017/S0021853714000619.

Gay, John et al. 1995. *Lesotho's long journey: Hard choices at the crossroads*. Maseru, Lesotho: Sechaba Consultants.

Gay, John, and David Hall. 1994. *Poverty in Lesotho, 1994: A mapping exercise*. Lesotho: Sechaba Consultants.

Gay, Judith. 1980. "Basotho women's options: A study of marital careers in rural Lesotho." Ph.D. dissertation, University of Cambridge.

———. 1985. "'Mummies and babies' and friends and lovers in Lesotho." *Journal of Homosexuality* 11 (3–4): 97–116.

Geigy, Rudolf, and Georg Höltker. 1951. "Mädchen-initiationen im Ulanga-Distrikt von Tanganyika." *Acta Tropica* 8: 289–344.

Gelfand, Michael. 1979. "The infrequency of homosexuality in traditional Shona society." *Central African Journal of Medicine* 25(9): 201–2.

———. 1985. "Apparent absence of homosexuality and lesbianism in traditional Zimbabweans." *Central African Journal of Medicine* 31: 137–38.

Gevisser, Mark. 1995. "A different fight for freedom: A history of South African lesbian and gay organisation from the 1950s to the 1990s." In *Defiant desire: Gay and lesbian lives in South Africa*, eds. Mark Gevisser and Edwin Cameron, 14–86. New York: Routledge.

———, and Edwin Cameron, eds. [1994] 1995. *Defiant desire: Gay and lesbian lives in South Africa*. Johannesburg: Ravan Press. Reprint. New York: Routledge.

Gibbon, Edward. [1781] 1925. Vol. 4, *The history of the decline and fall of the Roman Empire*. 6th ed. London: Methuen.

Giles, Linda. 1987. "Possession cults on the Swahili coast: A re-examination of theories of marginality." *Africa* 57(2): 234–58.

Gill, Debby. 1992. *Lesotho: A gender analysis*. Lesotho: Sechaba Consultants.

Gluckman, Max. 1950. "Kinship and marriage among the Lozi of Northern Rhodesia and the Zulu of Natal." In *African systems of kinship and marriage*, eds. A. R. Radcliffe-Brown and D. Forde, 166–206. New York: Oxford University Press.

Goldschmidt, Walter. 1967. *Sebei law*. Los Angeles: University of California Press. (Reports male transvestism and denial of homosexuality [135–37].)

Gorer, Geoffrey. [1935] 1962. *Africa dances*. New York: Norton.

Graere, R. P. 1929. "L'art de guérir chez les Azande." *Congo* 1: 361–582.

Greenberg, David F. 1988. *The construction of homosexuality*. Chicago: University of Chicago Press.

Greenberg, Joseph H. 1941. "Some aspects of Negro-Mohammedan culture contact among the Hausa." *American Anthropologist* 43: 51–61.

Grigsby, William J. 1996. "Women, descent, and tenure succession among the Bambara of West Africa. *Human Organization* 55: 93–98.

Grottanelli, Vinigi. 1988. *The python killer: Stories of Nzema life*. Chicago: University of Chicago Press.

Grützer, H. 1877. "Die Gebräuche der Basuto." *Verhandlungen der Berliner Gesellschaft für Anthropologie, Ethnologie, und Urgeschichte*, 76–92.

Gunther, John. 1955. *Inside Africa*. New York: Harper and Brothers.

Haberlandt, Michael. 1899. "Conträre Sexual-Erscheinungen bei der Neger-Bevölkerung Zanzibars." *Zeitschrift für Ethnologie* 31(6): 668–70.

Hackman, Melissa. 2018. *Desire work: Ex-gay and pentecostal masculinity in democratic South Africa*. Durham, NC: Duke University Press.

Hallpike, Christopher Robert. 1972. *The Konso of Ethiopia*. Oxford: Oxford University Press.

Halperin, David M. 1989. "Sex before sexuality: Pederasty, politics, politics, and power in classical Athens." In *Hidden from history*, eds. M. Duberman et al., 37–53. New York: New American Library.

Hambly, Wilfred D. 1934a. *The Ovimbundu of Angola*. Chicago: Field Museum.

———. 1934b. "Occupational ritual, belief and custom among the Ovimbundu." *American Anthropologist* 36: 156–67.

———. 1937. *Source book for African anthropology*. Chicago: Field Museum.

Hammer, Wilhelm. 1909. "Leibesleben und -Leiden in West-Mittelafrika." *Geschlecht und Gesselschaft* 4: 193–201. (On Duala refinement [199].)

Hannequin, Brigitte. 1990. "The state, patriarchy, and development: The case of a Mossi village in Burkina Faso." *Canadian Journal of African Studies* 24: 36–49.

Hanry, Pierre. 1970. *Erotisme africain: Le comportement sexuel des adolescents guinéens*. Paris: Payot.

Harpending, Henry. 1990. "Herero households." *Human Ecology* 18: 417–39.

Harries, Patrick. 1990. "Symbols and sexuality: Culture and identity in the early Witwatersrand mines." *Gender and History* 11(3): 318–36.

———. 1993. "Through the eyes of the beholder: Junod and the notion of primitive." *Social Dynamics* 19: 1–10.

———. 1994. *Culture, and identity: Migrant laborers in Mozambique and South Africa*. Portsmouth, NH: Heinemann.

Hartman, Keith. 1992. "AIDS, race and sexuality in South Africa." *San Francisco Bay Times* 14(2) (October 22): 16–17.

Hayes, Jarrod. 2000. *Queer nations: Marginal sexualities in the Maghreb*. Chicago: University of Chicago Press.

Head, Bessie. 1974. *A question of power*. London: Heinemann.

Hellwald, Friedrich von. 1886. *Halithea-Landrace*. 2 vols. Breslau: Eduard Trewendt.

Hemphill, Essex, ed. 1991. *Brother to brother: New writings by black gay men*. Boston: Alyson.

Hendriks, Aart, Rob Tielman, and Evert van der Veen, eds. 1993. *The third pink book: A global view of lesbian and gay liberation and oppression*. Buffalo, NY: Prometheus Books.

Hennessy, Rosemary. 1995. "Incorporating queer theory on the Left." In *Marxism in the Postmodern Age*, eds. Antonio Callari et al., 266–75. New York: Guilford Press.

Herdt, Gilbert, ed. 1984. *Ritualized homosexuality in Melanesia*. Berkeley: University of California Press.

———. 1994. *Third sex, third gender*. New York: Zone.

———. 1999. *Sambian sexual culture*. Chicago: University of Chicago Press.

Herskovits, Melville J. 1937a. *Life in a Haitian valley*. New York: Knopf.

———. 1937b. "A note on 'woman marriage' in Dahomey." *Africa* 10: 335–41.

———. 1938. *Dahomey: An ancient West African kingdom*. New York: Augustine.

Hill, Polly. 1967. *Rural Hausa*. New York: Cambridge University Press.

Hirn, Yrjö. 1900. *The origins of art: A psychological & sociological inquiry*. London: Macmillan.

Holleman, J. F. 1969. *Shona customary law: With reference to kinship, marriage, the family and the estate*. Manchester: Manchester University Press.

Hollis, Alfred Claud. 1905. *The Masai*. Oxford: Clarendon Press.

———. 1909. *The Nandi*. Oxford, UK: Clarendon Press.

Holmes, Rachel. 1995. "The Winnie Mandela trial and the politics of race and sexuality." In *Defiant desire: Gay and lesbian lives in South Africa*, eds. Mark Gevisser and Edwin Cameron, 284–94. New York: Routledge.

Hrdy, Daniel B. 1987. "Cultural practices contributing to the transmission of HIV in Africa." *Review of Infectious Diseases* 9: 1109–19.

Huber, Hugo. 1968. "'Woman-marriage' in some East African societies." *Anthropos* 63: 745–52.

Hulstaert, Gustave. 1938a. *Le mariage des Nkundó*. Brussels: Librairie Falk.
———. 1938b. *Les sanctions coutumières contre l'adultere chez les Nkundó*. Brussels: G. Van Campenhout.
Huntingford, George W. B. 1953. *The Nandi of Kenya: Tribal control in a pastoral society*. London: Routledge and Kegan Paul.
———. 1973. "Nandi of Western Kenya." In *Cultural source materials for population planning in East Africa: Beliefs and practices*, ed. Angela Molnos, 406–14. Nairobi: East African Publishing House.
Hutchinson, T. J. 1861. *Ten years' wanderings among the Ethiopians; with sketches of the manners and customs of the civilized and uncivilized tribes, from Senegal to Gaboon*. London: Hurst and Blackett.
Hyam, Ronald. 1990. *Empire and sexuality: The British experience*. New York: Manchester University Press.
Imperato, Pascal J. 1977. *African folk medicine: Practices and beliefs of the Bambara and other peoples*. Baltimore, MD: York. (Mentions that "homosexuals seek refuge today in large towns in Mali or in cities and towns in adjacent countries" [42].)
1996 CIA Factbook. 1996. United States, Central Intelligence Agency. http://www.gutenberg.org/cache/epub/27675/pg27675-images.html. Accessed September 5, 2020.
Irle, Johann J. 1906. *Herero: Ein Beitrag zur Landes-, Vols- und Missionskunde*. Gütersloh: C. Bertelsmann.
Isaacs, Gordon, and Brian McKendrick. 1992. *Male homosexuality in South Africa*. Cape Town: Oxford University Press.
Jäger, Gustav. 1886. *Handwörterbuch der Zoologie, Anthropologie, und Ethnologie*. Vol. 4, *Halithea-Landrace*. Breslau: Eduard Trewendt.
Jackson, Margaret. 1987. "'Facts of life' or the eroticization of women's oppression? Sexology and the social construction of heterosexuality." In *The cultural construction of sexuality*, ed. Pat Caplan, 52–81. London: Tavistock.
Jacobs, Sue-Ellen, and Jason Cromwell. 1992. "Visions and revisions of reality: Reflections on sex, sexuality, gender and gender variance." *Journal of Homosexuality* 23(4): 43–69.
Jarric, Petrus. 1616. *Thesarus indicus*. Köln: Coloniæ Agrip.
Jayawardene, Sureshi M. 2019. "Language in Africa." In *Global encyclopedia of lesbian, gay, bisexual, transgender, and queer history*, eds. Howard Chiang et al., 903–909. Farmington Hills, MI: Charles Scribner's Sons.
Jeater, Diana. 1993. *Marriage, perversion, and power: The construction of moral discourse in Southern Rhodesia, 1894–1930*. Oxford: Clarendon.
Jeffreys, Sheila. 1989. "Does it matter if they did it? In *Not a passing phase: Reclaiming lesbians in history 1840–1985*, ed. Lesbian History Group, 19–28. London: Woman's Press.

Jenness, Valerie. 1992. "Coming out: Lesbian identities and the categorization problem." In *Modern homosexualities: Fragments of lesbian and gay experience*, ed. Ken Plummer, 65–74. London: Routledge.

Johnson, Cary A. 1986. "Inside gay Africa." *New York Native* (March 3): 29, 32.

Johnston, Harry H. 1884. *The River Congo from its mouth to Balobo*. London: Low, Marston, Searle, and Rivington. ("Unnatural crimes are unknown among them [the "indolent, fickle and sensual" Bakongo of Pallaballa] where they have not come under European influence, and they have no word in their language to correspond with what is a common term of almost playful opprobrium among the English lower classes" [404]; "Phallic worship in various forms prevails; it is not associated with any rites that might be called particularly obscene" [405]; "Connected, no doubt with this phallic worship are the Nkimba initiation ceremonies of the Lower Congo [River] which in varying forms may be traced among the 'manhood initiation' rites found among most Bantu peoples" [406].)

———. 1897. *British central Africa*. London: Methuen. (Asserts that "common to the greater part of Pagan Tropical Africa . . . [male initiation ceremonies are] said to be of a slightly obscene character. . . . Much good advice is said to be given to the boys, by these elderly instructors, but there is also much loose talk and the boys are thoroughly enlightened as to sexual relations" [409].)

Jones, Christopher. 1996. "Foreign tongues untied." *Washington Blade* (February 16): 39–41.

Junker, Wilhelm. 1892. *Travels in Africa*. London: Chapman and Hall. (Reports that Azande King Bakangi was accompanied everywhere by his "catamites" [3–4].)

Junod, Henry. [1912] 1927. *Life of a South African tribe*. London: MacMillan.

Kakonge, Meli, and Pierre Erng. 1976. "Comportments sexuels chez les Baushi de Kinama (Shaba, Zaïre)." *Psychopathologie africaine* 12: 5–33.

Kandt, R. 1905. *Caput Nili. Eine empfindsame Reise zu den Quellen des Nils*. Berlin: Dietrich Reimer.

Kagwa, Apolo. [1918] 1934. *The customs of the Baganda*. New York: Columbia University Press.

Karp, Ivan. 1974. "Traditional Southern Iteso social structure." *Southeastern Review* 1: 110–22.

———, and Patricia Karp. 1973. "The Iteso of the Kenya-Uganda border." In *Cultural source materials for population planning in East Africa: Beliefs and practices*, ed. Angela Molnos, 385–98. Nairobi: East African Publishing House.

———, et al. 1983. "Reading *The Nuer*." *Current Anthropology* 24: 481–92.

Karsch-Haack, Ferdinand. 1911. *Das gleichgeschlechtliche Leben der Naturvölker*. Munich: Ernst Reinhardt. Reprint. New York: Arno Press, 1975.

Kendall, [Kathryn]. 1986. "From lesbian heroine to devoted wife: Or, what the stage would allow." *Journal of Homosexuality* 12 (3–4): 9–22.

————. 1990. "Finding the good parts: Sexuality in women's tragedies in the time of Queen Anne." In *Curtain calls: An anthology of essays on eighteenth-century women in theatre*, eds. Mary Ann Schofield and Cecilia Macheski, 165–76. Columbus: Ohio University Press.

————. 1993. "Ways of looking at Agnes de Castro." In *Upstaging big daddy: Directing theatre as if race and gender matter*, eds. Ellen Donkin and Susan Clement. Ann Arbor: University of Michigan Press.

————. 1998. "Mpho 'M'atsepo Nthunya and the meaning of sex." *Women's Studies Quarterly* 26(3/4): 220–25.

Kenyatta, Jomo. 1938. *Facing Mount Kenya*. London: Martin Secker and Warburg.

Kershaw, Gretha. 1973. "The Kikuyu of Central Kenya." In *Cultural source materials for population planning in East Africa: Beliefs and practices*, ed. Angela Molnos, 47–59. Nairobi: East African Publishing House. ("Sodomy seems to have been practiced during certain Mau Mau rites with the express intent of rendering participants unclean to the point that they could not return to the normal population and so had to keep solidarity with others in like state" [51].)

Khan, Badruddin. 1997. "Not-so-gay life in Pakistan in the 1980s and 1990s." In *Islamic Homosexualities*, eds. Stephen O. Murray and Will Roscoe, 275–96. New York: New York University Press.

Kidd, Dudley. 1904. *The essential Kaffir*. London: Adam and Charles Black.

Kirby, Percival R. 1942. "A secret musical instrument: The ekola of the Ovakuanyama of Ovamboland." *South African Journal of Science* 38: 345–51.

Kleis, Gerald W., and Salisu A. Abdullahi. 1983. "Masculine power and gender ambiguity in urban Hausa society." *African Urban Studies* 16: 39–53.

Klockmann, Thomas. 1985. "Vom Geheimnis menschlicher Gefühle: Günther Tessmanns Pangwe-Monographie im Lichte seiner Lebenserinnerungen sowie neurer Forschungen." *Wiener Ethnohistorische Blätter* 29: 3–20.

Kolb, Peter. 1719. *Caput Bonae Spei hodiernum; das ist, Vollständige Beschreibung des africanischen Vorgebürges der guten Hofnung*. Nuremburg: P. C. Monath. Translated by Medley, *The present state of the Cape of Good-Hope*. London: W. Innys and R. Manby, 1731–38. Reprint. New York: Johnson Reprint Corp, 1968.

Krapf, Johann Ludwig. 1882. *A dictionary of the Suaheli language*. London: Trübner.

Krige, Eileen Jensen. 1938. "The place of the Northeastern Transvaal Sotho in the Bantu complex." *Africa* 11: 265–93.

————. 1965. *The social system of the Zulus*. Pietemaritzburg, South Africa: Shuter and Shooter.

————. 1974. "Woman-marriage, with special reference to the Lovedu." *Africa* 44: 11–36.

————, and Jacob Daniel Krige. [1943] 1947. *The realm of the rain queen: A study of the pattern of Lovedu society*. Oxford: Oxford University Press.

Krige, Jacob Daniel, and Eileen Jensen Krige. 1954. "The Lovedu of the Transvaal." In *African worlds: Studies in the cosmological ideas and social values of African peoples*, ed. Cyril Daryll Forde, 55–82. New York: Oxford University Press.

Kroeber, Alfred Louis. 1955. "Linguistic time depth results so far, and their meaning." *International Journal of American Linguistics* 21: 91–104.

Krouse, Matthew, and Kim Berman, eds. 1993. *The invisible ghetto: Lesbian and gay writing from South Africa*. Johannesburg: Cosaw.

Kulick, Don. 1998. *Practically women*. Chicago: University of Chicago Press.

La Fontaine, Jean S. 1959. *The Gisu of Uganda*. London: International African Institute.

Labat, Jean Baptiste. 1732. Vol. 2, *Relation historique de l'Ethiopie occidentale: Contenant la description des royaumes de Congo, Angelle, & Matamba*. . . . Paris: C. J. B. Delespine le fils.

Lagae, C. R. 1923. "La naissance chez les Azande." *Congo* 1: 161–77.

Lallemand, Suzanne. 1976. "Biological mothers and foster-mothers among the Mossi." *L'Homme* 16: 109–24.

Lambek, Michel. 1981. *Human spirits: A cultural account of trance in Mayotto*. Cambridge: Cambridge University Press.

Langle, Fleuriot de. 1876. "Croisières à la côte d'Afrique. *Le Tour du Monde* 31: 241–304.

Lanham, Peter, and A. S. Mopeli-Paulus. 1953. *Blanket boy's moon*. London: Collins.

Larken, P. M. 1926–27. "Impressions of the Azande." *Sudan Notes and Records* 9: 1–55; 10: 85–134.

Larson, Ann. 1989. "Social context of human immunodeficiency virus transmission in Africa: Historical and cultural bases of East and Central African sexual relations." *Review of Infectious Diseases* 11: 711–31.

Lasnet, Alexandre. 1899. "Notes d'ethnologie et de la médicine sur les Sakalaves du Nord-Ouest [Madagascar]." *Annales d'hygiène et de médecine coloniale* 2: 471–97.

Laubscher, Barend J. F. 1937. *Sex, custom and psychopathology: A study of South African pagan natives*. London: Routledge and Kegan Paul. (Tenuous generalizations from Queenstown Mental Hospital cases and reports of magistrates on indigenous psychodynamics [157–58, 283–84].)

Laurance, Jeremy C. D. 1957. *The Iteso: Fifty years of change in a Nilo-Hamitic tribe of Uganda*. Oxford: Oxford University Press.

Laurent, Émile. 1911. "Les Sharimbavy de Madagascar." *Archives d'Anthropologie Criminelle* 26: 241–48.

Leakey, Louis S. B. 1977. *The southern Kikuyu before 1903*. 3 vols. New York: Academic Press.

Lebeuf, Annie M. D. 1963. "The role of women in the political organization of African societies." In *Women of Tropical Africa*, ed. Denise Paulme, 93–120. Berkeley: University of California Press.

Lee, S. G. 1969. "Spirit possession among the Zulu." In *Spirit mediumship and society in Africa*, eds. J. Beattie and J. Middleton, 128–56. London: Routledge & Kegan Paul.

Leighton, Alexander et al. 1963. *Psychiatric disorders among the Yoruba*. Ithaca, NY: Cornell University Press.

Lenz, Oskar. 1884, 1892. *Timbuktu*. 2 vols. Leipzig: P. A. Brockhaus. (Reports that high officials kept numbers of castrated Negro boys for pederastic purposes [1: 248].)

Lessik, Alan. 1996. "Marching to Pretoria." *San Francisco Frontiers*, January 18, pp. 22–24. (Journalistic account of new lesbigay openness in traditional Afrikaaner stronghold.)

Leupp, Gary P. 1995. *Male colors: The construction of homosexuality in Tokugawa Japan*. Berkeley: University of California Press.

Levine, Donald N. 1965. *Wax and gold: Tradition and innovation in Ethiopian culture*. Chicago: University of Chicago Press.

Lewis, Ethelreda. [1934] 1984. *Wild deer*. Cape Town: David Philip.

Lewis, Ioan. M. 1966. "Spirit possession and deprivation cults." *Man* 1: 307–29. Reprinted in *Religion in Context*, 23–50. Cambridge: Cambridge University Press, 1986.

———. 1973. "The Somali of Somalia and Northeastern Kenya." In *Cultural source materials for population planning in East Africa: Beliefs and practices*, ed. Angela Molnos, 428–41. Nairobi: East African Publishing House. ("Celibacy has no positive value in Somali culture and would be regarded as extremely strange, a sure indication that the person concerned was not a true man and potentially a homosexual, a condition which has no positive value in Somali culture and indeed is highly scorned" [434].)

Lhote, Henri. 1955. *Les Touaregs du Hoggar*. Paris: Payot. ("The Iklan have very corrupt mores and practice pederasty" [28, HRAF translation].)

Lienhardt, Peter. 1968. *The medicine man: Swifa ya Nguvumali, by Hasani bin Ismail*. Oxford: Oxford University Press.

Linton, Ralph. 1933. *The Tanala, a hill tribe of Madagascar*. Chicago: Field Museum.

Livermon, Xavier. 2019. "Archives in Africa." In *Global encyclopedia of lesbian, gay, bisexual, transgender, and queer (LGBTQ) history*, ed. Howard Chiang, 91–95. Farmington Hills, MI: Charles Scribner's Sons.

Livingstone, David. 1857. *Missionary travels and researches in South Africa*. London: John Murray.

———. 1865. *Narrative of an expedition to the Zambesi and its tributaries*. London: John Murray.

Lorber, Judith. 1994. *Paradoxes of gender*. New Haven: Yale University Press.

Lorde, Audre. 1984. *Sister outsider*. Trumansburg, NY: Crossing Press.

Louw, Ronald. 1996. "Same-sex desire and African culture: Untraditional traditional weddings in the 1950s in Durban, South Africa." Paper presented at the African Studies Association annual meeting, San Francisco.

Luirink, Bart. 1995. "Zimbabwe's gays live in fear of the future." *Johannesburg Weekly Mail and Guardian*, September 22.

MacDermot, Brian H. 1972. *The cult of the sacred spear: The story of the Nuer tribe in Ethiopia*. London: Hale.

Macgregor, J. K. 1909. "Some notes on Nsibidi." *Journal of the Anthropological Institute of Great Britain and Ireland* 39: 209–19.

Mack, Mehammad Amadeus. 2019. "Maghreb." In *Global encyclopedia of lesbian, gay, bisexual, transgender, and queer history*, eds. Howard Chiang et al., 985–90. Farmington Hills, MI: Charles Scribner's Sons.

Maclean, John. [1858] 1906. *A compendium of Kafir law and customs*. Grahamstown, South Africa: J. Slater.

Madan, Arthur Cornwallis. 1902. *English-Swahili dictionary*. Oxford: Clarendon Press.

Makin, William J. 1933. *Red Sea nights*. New York: National Travel Club. (58).

Maloka, Edward Tshidiso. 1995. "Basotho and the mines: Towards a history of labor migrancy." PhD dissertation, Department of Historical Studies, University of Cape Town.

Mamaki. 1993. "The gathering." In *The invisible ghetto: Lesbian and gay writing from South Africa*, eds. Matthew Krouse and Kim Berman, 2–3. Johannesburg: Cosaw.

Manalansan, Martin F., IV. 1991. "Neo-colonial desire." *Society of Lesbian and Gay Anthropologists Newsletter* 13: 37–40.

Maquet, Jacques J. 1961. *The premise of inequality in Rwanda*. New York: Oxford University Press.

———. 1972. *Africanity: The cultural unity of Black Africa*. New York: Oxford University Press.

Marriage, Diane J. 1993. *Perversion and power: The construction of moral discourse in southern Rhodesia, 1890–1920*. Oxford: Clarendon.

Martin, Maurice. 1912. *Au coeur de l'Afrique équatoriale*. Paris: Libraire Chapelot. (13–59, 164, 187–88.)

Massad, Joseph A. 2007. *Desiring Arabs*. Chicago: University of Chicago Press.

Matebeni, Zethu, ed. 2014. *Reclaiming Afrikan: Queer perspectives on sexual and gender identities*. Cape Town: Modjaji Books.

Mathuray, Mark. 2019. "Literature, African (Anglophone)." In *Global encyclopedia of lesbian, gay, bisexual, transgender, and queer history*, eds. Howard Chiang et al., 952–64. Farmington Hills, MI: Charles Scribner's Sons.

Matory, J. Lorand. 1986. "Vessels of power: The dialectical symbolism of power in Yoruba religion and polity." MA thesis, Department of Anthropology, University of Chicago.

———. 1994. *Sex and the empire that is no more: Gender and the politics of metaphor in Oyo Yoruba religion*. Minneapolis: University of Minnesota Press.

Mbaye, Aminata Cécile. 2019. "Repenser les discours sénégalais contemporains sur l'homosexualité à la lumière de Boy-Wives and Female Husbands." *Canadian Journal of African Studies* 52(3): 357–359. doi: 10.1080/00083968.2018.1546604. Accessed May 13, 2020.

McCall, John C. 1996. "Portrait of a brave woman." *American Anthropologist* 98: 127–36.

McNeil, Donald, Jr. "Free Namibia stumps the naysayers." *New York Times*. November 16, 1997.

Meek, Charles K. 1925. *The northern tribes of Nigeria: An ethnographical account of the northern provinces of Nigeria together with a report on the 1921 decennial census*. 2 vols. London: Oxford University Press.

Merriam, Alan P. 1971. "Aspects of sexual behavior among the Bala (Basangye)." In *Human Sexual Behavior*, eds. D. Marshall and R. Suggs, 71–102. New York: Basic Books.

———. 1974. *An African World: The Basongye village of Lusupa Ngye*. Bloomington: Indiana University Press. (319–21).

Messing, Simon D. 1957. "The highland-plateau Amhara of Ethiopia." PhD dissertation, Department of Anthropology, University of Pennsylvania.

———. 1959. "Group therapy and social status in the Zar cult of Ethiopia." In *Culture and mental illness*, ed. M. K. Opler, 319–32. New York: Macmillan.

Middleton, John. 1992. *The world of the Swahili: An African mercantile civilization*. New Haven: Yale University Press.

Miller, Christopher L. 1990. *Theories of Africans*. Chicago: University of Chicago Press.

Miller, Neil. 1992. *Out in the world*. New York: Random House.

Molnos, Angela, ed. 1973. *Cultural source materials for population planning in East Africa: Beliefs and practices*. Nairobi: East African Publishing House.

Monrad, Hans Christian. 1822. *Bidrag til en Skildring af Guinea-Kysten og dens Indbyggere*. Copenhagen: A. Seidelin.

Moodie, T. Dunbar, Vivienne Ndatshe, and British [Mpande Wa] Sibuyi. 1988. "Migrancy and male sexuality in the South African gold mines." *Journal of Southern African Studies* 14(2): 228–56.

———. 1989. "Migrancy and male sexuality in the South African gold mines." In *Hidden from history: Reclaiming the gay and lesbian past*, eds. M. Duberman et al., 411–25. New York: New American Library.

———. 1994. *Going for gold: Men's lives in the mines*. Berkeley: University of California Press.

Moore, Sally F. 1994. *Anthropology and Africa: Changing perspectives on a changing scene*. Charlottesville: University Press of Virginia.

Morris, Donald R. 1965. *The washing of the spears: A history of the rise of the Zulu nation under Shaka and its fall in the Zulu War of 1879*. New York: Simon and Schuster.

Moses, Stephen et al. 1994. "Sexual behavior in Kenya: Implications for sexually transmitted disease transmission and control." *Social Science and Medicine* 39: 1649–56.

Msibi, Thabo. 2014. "Contextualising 'dirty work': A response to Janice Irvine (2014)." *Sexualities* 17(5–6): 669–673.

Mudimbe, V. Y. 1988. *The invention of Africa*. Bloomington: Indiana University Press.

———. 1994. *The idea of Africa*. Bloomington: Indiana University Press.

Mueller, Martha B. 1977. "Women and men in rural Lesotho: The periphery of the periphery." PhD dissertation, Department of Politics, Brandeis University.

Munroe, Robert L., and Ruth H. Munroe. 1977. "Male transvestism and subsistence economy." *Journal of Social Psychology* 103: 307–8.

———, John W. Whiting, and David Hally. 1969. "Institutionalized male transvestism and sex distinctions." *American Anthropologist* 71: 87–91.

Murdock, George Peter. 1959. *Africa: Its peoples and their culture history.* New York: McGraw-Hill.

———. 1967. *Ethnographic atlas.* Pittsburgh: University of Pittsburgh Press.

———. 1981. *Atlas of world cultures.* Pittsburgh: University of Pittsburgh Press.

Murray, Stephen O. 1984. *Social theory, homosexual realities.* Gai Saber Monograph, no. 3. New York: Gay Academic Union.

———. 1987. "A Note on Haitian (in?)tolerance of homosexuality." In *Male homosexuality in Central and South America,* 92–100. New York: Gay Academic Union.

———. 1992a. *Oceanic homosexualities.* New York: Garland Press.

———. 1992b. "Emergent gay homosexuality in contemporary Thailand." In *Oceanic homosexualities,* 387–96. New York: Garland. (Rev. in Murray 1999.)

———. 1994. "Subordinating Native American cosmologies to the empire of gender." *Current Anthropology* 35(1): 59–61.

———. 1995a. *Latin American male homosexualities.* Albuquerque: University of New Mexico Press.

———. 1995b. "Some Southwest Asian and North African terms for homosexual roles." *Archives of Sexual Behavior* 24: 623–29.

———. 1996a. *American gay.* Chicago: University of Chicago Press.

———. 1996b. "Male homosexuality in Guatemala: Possible insights and certain confusions of sleeping with natives as a source of data." In *Out in the field: Reflections of lesbian and gay anthropologists,* eds. W. Leap and E. Lewin, 236–60. Urbana: University of Illinois Press.

———. 1997a. "Explaining away same-sex sexuality when it obtrudes on anthropologists' attention." *Anthropology Today* 13(3): 2–5.

———. 1997b. "The Omani khanith." In Stephen O. Murray and Will Roscoe, *Islamic homosexualities,* 244–55. New York: New York University Press.

———. 1997c. "The will not to know: Accommodations of homosexuality in Islamic societies." In Stephen O. Murray and Will Roscoe, *Islamic homosexualities,* 14–54. New York: New York University Press.

———. 1999. *Homosexualities.* Chicago: University of Chicago Press.

———, and Will Roscoe. 1997. *Islamic homosexualities.* New York: New York University Press.

Mushanga, Musa T. 1973. "The Nkole of southwestern Uganda." In *Cultural source materials for population planning in East Africa: Beliefs and practices,* ed. Angela Molnos, 174–86. Nairobi: East African Publishing House.

Mwambia, Salome P. K. 1978. "The Meru of Central Kenya." In *Cultural source materials for population planning in East Africa: Beliefs and practices*, ed. Angela Molnos, 60–67. Nairobi: East African Publishing House.

Mwangi, Evan. 2017. *Translation in African contexts: Postcolonial texts, queer sexuality, and cosmopolitan fluency*. Kent, OH: Kent State University Press.

Nadel, Siegfried F. 1942. *A black Byzantium: The kingdom of Nupe in Nigeria*. New York: Oxford University Press.

———. 1947. *The Nuba*. Oxford: Oxford University Press.

———. 1952. "Witchcraft in four African societies." *American Anthropologist* 54: 18–29.

———. 1954. *Nupe religion*. London: Routledge and Kegan Paul.

———. 1955. "Two Nuba religions." *American Anthropologist* 57: 661–79.

Nanda, Serena. 1990. *Neither man nor woman: The hijra of India*. Belmont, CA: Wadsworth.

Naqvi, Nauman, and Hasan Mujtaba. 1996. "Two Baluchi *buggas*, a Sindhi *zenana*, and the status of *hijras* in Pakistan." In Stephen O. Murray and Will Roscoe, *Islamic Homosexualities*, 262–66. New York: New York University Press.

Ndatshe, Vivienne. [1982] 1993. "Two miners." In *The invisible ghetto: Lesbian and gay writing from South Africa*, eds. Matthew Krouse and Kim Berman, 45–51. Johannesburg: Cosaw.

———, and Mpande wa Sibuyi. 1993. "Love on the mines." In *The invisible ghetto: Lesbian and gay writing from South Africa*, eds. Matthew Krouse and Kim Berman, 45–51. Johannesburg: Cosaw Publishing.

Needham, Rodney. 1973a. "The left hand of the *mugwe*: An analytical note on the structure of Meru symbolism." In *Right and left: Essays on dual classification*, 109–27. Chicago: University of Chicago Press.

———. 1973b. "Right and left in Nyoro symbolic classification." In *Right and left: Essays on dual classification*, 299–341. Chicago: University of Chicago Press.

Nero, Charles I. 1991. "Toward a black gay aesthetic." In *Brother to brother: New writings by black gay men*, ed. Essex Hemphill, 229–52. Boston: Alyson.

Newman, James L. 1995. *The peopling of Africa*. New Haven: Yale University Press.

Ngubane, Harriet. 1977. *Body and mind in Zulu medicine*. New York: Academic Press.

Nicole, Kreisbefehlshaber. 1903. "Dis Diakite-Sarrakolesen." In *Rechtsverhältnisse von Eingeborenen Völkern in Afrika und Ozeanien*, comp. S. R. Steinmetz, 93–138. Berlin: Julius Springer Steinmetz. (Men viewed as crazy rather than duplicitous live with/as women and receive presents from admirers in the Bezirk Sahel group.)

Nicolson, Nigel. 1973. *Portrait of a marriage*. London: Weidenfeld and Nicolson.

Njau, Rebeka. 1975. *Ripples in the pool*. Nairobi: Transafrica.

Nkoli, Simon. 1993. "This strange feeling. "In *The invisible ghetto: Lesbian and gay writing from South Africa*, eds. Matthew Krouse and Kim Berman, 19–26. Johannesburg: Cosaw.

———. 1995. "Coming out as a black gay activist in South Africa." In *Defiant desire: Gay and lesbian lives in South Africa*, eds. Mark Gevisser and Edwin Cameron, 249–57. New York: Routledge.

Norris, Robert. 1789. *Memoirs of the reign of Bossa Abadee, King of Dahomy.* London: W. Lowndes. (Mentions castrated men in the royal court [422].)

Nthunya, Mpho 'M'atsepo. 1995. "'M'alineo chooses me." In *Basali! Stories by and about Basotho Women*, ed. K. Limakatso Kendall, 4–7. Pietermaritzburg, South Africa: University of Natal Press.

———. 1997. *Singing away the hunger: Stories of a life in Lesotho*, ed. K. Limakatso Kendall. Bloomington, IN: Indiana University Press, 1997. First published 1996 by University of Natal Press, Pietermaritzburg, South Africa. Reprint.

Nyeck, S. N., and Marc Epprecht, eds. 2013. *Sexual diversity in Africa.* Montreal: McGill-Queen's University Press.

Obbo, Christine. 1976. "Dominant male ideology and female options: Three African case studies." *Africa* 46: 371–89.

———. 1980. *African women: Their struggle for economic independence.* London: Zed Press.

———. 1995. "Gender, age, and class: Discourses on HIV-transmission and control in Uganda." In *Culture and sexual risk*, eds. Han ten Brummelhuis and Gibert Herdt, 79–96. Amsterdam: Gordon and Breach.

Oboler, Regina Smith. 1980. "Is the female husband a man?" *Ethnology* 19: 69–88.

———. 1985. *Women, power, and economic change: The Nandi of Kenya.* Stanford: Stanford University Press.

O'Brien, Denise. 1977. "Female husbands in southern Bantu societies." In *Sexual stratification: A cross-cultural view*, ed. Alice Schlegel, 109–26. New York: Columbia University Press.

Oliver, Roland, and J. D. Fage. 1966. *A short history of Africa.* Baltimore, MD: Penguin.

O'Malley, Jeffrey et al. 2018. *Sexual and gender minorities and the Sustainable Development Goals.* New York: United Nations Development Programme.

Orubuloye, I. O., John C. Caldwell, and Pat Caldwell. 1993. "African women's control over their sexuality in an era of AIDS: A study of the Yoruba of Nigeria." *Social Science and Medicine* 37: 859–72.

Osinubi, Taiwo Adetunji. 2019. "Cinema, African (Anglophone)." In *Global encyclopedia of lesbian, gay, bisexual, transgender, and queer history*, eds. Howard Chiang et al., 332 – 43. Farmington Hills, MI: Charles Scribner's Sons.

Overbergh, Cyrille van. 1908. *Les Basonge.* Brussels: A. de Wit. (3: 76, 254).

———, and Edouard de Jonghe. 1907. *Les Mayombe.* Brussels: A. de Wit. (114, 281).

Palou, Francisco. [1787] 1913. *Life and apostolic labors of the venerable Father Junipero Serra.* Translated by C. Scott Williams. Pasadena, CA: George Wharton James.

Parin, Paul, Fritz Morgenthaler, and Goldy Parin-Metthey. 1980. *Fear thy neighbor as thyself.* Chicago: University of Chicago Press.

Parkin, David J. 1973. "Luo of Kampala, Nairobia and Western Kenya." In *Cultural source materials for population planning in East Africa: Beliefs and practices*, ed. Angela Molnos, 330–39. Nairobi: East African Publishing House.

Parrinder, Edward Geoffrey. 1976. *Mysticism in the world's religions*. London: Sheldon Press. (Reports cross-dressing Dahomey shamans being called wives of the possessing god [79].)

Patron. Eugene. 1995. "Africa: Heart of lavender." *Harvard Gay and Lesbian Review* 2(4): 22–24.

Paszat, Emma. (Forthcoming). "Sexuality politics, scientific manipulation, and the Anti-Homosexuality Act, 2014." *Sexualities*.

Paulitschke, Philipp Viktor. 1893. *Ethnographie Nordost-Afrikas*. Berlin: G. Reimer. (Mentions that the "vice of sodomy exists among the Oromó" [172]).

Pechuel-Loesche, Eduard. 1907. *Volkskunde von Loango*. Stuttgart: Strecker and Schroder.

Pedrals, Dennis Pierre de. 1950. *La vie sexuelle en Afrique noire*. Paris: Payot.

Peristiany, Jean G. 1939. *The social institutions of the Kipsigis*. London: George Routledge. (Sodomy is "far from unknown" in this tribe east of Lake Victoria in Kenya because precedents and a proverb were cited at a trial [55].)

Phelan, Shane. 1993. "Coming out: Lesbian identity and politics." *Signs* 18: 765–90.

Phillips, Oliver. 1997a. "Zimbabwean law and the production of a white man's disease." *Social and Legal Studies* 6(4): 471–91.

———. 1997b. " 'Venus monstrosa' and 'unnatural offences': Homosexuality and the law in Zimbabwe." In *Socio-legal control of homosexual behaviour*, eds. R. Green and D. West, 43–49. London: Plenum.

———. 1997c. "Zimbabwe." In *Sociolegal control of homosexuality: A multi-national comparison*, eds. Donald West and Richard Green, 43–56. New York: Plenum.

Phimister, Ian. 1988. *An economic and social history of Zimbabwe: Capital accumulation and class struggle, 1890–1948*. London.

———. 1996. "Mines, men, migration, and death." *Zimbabwe Review* (January): 12–14.

Pittin, Christin. 1983. "Houses of women: A focus on alternative life-styles in Katsina City." In *Female and male in West Africa*, ed. C. Oppong, 291–302. London: Allen and Unwin.

Poewe, Karla O. 1982. *Reflections of a woman anthropologist: No hiding place*. San Francisco: Academic Press.

Poirier, Guy. 1993. "French renaissance travel accounts: Images of sin, visions of the New World." *Journal of Homosexuality* 25: 215–29.

Porter, Mary A. 1992. "Swahili identity in post-colonial Kenya: The reproduction of gender in educational discourse." PhD dissertation, Department of Anthropology, University of Washington.

———. 1995. "Talking at the margins: Kenyan discourses on homosexuality." In *Beyond the lavender lexicon*, ed. W. Leap, 133–54. New York: Gordon and Breach.

Potash, Betty. 1978. "Some aspects of marital stability in a rural Luo community." *Africa* 48: 380–97.

Potman, Gerben, and Huub Rujigrok. 1993. "Male homosexuality in West Africa." In *The third pink book: A global view of lesbian and gay liberation and oppression*, eds. A. Hendriks, R. Tielman, and E. van der Veen, 165–70. Buffalo, NY: Prometheus.

Presley, Cora Ann. 1992. *Kikuyu women, the Mau Mau rebellion, and social change in Kenya*. Boulder, CO: Westview Press.

Prins, Adriaan H. J. 1961. *The Swahili-speaking peoples of Zanzibar and the East African coast (Arabs, Shirazi and Swahili)*. London: International African Institute.

Purchas, Samuel. 1625. Vol. 2, *Purchas, his pilgrimes*. London: William Stansby. (Quotes a 1606 Jesuit report [1558].)

Rachewiltz, Boris de. 1964. *Black eros: Sexual customs of Africa from prehistory to the present day*. New York: Lyle Stuart. (180, 191, 282).

Radcliffe, Dee. 1993. "Confessions of a failed lesbian separatist." In *The invisible ghetto: Lesbian and gay writing from South Africa*, eds. Matthew Krouse and Kim Berman, 192–95. Johannesburg: Cosaw.

Radcliffe-Brown, A. R., and Daryll Forde. 1950. *African systems of kinship and marriage*. New York: Oxford University Press.

Raftopolous, Brian. 1995. "Nationalism and labour in Salisbury, 1953–1965. *Journal of Southern African Studies* 21(1): 79–94.

Rautanen, M. 1903. "Die Ondonga." In *Rechtsverhältnisse von Eingeborenen Völkern in Afrika und Ozeanien*, comp. S. R. Steinmetz, 326–45. Berlin: Julius Springer Steinmetz.

Reade, Winwood. 1864. *Savage Africa*. London: Smith, Elder. (424).

Richardson, Diane. 1992. "Constructing lesbian sexualities." In *Modern homosexualities*, ed. Ken Plummer, 187–99. London: Routledge.

Rivière, P. G. 1971. "Marriage: A reassessment." In *Rethinking kinship and marriage*, ed. Rodney Needham, 57–74. London: Tavistock.

Roberts, Brian. 1975. *The Zulu kings*. New York: Scribner.

Roberts, Matthew W. 1995. "Emergence of gay identity and gay social movements in developing countries: The AIDS crisis as catalyst." *Alternatives* 20: 243–64.

Robertson, Claire. 1987. "Developing economic awareness: Changing perspectives in studies of African women, 1976–1985." *Feminist Studies* 13: 97–137.

Rodriguez, S. M. 2018. *The Economies of Queer Inclusion: Transnational Organizing for LGBTI Rights in Uganda*. London: Rowman & Littlefield.

Roof, Judith. 1994. "Lesbians and Lyotard: Legitimation and the politics of the name." In *The lesbian postmodern*, ed. Laura Doan, 46–67. New York: Columbia University Press.

Roscoe, John. 1907. "A cow tribe of Enkole in the Uganda protectorate." *Journal of the Royal Anthropological Institute* 37: 93–118.

———. 1911. *The Baganda: An account of their native customs and beliefs*. London: Macmillan. (80).

Roscoe, Will. 1988. "Making history: The challenge of gay and lesbian studies." *Journal of Homosexuality* 15: 1–40.

———. 1991. *The Zuni man-woman*. Albuquerque: University of New Mexico Press.

———. 1994. "How to become a berdache: Toward a unified analysis of gender diversity." In *Third sex, third gender*, ed. Gilbert Herdt, 329–72. New York: Zone.

———. 1995. "Was We'wha a Homosexual?: Native American survivance and the two-spirit tradition." *GLQ: A Journal of Lesbian/Gay Studies* 2(3): 193–235.

———. 1996. "Priests of the goddess: Gender transgression in ancient religions." *History of Religions* 35(3): 295–330.

———. 1997. "Precursors of Islamic male homosexualities." In Stephen O. Murray and Will Roscoe, *Islamic homosexualities*, 55–86. New York: New York University Press.

———. 1998. *Changing Ones: Third and fourth genders in native North America*. New York: St. Martin's.

Roux, J. 1905. "Notes sur un cas d'inversion sexuelle chez une Comorienne." *Bulletin de la Société d'Anthropologie* 6: 218–19.

Rowse, J. A. 1964. "The purge of Christians at Mwanga's court." *Journal of African History* 5: 55–71.

Russell, Mrs. C. E. B. 1970. *General Rigby, Zanzibar, and the slave trade*. New York: Negro Universities Press.

Sacleux, Charles. [1891] 1949. *Dictionnaire Français-Swahili*. Paris: Institut d'ethnologie.

Sahlins, Marshall D. 1961. "The segmentary lineage: An organization of predatory expansion." *American Anthropologist* 63: 322–46.

Sandgren, David P. 1989. *Christianity and the Kikuyu: Religious divisions and social conflict*. New York: Peter Lang.

Saran, A. B. 1964. "The interrelation of social organization, ethos and ethics among the Azande." *Eastern Anthropologist* 17: 73–85.

Sayagues, Merceds. 1996. "Zimbabwe gays bring the issue into the open." *Africa Information Afrique* (September 18).

Scarnecchia, Timothy. 1993. "The politics of gender and class in the creation of African communities, Salisbury, Rhodesia, 1937–1957." PhD dissertation, Department of Afroamerican and African Studies, University of Michigan.

Schapera, Isaac. 1930. *The Khoisan peoples of South Africa*. London: G. Routledge and Sons.

———. 1933. "Premarital pregnancy and native opinion: a note on social change." *Africa* 6: 59–89.

———. 1937. *The Bantu-speaking tribes of South Africa*. London: G. Routledge and Sons.

———. 1938. *A handbook of Tswana law and custom*. New York: Oxford University Press.

———. 1979. "Notes on some Herero genealogies." *African Studies* 38: 17–42.

Schenkel, R. 1971. "Le vécu de la vie sexuelle chez les Africains acculturés du Sénégal." *Psychopathologie africaine* 7: 313–58. (Mentions homosexual clubs in Dakar [279].)

Schild, Maarten. 1992. "Islam." In *Sexuality and eroticism among males in Moslem societies*, eds. Arno Schmitt and Jehoeda Sofer, 179–88. Binghamton, NY: Harrington Park Press.

Schmidt, Elizabeth. 1992. *Peasants, traders, and wives: Shona women in the history of Zimbabwe, 1870–1939*. Portsmouth, NH: Heinemann.

Schmitt, Arno, and Jehoeda Sofer. 1992. *Sexuality and eroticism among males in Moslem societies*. Binghamton, NY: Harrington Park Press.

Schneider, Wilhelm. 1885. Vol. 1, *Die Naturvölker*. Münster: Erster Theil.

Schoenmaeckers, R. C., I. H. Shah, R. Lesthaeghe, and O. Tambashe. 1981. "The child-spacing tradition and the post-partum taboo in tropical Africa." In *Child-spacing in tropical Africa*, eds. Hilary Page and Ron Lesthaeghe, 25–72. New York: Academic Press.

Schoepf, Brooke Grundfest. 1995. "Culture, sex research and AIDS prevention in Africa." In *Culture and sexual risk*, eds. Han ten Brummelhuis and Gibert Herdt, 29–52. Amsterdam: Gordon and Breach.

Schraeder, Peter J., ed. 2020. *Understanding contemporary Africa*. 6th ed. Boulder, CO: Lynne Rienner Publishers.

Schultze, Leonhard. 1907. *Aus Namaland und Kalahari*. Jena: G. Fischer.

Schweinfurth, Georg. 1872. "Tagebuch einer Reise zu den Niam-Niam und Monbalu." *Zeitscrhift für Erdkunde zu Berlin* 7: 385–475.

Seligman, C. G., and Brenda Seligman. 1932. *Pagan tribes of the Nilotic Sudan*. London: Routledge and Kegan Paul. (They mention that "a Dinka widow may 'marry' a girl, whose children will be counted to the deceased" and provide two instances among iron-working Cics [164–65].)

Shepherd, Gill. 1978a. "Transsexualism in Oman?" *Man* 13: 133–39.

———. 1978b. "Oman xanith." *Man* 13: 663–65.

———. 1987. "Rank, gender and homosexuality: Mombasa as a key to understanding sexual options." In *The cultural construction of sexuality*, ed. Pat Caplan, 240–70. London: Tavistock.

Shostak, Marjorie. 1983. *Nisa: The life and words of a !Kung woman*. New York: Random House. (Nisa recalls "my girlfriends started to play sexually with each other. They'd put saliva in their hands, rub it onto their genitals, and touch genitals together"—though Nisa considered the saliva disgusting [115].)

Sibuyi, Mpande wa. [1987] 1993. "*Tinoncana etimayinini*: The wives of the mine." In *The invisible ghetto: Lesbian and gay writing from South Africa*, eds. Matthew Krouse and Kim Berman, 52–64. Johannesburg: Cosaw.

Signorini, Italo. 1971. "Angawale azzale: il matrimonio tra individui dello stesso sesso negli Nzema del Ghana sud-occidentale." *Rassegna Italiana di Sociologia* 12: 529–45.

Simmons, Ron. 1991. "Some thoughts on the challenges facing black gay intellectuals." In *Brother to brother: New writings by black gay men*, ed. Essex Hemphill,
211–27. Boston: Alyson.

Smith, Edwin M., and Andrew M. Dale. 1920. *The Ila-speaking peoples of northern
Rhodesia*. 2 vols. London: Macmillan.

Smith, Mary F. 1954. *Baba of Karo: A woman of the Muslim Hausa*. London: Faber
and Faber. Reprint. New Haven: Yale University Press, 1981.

Smith, Michael S. 1991. "African roots, American fruits: the queerness of Afrocen-
tricity." *Outweek*, February 27, pp. 30–31, 78.

Somé, Malidoma Patrice. 1993. "Gays as spiritual gate keepers." *White Crane Newsletter* 4(9): 1, 6, 8. (Interview of Somé by Bert Hoff.)

————. 1994. *Of water and the spirit: Ritual, magic, and initiation in the life of an
African shaman*. New York: Putnam.

Southall, Aidan W. 1973. "The Luo of South Nyanza, Western Kenya." In *Cultural
source materials for population planning in East Africa: Beliefs and practices*, ed.
Angela Molnos, 340–51. Nairobi: East African Publishing House.

Southwold, Martin. 1973. "The Baganda of Central Uganda." In *Cultural source
materials for population planning in East Africa: Beliefs and practices*, ed. Angela
Molnos, 163–73. Nairobi: East African Publishing House.

Soyaux, Herman. 1879. *Aus West-Afrika, 1873–1876*. 2 vols. Leipzig: F. A. Brockhaus.

Spartacus guide. 1993. 21st ed. Amsterdam: Spartacus.

Spiro, Melford E. 1993. "Is the Western conception of the self 'peculiar' within the
context of world cultures?" *Ethos* 21: 107–153.

Stayt, Hugh A. [1931] 1968. *The BaVenda*. London: Oxford University Press.

Steinmetz, S. R., comp. 1903. *Rechtsverhältnisse von Eingeborenen Völkern in Afrika
und Ozeanien*. Berlin: Julius Springer. (A compilation of missionary observations; 38–39, 111, 159, 210, 232, 288, 333–34, 376).

Steward, Samuel M. 1982. Introduction to reprint of *Quatrefoil* by James Barr.
Boston: Alyson.

Stoler, Ann L. 1995. *Race and the education of desire*. Durham: Duke University Press.

Stoll, Otto. 1882. *A dictionary of the Swaheli language*. London: Trübner.

Strobel, Margaret. 1975. "Women's wedding celebrations in Mombasa, Kenya."
African Studies Review 18(3): 35–45.

————. 1976. "From Lelemama to lobbying: Women's associations in Mombasa,
Kenya." In *Women in Africa*, eds. Nancy J. Hafkin and Edna G. Bay, 183–211.
Stanford: Stanford University Press.

————. 1979. *Muslim women in Mombasa, 1890–1975*. New Haven: Yale University Press.

Sudarkasa, Niara. 1973. *Where women work: A study of Yoruba women in the mar-
ketplace and the home*. Publication No. 53, University of Michigan Anthropology Museum.

————. 1977. "Women and migration in contemporary Africa." *Signs* 3: 178–89.

———. 1986. "The status of women in indigenous Africa." *Feminist Studies* 12: 91–103. Reprinted in *Women in Africa and the African diaspora*, eds. R. Terborg Penn, S. Harley, and A. Rushing, 25–42. Washington, DC: Howard University Press.

Sweetman, David. 1971. *Queen Nzinga: The woman who saved her people.* London: Longman.

———. 1984. *Women leaders in African history.* Oxford: Heinemann.

Symons, Johnny. 1994. "Out in Africa." (Twenty-minute video of interviews with gay men from Zimbabwe and South Africa.)

Taberer, H. M. 1907. "Unnatural native vice enquiry, 1907." *Archives of the Transvaal Chamber of Mines.* N. Series, File N.35, Johannesburg.

Talbot, Percy Amaury. 1926. *The peoples of southern Nigeria: A sketch of their history, ethnology and languages, with an abstract of the 1921 Census.* 4 vols. London: Oxford University Press.

———. 1927. *Some Nigerian fertility cults.* London: Oxford University Press. (37–39).

———. 1932. *Tribes of the Niger Delta: Their religions and customs.* New York: Barnes and Noble. (On 195–96, he mentions that barren women can acquire a wife, who is impregnated by her husband or by other males in the household, and that the female husband leaves her property to the children of that wife.)

Tamale, Sylvia. 2011. *African sexualities: A reader.* Cape Town: Pambazuka.

Tanner, Ralph E. 1969. "The East African experience of imprisonment." In *African penal systems*, ed. Alan Milner, 295–315. New York: Praeger.

Tauxier, Louis. 1912. *Les noirs du Soudan: Pays Mossi et Gourounni.* Paris: Émile LaRose.

Taylor, Brian K. 1962. *The western lacustrine Bantu.* London: International African Institute.

Tcheuyap, Alexie. 2019. "Cinema, African (Francophone)." In *Global encyclopedia of lesbian, gay, bisexual, transgender, and queer history*, eds. Howard Chiang et al., 343–47. Farmington Hills, MI: Charles Scribner's Sons.

Tessman, Günther. [1904] 1913. *Die Pangwe.* Berlin: E. Wasmuth.

———. 1909. "Religionsformen der Pangwe." *Zeitschrift für Ethnologie* 41: 874–89.

———. 1921a. "Die Homosexualität bei den Negern Kameruns." *Jahrbuch fur sexuelle Zwischenstufen* 21: 121–38.

———. 1921b. *Ajongs erzählungen: marchen der Fangneger.* Berlin: Pantheon-Verlag.

———. 1932. "Die Völker und Sprachen Kameruns." *Petermanns Geographische Mitteilungen* 78: 70–115, 184–90.

———. 1934. *Die Bafia und die Kultur der Mittelkamerun-Bantu.* Stuttgart: Strecker und Schroder.

Teunis, Niels. 1996. "Homosexuality in Dakar: Is the bed the heart of a sexual subculture?" *Journal of Gay, Lesbian, and Bisexual Identity* 1: 153–70.

Thai, Bethuel. 1996. "Laws tough on Basotho women." *Sowetan*, September 27, p. 17.

Thomas, Northcote W. 1914. *Law and custom of the Ibo of the Asaba District, south Nigeria*. London: Harrison and Sons. (Distinguishes variations from village to village in inheritance rights depending upon whether the wife produces sons or daughters before or after the female husband's death. There is no information on sleeping arrangements [83–85].)

Tönjes, Hermann. 1871. *Ovamboland*. Berlin: Warned. (Mentions *omaxenge*, "passive pederasts," among the Ukuanjama of Ovamboland [155].)

Torday, Emil, and Thomas Athol Joyce. 1905. "Notes on the ethnography of the Ba-Mbala." *Journal of the Anthropological Institute of Great Britain and Ireland* 35: 398–426.

———. 1906. "Notes on the ethnography of the Ba-Yaka." *Journal of the Anthropological Institute of Great Britain and Ireland* 36: 39–59.

Tosh, John. 1978. *Clan leaders and colonial chiefs in Lango: The political history of an east African stateless society, c. 1800–1939*. New York: Oxford University Press.

Trevisan, Joño. 1986. *Perverts in paradise*. London.

Trueman, Matt. 2016. "Review: pigs and dogs (Royal Court)." *WhatsOnStage.com*. http://www.whatsonstage.com/london-theatre/reviews/pigs-and-dogs-royal-court_41351.html. Accessed May 23, 2018.

Turnbull, Colin M. 1962. *The forest people*. Garden City, NY: Doubleday.

———. 1965. *Wayward servants: The two worlds of the African pygmies*. New York: Museum of Natural History Press.

———. 1972. *The mountain people*. New York: Simon and Schuster. (Among the Ugandan Teso people he called Ik, Turnball observed young men affectlessly masturbating each other, oblivious of the presence of others [254].)

———. 1986. "Survival factors among Mbuti and other hunters of the equatorial African rain forest." In *African pygmies*, ed. L. Cavalli-Sforza, 103–23. San Diego: Academic Press.

Turner, Victor W. 1967. *Forest of symbols: Aspects of Ndembu ritual*. Ithaca, NY: Cornell University Press.

Tutu, Desmond. 1996. "Foreword." In *We were baptized too: Claiming God's grace for lesbians and gays*, eds. M. B. Alexander and James Preston. London: John Knox.

Tuupainen, Maija. 1970. "Marriage in a matrilineal African tribe: A social anthropological study of marriage in the Ondonga tribe in Ovamboland." *Transactions of the Westermarck Society* 18.

Uchendu, Victor C. 1965. *The Igbo of southeast Nigeria*. New York: Holt, Rinehart and Winston.

Uganda. Ministry of Health. 2014. *Scientific statement on homosexuality*. https://www.transcend.org/tms/2014/03/uganda-scientific-statement-from-the-ministry-of-health-on-homosexuality/. Accessed September 12, 2020.

van Onselen, Charles. 1976. *Chibaro: African mine labor in southern Rhodesia, 1900–1933*. London: Pluto Press.

————. 1982. *Studies in the social and economic history of the Witwatersrand, 1886–1914.* Vol. 2, *New Nineveh.* Johannesburg: Ravan Press.

————. 1984. *The small matter of a horse: The life of "Nongoloza" Mathebula, 1867–1948.* Johannesburg: Ravan Press.

Velten, Carl. 1910. *Suaheli-Worterbuch.* Berlin: Selbstverlag des Verfassers.

Verdon, Michel. 1982. "Where have all their lineages gone?: Cattle and descent among the Nuer." *American Anthropologist* 84: 566–79.

Vicinus, Martha. 1994. "Lesbian history: All theory and no facts or all facts and no theory?" *Radical History Review* 60: 57–75.

Vilakazi, Absolom. 1962. *Zulu transformations.* Pietermaritzburg, South Africa: University of Natal Press.

Viljoen, Frans. 2019. "Botswana court ruling is a ray of hope for LGBT people across Africa." *The Conversation,* June 12, 2019. https://theconversation.com/botswana-court-ruling-is-a-ray-of-hope-for-lgbt-people-across-africa-118713. Accessed April 16, 2020.

Vimbela, Vera. 1995. "Climbing on her shoulder: An interview with Umtata's 'first lesbian.'" In *Defiant desire: Gay and lesbian lives in South Africa,* eds. Mark Gevisser and Edwin Cameron, 193–97. New York: Routledge.

Wagner, Gunter. 1949. *The Bantu of north Kavirondo.* 2 vols. London: Oxford University Press.

Wald, Benji. 1994. "Sub-Saharan Africa." In *Atlas of the world's languages,* eds. C. Moseley and R. Asher, 289–309. New York: Routledge.

Watts, Raleigh. 1992. "The Polynesian *mahu.*" In Stephen O. Murray, *Oceanic homosexualities,* 171–84. New York: Garland.

Weeks, John H. 1909. "Anthropological notes on the Bangala of the Upper Congo River." *Journal of the Anthropological Institute of Great Britain and Ireland* 39: 97–136, 416–59.

Weine, Ferdinand. 1848. *Expedition zur Entdeckung der Quellen des Weissen Nil.* Berlin: G. Reimer.

Weiss. Max. 1910. *Die Völkerstämme im Norden Deutsch Ost-Afrikas.* Berlin: C. Marechner. (299–300).

Werner, Alice. 1906. *Natives of British central Africa.* London: Constable. (Discusses female sexual instruction in initiation ceremonies without any indication of nonverbal instruction [126].)

Weston, Kath. 1993. "Lesbian/gay studies in the house of anthropology." *Annual Review of Anthropology* 22: 157–85.

————. 1996. *Render me, gender me.* New York: Columbia University Press.

Wetherell, Iden. 1995a. "Mugabe cracks down on gay rights." *Johannesburg Weekly Mail and Guardian,* August 4–10, p. 15.

————. 1995b. "No sex please, it's subversive." *African Agenda* 1(7): 23–24.

————. 1996. "Mugabe's unholy war." *Southern African Report* 11(4): 13–14.

Whitam, Frederick L., and Robin M. Mathy. 1986. *Male homosexuality in four societies: Brazil, Guatemala, the Philippines, and the United States.* New York: Praeger Publishers.

White, C. M. N. 1953. "Notes on the circumcision rites of the Balovale tribes." *African Studies* 12: 41–56.

Wikan, Unni. 1977. "Man becomes woman: Transexuals in Oman as a key to gender roles." *Man* 13: 304–19.

———. 1978a. "The Omani xanith: a third gender role?" *Man* 13: 473–75.

———. 1978b. "The Omani xanith." *Man* 13: 667–71.

———. 1982. *Behind the veil: Women in Oman.* Baltimore: Johns Hopkins University Press.

Williams, Walter L. *1986. The spirit and the flesh: Sexual diversity in American Indian culture.* Boston: Beacon Press.

Wilson, Godfrey M. 1936. "An introduction to Nyakyusa society." *Bantu Studies* 10: 253–91.

———. 1957. "Male prostitution and homosexuals." Appendix to *Mombasa Social Survey.* Nairobi: Government Printer.

Wilson, Monica. 1951. *Good company: A study of the Nyakyusa age-villages.* London: Oxford University Press. (Quotations are from the 1963 paperback, Boston: Beacon Press.)

———. 1977. *For men and elders: Change in the relations of generations and of men and women among the Nyakyusa-Ngonde people, 1875–1971.* New York: Africana.

Winkler, John J. 1990. *The constraints of desire: The anthropology of sex and gender in ancient Greece.* New York: Routledge.

Winter, Edward Henry. 1959, 1965. *Beyond the mountains of the moon: The lives of four Africans.* Urbana: University of Illinois Press. (In the recollection of a Bwamba [from central Africa] about the isolation of initiation, "The old man who was looking after the boys used to take out his penis and say, 'Come blow it like a whistle,' and if the boy did not blow it, he was beaten" [163].)

Wolf, Eric. 1982. *Europe and peoples without history.* Berkeley: University of California Press.

Woods, Gregory. 1994. "Poems of black African manhood." *Perversions* 1(1): 22–37. (Reviews various heterosexist manifestations of castration anxiety and contemptuous South African allusions to prison debasement, shading from hatred to more recent incomprehension.)

Worthman, Carol M., and John W. M. Whiting. 1987. "Social change in adolescent sexual behavior, mate selection, and premarital pregnancy rates in a Kikuyu community." *Ethos* 15: 145–65.

X, Jacobus. 1893. *L'amour aux colonies.* Paris: Isidore Liseux. Translated as *Untrodden fields of anthropology: Observations on the esoteric manners and customs of semi-civilized peoples . . . by a French army-surgeon.* 2 vols. Paris: Librarie de medecine, folklore et anthropologie, 1898. Reprint. Huntington, NY: R. E. Krieger, 1972.

Yusuf, Ahmed B. 1974. "A reconsideration of urban conceptions: Hausa urbanization and the Hausa rural-urban continuum." *Urban Anthropology* 3(2): 200–21.

Zita, Jacquelyn N. 1992. "Male lesbians and the postmodern body." *Hypatia* 7(4): 106–27.

Index

Note: *Italics* indicate information appears in a table.